The JAPANESE THRUST
into SIBERIA, 1918

STUDIES OF
THE RUSSIAN INSTITUTE
COLUMBIA UNIVERSITY

The JAPANESE THRUST into SIBERIA, 1918

By JAMES WILLIAM MORLEY

COLUMBIA UNIVERSITY PRESS

NEW YORK, 1957

COPYRIGHT © 1954
COLUMBIA UNIVERSITY PRESS, NEW YORK
FIRST PUBLISHED IN BOOK FORM 1957

PUBLISHED IN
GREAT BRITAIN, CANADA,
INDIA, AND PAKISTAN
BY THE OXFORD UNIVERSITY PRESS
LONDON, TORONTO,
BOMBAY, AND KARACHI

LIBRARY OF CONGRESS
CATALOG CARD NUMBER: 57–5805

MANUFACTURED IN THE
UNITED STATES OF AMERICA

THE RUSSIAN INSTITUTE
OF COLUMBIA UNIVERSITY

The Russian Institute was established by Columbia University in 1946 to serve two major objectives: the training of a limited number of well-qualified Americans for scholarly and professional careers in the field of Russian studies and the development of research in the social sciences and the humanities as they relate to Russia and the Soviet Union. The research program of the Russian Institute is conducted through the efforts of its faculty members, of scholars invited to participate as Senior Fellows in its program, and of candidates for the Certificate of the Institute and for the degree of Doctor of Philosophy. Some of the results of the research program are presented in the Studies of the Russian Institute of Columbia University. The faculty of the Institute, without necessarily agreeing with the conclusions reached in the Studies, believe that their publication advances the difficult task of promoting systematic research on Russia and the Soviet Union and public understanding of the problems involved.

The faculty of the Russian Institute are grateful to the Rockefeller Foundation for the financial assistance which it has given to the program of research and publication.

178895

STUDIES OF

THE RUSSIAN INSTITUTE

COLUMBIA UNIVERSITY

Soviet National Income and Product in 1937
BY ABRAM BERGSON

Through the Glass of Soviet Literature: Views of Russian Society
EDITED BY ERNEST J. SIMMONS

The Proletarian Episode in Russian Literature, 1928–1932
BY EDWARD J. BROWN

Management of the Industrial Firm in the USSR: A Study in Soviet
Economic Planning
BY DAVID GRANICK

Soviet Policies in China, 1917–1924
BY ALLEN S. WHITING

Ukrainian Nationalism, 1939–1945
BY JOHN A. ARMSTRONG

Polish Postwar Economy
BY THAD PAUL ALTON

Literary Politics in the Soviet Ukraine, 1917–1934
BY GEORGE S. N. LUCKYJ

The Emergence of Russian Panslavism, 1856–1870
BY MICHAEL BORO PETROVICH

Bolshevism in Turkestan, 1917–1927
BY ALEXANDER G. PARK

The Last Years of the Georgian Monarchy, 1658–1832
BY DAVID MARSHALL LANG

Lenin on Trade Unions and Revolution, 1893–1917
BY THOMAS TAYLOR HAMMOND

The Japanese Thrust into Siberia, 1918
BY JAMES WILLIAM MORLEY

To Bobbie

NOTE ON
TECHNICAL PROBLEMS

To clarify the chronology, all dates, including those given in Russian sources according to the "old style," have been converted to the Gregorian calendar unless otherwise indicated. Of course, for any specific event, the date and time are given according to the Gregorian calendar for the place in which the event occurred, so that, to compare events in such widely scattered points as London, Moscow, Tokyo, and Washington, the reader will need to make the adjustment appropriate to the difference in time zones.

Unless otherwise indicated, all translations in this study were made by the author.

In transliterating Russian proper names and words into the Latin alphabet, the modified Library of Congress system favored by the Russian Institute, Columbia University, has been followed, omitting diacritical marks. In transliterating Chinese, the Wade-Giles system has been followed. For Japanese, a modified Hepburn system was used.

Except in the Preface, Japanese personal names have been given in accordance with Japanese usage: that is, the family name first, the given name last.

PREFACE

Although nearly forty years have elapsed since the Russian Revolution of 1917 and the inter-Allied intervention in Siberia in 1918, many critical phases of these events have not yet been adequately studied, and many critical problems raised by them have not yet been solved. How the revolution penetrated Siberia, for example, has been largely ignored. Why the Allies intervened in Siberia has been left largely to the contentions of American apologists and Soviet propagandists, who have usually found satisfaction in placing major responsibility on the Japanese, or to Japanese officials, who have sought to return the responsibility to the Allies. The effect has been to weaken the free nations, first, by depriving them of valuable experience in devising effective policies to combat the expansion of communism, and second, by dividing them with mutual misunderstanding of each other's political processes and problems. In the hope that it will contribute to the cause of freedom, this study attempts to answer as fully and as fairly as may be the question: What led Japan to intervene in Siberia in the summer of 1918?

There are four major elements in the equation. First is the power structure within the Japanese government in the period of 1917 to 1918. What specific individuals and groups were in a position to influence the decision, what were their other policies, and what were their relations to each other? Most of this information is available in published Japanese sources. Second is the objective situation which Japanese policy makers faced in the early months of the revolution in Siberia. Soviet archival publications, the memoirs of leading Russian and non-Russian participants, and the reports of American and Japanese official observers are valuable here. Thirdly, while it is unnecessary for the purpose to analyze in detail the motives and objectives of the Western powers, it is essential to investigate their activities in the region as known by the Japanese and to study their representations to the Japanese government. This has been facilitated by the studies of other scholars, published biographies, memoirs, the published and unpublished papers of the archives of the United States Department of State, and especially the reports of Japanese officials as preserved in the official and hitherto classified archives of the Japanese War, Navy, and Foreign Ministries. Finally, it was the exceptional opportunity to study these Japanese archival materials, in addition to certain other unpublished Japanese manuscripts and published Japanese memoirs, which made it possible to find an answer to the ultimate question: how did the Japanese policy makers respond to these various domestic and international pressures?

For the financial support which enabled me to carry on this research, I am deeply indebted to Columbia University, for the award of the Lydig Fellowship, 1947–48; to the Social Science Research Council, for granting me an Area Research-Training Fellowship for study in Washington, D.C., and in Japan, 1950–52; and to Union College for grants in aid of research, 1954–55. Nor could it have been completed without the help of many friends. For their scholarly example, their constant advice, and their warm friendship and inspiration, I should like to thank four men in particular: Mr. Ryusaku Tsunoda, recently retired curator of the East Asiatic Collection of Columbia University; Professor Philip E. Mosely, formerly director of the Russian Institute, Columbia University, now director of studies, Council on Foreign Relations; Professor Hugh Borton, formerly director of the East Asian Institute, Columbia University, now president of Haverford College; and Mr. Ken Kurihara, chief of the Diplomatic Documents Compilation Office of the Japanese Foreign Ministry.

I should like, too, to express my gratitude to the many members of the Columbia University faculty and library staff who helped me: especially Dr. John A. Krout, formerly chairman of the Department of History, now vice president and provost of the university; Professors L. Carrington Goodrich, Henry Graff, John Hazard, Franklin Ho, Nathaniel Peffer, Geroid T. Robinson, Sir George Sansom, Osamu Shimizu, and C. Martin Wilbur; Mr. Howard Linton, librarian of the East Asiatic Library, and his able assistants, particularly Miss Miwa Kai and Mr. Philip Yampolsky, who facilitated my use of that excellent collection and helped by securing volumes from other libraries, including the Chinese Collection of the Harvard-Yenching Institute Library, the Japanese Collection of the University of Michigan and the National Diet Library in Tokyo.

I am also grateful to Mr. Helmer Webb and the staff of the Union College Library for their help in securing distant volumes and to President Carter Davidson of Union College for granting me a leave of absence from 1950 to 1952, in order to pursue my research in Washington, D.C., and in Japan, and for his constant encouragement.

In Washington, my thanks are due to the staffs of the U.S. Army War College Library; the U.S. War Department Library; the National Archives Library; the Library of Congress, especially to Dr. Edwin G. Beal, Jr., chief of the Japanese Section, and his assistants, Miss Takeshita and Mr. Kuroda, and to Mr. John Dorosh, curator of the Russian Room; and to the National Archives, where Miss Elizabeth Bethel of the War Records Division assisted me in the use of the Japanese War and Navy Ministry Archives.

Space does not permit me even to mention the names of all the many Japanese scholars and diplomats who helped me in my researches in Japan. No wandering scholar can ever have been received more graciously nor helped more generously in any country. Of the many, however, I should like to acknowledge here a few: particularly Professor Fumihiko Tachikawa of Kyōto University, Professor Tatsuji Takeuchi of Kwansei Gakuin University, Professor Seizaburo Shinobu of Nagoya University, Professor Kōsaku Tamura of Chūō University, Professor Yoshitake Oka and especially Professor Toshio Ueda of Tokyo University, all of whom gave helpful advice and generous permission to use their personal and university libraries. Of the staff of the National Diet Library, I should like to thank Professor Sadabumi Fujii, chief of the Reference Section of the Ueno Library Branch, both for his own help and for securing for me at one stage of the project two able young assistants, Miss Kazuko Ishikawa and Miss Tomoko Ishikawa; Mr. Taijiro Ichikawa, director of the Division of International Affairs; Mr. Takeshi Saito, director of the Legislative Reference Section of the General Research Department; Professor Toshikane Ōkubo, director of the Archives of Constitutional Government, Diet Building Branch; and Mr. Nobutaka Matsuda, chief of the Foreign Ministry Library Branch, and his diligent assistant, Mr. Shoji Sakamaki. I would express my special gratitude to the many officials of the Foreign Ministry, including, in addition to Mr. Ken Kurihara, Mr. Kijiro Miyake, formerly chief of the Archives Section, and Mr. Masao Ibaraki of the Investigation Bureau. I am also deeply grateful for the willingness of many former diplomatic officials to help me clarify various points with which they were familiar from personal experience; among them, Mr. Suemasa Okamoto, Mr. Shigeru Shimada, Mr. Teiji Tsubogami, Mr. Makoto Yano, and in particular, Mr. Kimitomo Mushakoji. And I shall never forget the many hours freely given me by Mr. Bunshiro Satō, formerly of Peers College, to help me in the study of *kambun* and various phases of Japanese culture. Mr. Chihiro Hosoya, whose excellent study appeared too late for me to use, was kind enough to read an early draft.

I wish to express my thanks also to Miss Matilda L. Berg and Miss Barbara Melissa Voorhis of Columbia University Press. Both in style and in form this book has benefited from their careful editing.

For the constant encouragement of my parents and for the love and sacrifice of my family, who shared the irregular life of a wandering student with me, no words are adequate.

These excellent friends are in no way responsible for the conclusions expressed here. With some of my judgments, they may in fact disagree. I would only assure them and the reader that I have written with no other concern than for the truth. I have tried to follow the dictum of Confucius, "to write without embellishment," in the conviction that sincere talk among friends is the best way to promote a sympathetic understanding between the great peoples of Japan and the world.

New York   JAMES WILLIAM MORLEY
January, 1957

CONTENTS

I. Samurai in Siberia 3

II. Clansmen and Politicians 8

III. Enemies and Allies 28

IV. Reconnaissance in Siberia 60

V. The Manchurian Sanctuary 83

VI. International Complications 110

VII. A Crisis Weathered 136

VIII. The Army's Problems 161

IX. Unruly Protégés 188

X. Unaccommodating Allies 213

XI. The Impasse Broken 233

XII. A Decision Forced 260

XIII. Hidden Meanings 291

CHRONOLOGY 315

APPENDIXES 323

BIBLIOGRAPHY 369

INDEX 381

MAP: The Amur Basin, 1917–1918 5

The JAPANESE THRUST
into SIBERIA, 1918

I. SAMURAI IN SIBERIA

In August, 1918, the east Siberian port of Vladivostok presented a strange sight. The harbor, once the powerful base of Russia's Japan Sea fleet, bristled with Allied men-of-war: the *Brooklyn,* flagship of the United States' Asiatic Fleet, the British cruiser *Suffolk,* the Chinese *Hai Jung,* and the warships *Iwami, Asahi,* and *Asakage* from the island empire of Japan. The docks, once the scene of busy stevedore gangs, now groaned under mountains of unmoved supplies. Up in the city, the low-lying wooden buildings no longer rang with the songs of Russian sailors or the clumping of Russian army boots. For Vladivostok, "Lord of the East," was no longer a Russian city. It was an Allied city, thronged with the troops of many nations, gathering now to jump off on one of the most bizarre and least understood military adventures in modern times: the Inter-Allied intervention in Siberia.

What were these Allied troops doing there? How did they come to be there? According to the official announcements at the time, the purpose of the British was to bring economic relief to the Russian people and assist them against the Germans;[1] the purpose of the Americans was "to steady" Russian efforts at "self-government or self-defense," to rescue a corps of valiant Czechoslovak soldiers who were being prevented from reaching the Western front by unruly Austrian and German prisoners of war in Siberia, and

[1] Memorandum from the British chargé to the secretary of state, August 8, 1918, U.S. Department of State, *Papers Relating to the Foreign Relations of the United States* (hereinafter, *USFR, 1918, Russia*) (Washington: G.P.O., 1932), II, 333–34.

eventually to extend economic aid;[2] while the purpose of Japan was simply to be of assistance to its allies.[3] But the actions of the powers spoke louder than their declarations. For two years the British, the French, and the Czechoslovaks fought to strengthen an anti-Bolshevik front in western Siberia; the Americans concentrated on policing and rehabilitating the railroads in the East; and the Japanese, refusing to go beyond Lake Baikal, settled down to contest the Amur basin with both the Americans and the Bolsheviks. The contrast between preliminary declarations and subsequent actions was perhaps most pronounced in the Japanese case. Even after the Western Allies had withdrawn their troops in 1920, the Japanese remained for two more years and did not finally evacuate northern Sakhalin until 1925. Moreover, at the height of the expedition, they were willing to support a force of from three and a half to four and a half divisions in the field at one time, far more than the British, French, and American troops combined; nor did they shrink from expending a final total of over one billion yen.[4]

These facts have led many charges to be levied at the Allied governments, particularly at Japan. Even before the operations were begun, Soviet spokesmen were saying that "the imperialists of Japan wish to strangle the Soviet Revolution, to cut off Russia from the Pacific Ocean, to seize the rich territories of Siberia, and to enslave the Siberian workers and peasants." [5] Soviet historians have generally followed this line ever since.[6] The American commander,

[2] Acting secretary of state to Morris (in Tokyo), August 3, 1918, *ibid.*, II, 328–29.

[3] Memorandum from Ishii (in Washington) to the acting secretary of state, received August 2, 1918, *ibid.*, II, 324–25.

[4] For a detailed summary of Japanese military and naval operations, see Japan, Sambō Hombu, *Taishō Shichi-nen naishi Jūichi-nen Shiberia Shuppei-shi* (Tokyo, 1924), I, Appendix, 111–37.

[5] Proclamation of the Council of People's Commissars, April 5, 1918, published in *Ranee Utro*, No. 57, April 6, 1918, quoted in James Bunyan, *Intervention, Civil War and Communism, April–December, 1918* (Baltimore: Johns Hopkins Press, 1936), pp. 68–69.

[6] For an interesting recent shift in Soviet interpretation, however, one in which the entire onus for the expedition is laid on the United States, see A. Gulyga, "Nachal'nyi Period Antisovetskoi Interventsii S.Sh.S. (1917–1918 gg.)," *Voprosy Istorii*, III (1950), 3–25.

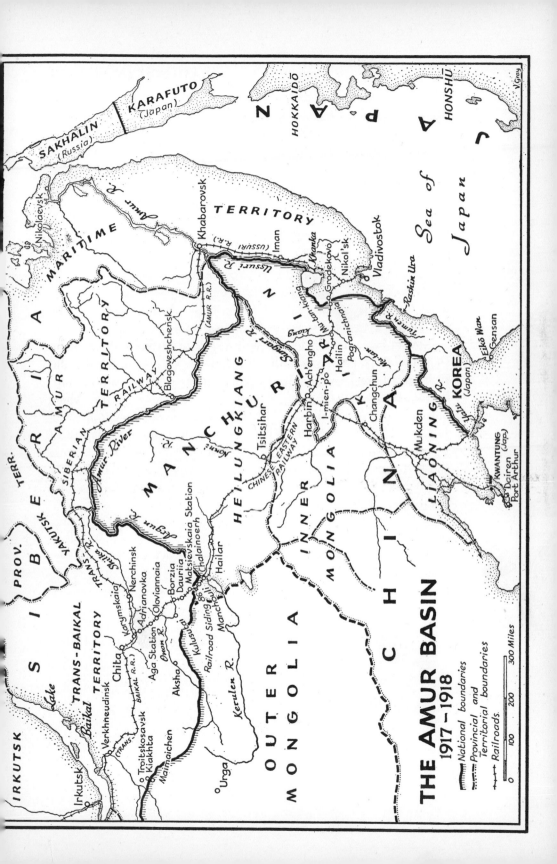

THE AMUR BASIN
1917–1918

—— National boundaries
----- Provincial and
      Territorial boundaries
-+-+- Railroads

0   100   200   300 Miles

General Graves, came roughly to the same conclusion;[7] and later American scholars, relying principally on Russian monographs and American records in the Department of State, have tended to agree, insisting that Japan was the leader and that America intervened primarily to keep a check on it.[8]

Until recently, there has been no way to ascertain the truth of these charges. Even now, many facts about the expedition are still under seal in official archives. This is especially true for Great Britain and France; but it is also still partly true for the United States, where many of the War Department's records are still unavailable; and, in spite of the publication by various authorities in the Soviet Union of many useful memoirs and official papers relating to the expedition, Siberia's role in the Russian Revolution is still largely a *terra incognita* in Russian historiography.

Now at last a new and valuable mine of material has been made available in Japan. Since the Second World War, the official archives of the Japanese War, Navy, and Foreign Ministries have been opened, valuable diaries and other books by or about important Japanese leaders of the time have been published, and Japanese officials and scholars have taken a new and vital interest in lighting up the dark corners of the history of the recent past. For the first time it becomes possible to say with some authority why the Japanese intervened in Siberia in 1918; and the answer is important, for it throws valuable light on the history of Japan's continental aspirations, which have been one of the basic determinants of the international relations of the Far East for the past half century and more. It also helps to illuminate Japan's strained relationship with the Soviet Union. In addition, while the details are incomplete and perhaps dangerous for a Westerner to interpret, they are full enough to tell us not only why the decision was taken,

[7] William S. Graves, *America's Siberian Adventure, 1918–1920* (New York: Jonathan Cape and Harrison Smith, 1931), p. 342.

[8] See, for example, such recent studies as Pauline Tompkins, *American-Russian Relations in the Far East* (New York: Macmillan, 1949), p. 85; and John Albert White, *The Siberian Intervention* (Princeton: Princeton University Press, 1950), pp. 172, 189, and *passim;* both of these agree in general with the earlier interpretation of A. Whitney Griswold, *The Far Eastern Policy of the United States* (New York: Harcourt, Brace, 1938), pp. 223–68.

but also how and by whom. They take us behind the screen of
news reports, diplomatic notes, and speeches in parliament, into a
world rarely visited, the inner world of private villas and secret
council chambers, where the clansmen and politicians of prewar
Japan decided the fate of the empire.

A preliminary word of caution is necessary. In constitutional
form, the Japanese government was a monarchy, over which the
emperor was sovereign. On the other hand, the emperor exercised
his power either through or with the consent of such bodies as
courts, a parliament, a privy council, and a cabinet. Some of these
constitutional forms and practices may suggest analogies to those
in Western political systems from which, indeed, the inspiration
for them was partly drawn. The Western student of Japanese
politics must, therefore, be doubly on his guard lest he be tempted
to assume at times that, because Japan had an emperor, its government functioned like that of Louis XIV; or, that because it had a
parliament, that body exercised the same powers as the parliament
in modern Britain; or, that because the position of the military was
exceptional, the military leaders exercised the authority of a Hitler
or a Mussolini. The Japanese government was a unique government. The old wine of centuries of Japanese political experience
under feudalism had been poured into new bottles imported from
the West. The labels were therefore often misleading—the bottles
themselves were sometimes unable to stand the pressure. To understand why the Japanese government intervened in Siberia in 1918,
it is essential from the beginning to look within and behind its
constitutional forms in order to determine the actual political forces
at work. What individuals, what cliques, and what coalitions were
in a position in 1918 to make or to influence such a decision? In
short, who ruled Japan in 1918?

II. CLANSMEN AND POLITICIANS

The Elder Statesmen

The reign of Taishō Tennō, from 1912 to 1926, was for Japan a time of storm and stress. Japan was then like a young man who still hears the counsel of his parents but does not yet have a sure understanding within himself of the person he would or could be; who is now idealistic, now cynical, now gentle, now rough, now restrained, now dissolute, as one or another of his newly matured capacities or one or another of his newly found impulses struggles to rule him.

Young Japan had been held in tutelage for half a century while the able bureaucrats of the western clans, especially of Satsuma, Chōshū, Hizen, and Tosa, had striven to train and to equip it to play an independent role in the modern world. In the days gone by, they and their ancestors had watched the ominous "black ships" of the West poke their prows into Asian seas, their gunwales lined with the missionaries, the traders, and the cannon of the "hairy barbarian"; they had watched these "barbarians" swarm on the Indian coast, seize the rich East Indian archipelago, and force their way into China; and they had resolved that Japan would never be taken. Spurred on also by deep dissatisfaction with the weaknesses and inequalities of their own feudal system, they had risen up in 1867 to modernize Japan in the name of the emperor.

They had encouraged the development of a semicapitalistic economy over which preponderant influence was exercised by a few favored family combines, known as the *zaibatsu*. They had organized Western-type, yet clan-controlled, armed forces. They had designed a constitutional system of centralized government, democratic in appearance, but carefully constructed to preserve as much power as possible in the hands of a bureaucratic oligarchy. Through the schools and media of public expression, they had sought to discipline the nation with an emperor-centered, nationalistic ideology. And, finally, in the Sino-Japanese War, 1894–95, and the Russo-Japanese War, 1904–5, they had launched it on a course of cautious imperial expansion.

Now in the Taishō era, these founding fathers of the new Japan were passing away. Of the most important, those honored with the title of "genro" or elder statesman, only four were left when the era opened; and, in spite of the addition of two more to the group by 1918, when the decision was taken to intervene in Siberia, only three active genro were left: Field Marshal Prince Yamagata Aritomo, a wizened warrior of the Chōshū clan, now eighty years old, a man who had used nearly every high office of state to strengthen and glorify his emperor, his army, and his clan; Marquis Matsukata Masayoshi, eighty-three years old, a veteran financial administrator and protector of Satsuma clan interests; and Prince Saionji Kimmochi, an urbane court aristocrat whose foreign training and experience as president of the Seiyūkai political party, president of the Privy Council, and twice as premier, had led him to favor the strengthening of more peaceful and more liberal forces within Japanese society.

The genro were a peculiarly Japanese institution. They derived their authority not from the constitution, which did not even mention them, but from the traditional sanction of respect for eminent men. By 1916 they exercised their power, no longer by holding high offices (they had in fact given up most of their offices) but by calling on the almost feudal loyalties of contemporaries and juniors whom they had helped or could help to reach high positions. These networks of loyalty or factions were most strongly rooted in the bureaucracy, and they lived on despite the growing senility of their genro chieftains.

The two most powerful factions at the time of the Siberian expedition were the Satsuma clique and the Chōshū clique. The

Satsuma clique was made up of officials who looked for leadership to the former clansmen of the Satsuma fief in southern Kyūshū, particularly to Marquis Matsukata. In the Taishō era, it dominated the navy. It exerted a powerful influence among the ranks of the career officials of the Foreign Ministry, particularly in the ruling "Teidai" or Tokyo Imperial University faction, led by Vice Minister Shidehara Kijuro. In the House of Peers, it made its weight felt especially in the person of Baron Makino.

The Chōshū Clique

Perhaps the single most powerful force in the Japanese government in 1918 was the Chōshū clique, which included a broad range of civilian and military officials, most of whom had been born in the region formerly controlled by the Chōshū clan in southwestern Japan, and all of whom were loyal to the senior genro, Prince Yamagata. It is perhaps true to say that no one in Japan at the time, excluding the emperor, enjoyed greater prestige than Yamagata, and that no one, including the emperor, exercised more real authority. Nevertheless, the prince did not control his clique in the manner of a Western-style dictator. As a rule, he seems to have set the basic policy and, when disagreements arose from time to time within the clique, it was he who made the ultimate decision. Yet Yamagata was a cautious man. He listened carefully to the opinions of his senior advisers and his favorite juniors, treating them now as a commander would his staff, now as a benevolent father would his respectful children, seeking always to find the policy which, while true to his own purposes, would also best enable the clique to pull together toward the common objective and to attain that objective through the orderly processes of government.

By 1918, four men were high in the councils of the Chōshū clique. They were the retired privy councilor, Major General Viscount Miura Goro; the veteran civilian administrator, Viscount Hirata Tōsuke, Chōshū leader in the House of Peers; the able military administrator, Field Marshal Count Terauchi, former war minister, governor general of Korea, and finally premier; and the somewhat younger vice chief of the Army General Staff Head-quarters, Lieutenant General Tanaka Gi'ichi. It was clearly a clique in which the military dominated. It was also a clique which more or less dominated the military, a fact which gave it an almost impregnable position of power in the Japanese government.

There were several basic reasons for the extraordinary power of the military leaders in the Japanese government of the day. One was the habit of political behavior, ingrained during the centuries of feudal experience, of showing deference in public affairs to military men. Another was the law of the land, by which the military had fortified their traditional position.[1] By law, the service ministers had to be selected from the active or retired list of generals and admirals, which enabled the senior officers to exact conditions from a cabinet before permitting one of their number to serve. By law, except for purely administrative matters, the service ministers, like the chiefs of staff, were directly responsible only to the emperor, which, in practice, meant to the emperor's military advisers; in other words, to the military clique of which they were members. By law, their regular operating funds were placed beyond the control of the diet. Thus, the military were often able to pursue policies independent from those of the cabinet or, if necessary, to establish policies for the cabinet.

In 1916, when the Ōkuma government resigned, the Chōshū clique and their military followers had two particular concerns. One was that the next cabinet should secure diet approval for an expansion in the size of the army.[2] This was particularly dear to the heart of the army chief of staff, General Baron Uehara, who had shown his determination on this point in 1912 by using his office as war minister to break a recalcitrant cabinet. The other was that the government should follow their lead in foreign policy, at least in regard to the Asian continent.

In the early days of the Ōkuma cabinet, from 1914 to 1915, they had been incensed by Foreign Minister Katō's rather independent

[1] Itō Masanori, *Kokubō-shi* (Tokyo: Tōyō Keizai Shimpō-sha, 1941) Vol. IV of *Gendai Nihon Bummei-shi*, pp. 31–126.
[2] For an able account of Japan's military development, see Matsushita Yoshio, *Kindai Nihon Gunji-shi* (Tokyo: Kigen-shō, 1941).

way of handling the "twenty-one demands" and by his exclusive attachment to the alliance with Great Britain. The genro, under Yamagata's leadership, had become seriously worried by the growing anti-Japanese feeling in China and by the possibility of a white-race coalition returning to China in the postwar years and out-competing Japan in the Chinese market.[3] They had become convinced of the necessity of drawing closer to China and at the same time closer to the Allies, especially Russia. In the latter case, their purpose was quickly achieved. After engineering Katō's resignation in the summer of 1915, Yamagata had Katō's successor, Viscount Ishii, add Japan's signature to the Declaration of London[4] and, in 1916, sign the fourth secret treaty with Russia, an agreement which delimited the interests of the two powers in northeast Asia and pledged them to mutual defense.[5] The Chōshū clique and the army were now determined that the next cabinet should strengthen the Russian orientation and reach a settlement of the few issues still outstanding with that country.

The question of how to improve and strengthen relations with China was more complicated. Unlike Japan, China had been unable in the nineteenth century to solve the problems occasioned by a declining social order and the coming of the West. Long pent-up revolutionary forces had finally overthrown the dynasty in 1912, inaugurating a so-called republic, which by 1916 was disintegrating before the onslaught of locally based war lords. In this chaotic situation, what should be done to secure Japan's interests? In 1915, in the presidency of Yuan Shih-k'ai, Foreign Minister

[3] Memorandum from Inoue to Yamagata, August 9, 1914, in Sakatani Yoshiro, comp., *Segai Inoue Kō Den* (Tokyo, 1930), V, 367–69; and letter from Yamagata to each of the genro, mid-February, 1915, in Tokutomi I'ichiro, *Kōshaku Yamagata Aritomo Den* (Tokyo: Yamagata Aritomo Kō Kinen Jigyō-kai, 1933), III, 942–51.

[4] For a brief discussion in English, see Tatsuji Takeuchi, *War and Diplomacy in the Japanese Empire* (Garden City, N.Y.: Doubleday, Doran, 1935), pp. 196–203. See also Ishii Kikujiro, *Gaikō Yoroku* (Tokyo: Iwanami Shoten, 1930), pp. 117–24.

[5] The best account in English is Peter Berton, The Secret Russo-Japanese Alliance of 1916 (unpublished Ph.D. dissertation, Columbia University, 1955). The best account in Japanese is Japan, Gaimushō, *Nichi-Ro Kōshō-shi* (Tokyo, 1944), II, 315–34.

Katō had argued that Japan should take advantage of the weakness of China and the distraction of the Western powers to extract certain basic concessions.[6] Some army men had agreed and the "twenty-one demands" resulted.[7] But the "twenty-one demands" incited a strong anti-Japanese movement in China; and when Yuan made known his ambition to become emperor of a strong, centralized China, many Japanese—not only those inside the government, but those outside it as well—began to question the wisdom of dealing with him.

It was perhaps natural for the Chōshū clique and the military men to analyze the Chinese political situation in Japanese terms, and, in desiring a Sino-Japanese coalition policy, to think not so much of working with popularly supported Chinese bodies as of seeking out friendly factions and bolstering them with economic and military support. Accordingly, in 1915–16, following Katō's resignation, a group of high-ranking military and naval officers began to meet regularly in the office of Koike Chōzō, chief of the Political Affairs Bureau of the Foreign Ministry, to map out such a policy.[8] It was apparently this group, supported in the cabinet by members of the China League (Tai-Shi Rengōkai) and financed in part by the Okura and Kuhara zaibatsu, which helped to organize the secret financial and military support for Ch'en Ch'imei's uprising at Shanghai in December, 1915, for Ts'ai Ao's rebellion in Yunnan in 1916, and for the monarchist movement of

[6] Itō Masanori, Katō Kōmei (Tokyo: Katō Haku Denki Hensan I'inkai, 1929), II, 132–40.

[7] For example, Major General Machida Kei'u, military attaché at the legation in Peking, forwarded a memorandum to Tokyo on September 21, 1914, urging an over-all settlement with China, the details of which appear to have been integrated with the ideas of Foreign Minister Katō to form the so-called "twenty-one demands." Machida Kei'u, "Jikyoku ni kansuru Shiken," September 21, 1914, in JGK,MT 11281, I, 00744–56. The minister of war, General Oka Ichinosuke, even proposed that a military expedition be sent to support them, but he was not backed up by the genro. Kiyozawa Kiyoshi, Nihon Gaikō-shi (Tokyo: Tōyō Keizai Shimpō-sha Shuppan-bu, 1942), II, 356. The actual text of the demands was worked out by Koike Chōzō, chief of the Political Affairs Bureau of the Foreign Ministry. Tokugawa Iemasa (assistant to Koike Chōzō), "Gaimushō Kimmu-chū toriatsukaitaru Shoken," in Japan, Gaimushō Kiroku, "Sho-shūshi Kankei Zakken: Gaikō Shiryō-shū Kankei" (hereinafter, JGK,SKZ), III, 18.

[8] Tokugawa, "Gaimushō Kimmu-chū," JGK,SKZ, III, 18.

Prince Su in Manchuria and eastern Inner Mongolia, early in the same year.[9]

The death of Yuan Shih-k'ai in June, 1916, presented these Japanese planners with an exceptional opportunity. Instead of supporting local revolts, why not establish one of their protégés in control at Peking? From his post as governor general of Korea, the powerful Chōshū leader Marshal Terauchi immediately sent a trusted friend to Peking to see what might be done.[10] His friend was the young continental enterpriser Nishihara Kamezo, a man whose promotion of Japanese-Korean trade and whose interest in broader imperial problems had led Terauchi twice before to use him on confidential missions. On June 19, 1916, Nishihara left for Peking, where he conferred with Japan's chief representatives, including Minister Hioki, Councilor Obata, and Colonel Sakanishi. He also conferred with officials in the Chinese government, particularly with the northern warlord premier Tuan Ch'i-jui and his pro-Japanese coterie, including two graduates of Waseda University, Lu Tsung-yü, the foreign minister, and Ts'ao Ju-lin, successively minister of communications, minister of foreign affairs and finally minister of finance in Tuan's cabinets. Back home, a month later, Nishihara reported to Terauchi and to other members of the Chōshū clique, including Hirata Tōsuke, Yamada Shunzo of the House of Peers, and Shōda Kazu'e, then president of the Bank of Korea. It was apparently as a result of this mission that the Chōshū clique came to a firm decision on China policy: to stop supporting local revolutions in China; instead, it would back the warlord clique of General Tuan Ch'i-jui in its struggle for power in Peking and then seek to build a political, economic, and military coalition with it.[11]

---

[9] Nishihara Kamezo, *Yume no Shichi-jū-yo-nen: Nishihara Kamezō jiden* (Kumobara Mura, 1949), pp. 83–91, 142–50; and Kuzu Yoshihisa, *Tōa Senkaku Shishi Kiden* (Tokyo, 1935), II, 625–48.

[10] Nishihara, *Yume no Shichi-jū-yo-nen*, pp. 92–108.

[11] For a fairly full explanation of the Terauchi cabinet Chinese policy, see the memorandum, "Nisshi Shinzen to Sono Jigyō," drafted by Nishihara at the order of Terauchi on October 1, 1918, corrected by Terauchi on October 28, and then presented to Premier Hara in order to promote continuity in the policy; needless to say, Hara ignored it. Nishihara, *Yume no Shichi-jū-yo-nen*, pp. 277–83. Nishi-

Of course, the Chōshū clique desired that Japan should also clear up the growing misunderstandings with the United States and secure the support of China and the Western powers for its claims to the German colonies in Asia, which it had seized in the early days of the war. But these were policies that any Japanese government might be expected to pursue. The needs which the Chōshū clique felt to be uniquely critical were to expand the size of the armed forces, to strengthen the alliance with Russia, and to build a coalition with a Tuan-led government in China. These needs it was determined to fulfill through the new government.

To appreciate the power and interests of the Chōshū clique in the Terauchi government, which was proclaimed in October, 1916, and which later took the decision to intervene in Siberia, it will be useful to analyze briefly its formation.

Terauchi's "Transcendent" Cabinet

As early as December, 1915, Count Ōkuma, who was then premier, had told Yamagata that he would like to resign.[12] Liberals were attacking him for interfering in the elections and for antagonizing China; bureaucrats were also attacking him for his China policy and, in addition, for failing to achieve the navy's plans for expansion. The difficult job was to find a successor. Ōkuma's choice was Baron Katō Kōmei, leader of the largest party

---

hara, of course, should not be credited with devising the policy, although he was certainly instrumental in convincing his superiors that it could be carried out. The chief planner of the economic phase of the coalition policy seems to have been Gotō Shimpei, who was shortly to become Terauchi's home minister and later his foreign minister. Tsurumi Yūsuke, *Gotō Shimpei* (Tokyo: Gotō Shimpei Denki Hensan-kai, 1938), III, 535–656; and Shinobu Seizaburo, *Taishō Seiji-shi* (Tokyo: Kawade Shobō, 1951–52), II, 335–39. The chief planners of the military alliance seem to have been the army chief of staff, Marshal Uehara, and his vice chief, Lieutenant General Tanaka. Japan, Sambō Hombu, *Shiberia Shuppei-shi*, I, Appendix 5, 49–67; and Araki Sadao, comp., *Gensui Uehara Yūsaku Den* (Tokyo: Gensui Uehara Yūsaku Denki Hankō-kai, 1937), II, 119–20.

[12] Ōtsu Jun'ichiro, *Dai Nihon Kensei-shi* (Tokyo: Hōbunkan, 1927), VII, 820–35. Ōtsu's account of the formation of the Terauchi cabinet has been followed unless otherwise noted.

in the diet, the Dōshikai, which formed the heart of the coalition supporting the Ōkuma cabinet. Katō could be relied on, said Ōkuma, to continue his policies and to win parliamentary support for them; but the clan bureaucrats, particularly Yamagata, would not hear of a Katō cabinet. They had never considered the presidency of a political party either a necessary or a desirable prerequisite for the premiership. There were other ways to control the diet. Nor were they anxious to perpetuate the Ōkuma policies, certainly not the Katō phase of them. Katō stood for at least four things which they objected to: party government, the independence of the foreign ministry, the English rather than the new Russian orientation, and the enmity of China, which the "twenty-one demands" had engendered.

Prince Yamagata had had enough of Katō. This time he wanted a man of his own; and he had such a man in mind. Three influential Communications Ministry bureaucrats had previously taken advantage of the coronation ceremonies at Kyoto in November, 1915, to discuss politics; Baron Gotō Shimpei, Nakakoji Ren, and Baron Den Kenjiro.[13] Gotō, Nakakoji, and Den had agreed among themselves that the China issue should be exploited in order to bring down the Ōkuma cabinet and that the premiership should be offered to Yamagata's heir apparent, Field Marshal Count Terauchi. Gotō drew up a memorandum to this effect and circulated it to enlist support. Yamagata gave the plan his blessing.

Terauchi Masatake had been a soldier all his life. Born in 1851, the second son of a samurai retainer of the Yamaguchi clan in Chōshū, he had been adopted at an early age into the Terauchi family and started on a military career. After training first in the clan cadet corps and then in the military academy in Osaka, he was commissioned in 1871 a second lieutenant in the infantry of Japan's young imperial army. His mettle was tested immediately in the southwestern campaign to suppress the Satsuma rebellion, and he so distinguished himself that, despite the incapacitation

[13] Iwabuchi Tatsuo, *Sekai Go-jū-nen-shi* (Tokyo: Masu Shobō, rev. ed., 1947), pp. 285–86.

of his right arm through wounds, he was encouraged to stay in the service. He rose steadily to command a brigade in the Sino-Japanese War and shortly afterward was made vice chief of the Army General Staff Headquarters. In 1902 he became minister of war, a post which he held through the period of the Russo-Japanese War and until 1910, when he was appointed governor general of Korea. In the summer of 1916 at the age of sixty-four his appearance was no less distinguished than his record. He was short but powerfully built, his massive head set tightly on broad shoulders. As though to symbolize the origin of the military technique of which he was master, the lower half of his face seemed European, the determined line of his mouth and jaw accentuated by an iron grey moustache and close cropped goatee, but in the upper part of his face small, slitlike eyes and diagonal eyebrows stood out against a broad, bald forehead.

For a brief period in the summer of 1916 it seemed possible that some kind of coalition might be worked out. Ōkuma suggested that the command to form a cabinet be given jointly to Terauchi and Katō; and Yamagata agreed that Terauchi should be recalled from Korea to express his views. Reporting back on July 6, Terauchi immediately entered into conversations with Yamagata and Ōkuma. After three meetings with Ōkuma, the negotiations were broken off. Terauchi rejected outright Ōkuma's two demands: that he share power with Katō and that he agree to continue the Ōkuma policies. Undoubtedly speaking for Yamagata as well as himself, Terauchi declared that what was needed was a "government of national unity," a government not of any one political party, but a government above all parties and therefore one around which all could rally. The clan bureaucrats had decided to insist on a "transcendent cabinet," controlled by themselves. Against the Yamagata clique's determined opposition, Ōkuma could not win. He did make a last attempt to secure the emperor's approval of a Katō government, but Prince Ōyama as lord keeper of the privy seal was able to warn his fellow genro in time to prevent it.

Terauchi immediately set about selecting a cabinet loyal to

himself and to the Chōshū clique. For the key Home Ministry, he selected his early supporter and an advocate of the Sino-Japanese coalition, Baron Gotō. His other two early supporters, Nakakoji and Den, he rewarded with the Ministry of Agriculture and Commerce and the Communications Ministry, respectively. In the War Ministry, there was no reason to remove Lieutenant General Ōshima Ken'ichi; nor was there any reason to change Navy Minister Admiral Baron Katō Tomosaburo. The Foreign Ministry was a more difficult post to fill. Someone was needed who would be friendly to Chōshū policies and would also be able to get along with the Satsuma-inclined career officials. After a month's delay, it appears to have been decided that the safest solution would be for the premier himself to handle China policy, which he did largely by using Nishihara as his personal representative in China, and to appoint someone who would be acceptable to the ministry and who could at the same time be relied on to maintain the Russian tie. Terauchi finally selected a career diplomat with virtually no political ties of any kind, Viscount Motono Ichiro, who as ambassador to Russia had successfully negotiated the secret alliance. Shōda Kazu'e, president of the Bank of Korea and ardent supporter of the Sino-Japanese coalition policy, was made finance minister. The other less important posts were filled largely with bureaucratic friends from the days Terauchi served in the Katsura cabinet or as governor general of Korea.

It was clearly a Chōshū-controlled cabinet. It would be a mistake to conclude, however, that government policy was, therefore, dictated by the Chōshū clique.

Terauchi's Party Allies

The cabinet was only one, although admittedly the most important, organ in Japanese government and society in the late years of the First World War. We have already noted how the army had developed independent power. Similarly, other career services and government bodies had their own powers and in time developed their own *esprit de corps;* they were less powerful than the army, to be sure, but their wishes could not altogether be ignored. The *zaibatsu* had grown rich and powerful, hungry for political influence, and valuable to anyone seeking public office. Most important of all, the political parties were increasingly demanding control of the government; and, largely because of their power over legislation, especially appropriations, their demands had somehow to be appeased.

The political history of Japan between 1889 and 1918 has often been written in terms of a struggle for power between the bureaucratic forces led by the genro, and the popular forces led by the party leaders, with the result that the non-party or what the Japanese call "transcendent" cabinets have been looked on as organs of the genro while the infrequent "party" cabinets have been looked on as organs of the diet. While it is true that under various cabinets the balance of power between these forces shifted, it is of more fundamental importance to understand that, as time went on, both the genro and the party leaders came to realize that no cabinet, whether organized by party leaders or by bureaucrats, could rule effectively unless it was able to establish some kind of working understanding between a majority party or a majority coalition in the diet and one or more of the powerful clan cliques in the bureaucracy. It was highly desirable also to secure the active support of one or more of the *zaibatsu.*

In the past the cliques had tried various ways of securing these connections, including infiltration into their official hierarchies, marriage alliances, and the granting or withholding of government favors. Prince Saionji, for example, who had been less successful than his fellow genro in building a strong personal clique in the bureaucracy, was the brother of Baron Sumitomo, the great *zaibatsu,* and was also the past president of the Seiyūkai political party, whose head at the time of the Siberian expedition was Hara Kei, a man with extensive experience in the government bureaucracy and in the affairs of the Furukawa Mining

Company.[14] The same Seiyūkai party had also developed ties with the Chōshū clique and the Mitsui interests. On the other hand, the Satsuma clique had established working arrangements with the Mitsubishi interests and with the political party movement led by Count Ōkuma and Baron Katō, the latter being the brother-in-law of Baron Iwasaki, head of the Mitsubishi combine. Whereas in the Japanese tradition the cliques were like clans, each with its own lord and loyal samurai, the ties formed among the leaders of these cliques, the political parties, the zaibatsu, and other bureaucratic groups had come, by the time of the Siberian expedition, to resemble the shifting coalitions formed in earlier times among relatively equal feudal lords.

Terauchi, of course, had proclaimed his cabinet to be transcendent. He had rejected a coalition with Katō; he had further affronted Katō's party by appointing to cabinet posts men who had recently resigned from that party; and he had steadfastly refused to take men from any other party into his cabinet. It became immediately clear, however, that transcendent though the cabinet might be, it could not govern effectively without political party support. The problem was extremely serious since, on October 10, 1916, the day following the proclamation of the new cabinet, the three parties which had supported the former cabinet in the diet officially announced the formation of the Kenseikai or Constitutional party, headed by Baron Katō and dedicated to breaking the new government through opposition in the diet.[15]

When the thirty-eighth diet met on January 22, 1917, it was constituted as follows:[16]

Seiyūkai	111
Kokumintō	28
Kenseikai	200
Independents	42
Total	381

[14] For a recent study in English of such relationships, see Robert A. Scalapino, *Democracy and the Party Movement in Prewar Japan: The Failure of the First Attempt* (Berkeley: University of California Press, 1953), especially pp. 258–63.
[15] Itō Masanori, ed., *Katō Kōmei*, II, 228–33.
[16] Ōtsu, *Dai Nihon Kensei-shi*, VIII, 14.

It was obvious to everyone that the new government was headed for trouble. Yamagata's colleague, Hirata Tōsuke, took it upon himself to seek the necessary support for the government. There was no question that the Kenseikai would be hostile to the cabinet. The Kokumintō and Seiyūkai, on the other hand, as the opponents of the Ōkuma government and therefore of the newly formed Kenseikai, might feel differently. The Kokumintō, led by its founder Inukai Tsuyoshi, seemed uncompromising at first. Since its formation in 1910, the Kokumintō had been a vigorous champion of party government, and at its party convention in January, 1917, it determined to seek an alliance with the other parties to bring down the government.[17]

The best chance for diet support seemed to Hirata to be the Seiyūkai and the independents. The Seiyūkai had often cooperated with the Chōshū clique in the past and its president, Hara Kei, had often responded loyally to Yamagata's indulgence. Under Hara's leadership, the Seiyūkai at its January convention had declared that it would "follow a policy of complete independence"; but, behind this façade, Hirata knew that there were two factions struggling for power. The one, led by men like Noda Utarō, favored alliance with the Kenseikai and Kokumintō to bring down the cabinet. The other, led by men like the former bureaucrat Tokonami Takejiro, who had succeeded Gotō as president of the Railway Board in 1913, were more inclined to consider the benefits to be derived from cooperating with the cabinet in power.[18] In the general election of 1915 the Seiyūkai had been severely punished for its opposition. These men saw that cooperation might win not only the favor of Yamagata, without which the party could hardly hope to put its leader into power, but also the favor of the cabinet in a general election, which could help it recover its position in the diet. Hirata determined to work on the Seiyūkai. He talked with Baron Den and had him consult immediately with Tokonami. Tokonami then talked with Hara and the decision was taken: the Seiyūkai would continue

[17] *Ibid.*, VII, 851–56.
[18] *Ibid.*, VII, 836–38.

publicly to proclaim a policy of independence but would proceed privately to support the government.

This was only the first step. The cabinet's next problem was to cut down the size of the opposition and build up the Seiyūkai and other minor parties which might be amenable to government leadership. Two methods had often been employed in such a situation in the past: bribery of current diet members or dissolution of the diet and interference in the ensuing general election. The cabinet decided on the second alternative, for it was believed that the Ōkuma government had interfered so extensively in the election of 1915 that the diet was not really representative, that in fact a relatively free election would result in the kind of diet desired. An opportunity for dissolution arose on January 24, 1917, the third day of the session, when Inukai led the attack by introducing a resolution of "no confidence" in the government. Since the bill would undoubtedly pass by an overwhelming majority, Terauchi promptly dissolved the diet and called for a special general election on April 20.

The general election could be a powerful weapon in the hands of the government, so that it was well to be on the government's side. The Kokumintō, inclined from the experience under the Ōkuma cabinet to cooperate with the Seiyūkai rather than the Kenseikai, saw the wisdom of changing its policy. It too decided to cooperate unofficially with the government. Baron Gotō as home minister was given the job of securing a suitable diet; that is, of breaking the Kenseikai, and strengthening the Seiyūkai, the Kokumintō, and the independents. He did not believe it necessary to resort to extensive interference, but in his instructions to the local election officials, whom he called together in February, he made clear what was expected of them. He said:

The nation, especially its thinking classes, generally expected this dissolution from the very beginning, and has shown its sympathy for other parties than the Kenseikai. Since the majority party is unnaturally large and the minority parties unnaturally small, the actual situation in the diet is not conducive to the smooth functioning of constitutional government, so that the nation, desiring a dissolution, hopes for a complete change in the future.[19]

The results were all that the cabinet had hoped for. The special thirty-ninth diet, which met on June 23, 1917, was constituted as follows:[20]

Seiyūkai	160
Kenseikai	119
Kokumintō	35
Independents	67
Total	381

The Kenseikai's majority had been broken and the other groups built up to such a point that the Terauchi cabinet might be able to weather the parliamentary storm if the support of the Seiyūkai and the Kokumintō could be relied upon, and if a sufficient number of the independents could be rallied into a pro-government party. All these "if's" were realized. The friendliness of the cabinet during the election won a reciprocal feeling of gratitude from the Seiyūkai, the Kokumintō, and from among the independents. Baron Gotō persuaded forty-two of the independents to form a pro-government party, which called itself, first, the Ishinkai, later, the Shinseikai. While this last was the only true government party, so long as it held together and so long as the Seiyūkai and Kokumintō cooperated, the cabinet held theoretically a majority of 47 members in the thirty-ninth diet (June 23 to July 14, 1917) and of 61 members in the fortieth diet (December 27, 1917 to March 26, 1918).[21]

The Advisory Council on Foreign Relations

Gratifying though the election was, the Chōshū clique did not yet feel secure enough, particularly in the field of foreign policy. It worried lest some rival faction in the bureaucracy or some

[19] *Ibid.*, VIII, 7.
[20] *Ibid.*, VIII, 31.
[21] Party composition of the fortieth diet is given *ibid.*, VIII, 147.

party leader in the diet should frustrate its China and Western policies or destroy the united front which it hoped Japan could present at the peace conference to come. As early as May and June, 1916, before the Terauchi cabinet had been formed, the retired Chōshū bureaucrat, Miura Goro, seventy-year-old veteran of the War Ministry and the Privy Council, tried to solve the problem by persuading the heads of the three major parties in the diet (Katō of the Dōshikai, Hara of the Seiyūkai, and Inukai of the Kokumintō) to agree to remove foreign policy from the field of domestic party politics.[22] All three joined in making a declaration to that effect, but when Terauchi refused to work with Katō in the new cabinet the declaration was seriously weakened. At any rate, several of the Chōshū clique, particularly Hirata and Gotō, thought there was a better way, a way which might prevent not only party opposition, but also any possible bureaucratic opposition. They would invite representatives from each of the bodies on which the cabinet relied for its support to form an advisory committee to deliberate on important matters of foreign policy. The cabinet, of course, would still have final responsibility for that policy, and the independent command prerogatives of the military and naval authorities would remain unchanged. On the other hand, such an advisory body would form a convenient organ in which the foreign policies of the major political parties as well as those of the other important groups concerned could be coordinated under the guidance of the cabinet, thereby insuring the cabinet as much as possible against the danger of private obstruction or public attack.

In January, 1917, Baron Gotō began discussing the details with Viscount Itō Miyoji.[23] Itō was not a Yamagata man; he had been a protégé of that other great Restoration leader from Chōshū, Itō Hirobumi. As one of the drafters of the constitution and of many other fundamental laws, Itō Miyoji was perhaps even more concerned than his sponsor for the legal structure of the government.

[22] Itō, Katō Kōmei, II, 64–70.
[23] Kuribara Hirota, Hakushaku Itō Miyoji (Tokyo: Shinteikai, 1938), III, 68–69.

Appointed to the Privy Council in 1899, he was respected and trusted by the Yamagata clique as a guardian of the bureaucracy, the very embodiment of the law. It was he who drafted the ordinance establishing the Advisory Council on Foreign Relations.[24] The rough draft was discussed first with Foreign Minister Motono, Premier Terauchi, and probably others; finally, in May, 1917, Itō secured Yamagata's approval.

The stage was set. On June 2, Baron Katō Kōmei, Hara Kei, and Inukai Tsuyoshi were invited to confer with Terauchi at the Prime Minister's official residence.[25] Terauchi reviewed the need for a strong, consistent foreign policy, much as Miura had done the year before. He then invited them to participate with representatives of various organs of the government in a special advisory council. Hara and Inukai readily accepted. They had already experienced the benefits of cooperation in the general election and their parties had already decided on a policy of unofficial cooperation. Katō hesitated. His party had suffered seriously in the general election and he himself had been under vigorous attack by the bureaucrats, particularly for his foreign policy in the Ōkuma cabinet. To yield to the prime minister's request would mean abandoning two firm principles: responsible party government and the independence of the Foreign Ministry. Three days later Katō gave his answer: if the government wanted the advice of the party leaders, it should take them into the cabinet; otherwise, it should make its own policy and be ready to accept responsibility for it.

By this time, the Kenseikai's control of the diet had been broken, so that Katō's approval was not indispensable. On June 5, 1917, the Advisory Council on Foreign Relations was established by imperial ordinance.[26] Directly under the emperor and presided over by the premier, the council was to deliberate on "important matters relating to the general situation." Its initial members were appointed by the emperor and were given the title of ministers

[24] Rinji Gaikō Chōsa I'in-kai.

[25] Itō, *Katō Kōmei*, II, 260–67.

[26] Gazetted in the *Kwampō Gōgai*, June 7, 1917, quoted in Kuribara, *Haku-shaku Itō Miyoji*, III, 66–67.

of state. They included Field Marshal Count Terauchi Masatake (premier), Viscount Dr. Motono Ichiro (foreign minister), Baron Gotō Shimpei (home minister), Lieutenant General Ōshima Ken'ichi (war minister), Admiral Baron Katō Tomosaburo (navy minister), Viscount Itō Miyoji (privy councilor), Viscount Hirata Tōsuke (member of the House of Peers), Baron Makino Shinken (member of the House of Peers), Hara Kei (member of the House of Representatives and president of the Seiyūkai), and Inukai Tsuyoshi (member of the House of Representatives and president of the Kokumintō).

In terms of official organs of the government, the advisory council is seen to have represented the premier, the two military bureaucracies (the army and the navy); the two most important civilian bureaucracies (the Foreign and Home ministries); the Privy Council, whose approval was needed for all treaties and any other important measures the emperor cared to refer to it; and the two houses of the diet, which together exercised legislative, including budgetary control. An analysis in terms of the unofficial cliques and groups represented is even more enlightening. Except for Motono, who was relatively isolated, and Itō, who was inclined toward independence although he often cooperated with the Chōshū leadership, the members of the advisory council fell neatly into three powerful groups: the Chōshū clique (Terauchi, Gotō, Ōshima, and Hirata), the Satsuma clique (Makino and Katō), and the Seiyūkai and Kokumintō political parties (Hara and Inukai). Perhaps nowhere is there better revealed the true coalition nature of this so-called last of the bureaucratic cabinets.

Terauchi continued to proclaim the transcendent character of his "government of national unity" and Hara and Inukai continued publicly to declare the independence of their parties; but in practice the Terauchi government was now a coalition between the Chōshū bureaucrats on the one hand, and the Satsuma clique and the leaders of the Seiyūkai, the Kokumintō, and the Ishinkai political parties on the other. Terauchi, who was pictured publicly as the military strong man, the superparty leader, had in fact to play the role of a politician, mediating among various forces, none of which he could control.

During his first year in office Terauchi played this role to good effect. He encouraged the army to develop plans to increase its strength.[27] He satisfied the Satsuma clique by twice securing special appropriations from the diet to enlarge the naval establishment.[28] Support for Japan's postwar claims were won secretly from the British, the French, and the Russians;[29] and Ambassador Ishii managed to smooth out relations with the United States.[30] For a while the Chōshū clique's Chinese policy was thwarted by Tuan Ch'i-jui's loss of office shortly after Terauchi came to power; but, largely through the agency of Terauchi's personal representative Nishihara, Tuan was encouraged to recover the premiership by force, in July, 1917, and to enter into concrete discussions concerning economic and military ties with Japan.[31]

The Terauchi government was thus moving smoothly along its appointed course when suddenly it was challenged by a wholly new situation: the Russian Revolution and its spread eastward.

[27] Araki, Gensui Uehara Yūsaku Den, II, 114–17.

[28] Matsushita, Kindai Nihon Gunji-shi, pp. 227–29.

[29] Shinobu Seizaburo, Kindai Nihon Gaikō-shi (Tokyo: Kenshin-sha, rev. ed., 1948), p. 228; the same author's Taishō Seiji-shi, II, 345–46; and British ambassador to the Japanese foreign minister, February 16, 1917, in John V. A. MacMurray, Treaties and Agreements with and concerning China, 1894–1919 (New York: Oxford University Press, 1921), II, 1368.

[30] After two months' negotiations in Washington, Ishii managed on November 2, 1917, to conclude with Secretary of State Lansing an agreement often referred to as the Lansing-Ishii agreement, in which Japan undertook to respect China's independence and territorial integrity and the United States agreed to recognize Japan's "special interests" in China. Ishii, Gaikō Yoroku, pp. 136–48.

[31] For Nishihara's part in these events, see the discussion of his fourth trip to China, June 3 to August 3, 1917, in Nishihara, Yume no Shichi-jū-yo-nen, pp. 196–211.

III. ENEMIES AND ALLIES

When news reached Tokyo of the Bolshevik seizure of power in Petrograd on November 7, 1917, the Japanese leaders were no more prepared than the leaders of any other Allied government to deal with the complex problems which were soon to confront them, but they were determined from the beginning that developments in Russia should not be permitted to distract them from their fundamental policy of "Asia first" or, more specifically, "China first." At the same time, they were anxious, if possible, not to permit the Russian Revolution to weaken the ties they had so laboriously built with England, France, and America. Obviously, the basic problem was how to develop a new Russian policy that would reconcile these two needs.

Asia First

It was clear to the Japanese that their Western Allies would be seriously affected by the Russian Revolution, for the new rulers in Petrograd had announced on the day of their coup that they meant to take Russia out of the First World War. For three and a half years the Russians had held down the eastern front while the British, the French, and the Italians had fought to a draw in the west and the south. If now, in violation of the Declaration of London, Russia were to sign a separate peace with the Central Powers, thus enabling Germany and Austria-Hungary to replenish their supplies from the fields and mines of the Ukraine, to cut off Rumania, and to shift their eastern legions to the western front, Britain, France, and Italy might well face disaster.

Obviously, in such circumstances the first thought of the Western Allies would be to do all in their power to rebuild an eastern front; and the Japanese leaders could guess what the procedure would be: a request to Japan to send a major military expedition to European Russia. The proposal had first been broached and rejected in 1915. Again, early in 1917 British Foreign Secretary Balfour had tried to persuade Russia and Japan to enter into concrete negotiations for such an expedition, but Japan's military attaché in London, General Inagaki, had made clear that his country would require a high price to send its troops out of east Asia; and Balfour had agreed with Russian Minister Nabokov that the price suggested, including transfer of the Chinese Eastern Railway branch northward to Harbin and the demilitarization of Vladivostok, was too high.[1]

Despite the failure of these preliminary talks, Western newspapers revived the idea again and again during the summer of 1917.[2] France broached the subject at the Inter-Allied Conference on July 25–26,[3] and brought it up again with Russia in the fall.[4] As plans were being made during these months for another Inter-Allied Conference on the Russian problem,[5] the Chōshū clique in Japan became convinced that another and stronger plea for a

[1] Balfour mediated these negotiations indirectly through Lt. Col. Charles à Court Repington, his close personal friend and then military correspondent of the London *Times*, between January 14 and March 4, 1917. Charles à Court Repington, *The First World War, 1914–1918: Personal Experiences* (Boston: Houghton Mifflin Co., 1920), I, 432–77. Nabokov seems to have been approached by someone again in the summer of 1917, when he records that he conveyed to the Russian high command a suggestion he had received to send 200,000 Japanese troops to the Russian front, but that this was rejected as "impracticable." Constantin Nabokov, *The Ordeal of a Diplomat* (London: Duckworth, 1921), p. 244.

[2] Ōtsu Jun'ichiro, *Dai Nihon Kensei-shi* (Tokyo: Hōbunkan, 1927), VIII, 294–98.

[3] David Lloyd George, *War Memoirs of David Lloyd George* (Boston: Little, Brown, 1936), V, 91–93.

[4] J. Noulens, *Mon ambassade en Russie soviétique 1917–1919* (Paris, 1933), II, 46.

[5] Memorandum from British embassy to Department of State, September 10, 1917, in *USFR, 1917: Supplement 2: The World War*, I, 197–98; Secretary of State Lansing to Wilson, October 3, 1917, *ibid.*, I, 222–23; and Francis (in Petrograd) to Lansing, October 15, 1917, *ibid.*, I, 254.

Japanese expedition was in the offing. Lest the government's resolution waver under increased Allied pressure, the Chōshū leaders decided in October to secure a prior commitment to reject any such proposal that might be made. Accordingly, the Army General Staff Headquarters prepared a report and submitted it to the cabinet.[6]

Entitled "Analysis of a European Expedition," the report examined in detail the physical problems involved in any major expedition to European Russia, including the difficulties of transportation, the cost of supplies and of reorganizing Japan's administrative structure. It concluded that while such an expedition would be possible, it would require an extraordinary expenditure of money and effort. "The question is," said the army, "would it be worth the sacrifice it would entail?"

Declaring emphatically that it would not, the army reminded the cabinet of the basic assignment which the Chōshū clique had given it: to strengthen Japan's position in east Asia so that it would be able, after the war, to withstand the competition of the Western powers in China. For the sake of this policy, the army had refused for three and a half years to divert any major force to Europe. The Allies knew that. In fact, the Japanese army argued, it was precisely because the Allies did know it and precisely because they wished to defeat Japan's purposes in east Asia that they had pressed and would press again for a Japanese expedition. The Japanese government needed to see that fact just as clearly. It needed to be on its guard lest the Russian Revolution confuse it about the Allies' true purposes and distract it from the scene of its major responsibility. That scene was China. Of course, if the Allies were willing to defray the expenses and provide the supplies for Japan to operate wherever it chose, that might be something else; but, until they were prepared to do so, or until the Japanese government had secured "Japan's political and economic supremacy in China," the cabinet had better leave European Russia alone and devote all of its energies to "solving the China problem."

The army's views made good sense to the cabinet, apparently

[6] Ōshū Shuppei ni kansuru Kenkyū," in Japan, Sambō Hombu, *Taishō Shichinen naishi Jūichi-nen Shiberia Shuppei-shi* (1924), I, Appendix, 7–28.

even to its independent-minded foreign minister, Viscount Motono. When the Bolshevik coup of November 7 finally caused the Allies to schedule for November 29 the frequently postponed Inter-Allied Conference on the Russian problem at Paris, the Japanese cabinet, pressed no doubt by the Chōshū clique and the army, decided to take the next step of seeking support for its policy from the entire governing coalition. A meeting of the Advisory Council on Foreign Relations was called at the prime minister's official residence on November 12.[7] Here, Foreign Minister Motono explained why the cabinet feared that the Allies would use the forthcoming Paris conference as an opportunity to urge Japan to send an expedition to Europe and argued that practical considerations made it impossible for Japan to comply. To Motono's relief, party and bureaucratic members alike agreed. No time was lost in sending instructions to Japan's representatives in London and Paris.[8]

Although the extremely meager reports of this council meeting do not say so, it must also have discussed the attitude Japan should take toward the Bolshevik regime. The council seems to have decided that, for the time being, Japan would not recognize the Soviet government and would not join it in negotiating with Germany. One important reason, no doubt, was a strong desire to show sympathy for the wartime plight of Japan's Western Allies, but not to the extent of sending troops to aid them.

Confusion at Paris

The soundness of the Chōshū clique's preliminary estimate of the situation was confirmed at the Inter-Allied Conference at Paris, November 29–December 3, 1917.[9] In the course of the discussions,

---

[7] Hara Kei, *Hara Kei Nikki*, ed. Hara Kei'ichiro (Tokyo: Kengensha, 1950–52), VII, 266.

[8] Japan, Sambō Hombu, *Shiberia Shuppei-shi*, I, 31–32.

[9] Minutes of the Inter-Allied Conference have never been published. Partial reports by Colonel House and other American representatives can be found in *USFR, 1917, Supplement 2: The World War*, I, 334–445. See also Edward Mandell House, *Intimate Papers of Colonel House*, ed. Charles Seymour (Boston: Houghton Mifflin, 1926–28), III, 246–315. For a British account, see Lloyd George, *War Memoirs*, V, 108–110. A copy of the complete text or at least the

the proposal for a Japanese expedition to European Russia was made by Field Marshal Foch, though in a form slightly different from what the Japanese had expected. He urged not a solely Japanese expedition to European Russia, but a joint operation conducted by Japan and America.

"Russia," declared Foch, "is in a state of anarchy and disorder which imperils its military and political power and its economic riches." The West, he went on, is threatened with a collapse of the Russian forces and the isolation and consequent destruction of the Rumanian forces on the southeastern front. Not only would this detract from the military power of the Allies, but it would enable Germany to extend at will its conquests deep into Russia, seizing the Russian industrial plant and natural resources. Germany would thereby be enabled enormously to enhance its offensive power in the West and to build for itself a base from which to menace Korea and jeopardize "the economic development of the lands of the Far East."

The only way to prevent this catastrophe, said Foch, was to bolster the still strong Rumanian forces and, under British and French direction (to which the Rumanians had already agreed) have them serve as a nucleus around which to group organized pro-Allied elements in southern Russia, such as the Cossacks, the Caucasian peoples, and the Czechoslovaks. In order to build such a southeastern coalition, the British and French would of course require a protected route of communication, such as only the Trans-Siberian Railroad could provide. The European Allies, he went on, were in no position to seize the railway. On the other hand, Japan and the United States, by reason of geographic location, military power, and national interest, were ideally suited for just such an operation. Specifically then, Foch proposed that Japanese and American troops should "take possession of the Trans-Siberian

---

substance of the important proposal by Marshal Foch referred to below, will be found in Appendix A, below, entitled "Memorandum au sujet des mesures à prendre à l'égard de la Russie"; this was transmitted to Japan's Ambassador Matsui and has been preserved in the Japanese Foreign Ministry archives in the file entitled "Rokoku Kakumei Ikken: Shuppei Kankei: Hon Mondai Shinchoku Keika" (hereinafter, *JGK, RKI, SK, HMSK*), pp. 95–100.

Railroad at Vladivostok first, then at Harbin, and from there to Moscow, by means of detachments which would extend their action progressively along the line." It was simply a "security measure" to be accomplished by "police detachments." Once the line was secured, increased supplies could be sent to the southeastern front, preparing "further military aid to the combatants" as needed, and acting to prevent German penetration across Russia and Siberia.

Slightly different though this was from the proposal that had been expected, the Japanese representatives, Ambassadors Chinda and Matsui, felt confident in rejecting it.[10] So did the American representative, Colonel House, who insisted that, far from rallying the Russian people to the Allied cause, intervention of this kind would drive them even more securely into the arms of the Germans. Balfour might have been expected to challenge this view. It will be remembered that earlier in the year he had tried to arrange for a Japanese expedition, and, since November 1, he had pressed Lord Reading to sound out the Americans on the possibility of either supporting a Japanese expedition or sending one of their own.[11] He must certainly also have discussed the problem with Britain's ally across the Channel, so that the "Foch plan" would appear to be as much British as French. However, at the conference Balfour joined the opposition. He seems to have decided that Britain would be better able to persuade Japan and America to change their minds later if it appeared sympathetic to their views then. The Japanese must have been gratified, but hardly deceived.

The Japanese policy of withholding immediate recognition from the Soviet regime and of refusing to join it in peace negotiations with Germany was in harmony with the views of its allies. On the other hand, the Japanese delegates must have been confused, as their government certainly was in the months that followed, by the argument between the British and French delegates over the appropriate attitude toward the Bolsheviks if they persisted in

[10] Japan, Gaimushō, *Shiberia Shuppei Mondai, Dai Ippen: Shiberia Shuppei ni itaru Kōshō Keika* (November, 1922), pp. 3–6.

[11] British Ambassador Reading to Secretary of State Lansing, November 1, 1917, *USFR, 1918, Russia,* II, 1–2.

getting out of the war. Clemenceau was emphatic. To him, Russia's discussions with Germany were an outright violation of Soviet obligations under the London Declaration and could not be condoned in word or deed. Baron Sonnino was equally adamant. Colonel House agreed. The British, however, were differently inclined. The French were being too emotional and too legalistic. Lloyd George urged his colleagues to remember that the central objective now was to keep Russia out of Germany's hands; and the way to do that was certainly not to condemn it for an act it would very probably commit anyway. Would it not be better to "release Russia from her promise to continue the war," to establish some kind of unofficial liaison with the Soviet authorities, and then to offer a reconsideration of war aims in the light of the changed circumstances? Might it not be possible by such a course to wean the new government in Petrograd away from the Germans and, even if it could not be persuaded to give up the peace negotiations, at least to encourage it to insist on terms favorable to the Allies? In the months that followed, the French and the Americans were to see some merit in this proposal, but at Paris the disagreement was strong.

What made the British attitude toward Petrograd difficult for the Japanese to understand was the next proposal made by Lloyd George: while the Allies were conciliating the Bolshevik regime in Petrograd, Lloyd George felt they should also give active support to various anti-Bolshevik organizations, such as General Kaledin's, then being formed in southern Russia. The fact that such movements were fighting Petrograd would, Lloyd George admitted, embarrass the Allies' relations with the Soviet regime; but, he insisted, a policy of support was amply justified by the fact that these anti-Bolshevik regimes were also anti-German, and the Allies must lose no opportunity to encourage any force in Russia which opposed the Central Powers. To the French, this made much better sense than the other British proposal. Apparently it was agreed to develop a concrete plan through future negotiations. It would appear from subsequent actions that this proposal also made good sense to the Japanese; but, coupled with a conciliatory policy toward the

Bolshevik regime in Petrograd, it left the Japanese government confused as to the ultimate course the British government proposed to take. In short, did the British really favor the Bolshevik government or did they oppose it? How deep was their disagreement with the French? And on which side were the Americans?

Danger in the East

While the discussions at Paris were beginning to give the Japanese government some idea of the complications the Russian Revolution was to cause in its relations with the West, the spread of Bolshevik activity eastward was beginning to arouse the Japanese leaders to a different set of problems in its relations with east Asia. The November 7 coup in Petrograd served as a signal for Bolshevik groups throughout the vast reaches of the Russian lands to rise up locally and attempt to establish the Soviet regime. Aided by the prestige of events in Petrograd, by indecision in the ranks of their opponents, and by the guns of radical servicemen returning from the front, Bolshevik power began flowing eastward. The Bolsheviks were not immediately successful everywhere, for they were in most areas a small minority; but they made steady progress. Achinsk and Omsk fell on November 10,[12] Krasnoiarsk, the following day,[13] Barnaul, soon after.[14] Farther eastward, in Irkutsk, Chita, Blagoveshchensk, and Khabarovsk, the Bolsheviks had too little strength to move rapidly; but their feverish activity at Vladivostok and Harbin presaged a determined fight for all of Asiatic Russia.

[12] V. V. Maksakov and A. Turunov, *Khronika Grazhdanskoi Voiny v Sibiri (1917–1918)* (Moscow: Gosizdat, 1926), p. 47. It should be recognized that authoritative data on the takeover in each city seems not yet to be available, and published accounts differ; for example, the date of the soviet accession to power in Omsk is placed as late as December 6, 1917, in Sibirskii Kraevoi Sovet Professional'nykh Soiuzov, *Profsoiuzy Sibiri v Bor'be za Vlast' Sovetov, 1917–1919 gg.*, comp. V. Shemelev and ed. V. Vegman (Novosibirsk, 1928), p. 44.

[13] A. Pomerantseva, "V Krasnoiarske," in Vsesoiuznaia Kommunisticheskaia Partiia, Tsentral'nyi Ispolnitel'nyi Komitet, Sekretariat Glavnoi Redaktsii Istorii Grazhdanskoi Voiny v SSSR, *Sergei Lazo: Vospominaniia i Dokumenty*, comp. G. Reikhberg, A. Romanov, and P. Krol' (Moscow: Gosizdat, 1938), pp. 11–12.

[14] V. Vilenskii-Sibiriakov, "Bor'ba za Sovetskii Sibir'," *Severnaia Aziia*, II, No. 3 (1926), 47–66.

To the Japanese, revolution in European Russia was one thing; a revolution in Asiatic Russia, another. By 1917 Japan had developed important interests in that area: it had invested heavily in Russian government bonds,[15] and had built up a highly lucrative wartime trade with Russia's Asiatic ports (in 1916, these ports of entry, like Vladivostok and Harbin, had become Japan's third largest export market, being outranked only by the United States and China).[16] More and more Japanese companies had established branch offices in the key cities of northern Manchuria and eastern Siberia; and more and more Japanese nationals had taken up residence there.[17] How was the Japanese government to protect these interests in the face of the spreading civil war?

More important, how was the empire now to protect its northern border on the Asian continent? Ever since the first Russians visited Japan in the late eighteenth century, the Japanese had lived in fear of the north. It was, in fact, not until the conclusion of the fourth secret agreement in 1916 that they had at last been able to strike a relative balance with Russian imperial interests along a long line stretching from the Kuriles to Sakhalin, to Korea, across Manchuria into Mongolia. Now the balance was destroyed. The Bolsheviks were publishing the secret agreements and denouncing the tsarist diplomacy which made them possible.[18] If they were to succeed in extending their authority over Russia's Far Eastern realm, would they not renew Russia's traditional drive southward?

[15] Japanese holdings of Russian government bonds are said to have amounted by 1918 to 255,949,323 yen. Uchisaburo Kobayashi, *The Basic Industries and Social History of Japan, 1914–1918* (New Haven: Yale University Press, 1930), p. 260.

[16] Japan's exports to Asiatic Russia in 1916 were valued at 117,693,478 yen; exports to the United States, at 340,244,817 yen; and to China, at 192,712,626 yen. Kakujiro Yamasaki and Gotaro Ogawa, *The Effect of the World War upon the Commerce and Industry of Japan* (New Haven: Yale University Press, 1929), p. 11.

[17] According to Ambassador Shidehara's report at the Washington conference, there were "no less than 9,717" Japanese living in Asiatic Russia in 1917. Japan, Gaimushō, "Gaimushō Kōhyō," No. 2 (January 20, 1922), in *Gaimushō Kōhyō-shū*, No. 3 (1922), p. 17.

[18] See, for example, Trotsky's address of November 27, 1917, translated in Francis (in Petrograd) to Secretary of State Lansing, November 27, 1917, *USFR, 1918, Russia*, I, 248–49.

Would they not then threaten not only Japan's interests in Asiatic Russia, but its interests in Korea, southern Manchuria, and China as well, perhaps even the security of the home islands themselves? Or suppose the Bolsheviks were really agents of the Central Powers, as some Allied leaders suspected. It was not inconceivable that they might reintroduce German power into the East. After all, was there not already the nucleus of a German Asian army in the prisoner-of-war stockades in Asiatic Russia? [19] Might not these men be released to establish control there and later perhaps be sent to attack Japan's continental positions?

Thus, the spread of the Russian Revolution eastward forced Japanese leaders to shift their immediate attention from China to Asiatic Russia and presented them with a difficult decision. Would it be wiser for Japan to assume that the Bolsheviks would win and therefore try to conciliate them, in the hope that eventually a mutually satisfactory division of northeast Asia could again be worked out? Or, would it not be safer for Japan to oppose the Bolsheviks, taking advantage of the civil war to extend Japanese influence over that part of the former Russian empire in which Japan had the greatest interest, namely, the vast, triangular Amur river basin, which stretched along the Japanese empire's northern border from Lake Baikal to the sea? Here the Bolsheviks were extremely weak. Here the Japanese were in a position geographically to exert a major, perhaps a decisive, influence.

The enormously complicating factor, of course, was that Japan was not the only outside power with interests in the Amur basin or in Asiatic Russia in general. The Western Allies also had trade relations, investments, and nationals to protect. They too had other Asian imperial interests for whose security they were concerned. Japan had often been acutely reminded of this fact in the past. It

[19] According to official Russian data, presumably for 1917 before the dissolution of the armed forces, some 50,694 prisoners of war were being held in stockades east of Irkutsk; the great majority of these were Austro-Hungarians. USSR, Tsentral'noe Statisticheskoe Upravlenie, *Rossiia v Mirovoi Voine, 1914–1918 goda (v tsifrakh)* (Moscow: Gosizdat, 1925), pp. 40–41. The exact number, of course, was not known to the Japanese, thus permitting fear to double it many times.

was again reminded of it by developments in Vladivostok and Harbin in November and December, 1917.

The Question of Vladivostok

Vladivostok, "Lord of the East," was a naval base of great strategic importance, the only threat to Japanese hegemony in the Sea of Japan. Moreover, as the terminus of the Trans-Siberian rail system, it was one of the great emporia of trade between East and West. During the First World War it had come to serve as one of the chief avenues of supply for the Russian front. In fact, so great was the Allied supply effort and so crippled was the Trans-Siberian by the deterioration of equipment and the disaffection of employees that, by the winter of 1917–18, there had accumulated in Vladivostok about seven hundred tons of goods: cotton, railway truck wheels, a submarine, ammunition, automobiles, shoes, barbed wire, agricultural implements, and field guns.[20] Crammed into warehouses, piled on docks, and stacked in open fields, these military stores were valued in the fall of 1918 as high as one billion dollars.[21]

Vladivostok, like most Siberian cities, was predominately anti-Bolshevik. Nevertheless, following the coup in Petrograd, the Bolsheviks here as elsewhere tried to emulate the accomplishment of their comrades in the west. Their usual tactic was to try to win control of a local soviet or committee of representatives of radical workers and soldiers, then to form Red Guards out of the troops returning from the eastern front, and finally to use the strength of these guards to transfer all local authority to the soviet. On November 18, the Bolsheviks in Vladivostok succeeded in winning a

[20] According to an American estimate, 700–750 tons. J. E. Greiner, "The American Railway Commission in Russia," *Railway Review* (Chicago), LXIII, No. 5 (August 3, 1918), 171, cited in John Albert White, *The Siberian Intervention* (Princeton: Princeton University Press, 1950), p. 137. According to a British estimate, 635 tons. Chinda (in London) to Motono, January 1, 1918, *JGK, RKI, SK, HMSK*, p. 173.

[21] Carl W. Ackerman, *Trailing the Bolsheviki: Twelve Thousand Miles with the Allies in Siberia* (New York: Scribner's Sons, 1919), p. 42.

majority in the executive committee of the Vladivostok soviet.[22]
On December 1, they pushed through a resolution claiming a transfer of all local authority to the soviet, and three days later the Red
Guard prepared to enforce the claim. With the moderate majority
of citizens unprepared to put up effective resistance, the city was
in imminent danger of falling into Bolshevik hands.

Although discussions within the Japanese cabinet have never
been made public, it is clear that the Japanese navy was alarmed
by the extension of the Russian Revolution to Vladivostok. Fearing
that the lives and property of Japanese and other foreign nationals
would be endangered by the disorder accompanying an attempt by
the soviet to seize control of the city and believing that Bolshevik
control of the great base would threaten Japan's security on the
Sea of Japan, the Japanese naval authorities made preparations
early in November to send ships to Vladivostok, but they were restrained by the attitude of the British.[23] Foreign Minister Motono
was aware of Allied interest in the stores piled up at the port and
he was anxious not to jeopardize the alliance with Britain. So before ordering the ships to Vladivostok he took the precaution of
consulting with His Majesty's ambassador in Tokyo, Sir Connyngham Greene. To Motono's chagrin, Sir Connyngham vetoed the
plan, expressing Britain's hope that Japan would act only in con-
cert with the Allies. Apparently in preparation for such an action,
the British War Office had ordered a garrison battalion at Hong
Kong to hold itself in readiness.[24]

By December 10, the British had become more seriously concerned about the Bolshevik threat to Vladivostok.[25] Balfour now
agreed with Ambassador Chinda that "it would be a serious matter

[22] G. Reikhberg, "Bol'sheviki Dal'nego Vostoka v Bor'be s Iaponskoi Interventsiei, 1918–1922 gg.," *Proletarskaia Revoliutsiia*, III (1939), 77–78.

[23] Japan, Kaigun Gunreibu, *Taishō Yon-nen naishi Kyū-nen Kaigun Senshi*
(1924), I, 134.

[24] John Ward, *With the "Die-hards" in Siberia* (London: Cassell, 1920), p. 1.

[25] Chinda (in London) to Motono, January 1, 1918, in Japan, Gaimushō, *Shiberia Shuppei Mondai*, I, 3–4; *JGK, RKI, SK, HMSK*, pp. 103–9. The general
tenor of these talks is confirmed in Winston Spencer Churchill, *The World Crisis: The Aftermath* (London: Thornton Butterworth, 1929), p. 89.

if the considerable piles of material sent by the Allies to Vladivostok were to fall into German hands." But, still he did not think independent naval action by Japan would be appropriate. "It would," he was sure, "give rise to misunderstandings by the Russians." The action had better be undertaken by some power which was "generally recognized" as having "no territorial ambitions," preferably the United States. This was obviously not what the Japanese government had in mind. Japan had been working to eliminate Western power from Asia and certainly did not want the Russian Revolution to provide an excuse for increasing it. No, said Chinda, a purely American expedition could not be accepted. If the Allies were to send an expedition to Vladivostok, then, "in view of its position and natural right as well as its duty, Japan should conduct it."

The next day, the Allied consuls at Vladivostok added their pressure.[26] They urged the need for military forces in the city, and added that, while American troops were to be preferred until an Allied force could be organized, Japanese troops would be acceptable in the meantime. Finally, on December 26 the British returned to the idea of common Allied action.[27] Why not, suggested Lord Cecil, Britain's under secretary of state for foreign affairs, send a joint force, "in substance Japanese, with a few French, Americans, and British added for the sake of appearances?"

Allied Action at Harbin

The Japanese government was also made acutely aware of its allies' interest in the Amur basin by the growing crisis at Harbin. Legally, the north Manchurian part of the Amur basin had been recognized by Russia as Chinese territory since the seventeenth century; in fact, since the agreements of 1895–96, the area had been brought

[26] Caldwell (in Vladivostok) to Lansing, Dec. 11, 1917, USFR, 1918, Russia, II, 6.

[27] Morris (in Tokyo) to Lansing, January 7, 1918, USFR, 1918, Russia, II, 20; and a letter from Cecil to Balfour, January 8, 1918, in Blanche E. C. Dugdale, Arthur James Balfour, First Earl of Balfour, K.G.O.M., F.R.S., 1906–1930 (London: Hutchinson, 1936), p. 255.

increasingly under Russian control.[28] The zone of operations of the Chinese Eastern Railway became in large measure a protectorate of the Russian government and the railway company itself came to function as a kind of colonial administration, financed by the Russo-Asiatic Bank and controlled ultimately by the Russian Ministry of Finance.[29] The only effective elements of Chinese authority within the railway zone were the Central Customs House at Harbin and its branches at Manchouli and Pogranichnaia at either end of the line. By 1916, Russian influence had grown so strong that Japan had agreed secretly to recognize the zone as a sphere exclusively of Russian exploitation.[30]

As the seat of administration of the railway zone and consequently a point of great commercial and political importance, Harbin, like Vladivostok, was an early object of Bolshevik ambition in the Amur basin. Also as in Vladivostok, the Bolshevik faction was not particularly strong. On November 7, when the Bolsheviks tried to persuade the Harbin soviet to oust General Horvat, the tsarist-appointed managing director of the railway and governor of the railway zone, they were promptly voted down.[31] Instead, a left-wing coalition of Social Revolutionaries and Mensheviks, who held a moderate majority, formed a Committee of Public Safety, representing all parties and institutions of popular government; two members of the committee were attached to the railway administration.

The consular corps seems to have viewed this as a transition step to Bolshevik control or else they felt that the moderate socialists

[28] Japan, Gaimushō, Jōyaku-bu, *Ei-Bei-Futsu-Ro no Kakkoku oyobi Shina Kokkan no Jōyaku* (1924), *passim*.

[29] Japan, Sambō Hombu, "Sambō Tokugō Shina Dai 4 gō," May 3, 1918, in Japan, Gaimushō, "Rokoku Kakumei Ikken: Shiberia ni taisuru Beikoku no Riken Kito sono ta Taidō Zakken" (hereinafter, *JGK, RKI, SB*), pp. 342–49.

[30] By the secret Russo-Japanese agreements signed on July 30, 1907, July 4, 1910, July 8, 1912, and July 3, 1916. See Peter Berton, The Secret Russo-Japanese Alliance of 1916 (unpublished Ph.D. dissertation, Columbia University, 1955); Japan, Gaimusho, *Nichi-Ro Kōshō-shi* (Tokyo, 1944), II, 315–34; and Ernest Bateson Price, *The Russo-Japanese Treaties of 1907–1916 concerning Manchuria and Mongolia* (Baltimore: Johns Hopkins University Press, 1933).

[31] Moser (in Harbin) to Reinsch, November 17, 1917, in *USFR, 1918, Russia*, II, 2–3.

presented an equally serious threat to their interests. At any rate, on
November 10, 1917, British Consul Porter and United States Consul Moser formally recognized General Horvat as the "head of the
local administration." Their governments, they said, would not be
indifferent to his removal. The situation grew more tense when
on November 21 the soviet received an order from Lenin to assume
power and to appoint commissars to the customs stations for Manchurian trade.[32] On the following day the consular corps responded
by telling General Horvat that he had their full support to take
preventive action; and, in case outside aid should be needed, the
consuls demanded that he accept a "program for the intervention
of Chinese or of international police." [33] In fear of disorder, the
Japanese reinforced their consulate by bringing up additional
guards from Changchun on December 2.[34] From Peking the Russian minister pressed Horvat to accept the consuls' demand, pointing out that without their support he would be recognized by no
one.[35]

It was under these trying circumstances that Horvat came into
contact for the first time with an aggressive young Trans-Baikal
Cossack, who was to play a major role in the drama of the Siberian
expedition. Gregorii Semenov, according to his autobiography, was
born in 1891 in the small Cossack village Kuranzka, on the middle
reaches of the Onon river in southern Trans-Baikal Territory.[36]
Raised in the Cossack tradition and fired with tales of ancient Mongol greatness, he developed into a bold, brutal frontiersman. At the
age of twenty, following graduation from the Orenburg Cossack
School, he was assigned to the First Verhkneudinsk Regiment of

[32] Dmitrii Leonidovich Horvat, "Memoirs" (a manuscript in the Hoover Library), ch. IX, cited in White, *Siberian Intervention*, p. 79.
[33] Reported in *The Far Eastern Review* (Shanghai), XV, No. 3 (March, 1919),
298.
[34] Kuroda Koshiro, *Gensui Terauchi Hakushaku Den* (Tokyo: Gensui Terauchi Hakushaki Denki Hensanjo, 1920), p. 294.
[35] Reinsch (in Peking) to Lansing, December 6, 1917, *USFR, 1918, Russia*,
II, 5.
[36] This account of Semenov's early life is based on his *O Sebe* (Harpin: Zaria,
1938), pp. 1–75.

the Trans-Baikal Cossack Army and stationed first in Troitskosavsk on the border of Khalka (Outer Mongolia), later in Urga, the capital of that region. His fascination with Mongolian affairs and his extraordinary propensity for intrigue showed themselves at once. He cultivated the Mongol leaders; and in the disturbances which followed the declaration of Khalka's independence from China in December, 1911, he not only rescued the Chinese imperial resident at Urga as he was ordered to do, but on his own initiative deployed his troops to disarm and disperse the Chinese garrison there. This was too much for his superiors. They promptly recalled him and for the next six years kept him as far from Mongolian affairs as they could. For a while he was packed off to a military school in Chita. Then he was moved eastward to Maritime Territory, where he was assigned to border patrol duty along the Ussuri river. In August, 1914, his "hundred" was mobilized and sent to the southwest front, where he fought until January, 1917, when he was given command of the Third Hundred of the Third Verkhneudinsk Regiment on the Persian front.

While these years of service on distant fronts kept Semenov from intriguing with his Mongol friends in Trans-Baikalia and Khalka, they also gave him valuable experience in military leadership. Moreover, it seems to have been during his service in the west that he formed a friendship with Baron Ungern-Sternberg, a Russian officer of Baltic German extraction who was later to serve as Semenov's faithful lieutenant in the Trans-Baikal fighting and in 1920 was to attempt to carve out a great pan-Mongol state in northeast Asia. Semenov found the baron a kindred soul, an autocrat, a soldier, and a mystic dreamer as well. When the front began to crumble under revolutionary influences in the late winter and spring of 1917, the two friends were roused not to flight, but to heroic deeds. They realized that the empire was doomed unless a volunteer army could be raised quickly. Where could such an army be raised? They thought they knew the answer: from among the non-Russian peoples like themselves, especially in eastern Siberia. Semenov saw the Buriat Mongols as the nucleus of such a force.

His mind traveled back to the thirteenth century when the Mongol hordes swept into Europe. He saw himself as a kind of latter-day Genghis Khan, riding at the head of the nomads to save his tsar.

After disbandonment of the Second Cossack Corps Semenov was ordered back to the Ussuri Brigade. In May he wrote about his plan to War Minister Kerensky, whereupon he was ordered to Petrograd to explain it to Colonel Murav'ev, chief of the All-Russian Revolutionary Committee for Forming a Volunteer Army under the General Staff. For a moment, Semenov's head was turned by the bigger stage. He proposed a military *coup d'état* in favor of General Brusilov. Although Colonel Murav'ev cut this scheme short, he did fall in with Semenov's original proposal, so that when Semenov left the capital on July 26 he claims to have taken with him a commission from the supreme commander as military commissar of the Far East (Irkutsk and Priamur military districts, and the Chinese Eastern Railway Zone) and as commander of the Mongol Buriat Cavalry Regiment, to be formed at Berezovka near Verkhneudinsk on the Trans-Baikal Railway. He claimed also to carry "full authority" from the Petrograd soviet.

In August, Semenov, again in Trans-Baikalia, began his campaign. At a meeting at Verkhneudinsk he persuaded the Buryat Mongols of southern Trans-Baikalia to accept his leadership in raising a volunteer unit to enter the Russian army. The Karachens of Inner Mongolia and the Bargut Mongols of Outer Mongolia and northwestern Manchuria had been at odds since the 1916 Karachen revolt against the Chinese, at which time the Barguts had remained loyal to China. Semenov succeeded in bringing them together in conference and in persuading a part of them to join his forces.[37] Hardly had he begun to recruit when, in view of his support of Kornilov, he was ordered by Kerensky to desist, an order which he ignored. When the Provisional Government was overthrown, he has said that he used his special commission from the Petrograd soviet to secure authorization for his force from the chairman of the moderate united soviet in Irkutsk. But as the Bolsheviks increased their influence there, probably shortly after their victory in the

[37] *Ibid.*, pp. 76–7.

election to the soviet on November 28, Semenov fled to Chita, and thence to the prisoner-of-war stockade at Dauriia, where he was joined by Baron Ungern-Sternberg and other rightists. Here Semenov found the garrison undermined, the prisoners of war actually in control. He quickly formed a police unit of German and Turkish prisoners and placed them under Baron Ungern; a captain of the Turkish general staff, Prince Elhadin, he took on his staff; Berezovskii, the commandant and a Cossack member of the Chita soviet, was won over with the offer of an ensign's rank; and the officers of the garrison, led by their commander, Staff Captain Oparin, finally threw in their lot with him. Semenov then sought reinforcements in two directions. The upper Onon river was scoured for volunteers and horses; and Lieutenant Zhevchenko was sent to Harbin with a letter to General Horvat, asking his support in organizing the Russians in Russian territory or in the Chinese Eastern Railway Zone into volunteer units. This was early in December, 1917.

By this time Horvat was under heavy pressure from the Harbin soviet and the Committee of Public Safety on the one hand, and the Allied consuls, the Chinese, and the Russian minister on the other. He could hardly spare recruits for what appeared to be a nationalist Mongol movement and therefore rejected Semenov's overture. Meanwhile, the demands of the Harbin soviet became so insistent that on December 5 Horvat agreed to share the administration of the zone with it.[38] This news galvanized the Allied ministers in Peking to action. They called on the Chinese government to support the Horvat administration with troops. The Chinese government responded immediately, the local Chinese intendant, Sze Sheo-chang, declaring in Harbin not only that the Chinese government would oppose Bolshevik participation in the administration of the railway zone, but that Chinese troops were on their way from Kirin Province.[39]

[38] *Ibid.*, pp. 76–77, and *The Far Eastern Review* (Shanghai), XV, No. 3, 298. The sources actually say "the Bolsheviks," but probably the committee was meant.

[39] *The Far Eastern Review* (Shanghai), XV, No. 3, 298, and "Khronika Sobytii na Tikhom Okeane 1914–1918 gg.," *Tikhii Okean*, III, No. 9 (July–September, 1936), 299.

Sze's announcement cut the ground from under the moderate revolutionaries. Peaceful collaboration with Horvat being impossible, the arguments of the Bolsheviks for immediate seizure by the soviet attracted more support. On December 12 the Bolsheviks gained control of the local soviet, which now declared itself the sole organ of power.[40] The Mensheviks and Social Revolutionaries walked out. The soviet deputies immediately began to assume physical control of the railway administration.[41] On December 18 the soviet announced that Horvat and various other officials had been dismissed. Ensign Riutin remained as chairman of the soviet; Slavin was named chief of the financial section and commissar of the railroad administration in Horvat's place; and Arkus, later shot by Semenov, was named commissar of police.[42]

These developments frightened Semenov. His position in Dauriia was far from secure. Now, if the Chinese Eastern Railway Zone were sovietized, he might be squeezed in a Red vise. On the other hand, were the zone or a part of it secured by himself, it would be an excellent staging area, a privileged sanctuary, from which to launch his planned offensive against the Bolshevik forces in Trans-Baikalia. On the very day that the Harbin soviet announced Horvat's dismissal, December 18, Semenov with only seven men, arrived at Manchouli. Taking advantage of the disorder in the city and claiming to be the leader of a Mongol-Buryat regiment and to be acting for the Provisional Government, he outbluffed the Russian garrison of 1,500 men and demobilized it, arresting and deporting the Bolsheviks he found.[43] On the following day, December 19, he wired Horvat:

[40] G. Reikhberg, *Iaponskaia Interventsiia na Dal'nem Vostoke, 1918–1922 gg.: Kratkii Ocherk* (Moscow: Gosudarstvennoe Sotsial'no-Ekonomicheskoe Izdatel'-stvo, 1935), p. 8 (no source cited).

[41] *The Far Eastern Review* (Shanghai), XV, No. 3, 298.

[42] M. Ivanov, "Oktiabr' v Sibiri, V: 1917 god v Kharbine," *Proletarskaia Revoliutsiia*, No. 10 (October, 1922), p. 383.

[43] Their bodies are said to have arrived in sealed railway cars in Chita on January 3, 1918. USSR, Tsentralnyi Arkhiv RSFSR, Arkhiv Oktiabr'skoi Revoliutsii, *Iaponskaia Interventsiia 1918–1922 gg. v Dokumentakh*, ed. I. Mints (Moscow, 1934), p. 207. Matveev asserts that the Chinese helped Semenov. V. M. Matveev, "Bor'ba za Sovety v Zabaikal'e," in Vsesoiuznaia Kommunisticheskaia Partiia, *Sergei Lazo*, pp. 22–42.

Have disarmed and demobilized the Bolshevized garrison of Manchouli and evacuated it to Russia. Garrison's duties have fallen on my regiment. Awaiting your orders. CAPTAIN OF THE COSSACKS, SEMENOV

It was a bold action, but too remote from Harbin to offset the influence of the Chinese, who saw in Semenov no less than in the soviet a threat to Chinese sovereignty. On December 20, at the request of the allied consular corps the Chinese intendant brought up 4,500 troops from the Kirin army. He demanded that Horvat expel both the Bolsheviks and the Semenovists from the zone, and Horvat was forced to issue the required orders. Both Bolsheviks and Semenovists refused to obey and Horvat was powerless to compel them. Finally, on December 25, in response to the appeal of the acting Russian consul general, the Allied consular corps formally requested the Chinese forces to act.[44] At 3 A.M. on Christmas day, the Chinese staff handed an ultimatum to the Harbin soviet, giving it three days in which to dissolve the 618th Militia and send the militiamen and all other active Bolsheviks beyond the Manchurian border. Faced with overwhelming force, the soviet executive committee and the 618th Militia decided that evening to comply; but the Chinese commander was resolved to take no chances. At nine the next morning, writes one of the Bolshevik leaders:

I saw an unusual crowd of people in the street. Around the barracks of the 618th militia were stacked piles of rifles, surrounded by Chinese soldiers, and groups of curious people. . . . I decided to go to Comrade Riutin's quarters, but had hardly begun to approach his quarters when I saw that they were surrounded by Chinese soldiers. Not understanding what was happening, I turned back and went up to a group that had gathered to hear what they were saying about it. But, just as I began to turn, one of them, pointing to me, cried, "Here is where they did their deeds! Now they are going . . . good riddance! Gentlemen,

[44] Japan, Sambō Hombu, *Shiberia Shuppei-shi*, I, 13. See also Ayakawa Takeharu, *Waga Tairiku Keiei Shippai no Shinsō* (Tokyo: Heisho Shuppan-sha, 1935), pp. 586–87, where the number of disaffected railroad guards is placed at only two companies. In *The Far Eastern Review* (Shanghai), XV, No. 3, 298, the number of Chinese troops was reported at 3,500, and a week later, this was increased by seven thousand.

there is one of the soviet leaders!" Answering back, I lost myself in the crowd and decided not to go to the soviet.[45]

As soon as they had driven the Bolsheviks from Harbin, the Chinese forces began to spread out over the Chinese Eastern Railway Zone, establishing their own military control and threatening the Semenovist bases in the west. Thus, in the first two cities in the Amur basin to be threatened by the Bolsheviks, Vladivostok and Harbin, Japan was reminded immediately by its Western Allies and China that they too had interests in northeast Asia and that they too meant to protect them.

Nishihara's Proposal

The first reaction of the Japanese navy to the revolution on the continent had been to urge that warships be sent to Vladivostok. Three other Japanese groups reacted almost as quickly: the army, the Foreign Ministry, and a private pressure group centering around the prime minister's special representative, Nishihara Kamezō. If Nishihara's autobiography may be trusted, it was this last group which first formulated the basic concept of the Siberian expedition.

Nishihara tells how, on November 13, 1917, he was approached by a Japanese newspaperman, Otani Masao, who solicited his help in organizing a movement among political and academic leaders to awaken Japan to the threat posed by the Russian Revolution.[46] Nishihara agreed, and soon a nucleus was found among the members of the old Tai-ro Dōshikai, an expansionist society which had sprung from that parent of most expansionist societies in modern Japan, the Gen'yōsha or Black Ocean Society in Fukuoka. One of the most active agitators in the new movement seems to have been a twenty-year-old youth from Fukuoka named Nakano Jiro.[47] It

[45] Ivanov, "Oktiabr' v Sibiri: v Kharbine," p. 386. The Japanese army account states that two militia units were involved, the 559th as well as the 618th. Japan, Sambō Hombu, *Shiberia Shuppei-shi*, I.

[46] Nishihara Kamezō, *Yume no Shichi-jū-yo-nen: Nishihara Kamezō Jiden* (Kumobara Mura, 1949), pp. 223–25, 228.

[47] Among the names of the leaders of this pressure group mentioned by Nishihara are the following: Uejima Nagahisa, Shigeno Shujo, Muramatsu Sen'ichiro,

was through Nakano that Nishihara met, on December 10, 1917, a Russian émigré named Andreev. Andreev was convinced that, with Japan's help, Siberia could be organized into an independent anti-Soviet state. He hoped, he said, that Japan would support the movement for Siberian autonomy and would send representatives to negotiate with suitable Russian groups with a view to providing financial and military assistance. Nakano was enthusiastic about the prospects. Nishihara was won over. According to his own testimony, "the time for the Siberian expedition had come," and by December 19, 1917, he had won over both Premier Terauchi and Vice Chief of Staff Tanaka. Shortly thereafter, a young linguist, Yoshimi Enzō, was sent to the continent to work with Andreev; at the end of January, 1918, Andreev himself was replaced by a certain Sawano Hideo. The whole venture would appear to have been the private policy of certain members of the Chōshū clique; the foreign minister, for example, was not informed.[48]

Official records confirm that Yoshimi was sent to the continent at this time for the purposes Nishihara states. As will be seen presently, certain decisions taken by the army in mid-December lend some support to Nishihara's account of the conversion of Tanaka and Terauchi to intervention. Moreover, the role Nishihara claims to have played in regard to Russian policy is similar to the crucial one which he played in China policy in this same period. In both cases he would appear to have been an important personal representative of the premier's wishes. On the other hand, his influence need not be overemphasized, for certainly various regular branches

Oishi Masashi, Dr. Tateba Tongo, Dr. Tomizu Kannin, and the above-mentioned Ōtani Masao and Nakano Jiro. A public meeting was called by this group, ostensibly on Germany, in the Kanda youth hall in Tokyo on December 18, 1918. Other public rallies followed and articles supporting an independent Japanese expedition were sent to various newspapers and magazines. Nine doctors of law were enlisted in the cause and in March, 1918, Ōtani published their essays in a volume entitled Shuppei Ron (Arguments for an Expedition).

[48] Motono seems to have learned of Yoshimi's activities on March 18, 1918, for the first time. Yoshimi to Nishihara, March 18, 1918, enclosed in Hayashi to Motono, March 24, 1918, Japan, Gaimushō Kiroku, "Rokoku Kakumei Ikken: Han-Kagekiha Kankei" (hereinafter, JGK, RKI, HK), I; Motono to Hayashi, April 2, 1918; ibid., II; and Hayashi to Motono, April 4, 1918, ibid., I.

of the Japanese government—the navy, the army, and the foreign
ministry—were concurrently moving toward a similar decision.

The Army's Plans

Only one week after the Russian Revolution the Chōshū clique
had made a rapid start toward developing a new Russian policy
and had succeeded in winning the unanimous agreement of the
coalition supporting the Terauchi cabinet. It should be remembered, however, that this was achieved in behalf of policies that
were essentially negative, such as nonrecognition of the Soviet
regime, nonparticipation in German peace talks, and nonparticipation in a European expedition.

Obviously, such negative policies would not long suffice. In
November and December events in Vladivostok and Harbin led
the Chōshū clique and its leading backer, the army, to believe that
two positive policies were necessary: preparation for sending Japanese troops into the Russian Far East; and execution of the plan to
negotiate a military coalition between Japan and China. In accord
with the first of these two policies, before the end of November
the Army General Staff Headquarters drew up a "Plan to Send
Troops to the Russian Far East to Protect Foreign Residents." [49]
As the title suggests, one purpose of the expedition was to protect
"Japanese nationals living in strategic places in northern Manchuria and the Maritime Territory," but this was not the sole purpose. What was no doubt more important, the troops were to
"guard the railways and telegraph facilities," so that preparations
might be made "for military operations which may be undertaken
later." Significantly enough, the number of troops was decided not
only on the basis of the "number of residents" in those areas and
the "strength of Russian forces" there, but also on the basis of "the
convenience for military operations which may be undertaken later
and the desirability of occupying a commanding position in case
the Allies jointly send troops." The plan called for two tempo-

[49] An English translation of the text of this plan will be found in Appendix B,
below. Japan, Sambō Hombu, *Shiberia Shuppei-shi*, I, Appendix, 29–33.

rarily organized mixed brigades. The one, to be called the North Manchurian Temporary Detachment and placed under the command of the governor general of the Kwantung Leased Territory, was to be sent to northern Manchuria. Its main strength would be stationed at Harbin with elements at Tsitsihar and other strategic points. The other, to be called the Maritime Territory Temporary Detachment, with its own headquarters, was to be sent to the Maritime Territory. Its main strength would be stationed at Vladivostok with elements at Khabarovsk and other strategic points. Since the Japanese constitutional organization did not demand any consultation with civilian authorities on operational activities, the general staff began preparations immediately. Confidential orders were sent to the divisions concerned, to the Korean army, and to the Kwantung Government General, and the chiefs of the latter two organizations were called to Tokyo to discuss the plan confidentially.

By mid-December, Bolshevik activity in the Russian Far East, especially at Harbin and Vladivostok, seemed to the general staff to call for a much greater military effort. The general staff became convinced that in the Maritime Territory the Bolsheviks should be treated as enemies and that powerful military forces should be used to bolster such "moderate" Russian groups as might be striving to form regimes independent of the Soviet government.[50] For this purpose, the temporary detachment destined for the Maritime Territory needed to be expanded into a Maritime Territory expeditionary force, including, beside the mixed brigade, a wartime-organized division and supporting units. The Bolshevik threat to the southern Ussuri valley seemed so great that the force was to base its main strength partly at Vladivostok and partly at Nikol'sk-Ussuriisk, stationing strong elements at Khabarovsk, along the river and also at other necessary points to "suppress Bolshevik and other uprisings or hostile activities." The general staff clearly believed such a limited operation to be only a beginning, for the

---

[50] An English translation of the text of this revision of the November plan, begun in mid-December, 1917, and completed in January, 1918, will be found in Appendix C, below. *Ibid.*, I, Appendix, 35–36.

revised plan, adopted in January, charged the Maritime Territory expeditionary force secretly to "make preparations necessary for operations against Russia," operations that may be "expected to develop in the future" and, depending on circumstances, to "confiscate railroad rolling stock." [51] The plan for a north Manchurian temporary detachment was apparently shelved for the time in the face of the arrival of Chinese forces there. It is clear that by mid-December the Japanese military authorities were convinced that they should send an expedition at least into the Maritime Territory, where it would protect foreign nationals, seize control of the Trans-Siberian rail lines, and help local anti-Bolshevik groups to gain power.

Revolutionary developments in the Russian Far East also convinced the army authorities that no time should be lost in negotiating the long-desired military coalition with China. Japan could well argue that the revolution made some kind of joint action imperative. For one thing, in Siberia and north Manchuria both countries had nationals whose lives and property they were anxious to protect. Both were anxious to keep the disorder in European Russia from spreading into Siberia and north Manchuria. And both feared lest the Amur basin should fall prey to some powerful government, either to the Soviet republic, which might, for all they knew, be a German front, or to some protégé of Britain, France, or America. It would be easier to ward off the common danger through common action, and common action would be more effective under Japanese leadership. In addition, for the Japanese military authorities at least, the October Revolution made such an agreement absolutely necessary. To carry out their plans to use the railway zone as a staging area for the invasion of Siberia, the Japanese must have some understanding with the thousands of Chinese troops being rushed into north Manchuria. Such at least would seem to have been the reasoning of General Uehara, chief of the army general staff, and his vice chief, Lieutenant General Tanaka.

Several high-ranking officers of the Chinese army, including

[51] *Ibid.*

Field Marshal Chin Yün-p'eng and Lieutenant General Chu T'ung-feng, visited Japan on November 14–16, 1917, to inspect the army's special grand maneuvers. This provided an excellent opportunity for Tanaka to broach the subject.[52] He enlisted the aid of Major General Sakanishi Rihachiro and Lieutenant General Aoki Nobuzumi, military advisers in the president's office in Peking, and Major General Saitō Kijiro, military attaché in the legation there. They were instructed to call on such Chinese leaders as President P'ing Kuo-chang and Prime Minister Wang Shih-ch'ang and to urge them to win the Chinese government's assent to the following points:

1) a Sino-Japanese military agreement for common self-defense against the eastward advance of German and Austrian power;
2) agreement between military representatives of both countries on the exact military provisions;
3) a request by the Chinese government to Japan for weapons and munitions needed by the Chinese forces and an offer by China of the various raw materials necessary to manufacture them.[53]

The Foreign Minister's Plan

Meanwhile, similar ideas were taking shape in the minds of Viscount Motono and several of his intimates in the Foreign Ministry, including his two secretaries, Matsushima Hajime, a thirty-five-year-old career officer whom Motono had brought with him from the embassy in St. Petersburg, and Matsuoka Yōsuke, the thirty-eight-year-old American-educated diplomat, famous later as a proponent of Japanese expansion and known in 1917 as a bright but brash young man who, like many eager juniors in every bureaucracy, was not reluctant to press his opinions on his superiors. Like the military authorities, the Motono clique also seems to have come early to the conclusion that a Japanese expedition into

[52] Araki Sadao, comp., *Gensui Uehara Yūsaku Den* (Tokyo: Gensui Uehara Yūsaku Denki Hankō-kai, 1937), II, 119–120.
[53] *Ibid.*, II, 51.

northern Manchuria and Siberia east of Irkutsk would be highly
desirable.

Of course, the Motono clique may have been influenced by
cabinet discussions of the army's ideas or by private conversations
with lesser members of the Chōshū clique. On the other hand, it
should be remembered that Motono, except for his secretaries, was
a rather solitary figure, both in the Foreign Ministry and in the
government at large. Ever since his school days in France, he had
spent most of his life in Europe. In his long years abroad he had
become culturally a European, and he had married a French
woman. The soirées in St. Petersburg had become more congenial
to him than the geisha parties in Shimbashi. Some say he spoke
French with greater facility than Japanese. Certainly he understood
the politics of European capitals better than those of Tokyo, and
he enjoyed perhaps more close friendships abroad than at home.
There is little in his personality and nothing in the record to suggest that he exchanged views very often with his colleagues in the
government. Moreover, the policy drafts extant in the foreign
ministry from this period suggest that Motono and his secretaries
were doing their own thinking.[54]

[54] Four such drafts exist in the Foreign Ministry's archives. They are (1) "Shiberia Shuppei no Kyūmu" (The Urgent Need for a Siberian Expedition), classified "secret," an original memo, brush-written on Foreign Ministry paper, Japan,
Gaimushō Kiroku, "Rokoku Kakumei Ikken: Teikoku no Taidō" (hereafter, *JGK,
RKI, TT*), I, 0184–220; (2) "Tōbu Shiberia Shuppei oyobi Nisshi Kyōdō Jiei-
saku Jikkō-an" (Proposal for the Execution of Policy of an East Siberian Expedition and Joint Sino-Japanese Defense), classified "secret," an original memo,
brush-written on Foreign Ministry paper, *ibid.*, I, 0221–230; (3) "Teikoku Gaikō
Seisaku no Kisō no Hitsuyō" (The Neccesity for a Fundamental Change in the
Foreign Policy of the Empire), *ibid.*, I, 0231–242; (4) "Tai-Tō-Roryō Sochi ni
kansuru Ken" (Matters Relating to Measures to Be Taken with Reference to
Eastern Russia), memorandum on unmarked stationery, *ibid.*, I, 0036–43. Although all four are undated and unsigned, after consultation with the then chief
of the second (Asian) section of the Political Affairs Bureau, Ambassador Mushakoji Kimitomo (later ambassador to Germany), and the present chief of the Office
for the Compilation of Diplomatic Documents, Mr. Kurihara Ken, I have tenta-
tively concluded that these memoranda were policy drafts prepared by either the
foreign minister, Viscount Motono, or for him by his secretaries, possibly for
presentation to the cabinet, although whether they were so presented is doubtful.
The fourth memorandum, from internal evidence, seems more likely to have been
submitted by some official in either eastern Siberia or northern Manchuria, possibly someone like Consul General Satō Naotake at Harbin (later ambassador to

According to these policy drafts, the Motono clique was intensely preoccupied by the German problem, feeling that the danger of the Russian Revolution was not that it might bring the Bolsheviks to power, but that it might open up all Russia to German penetration, permitting Germany not only to take over that vast land, but eventually to "lay its hands overland on China, in particular, on Manchuria and Mongolia." It was also seriously disturbed by the possibility that the weakness of the Bolsheviks and the threat of German expansion might, as Foch suggested, bring American troops to intervene—a prospect hardly less threatening to Japan than German intervention.

To meet this double threat, the Motono clique argued, Japan needed to strengthen its ties with the Allies and, as quickly as possible, to conclude a joint defense agreement with China. At the same time, it needed to move quickly into the Amur basin. It should not hesitate to seize the opportunity to "implant its natural influence in northern Manchuria," to acquire the northern half of Sakhalin, and to help the "moderate," anti-Bolshevik elements in the Russian Far East set up an autonomous regime. Thus, Japan could at last close the northern gateway, securing its "independent defense" and establishing its "predominant position in the Orient."

Such a policy would require a military expedition, not to European Russia, of course, but to the Amur basin. There, in the name of defense against "the eastward penetration of German influence," Japanese troops could "occupy strategic points," take over the railroads, immobilize the German and Austrian prisoners of war, and support the political ambitions of the "constructive elements."

In all of these details, the Motono clique's proposed expedition accorded well with the army's plans. Both groups were thinking primarily in terms of Japan's future position in east Asia and both were inclined to feel that the challenge of the Russian revolution could best be met by a Japanese military expedition to the Amur basin.

---

the Soviet Union). Internal evidence as well as archival classification establish that all four were written in the period between the Russian revolution in November, 1917, and the Treaty of Brest-Litovsk in March, 1918.

Beyond this, the Motono clique was giving serious attention to the problem of conciliating the Allies. It was exceedingly anxious to avoid arousing their suspicion and seems to have been convinced that this could be done by successfully integrating a Japanese expedition to the Amur with simultaneous Allied operations in European Russia, such as the British and the French were primarily interested in. Instead of American and Japanese troops jointly occupying the Trans-Siberian Railroad as Foch had proposed, that great rail system could be divided into zones: the Japanese exclusively taking over the eastern Siberian railroads, the Allies occupying the western Siberian and Turkestan lines leading to southern Russia. Each of the powers might encourage "constructive" elements in its own zone to establish themselves in power locally. Eventually these regimes might be brought together to form a "moderate" all-Russian government. In this way, Japan could secure its interests in east Asia and the Allies could secure theirs in the west. Of course, before Japanese operations could safely be undertaken, it would be necessary to negotiate an understanding with the Allies, conclude the defense pact with China, and await a suitable occasion, such as might possibly be presented by Allied pressure on Japan for an expedition, by serious threats to "the lives and property of Japanese or other foreign nationals," or by the further extension of German power into the Far East, either directly or indirectly through the Bolsheviks.

Interventionists versus Noninterventionists

With the Japanese navy anxious to send a detachment to Vladivostok, the army preparing to send an expedition to the Amur basin, and the Motono clique in the Foreign Ministry convinced of its necessity, it would appear that, within a few weeks of the Bolshevik coup in Petrograd, the Japanese cabinet and, therefore, the Chōshū clique, had come to agree generally that intervention in the Amur basin would be desirable. On the other hand, the failure of the general staff to consider in their plans certain problems which the Motono clique felt to be important and the absence of

any reference in the military and diplomatic archives to the contrary, compel one to conclude that the cabinet and therefore the
Chōshū clique had not yet agreed on a way to harmonize the
project for an expedition with the proposals of the Allies nor on the
exact circumstances that would justify its launching. They were,
however, fully aware that no planning they might do would be
very effective unless it had the support of the various groups which
were supporting the cabinet: the genro, the armed services, the
political parties, the Satsuma clique, and others, whose influence
was expressed in the Advisory Council on Foreign Relations. They
decided to seek its support immediately for the general idea of
intervention.

They must have been aware that such a general decision would
be difficult to secure. It would involve many serious questions,
such as questions of Asian policy, Western policy, budgetary appropriations, military strength, and bureaucratic rivalries. These
questions would be bound to affect the members of the advisory
council and the interests they represented, in many different ways.
But the danger was pressing and one can almost hear Terauchi say
that politics would have to be "transcended." Apparently with no
prior briefing of the members of the council, Terauchi called a
meeting for December 17.

Here, for the first time Motono presented to the council his
views on the Russian situation and urged upon it the necessity of
deciding on a policy of intervention.[55] He had hoped, no doubt, for
a vigorous discussion; and he certainly must have counted on his
cabinet colleagues to back him up; but the cabinet members maintained a cautious silence, waiting to see how the others would
react. The independent-minded Itō responded with gratifying sup-

[55] A draft proposal to the Advisory Council on Foreign Relations, dated December 17, 1917, ibid., I, 0003–13, unsigned, but whose contents agree with the
views Motono is reported to have expressed at that meeting is assumed here to
be the draft of Motono's speech to the council. Hara was not present at this
meeting but learned what transpired from Motono, whom he visited two days
later. This speech, taken together with the one Motono delivered to the council
on Dec. 27, accords generally with the views developed in the four policy drafts
discussed above in connection with the Motono clique. Hara, Hara Kei Nikki,
VII, 294–95.

port.[56] Baron Makino expressed his opposition. The others said nothing. Unfortunately, the key member, the president of the Seiyūkai party, Hara Kei, was absent, so that no immediate decision could be hoped for. It was decided to continue the discussion at a meeting on December 27.

The next ten days were critical ones for the Japanese government. In the interval Baron Makino worked rapidly to rally the opposition. He may have talked with his old friends in the Shidehara clique in the Foreign Ministry. He certainly conferred with Marquis Saionji.[57] Most important of all, he reached Hara and found him similarly convinced that the situation in Russia was too "unknown" and the danger to Japanese nationals not yet great enough to justify sending troops to Siberia.[58] Thus, as a reaction to Motono's proposal on December 17, a powerful anti-interventionist bloc was formed, representing the Satsuma clique, the Seiyūkai party, the genro, Saionji, and possibly the Shidehara clique in the Foreign Ministry.

Against the opposition of this bloc, Motono could not prevail. His vigorous speech before the council on December 27, in which he painted a frightening picture of "all eastern Siberia passing under German control" and "thousands of Japanese and Allied nationals" being "extremely disturbed and their lives and property daily endangered," again elicited the support of Viscount Itō, but it failed to influence the other members.[59] Makino returned to the attack. Hara joined him, warning of ominous possibilities: "Even were we to send only one private it would be the beginning of a great war," [60] and Russia would recognize it as such. He agreed that German influence was mounting in Russia, but that fact seemed to him to make an expedition less, not more advisable. It

[56] Ibid., VII, 245, 300.
[57] Ibid., VII, 300.
[58] Ibid., VII, 295, 298.
[59] An undated, unsigned "view," extant in the archives of the Foreign Ministry in JGK, RKI, TT, I, 0028–35, is here assumed to be the draft of Motono's speech to the council on December 27, 1917. Its general tenor agrees with what Hara reports Motono to have said (Hara, Hara Kei Nikki, VII, 303–4) and it is in the form for such a report and is appropriately filed.
[60] Hara, Hara Kei Nikki, VII, 303–4.

meant that in embarking upon an expedition Japan would be fighting both Germany and Russia. Suppose then that peace were declared on the western front, leaving Japan to fight them both in Siberia? Was Motono prepared for that? The army had better be greatly strengthened before sending troops abroad.

The meeting was tense and the portent ominous. War Minister Ōshima revealed that he at least had not been brought into Motono's confidence, by insisting that he could see no difference between Motono's plan and Foch's plan. The other cabinet members, obviously worried by the opposition, said little. The elder Chōshū bureaucrat, Hirata Tōsuke, tried to find common ground by agreeing that "there could be no expedition without adequate preparation"; but the division of opinion was too deep for easy compromises. Motono had gone too far too rapidly. The governing coalition was deeply split.

Japan's problem of devising a suitable Russian policy had now been made more difficult than ever. Not only would it be necessary to resolve the possible conflict between its own interests and those of the Allies, but some way must be found to reconcile the differences between the interventionists and the noninterventionists within its own Advisory Council on Foreign Relations. Many months were to pass before a decision could be reached. Meanwhile, the interventionist-minded groups refused to wait idly. Each began to pursue its own plans on its own initiative.

IV. RECONNAISSANCE IN SIBERIA

Disturbed though the Japanese army and navy may have been by the sharp conflict precipitated by Motono in the Advisory Council on Foreign Relations, they were prepared neither by necessity nor by tradition to postpone their plans indefinitely, and the prime minister gave them every encouragement to proceed.

The Race to Vladivostok

The first to act was the navy. Since early November they had been scanning the northern seas, watching with increasing apprehension the growth of Bolshevik power at Vladivostok, convinced that naval intervention there was necessary, but restrained by the refusal of their ally, Britain, to approve their plans. Early in February the restraints were broken.

From the beginning the British government had agreed that protection of the stores at Vladivostok required some kind of military action. Either it did not trust Japan to do the job or, as Lord Cecil said, it honestly feared that what it called the "constructive elements" in Russia would not trust Japan. On the other hand, Japanese desires could not be ignored and, furthermore, Japanese ships and men were indispensable. At least since December 10, 1917, the British had been trying to satisfy both requirements of the situation by urging Japan to consider joint operations with the Allies, Japan to send the "principal forces," Britain to send "token forces" from its garrison at Hong Kong, and America to send a few troops from the Philippine Islands. Japanese diplomats had steadily refused to consider such a proposal and it began to appear that no action would be taken when Britain decided, sometime in late December, to force the issue.

On January 1, 1918, Lord Cecil informed Ambassador Chinda in London that the British government had already taken two actions.[1] The idea of a joint operation at Vladivostok had been broached to the United States, and HMS *Suffolk* had "already been ordered up" to Vladivostok. Unfortunately, the United States had "refused to take action"; therefore Cecil requested the Japanese government to join in exerting pressure on the American government.

This struck Ambassador Chinda as simply a return to the joint-intervention proposal although in a more limited sphere of action than hitherto suggested; and he did not hesitate to repeat his contention of December 10, 1917, namely:

If it develops that it will be necessary to use troops, then . . . the geographical position of Japan makes it a matter of natural right and duty for it to undertake such operations alone; and the current proposal for each ally to send an expeditionary force, in view of the position of the Empire and the feelings of the people, would, I believe, arouse heated discussion and invite very grave disorder, just as would an American expedition.

When, two days later in Tokyo, Foreign Minister Motono read Chinda's report of the conversation, he reacted in similar vein and even more strongly. "It was difficult to understand," he is reported to have told the British ambassador in Tokyo, "why the British government had negotiated with the American government about an expedition to Vladivostok without first consulting with the Imperial government." [2] But he seems to have sensed no emergency. It was the prime minister who saw the key phrase in Chinda's report.

HMS Suffolk had "already been ordered up!" So Britain was doing exactly what it had objected to Japan's doing: taking independ-

---

[1] Chinda to Motono, January 1, 1918, in Japan, Gaimushō, *Shiberia Shuppei Mondai: Dai Ippen: Shiberia Shuppei ni itaru Kōshō Keika* (November, 1922), p. 5. Official British and American records relating to these alleged Anglo-American talks in December, 1917, have not so far been published.

[2] *Ibid.*, I, 5.

ent action at Vladivostok! The plea of the consular corps and the request of the British government had not stirred Terauchi; but he was not prepared to see Britain establish itself in the Japan Sea. Prime Minister Terauchi's chunky frame shook as he thundered, "Somehow our ships have got to enter Vladivostok first!" [3] The navy minister, Admiral Baron Katō Tomosaburo, agreed. It was immediately decided to dispatch the *Iwami* and the *Asahi*. On January 5 the navy minister instructed Admiral Baron Katō Sada-kichi, commander in chief, Kure naval base: "Complete immediately preparations for departure of *Iwami*. In particular, organize and take aboard one company of marines (a total of 100 men, including officers)." [4] For service as an icebreaker, he requisitioned the *Kamigawa Maru*, a 1,464-ton steamer of the Nippon Yūsen KK.

That evening, following a banquet at court, Navy Minister Katō discussed with several high officers the plans for the operation. [5] After informing them of the decision, he asked whom they would recommend to command the Fifth Squadron that would have to be organized. Rear Admiral Abo, chief of the operations section of the naval general staff, recommended the forty-eight-year-old commandant of the naval gunnery school, Rear Admiral Katō Kanji (Hiroharu). [6] Katō was to achieve great prominence later as naval delegate at the Washington conference and even more during the negotiation of the London naval treaty of 1930, when he served as chief of the navy general staff. His experience had been wide. From 1899 to 1902 he had been sent to study in Russia, where, it

[3] Fukunami Sadao and Ishihara Kitao, *Katō Kanji Taishō Den* (Tokyo: Katō Kanji Taishō Denki Hensan-kai, 1941), p. 667.

[4] Japan, Kaigun Gunreibu, *Taishō Yon Nen naishi Kyū Nen Kaigun Senshi* (1924), I, 135–36.

[5] Fukunami and Ishihara, *Katō Kanji*, pp. 662–64. This account is apparently based on a private manuscrpit of Admiral Abo and on a report, "Urajio no Keibi," by Admiral Fujita Hisanori, then a commander, who served as *kantai no sennin sambō* in the Fifth Squadron. The sources do not indicate that the chief of the navy general staff was consulted though he may have been present.

[6] Kanji and Hiroharu are variant readings of Katō's first name. The characters for Japanese personal names may frequently be read correctly in different ways. It is customary to read or pronounce them as the person himself prefers, but frequently, either because he expresses no preference or because variant readings are in common usage by his contemporaries, it is helpful to indicate these variants.

is interesting to note, he became friendly with a young military attaché named Tanaka Gi'ichi, destined to rise to the post of vice chief of the army general staff when the Siberian expedition began and later to win fame as one of Japan's foremost military politicians.[7] A protégé of Fleet Admiral Yamamoto Gombei, whom he served as adjutant, 1905–6, Katō was detailed to the retinue of His Imperial Highness Prince Fushimi Sadayoshi on his tour of England, Europe, and America in 1907 and two years later was appointed to serve as military attaché in London. In 1914 he commanded the southern detachment of three warships which convoyed Australian troopships as far as the Red Sea. At the conference on January 5, 1918, he was recommended by Admiral Abo as an officer of great "diplomatic ability" and "the best Russian expert in the navy."

The navy minister immediately agreed that Katō was the man and summoned him by telephone. Katō promptly accepted the assignment.[8] Among the important officers appointed to Katō's staff was Commander Yonai Mitsumasa, then recently returned from a tour as naval attaché in Russia, later to be five times navy minister and premier in 1939. On January 9, Rear Admiral Katō boarded the Iwami at Kure and weighed anchor that evening, setting his speed at nine knots; when he learned the next day that the British Suffolk had arrived at Sasebo for coaling and intended to leave on January 11 so as to arrive at Vladivostok on January 13 or 14, Katō ordered the engines pushed to the limit. Racing northward at a speed of thirteen knots, he nosed the Iwami into the ice-clogged harbor of Vladivostok at 9:30 A.M. on January 12, beating the Suffolk by two days.[9] The Asahi steamed up on January 18 and the following day became the rear admiral's flagship.

Katō had won the race, but he now faced a much more difficult job: carrying out the instructions of his naval superiors. They had not sent the squadron to Vladivostok merely to see what the British were up to—they wanted the Bolsheviks eliminated. According to

[7] Fukunami and Ishihara, Katō Kanji, pp. 343–53.
[8] Ibid., p. 665.
[9] Japan, Kaigun Gunreibu, Senshi, III, 8–9.

a summary of the oral instructions given Read Admiral Katō on January 6:

The object of dispatching warships to Vladivostok is, by showing our power and exerting pressure on the Bolsheviks, to maintain peace and order in the vicinity of Vladivostok in order to safeguard our rights and to protect the consular corps and subjects of the Empire and of friendly countries.[10]

The written instructions were more specific. Japan, Katō was told, had no "hostile feeling" toward Russia "in the widest sense," and hoped "to continue as before the friendly relationship" between the two countries. On the other hand, it was determined that Russia should not be Bolshevik-controlled, for the Bolsheviks were mere "puppets of Germany," engaged in "spreading tyranny in the Far East." "To the Bolsheviks under Lenin," his instructions went on to say, "we shall of course give no assistance, but shall destroy their power as quickly as possible and hope to establish a government under the moderates." Katō was cautioned, however, that these were only the navy's views, that the government was not yet prepared to take so strong a position, and that he should pursue these aims with utmost "caution, seriousness, and patience," consulting the consul general and resident Japanese officers at Vladivostok at every step, and "at an opportune time, without firing a rifle or landing a marine, but mainly by anchoring within the harbor, to show our strength and coerce them with so-called 'silent pressure.'" Katō was thus left with no doubt in his mind what the naval authorities wanted acheived; but within very narrow limits he was left on his own resources as to how to achieve it. Katō passed on the substance of these instructions to the captains of the *Iwami* and *Asahi,* adding only his own personal prejudice that the greatest precautions should be taken against "the ignorant masses, especially the greedy and depraved Jews," who are "instigated by Germany" to do the Japanese harm.[11]

One way to achieve the objective, Katō felt, was to try to calm

[10] *Ibid.,* I, 136. Although it is not recorded, internal evidence suggests that these instructions were given by the navy minister.

[11] *Ibid.,* III, 9–11.

the fears of the residents. Two days after his arrival, he had the Japanese consul general announce that the arrival of the warships was for no other purpose "than the natural obligation of our government to protect our nationals"; the consul general also professed the empire's strict intention to abstain from any interference in the internal affairs of Russia.[12] The previous day Katō had called in representatives of the Japanese residents and solicited their help in pacifying the Russians.[13] The Russian population clearly needed pacifying. On the very day of the consul general's announcement, the local soviet of soldiers' and workers' deputies protested vigorously that the arrival of Japanese warships was an infringement on Russian sovereignty.[14] And the next day the mayor of the city lodged a similar protest.

Thus, the Japanese were in naval command of the harbor when the British cruiser *Suffolk* arrived in Vladivostok on January 14 and the flagship of the United States's Asiatic fleet, the *Brooklyn*, arrived on March 1. And thus the navy took the first overt step toward Japanese intervention in the Russian civil war. It had acted not as a consequence of a deliberate decision by the government. Indeed, the cabinet probably was not consulted and the Advisory Council on Foreign Relations certainly was not. The step had been taken suddenly by the prime minister and the naval authorities for two reasons: to head off independent British naval action in Russian coastal waters, and to overawe the Bolsheviks and drive them from power in Vladivostok—at least in so far as the indecision of the Japanese government would permit.

"Silent Pressure"

Katō seems to have felt quite early that "silent pressure" was not going to be enough. Immediately upon his arrival he consulted with Consul General Kikuchi Giro, the Allied consuls, and the captain of the *Suffolk*. On the basis of these talks, he worked out with the

---

[12] *Ibid.*, III, 13.
[13] Fukunami and Ishihara, *Katō Kanji*, p. 673.
[14] Japan, Kaigun Gunreibu, *Senshi*, III, 13.

British ship captain a plan for the joint patrol of the residences of
allied nationals and the joint protection of their lives and property
in case disorder should spread.[15] Two landing units, the "Kō" and
the "Otsu," were organized from the marines aboard the *Iwami* and
Asahi. Two hundred and eighty men were to be provided by the
Suffolk. Two eventualities were provided for: if disorder ashore
threatened the foreign residents, the "Otsu" unit would be landed
for guard duty, the "Kō" following if necessary; and should these
troops unavoidably clash with Russian troops or rioters, the Japanese force should, under cover of the fleet guns, rescue refugees,
protect the ice breaker, and occupy the wireless station; meanwhile,
any hostile Russian naval craft would be sunk forthwith.

On February 4 there occurred an incident which almost brought
the landing craft to the dock. According to Katō's report, at 2:30
in the morning of that day a group of some forty armed men in
militia uniforms entered the Versailles Hotel and stole about one
million rubles in money and valuables.[16] The Allied consular corps
met the following day and drew up a protest to the president of the
Maritime district zemstvo council, demanding more adequate protection for foreign nationals. Admiral Katō made emergency preparations for a landing, but wired the Navy Ministry before proceeding. Had the central naval authorities felt free to expand operations
ashore, they might well have taken advantage of this incident; but
they did not. Cautiously, they informed the admiral that they
would take no steps until "after careful consideration" of further
reports on the situation as it developed and on the commander's
own views.

Apparently the commander believed that a landing could not
long be delayed. On February 10, he submitted a memorandum to
Consul General Kikuchi. Referring no doubt to the Versailles Hotel
robbery, he charged that "troops are plundering openly." [17] The
authorities were clearly unable to protect "the lives and property

---

[15] *Ibid.*, III, 15–16.

[16] *Ibid.*, III, 17–18. Substantially the same account is given in the report sent
by the American consul at Vladivostok to the secretary of state, February 4, 1918,
Record Group 84, American consulate, Vladivostok, 1918, XI, 800, No. 186.

[17] Japan, Kaigun Gunreibu, *Senshi*, III, 19–20.

of all foreign residents." A landing would soon be in order; nevertheless, a landing would almost inevitably involve fighting, in which case the consular corps would need to agree beforehand on the action to be taken if the Japanese forces were to operate effectively. In greater detail than in the January 20 plan, the commander outlined the steps he considered necessary in the event of an emergency. The first step should be to try to accomplish the mission by peaceful means, that is, to prevent the distribution of arms to marauding troops by seizing all weapons and sealing them in the customs-house, inspecting goods in transit at the railroad station, and placing a guard at the Volunteer Fleet office, where refugees would be gathered for evacuation. If these means proved insufficient, then as a second step an attempt should be made to induce the soviet and all furloughed soldiers and existing forces to turn over their weapons, and to move all foreign residents into a security zone. As a final step, the Allies must be prepared "to dissolve all forces here, seize their weapons, and force them to withdraw." Of course, "in any military emergency that might arise," the admiral wanted it clearly understood that his authority as supreme commander could not be interfered with. Furthermore, "if, as a result of an engagement, the entire city is occupied and the administration is placed under the joint control of all countries, all authority for preserving order should be entrusted to the supreme commander of the troops." The record is not clear whether the consular corps approved the admiral's plan. In any case, although it was never put into effect, it is of considerable interest in revealing that the admiral's thinking and planning had advanced far beyond the navy minister's original concept of "silent pressure." It shows, too, that navy officers were no less insistent than army officers that any Allied operations in the Russian Far East must be under the supreme command of Japan.

The Nakajima Mission

At about the same time the British decided to order *HMS Suffolk* to Vladivostok, the Japanese central military authorities became convinced that their own tentative plans for intervention could not be executed effectively without advance preparation on the Asian continent. For routine intelligence purposes, they had already a widespread apparatus in the area. Complete details are unavailable, but records of the War Ministry for this period show disbursements being made from secret funds for intelligence purposes by the general staff headquarters in Tokyo, by the China army, the Kwantung governor generalcy, the Korean army, and other major military commands.[18] The agents who eventually received these funds were organized into networks, those in each city or area reporting regularly, usually to an officer, who in turn forwarded the information to his commander. Reports of mutual interest from the army's agents as well as from its military attachés were usually passed on to the Ministry of Foreign Affairs or other ministry concerned.

In the period immediately following the October revolution in Petrograd, additional junior officers were sent out from Tokyo to expand this intelligence organization.[19] By late December, 1917, as the army's expeditionary plans were maturing, Chief of Staff Uehara and War Minister Ōshima felt that a special job needed to be done, requiring the services of senior officers. Uehara and Ōshima persuaded the prime minister; the prime minister in turn carefully consulted the Seiyūkai party president, Hara Kei, and won his agreement.[20]

The result was that early in January, 1918, Army General Staff Headquarters detailed two officers to the Russian Far East: Lieutenant Colonel Sakabe Tosuho, forty-year-old artillery officer then assigned to headquarters, and Major General Nakajima Masatake, forty-seven-year-old Russian specialist, intelligence chief of the

[18] Japan, Rikugunshō Kiroku, "Mitsu Dai Nikki" (hereinafter, JRK, MDN), 1918, IV. In March, 1918, for example, the Korean Army alone was disbursing secret funds to at least twenty-four individuals, of whom six were officers and the rest civilian agents, including the consul general at Harbin, Satō Naotake.

[19] For example, six additional junior officers in the guise of language and history students were sent in December, 1917, to reconnoiter on both sides of the Siberian border. MJ 490, dated December 7, 1917, JRK, MDN, 1918, II; MJ 494, dated December 10, 1917, ibid., 1918, II; and MJ 521, dated December 21, 1917, ibid., 1918, II.

[20] Hara Kei, Hara Kei Nikki, ed. Hara Kei'ichiro (Tokyo: Kengensha, 1950–52), VII, 309. Entry of January 1, 1918.

general staff, who had recently returned from an assignment at Russian general headquarters in Petrograd. Reconnaissance was a major objective, but reconnaissance with a purpose. The general staff had already made up its mind that a large-scale expedition would probably be necessary in order to support "moderate elements" in the Russian Far East. Nakajima and Sakabe were instructed to find those elements and build them into buffers against soviet expansion. As the chief of staff, General Baron Uehara, told them:

In the present situation, the empire must give serious consideration to stopping the eastward advance of the German and Austrian power. To do this, we shall try to have a barrier built, supported by the empire; but it must be done completely by the Russians.[21]

The premier developed this concept to Nakajima, explaining that "if a powerful dam can be built by having the Russians form moderate self-governing bodies in the Far East, the empire will have bodies to negotiate with and will supply them on loan with the funds or weapons they require." He is reported to have gone even farther to promise that, if the situation developed favorably, Japan would send troop support; however, this does not seem to accord with views expressed by the premier elsewhere, and probably reflects more accurately the attitude of the vice chief of the general staff, Lieutenant General Tanaka, who was also present. In the wake of Nakajima and Sakabe, a regular stream of intelligence officers began to flow into north China, Mongolia, and throughout the Amur basin in Siberia and north Manchuria.[22]

Political Conditions in Eastern Siberia

Even now, when, in spite of the losses which time has occasioned, perhaps more information is available for an over-all analysis of

[21] Japan, Sambō Hombu, *Taishō Shichi-nen naishi Jūichi-nen Shiberia Shuppei-shi* (Tokyo, 1924), III, 1046.

[22] For example, Uehara to Ōshima, February 12, 1918, MJ 56, JRK, MDN, 1918, II; Ōshima to Motono, February 14, 1918, Ō ju 212, Japan, Rikugunshō Kiroku, "Ō Ju Dai Nikki" (hereinafter, JRK, OJDN), May, 1918; Ishimitsu to Ōshima, March 5, 1918, MJ 101, JRK, MDN, 1918, II; Tanaka to Yamada, March 18, 1918, *ibid.*

the revolutionary conditions in the Amur basin than was available
to Nakajima, it is impossible to say with certainty what objective
situation he faced when he landed in Vladivostok on January 22,
1918. In the long past, many peoples had fled into the basin for
refuge or pushed down its rivers for conquest, leaving by 1918 a
scattered population of less than three million, dwarfed by the
enormous forests, the towering mountains, and the endless Amur.[23]
In the remote wastes of the northeast, primitive tribes still lived in
the Paleolithic age. Over the foothills and grasslands, more highly
developed Tungus, Buriats, and other indigenous peoples trapped
the fur-bearing animals, fished the streams, and herded their cattle
and goats. Only a few of these people had adopted the settled life
of the farmer. Most of the population were state peasants, who had
migrated only recently from European Russia to secure the greater
allotment of land and greater independence which the government
offered the Siberian pioneer. They did not hold some of the best
land, however; the broad valleys along the Chinese border had been
assigned largely to the Cossack minority. Another small minority,
made up of Russian officials, soldiers, intellectuals, a few industrial
workers, and Russian and foreign businessmen, were concentrated
in the key centers of transportation and administration along the
Trans-Siberian Railroad, Irkutsk being probably the only city with
a population exceeding 100,000.

The people of the Amur basin were also distinguished from
their western compatriots by their comparatively autonomous and
prosperous way of life. Even before the revolution in February,
1917, although subject in some instances to property qualifications,
most of the people in the area were accustomed to regulating their
own local affairs through their own locally elected elders, atamans,
dumas, and assemblies of various kinds; and most, if not all, had
enjoyed relatively good living. The state peasants, for example,
worked allotments averaging from twenty to forty acres per male.
The Cossacks held so much land that they had brought less than

[23] For a more detailed description of conditions in the Amur basin, see the author's "The Russian Revolution in the Amur Basin," soon to appear in *The
American Slavic and East European Review*.

10 percent of it under cultivation. Moreover, peasants, Cossacks, and persons from all walks of life had been drawing together, developing their skills in self-government and improving their living standard by participation in the expanding cooperative movement.

Perhaps it was their racial diversity, their scattered pattern of settlement, their local self-governing habits, and their relative prosperity which explain in large measure why the people of the Amur basin greeted the February Revolution with such quiet enthusiasm and why, when returning soldiers and political agitators tried to spread the gospel of extreme socialism, in the days following the October Revolution in Petrograd, the majority of the people of the Amur basin greeted them coldly.

It is as impossible now as it was at the time to ascertain exactly what their political feelings may have been in January, 1918; but a rough approximation may be made on the basis of the incomplete returns for the election to the Russian Constituent Assembly in November, 1917.

RETURNS OF THE ELECTION TO THE RUSSIAN CONSTITUENT
ASSEMBLY, NOVEMBER, 1917, BY PARTY GROUP[a]

Party	All Russia[b]	Percent	Amur Basin[c]	Percent
Moderate Socialists[d]	17,718,420	42	343,215	61
SD Bolshevik	9,844,637	24	81,102	14
Kadet, other non-socialist	3,249,019	8	33,336	6
Nationality,[e] other, unclassified	9,729,402	23	107,784	19
Totals[f]	41,686,876	100	565,437	100

[a] Adapted from Oliver Henry Radkey, *The Election to the Russian Constituent Assembly of 1917* (Cambridge: Harvard University Press, 1950), Appendix: pp. 77–80.

[b] The incomplete returns for All Russia, grouped here, represent some sixty election districts, twenty others being unrepresented either because no elections were held or because no returns are available.

[c] Even more incomplete than the figures for All Russia, here are grouped the available returns for Irkutsk Province, Transbaikal Territory and Amur Territory; no returns are available for Iakutsk, Kamchatka, the Chinese Eastern Railway Zone, nor presumably for the Maritime Territory, which is not mentioned in Radkey's list.

[d] Including SR, SD Menshevik, and minor socialist parties.

[e] Certain parties consisted of persons of one nationality only, and were devoted to the aims of that national group.

[f] Including joint lists not assigned to parties above.

In this tabulation, left-wing Social Revolutionaries are not distinguishable from right-wing; moreover, it would seem likely that revolutionary developments in European Russia and the intensified agitation by radical groups in the Amur basin in November and December, 1917, would have won more converts to the desirability of extreme measures; but even taking these factors into account, probably no more than one quarter at most favored a socialist dictatorship under Bolshevik leadership, probably no more than one tenth favored changes toward the other extremes of either democratic capitalism or tsarist imperialism, leaving perhaps as many as half the people still inclined to look to moderate socialists for leadership.

Nakajima must also have been aware that the moderate socialists were in control of most of the governing institutions. They had lost control of the central government in Petrograd, but the Siberian regionalists among them had held an extraordinary conference at Tomsk, December 18–28, 1917,[24] at which they had recognized the authority of the All-Russian Constituent Assembly to organize a central Russian authority, and, in addition, had called for elections in March to a regional constituent assembly to organize an autonomous government for Siberia. Meanwhile, the conference decided to set up a temporary "all-Siberian socialist authority," representing, if possible, all shades of socialist opinion.[25] A provisional Siberian council had been selected, composed of a president and six members. In accordance with the will of the conference, the council promptly appealed to all cooperative unions, national bodies, soviets, and the like to join in electing delegates to a provisional Siberian duma to serve as a temporary legislative organ. Except for

[24] The "Manifesto," issued by the conference and circulated to the diplomatic corps at Peking, *JGK, RKI, HK,* I; P. S. Parfenov, *Uroki Proshlogo, Grazhdanskaia Voina v Sibiri 1918, 1919, 1920 gg.* (Harbin, 1921), pp. 21–22; V. V. Maksakov and A. Turunov, *Khronika Grazhdanskoi Voiny v Sibiri,* 1917–1918 (Moscow: Gosizdat, 1926), p. 52; Dmitriev, "Oktiabr'skaia Revoliutsiia v Sibiri," *Severnaia Aziia,* III, No. 5–6 (1927), 8–9. Dmitriev seems to be in error in giving the dates of the sessions from December 6 to 12 (o.s.).

[25] From a declaration said to have been made by the conference, as quoted in Dmitriev, "Oktiabr'skaia Revoliutsiia v Sibiri," *Severnaia Aziia,* III, No. 5–6 (1927), 8–9.

the Bolshevik–left-wing Social Revolutionary-led soviets and the few organizations controlled by non-socialists, the response seems to have been enthusiastic. The All-Siberian Cooperative Congress, for example, meeting in early January, 1918, at Novo-Nikolaevsk, and showing a strong Social Revolutionary majority, not only adopted a plan for electing cooperative delegates to the duma, but adopted a schedule of payment by the cooperative unions to give it the necessary financial support.[26] Apparently the council expected to organize friendly troops returning from the front into regiments of its own and counted on the American railway missions and American capital to rehabilitate the Siberian railways.[27] It was hoping to establish connections with other regional governments, like the central Ukrainian rada at Kiev.[28] Finally, the recognition of foreign powers was sought.

Locally, in most zemstvos, dumas, committees of public safety, peasant congresses, and nationality conferences, the moderate socialists appear to have continued in the majority, even though they lacked a unified party organization. They were slow to cope with the mounting problems occasioned by breakdowns in the distribution of food and other goods and the disorder that mounted in the cities as lawless elements came out of hiding and embittered, often revolutionary, troops returned from the front. The moderate socialists seemed to lack the energy, the resourcefulness, or the courage to take advantage of their popular support.

Probably as a result of these weaknesses, they were losing ground to the Bolshevik and left-wing Social Revolutionary coalition of extremists, who, although a minority, were building a disciplined organization, soliciting vigorously the support of urban trade unionists, radical intellectuals, and veterans, organizing Red Guards, and plotting the seizure of power. They knew what they wanted and they knew how to get it. It has been said that the Bolshevik power

[26] On January 6, 1918, Parfenov, *Uroki Proshlogo,* pp. 22–25.

[27] From the report of the All-Siberian Cooperative Congress, summarized in *Narodnoe Delo,* No. 4, which is quoted *ibid.,* pp. 22–23.

[28] An agent was sent to the rada on December 31, 1917. Maksakov and Turunov, *Khronika,* p. 54.

in the Amur basin "was on decidedly clay feet";[29] but it had a daring head and hands of steel.

The strategy of the Bolsheviks was first to persuade their adherents to break away from the unified Social Democratic party organization, then to win control of the special class councils, known as soviets (which had been set up alongside the regular organs of the provisional government to represent what were felt to be the peculiar interests of the common people, usually the workers, soldiers, peasants, and sometimes the Cossacks), and finally, through the soviets, to seize complete authority over the state. By mid-January, 1918, they had made little headway in the Amur countryside but had been remarkably successful in the cities along the Trans-Siberian Railroad.

When Nakajima landed at Vladivostok on January 22, 1918, he must have realized fully that only the presence of the Allied warships in the harbor kept the Bolshevik-led soviet from seizing complete control of the city. If he did not know it already, he must soon have learned that Khabarovsk, capital city of the former Priamur governor generalcy, had already fallen to the socialist extremists.[30] There, on December 19, 1917, following vigorous agitation by radical trade unionists, soldiers from the garrison, and sailors from the Amur flotilla, the Bolshevik–left-wing Social Revolutionary bloc had gained control of the soviet and had begun immediately to organize a Red Guard. On December 24 they had arrested the provisional government's commissar. The following day, the Third Far Eastern Regional Congress of Soviets was held there, and on December 27, it proclaimed the authority of the soviets over the entire Russian Far East. On January 2, 1918, it had selected a new Bolshevik-controlled regional executive committee, forerunner of the Council of People's Commissars (Sovnarkom) to be organized in June.

[29] William Henry Chamberlain, *The Russian Revolution, 1917–1921* (New York: Macmillan, 1935), I, 424.

[30] "Khronika Sobytii na Tikhom Okeane 1914–1918 gg.," *Tikhii Okean*, III, No. 9 (July-September, 1936), 249–53; G. Reikhberg, *Iaponskaia Interventsiia na Dal'nem Vostoke, 1918–1922 gg., Kratkii Ocherk* (Moscow: Gosudarstvennoe Sotsial'no-Ekonomicheskoe Izdatel'stvo, 1935), pp. 7–8; Maksakov and Turunov, *Khronika*, p. 70.

At the western end of the basin, Irkutsk, capital city of the east Siberian region, had likewise fallen. Following a split with the united Social Democratic party on October 21, 1917, the Bolsheviks in Irkutsk had finally managed to gain control of the united soviet on November 28, whereupon they had organized a military-revolutionary committee, had begun recruiting Red Guards from among the Cossacks, military cadets, and infantry garrison, and on December 17 had begun moving their forces into the principal offices of the city.[31] For ten days, December 21–30, armed resistance had been put up by two of the military schools, a Cossack Hundred and some members of the officers' staff;[32] but, on January 4, 1918, the Irkutsk soviet was able to back its claim to plenary power in the "city of Irkutsk, province, and district," for itself and the district bureau. Immediately thereafter, the Third Congress of East Siberian Soviets met in the city and confirmed the action.[33]

The moderate socialist leaders were holding out more effectively in the central part of the basin. In Blagoveshchensk, the Bolshevik-left-wing Social Revolutionary bloc succeeded only on January 18 in winning a majority in the Amur territorial soviet; the moderate socialists continued to retain control in the municipal duma.[34] In Chita, capital of the Trans-Baikal Territory, the extremists had not even been able to capture the soviet. By early October, 1917, the Bolsheviks had split from the united Social Democratic party but

[31] Maksakov and Turunov, *Khronika*, pp. 50–52; U.S. Department of State archives, Record Group 84, American consulate, Vladivostok, 1918, XI, 800, No. 195 (American consul, Vladivostok, to secretary of state, February 1, 1918, enclosing a letter from an unnamed businessman in Irkutsk, dated December 17, 1917, describing the fighting at Irkutsk, December 8–17); R. T. Khaptaev, *Buriat-Mongoliia v Period Oktiabr'skoi Sotsialisticheskoi Revoliutsii* (Ogiz: Irkutskoe oblastnoe izdatel'stvo, 1947), pp. 25–26.

[32] Descriptions of the fighting will be found in the businessman's letter referred to above; in Sibirskii Kraevoi Sovet Professional'nykh Soiuzov, *Profsoiuzy Sibiri v Bor'be za Vlast' Sovetov, 1917–1919 gg.*, comp. V. Shemelev, ed. V. Vegman (Novosibirsk, 1928), p. 44; and in various memoirs included in Vsesoiuznaia Kommunisticheskaia Partiia, Tsentral'nyi Ispolnitel'nyi Komitet, Sekretariat Glavnoi Redaktsii Istorii Grazhdanskoi Voiny v SSSR, *Sergei Lazo, Vospominaniia i Dokumenty*, comp. G. Reikhberg, A. Romanov, and P. Krol' (Moscow: Gosizdat, 1938).

[33] Maksakov and Turunov, *Khronika*, p. 57.

[34] G. E. Reikhberg, "Bol'sheviki Dal'nego Vostoka v Bor'be s Iaponskoi Interventsiei, 1918–1922 gg.," *Proletarskaia Revoliutsiia*, III (1939), p. 77,

had been able to go no farther.[35] In fact, early in December, the moderate socialists, with the support of the Kadets, succeeded in concentrating all authority in the hands of a coalition body known as the People's Soviet.[36] Just before Nakajima's arrival in Vladivostok, several regiments, the First Chita and the First Nerchinsk Cossack, had returned from the front; the First Nerchinsk was also in the area; and all of these were friendly to the moderate socialist cause.[37] Indeed, they were at the very moment proving their loyalty by following Horvat's example in rejecting the help of the Semenovists.

Throughout December and January, Semenov had kept his agents circulating among the Cossack border villages, hunting for recruits and weapons. By the second week in January he had collected a regiment of 556 officers, civil officials, Barguts, Mongols, and Cossacks, not counting former prisoners of war and Chinese.[38] On January 11, he had sent a unit under Baron Ungern to the Cossack village of Oloviannaia on the bank of the Onon river, halfway to Chita. Ungern had disarmed the Red Guard there and gathered 175 rifles and four ammunition wagons before Red Guards from Chita, Karymskaia, and other near-by points drove him out. The next day the Red Guards had moved on Karymskaia and threatened Dauriia. It was at this point that Semenov learned that the anti-Bolshevik First Chita Cossack Regiment was returning to Chita. Hoping that the regiment was not only anti-Bolshevik, but anti-socialist as well, Semenov promptly appealed to the regiment's

[35] Reikhberg, *Iaponskaia Interventsiia,* pp. 6–7.

[36] *Ibid.,* p. 8; V. Sokolov, "Oktiabr' za Baikalom (Ianvar'-Fevral' 1918 g.)," *Proletarskaia Revoliutsiia,* No. 10 (October, 1922), p. 391. The date of the organization of the territorial People's Soviet is not certain. I have followed Reikhberg and Sokolov, who place it early in December. Other dates have been suggested: near January 5, by Maksakov and Turunov, *Khronika,* p. 57; and on January 11 (N.s or o.s.?), by Vsesoiuznaia Kommunisticheskaia Partiia (bol'shevikov), Chita Okruzhnyi Komitet, *Partizany* (Chita, 1929), p. 202; but, these dates may have become confused with dates of subsequent elections or decisions of one or more of the participating bodies.

[37] N. M. Matveev, "Bor'ba za Sovety Zabaikal'e," in Vsesoiuznaia Kommunisticheskaia Partiia, Tsentral'nyi Ispolnitel'nyi Komitet, Sekretariat Glavnoi Redaktsii Istorii Grazhdanskoi Voiny v SSSR, *Sergei Lazo,* pp. 24–25; A. Klark-Ansonova, "Drug," *ibid.,* p. 47.

[38] Gregorii Semenov, *O Sebe* (Harbin: Zaria, 1938), p. 86.

commander to join him at Chita. Then, without waiting for a reply, he ordered Lieutenant Savel'ev to lead about one hundred men northward to Chita.[39] Savel'ev quickly drove the Reds out of Oloviannaia, added 78 rifles and 12 swords to his armament, then pushed on to occupy Adrianovka. By the following day, the People's Soviet at Chita learned of the Semenovist advance and were terror-struck. Semenov was known to favor a military dictatorship and to have no sympathy for the moderate socialists. A delegation was rushed to Adrianovka to plead with Savel'ev to withdraw. Meanwhile, the First Chita Regiment had already reached Chita, disarmed the Red Guards there, and lent its support to the People's Soviet. Semenov was forced to withdraw. The stage appeared set in Chita for the consolidation of control by the People's Soviet over the Trans-Baikal Territory.

The Cossacks Supported

In view of the political complexion of the population of the Amur basin and the revolutionary developments which were taking place, it might be supposed that Nakajima would carry out his mission of offering support to "moderate self-governing bodies" in the area by negotiating with those governing organs supported by the majority in the basin and led by the moderate socialists. It might be thought that he would have talked immediately with members of the municipal duma in Vladivostok, the zemstvo representatives in Khabarovsk, or the delegates to the People's Soviet in Chita, or that he might have sought out the officers of the cooperatives; but, so far as is known, he did nothing of the kind. Nor does he seem to have given consideration to the provisional government at Tomsk. Instead, he concentrated his attention on former officers and on the Cossack armies and offered the support of the empire only to their right-wing elements.

Unfortunately, there are no official minutes, instructions, or re-

[39] This operation is confirmed in Matveev, "Bor'ba za Sovety v Zabaikal'e," p. 25; USSR Tsentral'nyi Arkhiv RSFSR, Arkhiv Oktiabr'skoi Revoliutsii, *Iaponskaia Interventsiia 1918–1922 gg. v dokumentakh*, ed. I. Mints (Moscow, 1934), p. 202.

ports to explain this fateful decision. Nor is it certain whether it was taken by Nakajima on his own authority or whether it had been preceded by extensive discussions in Tokyo. It may, of course, have been made on the basis of inadequate information about the size of the popular support for the moderate socialists, but it seems safer to imagine that other considerations were more important.

One consideration may have been a predisposition by the army to place primary emphasis on military strength; thus when aid to "moderate self-governing bodies" was specified, Nakajima clearly understood that only such bodies as had military strength were eligible for aid; and he must soon have learned, if he did not know before, that the most effectively organized military units available to oppose the socialist extremists were the Cossack armies. He must have known, however, that the People's Soviet in Chita did have military support, so that a second condition would appear to have been equally or more important: that the "moderate self-governing bodies" should be nonsocialist or antisocialist.

It seems probable from Nakajima's actions and from the actions and views of army men in the months which followed, that Japan's military leaders either did not understand, or at least did not attach great significance to, the differences between Mensheviks and Bolsheviks, or between left-wing and right-wing Social Revolutionaries. With what seems to be an all too common propensity to assume that other persons are like one's self and that other societies are like one's own, the Japanese military authorities may well have conceived of the situation in the Amur basin as similar to that in Japan, where socialism in any form was anathema, where popular support seemed irrelevant, and where moderation meant government by an oligarchy, backed by military, economic, and bureaucratic groups. In short, just as in the case of the Tuan clique in China, Japan's military leaders may have seen in the Cossack heads the closest counterpart to themselves, and to have considered, therefore, that they could be helped to power by methods familiar in Japan; and that, once in power, they could be depended upon as sound allies.

Another possible explanation cannot be ignored. The decision to support the Cossacks may have been taken in Tokyo in mid-December, 1917, by Terauchi and Tanaka, as a result of conversations with Nishihara and with the expedition-minded pressure group he had come to represent. Unfortunately, the Russian agent, Andreev, remains unidentified, and the only available source for these conversations, Nishihara's autobiography, has nothing to say on this point; but, as will presently be seen, at least one Cossack leader must certainly have been discussed, the aggressive Gregorii Semenov.

Whatever may be the real explanation, almost immediately upon his arrival in Vladivostok Nakajima turned his attention to the Ussuri Cossacks, who had traditionally manned one division to protect the Ussuri river borderland. At that moment they were holding a conference at Iman, some two hundred and fifty miles north of Vladivostok. In October, 1917, the Ussuri Cossack host had decided to give up its special privileges;[40] the present meeting was to determine its attitude toward the Soviet government and to select an ataman as leader.[41] Seizing the opportunity thus offered, Nakajima sent three agents to the conference. According to Japanese sources, a certain Major Dunlop was sent by the British.[42] Dunlop urged the Cossacks to declare for the Allies' side against the Bolsheviks and promised that, if they did so, "the Allies would give them considerable aid." No doubt covertly, the Japanese agents pressed for the same decision. This encouragement strengthened the Cossacks' own inclination finally to declare their hostility to the Soviet regime. The difficulty then was to find a suitable leader, suitable in the sense that he could command the allegiance of the Cossacks and at the same time secure aid from the British, or more important, from the Japanese. One of Japan's agents, a Russian by

[40] Maksakov and Turunov, *Khronika*, p. 45; Semenov (*O Sebe*, p. 46) reports that it had done so as early as May, 1917, but Semenov is frequently inexact as to dates.

[41] Japan, Sambō Hombu, *Shiberia Shuppei-shi*, III, 1048.

[42] Katō to vice chief of the navy general staff, Feb. 22, 1918, *JGK, RKI, HK,* I.

the name of Alekshin, backed by Nakajima, is reported to have been the determining influence in persuading the Cossacks to elect as ataman a young veteran of the Caucasian front, Ivan Kalmykov. Nakajima promised him aid and sent Captain Yokoo Noriyoshi, a young officer of the army in Korea, then in Vladivostok on intelligence duty, to help him.

Nakajima next gave his attention momentarily to the city of Blagoveshchensk, where he arrived on January 27.[43] Apparently finding no zemstvo or duma groups with whom he cared to deal personally, he contented himself with leaving a Russian employee[44] of the Kuhara Mining Company's branch office to rally what Russians he could, while he himself turned to the Amur Cossacks, who opened a conference of their own in the city on January 30. Here as at Iman, Nakajima succeeded in persuading the Cossacks under Ataman Gamov to decide for self-government in opposition to the Soviet regime. He then urged them to build up their strength and assigned Major Ishimitsu Makiyo, an intelligence agent from the Kwantung Government Generalcy, to maintain liaison with them.

It may be, of course, that Nakajima hoped to investigate the situation at Chita more thoroughly or at least to get in touch with the Semenovists in the southern part of the Trans-Baikal Territory; but, if so, he had waited too long. Sometime in early February, three more regiments arrived back in the territory from the Caucasian front: the First Verkhneudinsk, the Second Chita, and the Second Nerchinsk. They had, writes an old Bolshevik, "passed from the front lines through territory already sovietized, both Russian and Siberian. Everywhere they had been greeted by speeches, treated with meetings." [45] By the time they reached the sovietized eastern gateway at Irkutsk, they were so worked up that they arrested their officers and dropped them off the train.[46] At Verkhneudinsk, the home regiment seems to have detrained. The others pro-

---

[43] Japan, Sambō Hombu, *Shiberia Shuppei-shi,* III, 1046–47.
[44] The Japanese transliteration of this employee's name is given as Randouishefu. It has so far been impossible to identify him more accurately.
[45] V. Sokolov, "Oktiabr' za Baikalom (Ianvar'-Fevral' 1918 g.)," p. 389.
[46] P. Pozdeev, "Sovetizatsiia Zabaikalia v usloviiakh interventsii 1918 g.," *Proletarskaia Revoliutsiia,* XI, No. 34 (November, 1924), 185.

ceeded to Chita, led by such later famous Bolsheviks as Dmitrii Shilov, Zhigalin, Kirgizov, Baliasin, and Sergei Lazo.[47]

The position of the moderate socialists at Chita was not hopeless. They had the support of the First Chita Regiment. They could have called on the friendly First Nerchinsk Regiment to the east and could possibly have asked for support from the Semenovists.

The local Bolshevik leader, Sokolov, describes how, when the Bolshevized regiments arrived at Chita, their representatives went directly to the soviet of workers' and soldiers' deputies on February 15 and declared, "We have just established the Soviet power and have come to solve the problem with you. Are you ready?" [48]

Sokolov, who was also vice chairman of the people's soviet, replied that it was "too risky at the present time"; but, the newcomers proposed "to carry out the overturn nevertheless." The decision was taken and a revolutionary staff selected.

About noon of the next day a detachment occupied the offices of the People's Soviet. In the evening the all-powerful revolutionary staff called a meeting of the soviet and declared it open to Cossack elements.

The chairman tried to rely on the constitution. The Cossack elements, he said, do not represent all the population, nor even the majority of it. But the commissioner [Kirgizov of the revolutionary staff] declared he had nothing more to say.

He turned and left.

The [members of the People's] Soviet glanced around at each other with strained smiles.

The workers' group declared its support for an overturn and announced its withdrawal from the People's Soviet and its organizations.[49]

[47] Shilov became president of the Constituent Assembly of the Far Eastern Republic in 1922; Zhigalin became chief of staff of the Mamontov Partisan Army in Siberia in 1920; Kirgizov was later active in the Far Eastern Republic; Baliasin died while leading a partisan Cossack army against Semenov; and Lazo was soon to be appointed commander of the Red Guard on the Trans-Baikal front. Sokolov, "Oktiabr' za Baikalom (Ianvar'-Fevral' 1918 g.)," p. 389. Sokolov says that four regiments returned at this time but does not name them.

[48] *Ibid.* Maksakov and Turunov say that the First Revolutionary Zabaikal Division decided on February 10, 1918, to introduce the soviet structure into the territory; but, no source is given and the meaning is not clear. Maksakov and Turunov, *Khronika*, p. 58.

[49] Sokolov, "Oktiabr' za Baikalom (Ianvar'-Fevral' 1918 g.)," p. 389.

Thereupon the chairman bowed to the staff and dissolved the soviet.

The moderates had given up without a fight. All power was immediately assumed by the Soviet of Workers', Cossacks' and Soldiers' Deputies, headed by the local Bolshevik leader, Boris Sokolov.[50]

With the fall of Chita, Nakajima was cut off from easy access to the Semenovists. By mid-February, 1918, the Soviet tide was running so strongly in the Siberian part of the Amur basin that, for elements to build into an effective dam against it, the Japanese army would have to look to the Chinese Eastern Railway Zone in north Manchuria. Nakajima departed for Harbin.

[50] Maksakov and Turunov, *Khronika*, pp. 58–59, where the date for the takeover is given as February 15, 1918. Sokolov omits the date. The date used above, February 16, 1918, is found in Matveev, "Bor'ba za Sovety v Zabaikal'e," pp. 24–25; and in Vsesoiuznaia Kommunisticheskaia Partiia (bol'shevikov), Chita Okruzhnyi Komitet, *Partizany*, p. 202.

V. THE MANCHURIAN SANCTUARY

In the winter and spring of 1918 Harbin was a city of confusion. The administration was Russian: the former Chinese Eastern Railway administrator, General Horvat, continued in nominal authority, subject to a city council. But, since the sovietized railway guard had been expelled by the Chinese, actual control of the city was in the hands of Chinese troops. Political parties of every persuasion were demonstrating in the streets and circulating propaganda sheets. Refugees from Siberia and European Russia streamed steadily down from the border—Cossacks, duma and zemstvo leaders, monarchist generals, Chinese, Japanese, and Russian businessmen. The air was filled with talk of revolution and counterrevolution. Among the hundreds of would-be generals and dictators, four men stood out—Lieutenant General Domanevskii, Vice Consul Popov, Captain Semenov, and General Horvat.

Lieutenant General Domanevskii, formerly chief of staff of Russian forces along the Amur, had recently fled from Khabarovsk, bringing a plan for the Allies to form a force under a Russian commander, presumably himself, to take over the Trans-Siberian Railroad.[1] At first both Consul General Satō and Lieutenant Colonel Kurozawa were inclined to favor the general; but soon word came through that the Russian ambassadors in Peking and Tokyo had no confidence in him.[2] It became obvious that he had no troops to call on; he represented only himself.

[1] Satō to Motono, February 5, 1918, *JGK, RKI, SK, HMSK,* pp. 221–26.
[2] Motono to Satō, February 24, 1918, *JGK, RKI, HK,* I.

The Far Eastern Committee

The attention of the Japanese representatives was next attracted by an organization being formed around Vice Consul Popov, acting Russian consul general in Harbin, the Far Eastern Committee for the Defense of the Fatherland and the Constituent Assembly.[3] Apparently inspired or at least supported by the Russian legation in Peking,[4] the committee consisted of the following: Popov, who headed the Committee for Positive Aid, Rabulov,[5] deposed as governor of the Maritime Territory, who headed the Administrative Department; Alexandrov, chairman of the Executive Committee in Harbin, who chaired the Finance Department; and Colonel Nikitin, chairman of the Military Department and former commandant of the Irkutsk officers' school, a man with contacts among the officers' organizations which were being formed in various cities throughout Siberia.[6] Two things were needed if the committee was to be more effective than the host of other refugee committees in Harbin: money and troops.

For troops the committee looked first of all to the officers, estimated to number as many as twenty-five hundred, who were streaming into Harbin in the path of the Bolshevik advance in Siberia.[7] Sometime in the middle of February, 1918, the committee announced that Colonel Nikitin was forming a Far Eastern corps and ordered all officers to place themselves under the authority of

[3] The date of the organization of the committee is not clear. Mints gives January 30, 1918. USSR, Tsentral'nyi Arkhiv RSFSR, Arkhiv Oktiabr'skoi Revoliutsii, *Iaponskaia Interventsiia 1918–1922 gg. v dokumentakh*, ed. I. Mints (Moscow, 1934), p. 202. The Japanese Army General Staff Headquarters places it during the first ten days of February. Japan, Sambō Hombu, *Taishō Shichi-nen naishi Jūichi-nen Shiberia Shuppei-shi*, (Tokyo, 1924), III, 1051.

[4] According to Popov, as reported in Satō to Motono, Feb. 27, 1918, *JGK, RKI, HK*, I.

[5] The romanized form of the name, derived from the Japanese *kana* transliteration, is "Raburufu" in one source, "Raburoha" in another; I have been unable to identify the name in Russian, but assume it must be something like "Rabulov," which I have used here.

[6] According to Vice Consul Popov, as reported by Satō to Motono, February 23, 1918, *JGK, RKI, HK*, I.

[7] Kurozawa to Uehara, February 26, 1918, *ibid*, I.

the corps.[8] Captain Semenov was approached in the hope that he would lend the support of his troops at Manchouli and that he would place himself under the committee's direction. Meanwhile, intercession was made in his behalf with Horvat, whose backing, along with that of the Russian officials in Peking, the committee hoped to secure.

Semenov's Quest for Support

Although it is difficult to date accurately the actions of the Semenovists during this period, they were extremely busy. While scouring the southern part of the Trans-Baikal Territory for recruits and soliciting aid from every military unit which passed through Manchouli—whether Italian, Serb, or Bargut—Semenov was carrying on a vigorous military campaign and conducting far-reaching diplomatic negotiations.

He faced growing Communist strength in the north. Ungern's push to Oloviannaia on January 11, 1918, had been repulsed, and Savel'ev's offensive against Chita shortly thereafter had been turned back at Adrianovka. Following the fall of Chita to the soviet forces, the territorial Red Guards, led by Sergei Lazo, the daring young officer from Krasnoiarsk, drove the Semenovists steadily backward toward the border—and toward the Chinese.

From the time the Allies invited them into Harbin (the end of December, 1917), Chinese troops had been moving rapidly along the Chinese Eastern Railway to take over garrison duties throughout the zone.[9] According to Semenov, it was only through a combination of force and trickery that he was able to keep Hailar and Manchouli out of their hands.[10] Clearly he would need powerful aid from the outside if he were to avoid being crushed.

[8] Budberg dates this announcement February 11, 1918. Baron Aleksei Budberg, *Dnevnik Belogvardeitsa* (*Kolchakovskaia epopeia*) (Leningrad: Priboi, 1929), XII, 281–82. Whether this date is in the new or old style is not clear in the text. Satō dates it on February 22. Satō to Motono, February 22, 1918, *JGK, RKI, HK,* I.

[9] Saitō (in Peking) to Uehara, February 9, 1918, *JGK, RKI, HK,* I.

[10] Gregorii Semenov, *O Sebe* (Harbin: Zaria, 1938), pp. 80–85. Semenov's account here is unconfirmed, and may only be the product of a romantic imagination.

In late December, 1917, or early January, 1918, Semenov sent a certain Lieutenant Zhevchenko to talk with Russian and Allied leaders at Vladivostok, Peking, and Shanghai, probably also in Harbin.[11] The first part of the proposal was for the Allies to supply Semenov with weapons and money so as to enable him to rally a force of 3,000 to 4,000 men for an advance on Karymskaia, Chita, and Irkutsk, and finally to sweep the Bolsheviks completely out of the Trans-Baikal Territory. The Russian minister to China, Prince Kudashev, gave the plan his warm support. The Russian military attaché in Peking was also impressed and hoped that the Semenovists could be used eventually to take over the garrisoning of the railway from the Chinese.[12] The minister and the attaché agreed to work on the Allies.

A second part of Semenov's plan involved a man later to become very prominent in the history of the Siberian intervention, Rear Admiral Alexander Kolchak. A well-known Polar explorer, highly decorated defender of the Baltic in the early years of the war and later commander in chief of the Black Sea fleet, Kolchak (then forty-four) had just arrived in the Far East.[13] In the summer of 1917 Kerensky had discovered that Kolchak had agreed to head a union of secret, patriotic groups to suppress the Bolsheviks (interestingly enough, at about the same time Semenov was urging the same thing in Petrograd, though no connections between Kolchak and Semenov during this period are known); and so, in spite of the admiral's naval abilities, Kerensky had decided it was

[11] Semenov refers only to Zhevchenko's visit to Shanghai, saying he went in late December. His visit to Vladivostok is attested in Caldwell (Vladivostok) to Moser (Harbin), December 27, 1917, in U.S. Department of State archives, Record Group 84, American consulate, Vladivostok, "confidential correspondence," file 824. Knowledge of Zhevchenko's proposals in Harbin, together with the route of the railway, strongly suggest that he visited that city. Moser (Harbin) to Caldwell (Vladivostok), received December 28, 1918, *ibid.* The rest of his trip is described in Saitō to Uehara, February 22, 1918, *JGK, RKI, HK*, I. I have assumed that the reference to a Captain Gubichenko, negotiating for Semenov in Tokyo on February 18, results from a mistransliteration of Zhevchenko's name (mistransliterations of foreign names are extremely frequent in the Japanese archival sources). Japan, Sambō Hombu, *Shiberia Shuppei-shi*, III, 1077–78.

[12] Saitō to Uehara, February 9, 1918, *JGK, RKI, HK*, I.

[13] M. I. Smirnov, "Admiral Kolchak," *The Slavonic and East European Review*, XI, No. 32 (January, 1933), pp. 373–83.

politically wise to send him off on a junket to America to advise the United States government on a project for a landing in the Bosporus. Supposedly on his way home, he arrived in Japan in November, 1917. His activities during the first five months of the Bolshevik revolution are not known, but it is reasonable to assume that he maintained close contact and exchanged ideas with fellow anti-Bolsheviks in Japan and China. Gradually he began to emerge as a potential figure around whom the anti-Bolsheviks of the east might rally.

Semenov writes that late in December, 1917,[14] he sent his representative, Zhevchenko, to talk with the admiral in Shanghai. Japanese sources indicate that Zhevchenko was interested in securing financial backing.[15] Semenov tells us that he invited Kolchak to come to Manchouli to lead the anti-soviet movement.[16] Apparently, Semenov had in mind a deal: he would offer to accept Kolchak's leadership, at least for the time, if Kolchak in his turn would agree to support Semenov's forces; but this was inacceptable to Kolchak and his close supporters. Kolchak, along with Russian Consul General Putilov and Count Ezerski, wired Semenov their best wishes, but said the time was not yet ripe for Kolchak's emergence on the scene. They apparently preferred to wait to see what aid might be forthcoming from the Allies.

Allied Negotiations

The Russian minister to China, Prince Kudashev, approached the British minister first. The British had already decided to try to build up the anti-Bolsheviks in the Amur basin, as their negotiations with the Ussuri Cossacks indicate. They readily agreed to supply as much money as possible, 562,000 rubles monthly, it is said,[17] and detailed a certain Captain Denny to report at first hand

---

[14] Semenov, *O Sebe*, pp. 73–74.

[15] Nishihara says that Kolchak actually promised it. Nishihara Kamezo, *Yume no Shichi-jū-yo-nen: Nishihara Kamezō jiden* (Kumobara Mura, 1949), pp. 228–29.

[16] Semenov, *O Sebe*, pp, 73–74.

[17] Yoshizawa to Motono, February 3, 1918, *JGK, RKI, HK*, I.

on developments at Manchouli.[18] Beyond that, they urged Kudashev to enlist the support of the other Allies, particularly Japan.

On February 2, 1918, Prince Kudashev appealed to Yoshizawa Kenkichi, Japanese chargé in China, to secure from his government some 30 to 40 machine guns with ammunition, and some 3,000 rifles.[19] Two days later the British army authorities made the same request of Colonel Tanaka Kunishige, Japanese military attaché in London.[20] Once again the British revealed their primary concern for European Russia, for they spoke of having Semenov move west at least as far as Tomsk. In the following weeks the British government indicated a willingness to supply Semenov with £10,000 monthly.[21] It also kept up the pressure on Japanese representatives, now on Ambassador Chinda and Colonel Tanaka in London, now on Consul General Satō in Harbin, now on the chargé d'affairs in Peking, Yoshizawa Kenkichi, and the military attaché there, Major General Saitō Kijiro.[22]

What the British military authorities wanted was an agreement with the Japanese Army General Staff Headquarters, preferably worked out by the military attachés in Peking. Such an agreement would be less binding and less public than a convention between the two governments. Ambassador Chinda in London saw this point. He himself was anxious to keep Japan's hands free for any later large-scale expedition of its own, but he was equally anxious to fall in with the plans of the Western Allies so as to develop a close understanding with them. Consequently, Chinda recommended the British proposal to his government, and Colonel Tanaka forwarded the recommendation to the general staff.[23] From Peking, Chargé Yoshizawa also recommended aid to Semenov, in

[18] Saitō to Uehara, February 1, 1918, *ibid.*, I.

[19] Yoshizawa to Motono, February 3, 1918, *ibid.*, I; and diary entry February 3, 1918, in Araki, Sadao, comp., *Gensui Uehara Yūsaku Den* (Tokyo: Gensui Uehara Yūsaku Denki Hankō-kai, 1937), II, 142.

[20] The same Tanaka who in the fall of 1919, as chief of the second section (intelligence) of the Army General Staff Headquarters, led the successful fight within the government against a Japanese withdrawal from Siberia.

[21] According to the British minister in China. Yoshizawa to Motono, February 15, 1918, *JGK, RKI, HK,* I.

[22] Dispatches, February 1–24, 1918, *ibid.*, I.

[23] Chinda to Motono, February 10, 1918, *ibid.*, I.

line with the Anglo-French plans; at the same time he urged that negotiations for a Siberian expedition be entered into separately.[24] Major General Saitō felt that the sending of Japanese troops should be avoided since it would arouse the Russian people against the empire; but, he enthusiastically supported the Semenov plan.[25]

The British also pressed the American government to join in the project. On February 6, 1918, the British chargé in Washington informed the secretary of state that His Majesty's government, supported by the Russian minister in Peking, believed "it is clearly advantageous to the Allied cause to give any encouragement to any movement of purely Russian origin which had indications of being successful." [26] Such a movement Britain professed to find in the forces being rallied by Semenov. The statement recounted Semenov's plan, noted that the British government had decided to provide funds for munitions and clothing (the cost of which was expected to run, after the initial expenditure, at around £10,000 a month), and concluded by pointing out that of course it was a gamble, and therefore consideration should be given to the plan for Japanese intervention.

Washington preferred to remain aloof from any such arrangement; Paris, on the other hand, responded with alacrity, seizing on the Semenov plan as a substitute for one of its own which had failed to find acceptance. The rejection of the Foch plan in December, 1917, had not dampened the enthusiasm of the French government for Allied intervention. Moreover, the movement of the Japanese and British warships to Vladivostok in early January, 1918, convinced French leaders that their Allies were beginning to share their views. Accordingly, when reports of bloody street-fighting in Irkutsk reached Paris at about that time, the French decided to seize this as an immediate cause for intervention.

Apparently taking a leaf from Britain's book at Vladivostok, the French government decided to force Allied action by threatening to act alone. On January 8, Ambassador Jusserand in Washington

[24] Yoshizawa to Motono, February 17, 1918, *ibid.,* I.
[25] Saitō to Uehara, January 29, 1918, *ibid.,* I.
[26] Barclay to the secretary of state, February 6, 1918, *USFR, 1918, Russia,* II, 38–41.

informed the American government that events in Irkutsk had compelled his government to consider "the immediate sending to Harbin and thence to Irkutsk of the largest possible French force to be detailed from the corps of occupation in China." [27] France preferred not to act alone, the note went on to say, and hoped the Allies would cooperate with "new appropriations and supplies" in a joint expedition. The hope was expressed that "Russian military elements" would participate in order to give the expedition the appearance of an Allied action in support of "the Russian elements in Siberia that have remained true to the cause of the entente." [28] But the American government was unmoved. A week later it coldly denied that the pacification of Irkutsk and the assisting of prowar Russians were sufficient grounds for intervention in Siberia.

A French approach to the British government was similarly rebuffed. After several months of negotiations with America and with Japan, Britain saw no hope for an Allied expedition. The United States government would not participate, and Japan, according to Ambassador Chinda, would oppose any but a purely Japanese effort. The British government was in no position to undertake a major expedition and was in fact anxious not to be identified with one publicly, for fear of the effect on its negotiations with the Bolshevik government in Moscow.[29] It preferred instead to sponsor, jointly with the Allies, a Russian anti-Soviet military force and if possible a government of anti-Bolshevik Russians in the Amur basin.

It seems clear that the French also approached the Japanese government. As late as February 3 the French minister in Peking was telling the commander of the Japanese army in China of his government's feeling that "the present situation in Siberia is the same as

[27] French Ambassador Jusserand to the United States government, January 8, 1918, USFR, 1918, Russia, II, 20–21.

[28] The exact scope of the expedition as envisaged by the French is not clear, but probably was not limited to Irkutsk. The French consul general from Tientsin, who was sent to Irkutsk to investigate, is reported to have wired back the recommendation that an Allied (Japanese, British, French, and American) mixed brigade should be sent immediately to Irkutsk and should take over the railroads to the east. Commander of the Japanese army in China to Uehara, February 3, 1918, JGK, RKI, HK, I.

[29] According to the British military attaché in Peking, Saitō to Uehara, February 1, 1918, ibid., I.

during the Boxer incident" and that the French were determined to protect their interests.[30] At the same time, Major Bion de la Pomarède, the military attaché then assigned to the French missions in both Japan and China, arrived in Tientsin to confer with the Japanese commander about sending French troops either from the forces in China or from the native troops in Annam. While the archival records do not reveal explicitly the reaction to the French proposal, the insistence of the Japanese officials on keeping foreign troops out of the Amur basin and on preserving Japan's own freedom of action suggests conclusively that the reaction was less than favorable.

Thus, unable to get support for their own proposal, the French were casting about for an alternative when the Russian military attaché outlined the Semenov scheme to his Allied colleagues in Peking on January 29 and February 1.[31] Captain Pelliot was immediately dispatched to Manchouli to report on the actual situation there.[32] He seems to have been well impressed. On his return he urged support for Semenov's drive on Irkutsk, and also proposed that the occupied area be administered by a council, chaired by a "suitable Russian" under the supervision of the Allies and supported by the Cossacks.[33]

Meanwhile, Zhevchenko or Semenov appears to have been in touch with one or both of Nishihara's representatives, Yoshimi Enzō and Sawano Hideo, and to have received assurances that the Japanese government not only would give them arms, but would in the end send Japanese troops as well.[34] Zhevchenko left immediately to negotiate a concrete agreement in Tokyo. About February 4, Semenov came to Harbin to support the negotiations from there. These decisions were certainly known to the Japanese army, for on February 3 the vice chief of the Japanese Army General Staff Headquarters, Lieutenant General Tanaka, ordered Lieu-

[30] Commander of the Japanese army in China to Uehara, February 3, 1918, *ibid.*, I.
[31] Saitō to Uehara, February 1, 1918, *ibid.*, I, and Japan, Sambō Hombu, *Shiberia Shuppei-shi*, III, 1074.
[32] Saitō to Uehara, February 1, 1918, *JGK, RKI, HK*, I.
[33] Satō to Motono, February 18, 1918, *ibid.*, I.
[34] Nishihara, *Yume no Shichi-jū-yo-nen*, pp. 228–31.

tenant Colonel Kurozawa Jun, the chief Kwantung army staff agent, to Harbin to investigate Semenov's possibilities.[35] Two days later a Captain Sakabe at Manchouli was assigned to Kurozawa.[36] The Japanese officer more widely known for his liaison work with Semenov, Captain Kuroki Shinkei, seems not to have been assigned to that duty until the following month.[37]

Semenov in Harbin

The arrival of Semenov in Harbin early in February was therefore of some moment. His previous visits seem to have been largely futile errands to secure Horvat's permission to take over the arms of the former Russian frontier corps or to recruit among the railroad guards then in process of dissolution.[38] On this occasion he came primarily to negotiate with the powers. First, he secured the support of the British consul general. Then he turned to the Japanese representatives, especially to Consul General Satō, Lieutenant Colonel Kurozawa, the president of the Japanese association of Harbin, and the director of the office of the South Manchurian Railway Company. Representing himself as a man with no political connections, whose only interest was to fulfill his mission to restore order in the Far East, he claimed to have some 2,000 troops under his command at Manchouli. Because of Horvat's indecisiveness or outright opposition, he told them, he had been unable to secure enough arms and money to hold the Trans-Baikal Territory against the Bolsheviks; but he did have intimate relations with anti-Bolshevik groups throughout Siberia.[39] If only Japan would supply him with, say, 2,000 rifles, 20 machine guns, 6 mountain guns, two 6-inch artillery pieces, adequate ammunition, and enough

---

[35] Japan, Sambō Hombu, *Shiberia Shuppei-shi*, III, 1050, 1076.

[36] Kwantung army chief of staff to vice minister of war, February 5, 1918, MJ 50, *JRK, MDN* (February, 1918).

[37] Japan, Sambō Hombu, *Shiberia Shuppei-shi*, III, 1079.

[38] *Ibid.*, pp. 83–91. Semenov mentions having made at least three visits to Harbin in January and refers to none in February. His very important and extended visit in February is so well attested by a variety of sources as to warrant the conclusion that he has either mistakenly dated one or more of his January visits or has referred to them by the old-style calendar.

[39] Satō to Motono, February 14, 1918, *JGK, RKI, HK*, I.

money (perhaps 250,000 rubles), then he would be in a position to advance swiftly on Chita and Irkutsk and to clean out the territory. Of course, as the Allies surely wanted, he would hope not only to hold Irkutsk, but to push westward, perhaps linking up with similar anti-Bolshevik forces in the Cheliabinsk area; but whether he simply held Irkutsk or advanced, he would require the support of Japanese troops; what he hoped for was an immediate grant of munitions and money and a "firm decision" by the Japanese government to send troops to his aid.[40] The mention of Cheliabinsk as an ultimate objective and the request for a purely Japanese undertaking suggest that Semenov and his supporters as well as the French were being strongly influenced by British thinking, which was inclining more and more toward working secretly through Siberian elements like the Semenovists and the Ussuri Cossacks and through sizable Japanese forces as well, in order to choke the life out of the young Soviet Republic. At the same time the Allies would publicly maintain their freedom to negotiate with the Moscow authorities so long as life remained there.

Having talked with Semenov, Lieutenant Colonel Kurozawa wired headquarters in Tokyo on February 17, urging that money be supplied to Semenov immediately.[41] Support given now would enable him to secure the Trans-Baikal Territory, where his forces could serve as a nucleus around which "moderates" throughout the Far East could be rallied; moreover, "if he is helped now when his funds are about exhausted," Kurozawa pointed out, "he will rely heavily on Japan."

Consul General Satō was also greatly impressed by Semenov and supported his entire proposal. "A man of sound ability," he termed him[42] and urged that aid be sent immediately.[43] In addition, like the chargé in Peking, Yoshizawa Kenkichi, he was convinced

[40] Kurozawa to Uehara, February 19, 1918 (reporting conversation with Semenov on February 18), *ibid.*, I; and chief of staff, Kwantung army to Uehara, February 20, 1918 (reporting conversation between Semenov and director of South Manchurian Railway Company office in Harbin, same day), *ibid.*, I.

[41] Kurozawa to Tanaka, February 17, 1918, Japan, Sambō Hombu, *Shiberia Shuppei-shi*, III, 1076–77.

[42] Satō to Motono, March 12, 1918, *JGK, RKI, HK,* I.

[43] Satō to Motono, February 16, 1918, *ibid.*, I.

that a Japanese expedition was required. The Russians themselves, even the Cossacks, can never be counted on effectively to oppose the Bolsheviks, Satō warned. "They are like very sick men who, being unable to move their limbs, cannot stand without the aid of others." Yet, if the Bolsheviks were not driven out, they would permit the Germans to extend their influence in Siberia, thereby endangering the security of the empire and greatly strengthening the forces opposing the Allies. The interests of both the Allies and Japan required their elimination. A dual policy like Britain's, "on the one hand outwardly extending friendship to the Bolshevik government while on the other hand aiding the Semenov detachment which is trying to overthrow it," could achieve nothing, he thought. Decisive action was required; and if Japan did not take it, it had better watch out lest "north Manchuria be trampled on by China and Siberia itself be crushed by America." Send arms to Semenov, he urged, but accompany them with a Japanese expeditionary force, a small number to be used in advance units, the bulk to be kept in the rear where they could "prevent any interference by the Allies, especially America."

The crucial recommendation was probably Nakajima's. When Nakajima arrived in Harbin on February 21, 1918, he considered the claims of various aspirants for power. He promptly eliminated Lieutenant General Domanevskii, telling him that unless he "set up some kind of government organ which can be recognized as an independent government," no help would be forthcoming.[44] Colonel Nikitin had distinct possibilities, and Nakajima promised to support him if he would organize a government and occupy Vladivostok.[45] Semenov was also an impressive candidate, but, like Nikitin, he could not succeed alone. Nakajima was strongly attracted to Kurozawa's idea of incorporating their military efforts into the larger plans of the Far Eastern Committee and seems to have accepted the

---

[44] The name actually referred to here is "Major General Romanovskii," but this appears to be a mistake in transliteration as no such person is mentioned at this time in the dispatches. Japan, Sambō Hombu, *Shiberia Shuppei-shi*, III, 1051.

[45] *Ibid.*, III, 1052.

committee's contention that Semenov would subordinate his forces to its direction.

On February 24, Nakajima recommended to Tokyo that the committee be given sufficient arms to support a dual drive into Siberia: the Semenovists would advance westward on Chita and the forces to be recruited by Nikitin in the railway zone would advance eastward to the Ussuri and join with Kalmykov's Cossacks for a descent on Vladivostok.[46] In order to carry out this final operation, he urged that aid be given Kalmykov as well. Soon thereafter, Nakajima left for Vladivostok to talk with the Ussuri Cossacks.

Kalmykov's Flight

Shortly after Nakajima had departed for Harbin in mid-February, the Ussuri Cossacks, working with Britain's Major Dunlop, had conceived a plan for occupying the railroad station at Iman, where they had been meeting, thereby cutting off the Soviet elements in Vladivostok and securing the lower Maritime Territory. Such an operation, of course, would require both money and men; accordingly, a representative of Kalmykov had come to Vladivostok to appeal to the British consul.[47] The latter was prepared to give the money, but recommended that the men be sought from Japan;[48] he suggested a joint Japanese-British-Cossack conference and talked about it with Consul General Kikuchi on February 27, while the captain of HMS *Suffolk* approached Admiral Katō on the twenty-eighth. Both Kikuchi and Katō sought instructions from Tokyo.

Meanwhile, word of the decision at Iman reached the Soviets. Determined to crush the hostile Cossacks they set out immediately to arrest Kalmykov. The ataman managed to escape capture only by hiding in the British consulate on the morning of March 6. This provided an excellent opportunity for the joint conference sought

[46] Nakajima to Tanaka, February 24, 1918, *JGK, RKI, HK,* I.

[47] Japan, Sambō Hombu, *Shiberia Shuppei-shi,* III, 1048. A former teacher at the Eastern Institute in Vladivostok, whose name in the Japanese sources is transliterated variously as Menderin or Mendourin.

[48] Katō to vice chief of naval board, February 28, 1918, *JGK, RKI, HK,* I.

by the British consul general.[49] Consul General Kikuchi, who had received permission to attend "inconspicuously" only for the purpose of "reporting" the British and Cossack views,[50] came over that evening. Major Dunlop was also present. Although the available sources are not clear, Nakajima may also have attended the meeting; he is reported to have visited the British consulate early in March.

The plan outlined to Kikuchi and the others was the scheme, mentioned above, for the seizure of Iman as the first step toward driving the Bolsheviks out of the Maritime Territory. This, they hoped, would pave the way for Commissar Rusanov to call some kind of united assembly of municipal duma's and zemstvo's and to set up a government; they also hoped eventually to have the Ussuri Cossacks link up with the other Cossack forces in the Amur basin to restore order throughout the region.[51] Four thousand Cossacks could be rallied within two weeks, they promised, provided adequate support were forthcoming: 500,000 rubles as the first installment in an annual subsidy of 2,000,000 rubles; weapons, including 2,000 rifles, four machine guns and two field guns if possible, to be transferred preferably at Pogranichnaia or else at Harbin or Changchun; and support from Japanese forces, which they hoped could be stationed at Pogranichnaia, just across the Manchurian border on the Chinese Eastern Railway. Nakajima's recommendation of support for Kalmykov had already been forwarded to Tokyo from Harbin on February 24. The records do not reveal any further recommendation from him following this March 6 conference, but certainly he had not changed his mind. The official Japanese army history reports that he turned over a million rubles to Kalmykov at this time. On March 9 he even accompanied Kalmykov north to Iman to observe the mobilization of the Cossack forces.

Meanwhile, the British had also given Kalmykov some money;[52]

[49] Japan, Sambō Hombu, *Shiberia Shuppei-shi*, III, 1049.
[50] Motono to Kikuchi, March 4, 1918, *JGK, RKI, HK*, I.
[51] Kikuchi to Motono, March 7, 1918, *ibid.*, I.
[52] According to Japanese observers. Uemura to Tanaka, February 28, 1918, *JGK, RKI, HK*, I; and Kikuchi to Motono, March 7, 1918, transmitting a report by Lieutenant Colonel Sakabe, *ibid.*, I.

and on March 11 the British ambassador in Tokyo, Sir Connyngham Greene, sent a confidential memorandum to Foreign Minister Motono, indicating Britain's willingness "to consider" supplying the Ussuri Cossacks, but desiring first to know the views of the Japanese government.[53]

Unfortunately for the hopes of both Kalmykov and his backers, the mobilization failed. Kalmykov issued the call, but no one responded.[54] On March 13 the Cossack ataman was forced to flee to the border town of Grodekovo, only to have to seek almost immediately the safety of Pogranichnaia, on the Manchurian side of the border.

The Decision to Aid Semenov

Meanwhile, important decisions had already been taken in Tokyo regarding Kalmykov's rivals. With the Japanese military, diplomatic, and South Manchurian Railway Company representatives on the spot, as well as the Russian diplomatic officials and the governments of Britain and France unanimously recommending that Japan support Semenov, the authorities in Tokyo had quickly agreed. On February 18, 1918, Lieutenant Zhevchenko, who had recently arrived in Japan to represent Semenov, called on Lieutenant Colonel Araki Sadao of Army General Staff Headquarters.[55] Araki secretly introduced him to the appropriate army authorities and a deal was made: Japan was to supply 8 rapid-fire field guns, 1898 model; two 15-centimeter howitzers; 2,000 infantry rifles, 1897 model; 3,000 carbines, 1905 model; 50 machine guns, 1905 model; 200 pistols; 10,000 hand grenades; 10 grenade launchers; and 2,000 illuminating shells. For use with these weapons, the following ammunition was to be supplied: 10,000 rounds of shells and 5,000 rounds of shrapnel for the field guns; 2,000,000 rounds of machine-gun bullets; 1,000 rifle grenades; 7,500,000 rounds of carbine and rifle ammuni-

[53] Confidential memorandum from the British embassy, Tokyo, to the Japanese Ministry of Foreign Affairs, March 11, 1918 (English text), *ibid.*, I.

[54] Japan, Sambō Hombu, *Shiberia Shuppei-shi*, III, 1049.

[55] Japan, Sambō Hombu, *Shiberia Shuppei-shi*, III, 1077–78.

tion; and 20,000 rounds of pistol cartridges. On March 5 four mountain guns and the necessary ammunition were added.

For a few tense days the agreement was held up over financial matters. At first the Japanese authorities tried to secure some payment in exchange, offering the weapons at nearly half price, around two million yen. Zhevchenko countered with an offer of one million taels, which he claimed the Russian military attaché in Peking had agreed to pay. Nishihara says it was Kolchak who was expected to provide these funds.[56] At any rate, the Russian military attaché and the Russian minister in Peking, when appealed to, protested immediately that there was simply no money available.[57] Upon receipt of this news, Foreign Minister Motono, who had not been at all happy with the agreement, declared that the whole matter "should be dropped." Zhevchenko now called on Nishihara's friend Nakano Jiro, who in turn called on Nishihara, and Nishihara exerted all his influence on Terauchi, Motono, and Tanaka.[58]

"The fact is," Nishihara says he told Terauchi on February 24, "Japan agreed to assist the Siberian independence forces at the request of the Russian ambassador, with the idea that these independence forces would be used in conjunction with the Japanese troops which are presently to be sent." For Japan to quibble now over money was to behave like "a petty shopkeeper." "This is no time," he declared, "to be keeping accounts." Japan ought to "provide the weapons free of charge and even pay the war costs."

Terauchi thought Nishihara "made sense." On February 25, Motono seems also to have responded favorably to Nishihara's pressure, and on that day the war minister and the finance minister gave their official approval.[59] Thus, the Japanese War Ministry agreed to take over the expenses. Actually, according to Nishihara, he was able later to persuade the Kuhara *zaibatsu*, which had important interests in Russia and close relations with various expansionist societies, to defray these and subsequent expenses incurred

[56] Nishihara, *Yume no Shichi-jū-yo-nen*, pp. 228–29.

[57] Saitō to Tanaka, February 22, 1918, *JGK, RKI, HK,* I.

[58] Nishihara, *Yume no Shichi-jū-yo-nen*, pp. 228–29.

[59] Handwritten notation across copy of telegram, Satō to Motono, February 23, 1918, *JGK, RKI, HK,* I.

in the program to support Semenov.[60] It is interesting to note that Semenov's particular friend, with whom he made the arrangements in the Kuhara organization, was the ex-diplomat Koike Chōzō, who had been instrumental in drafting the so-called "twenty-one demands" in 1915.

Some arms remained in Harbin, but the bulk were sent through to Manchouli, where they began to arrive on March 20. In addition, to instruct Semenov's forces in the use of the weapons, the army detailed a squad of six officers and forty-three men from the seventh division, disguised in Russian uniforms, to accompany the shipments to Manchouli.[61]

The British and French seem to have arrived at a similar decision at about the same time. How much money they may have supplied is not clear, although it may have been in the vicinity of £10,000 from Britain and £5,000 from France.[62] In addition, the British seem to have agreed to send from their legation in Peking two field guns or two 5-inch mortars, with 800 rounds of ammunition. The French appear to have decided to send from their forces in Tientsin four 8-centimeter guns, with between 50,000 and 100,000 rounds of ammunition, and 100 hand grenades.[63] Several officers and men were sent by each government to accompany the shipments. Delivery was held up temporarily when the British and French protested against inspection and transportation charges on the South Man-

[60] Nishihara, *Yume no Shichi-jū-yo-nen*, p. 243.

[61] "Training the Semenov detachment in the handling of ordnance," Japan, Sambō Hombu, *Shiberia Shuppei-shi*, III, Appendix 6, 21–24.

[62] Yoshizawa to Motono, March 5, 1918, *JGK, RKI, HK*, I. Matveev asserts that in February, Britain and France gave Semenov 100,000 rubles and Japan via Kuroki gave him 2,906,428 rubles; but he cites no source. N. M. Matveev, "Bor'ba za sovety Zabaikal'e," in Vsesoiuznaia Kommunisticheskaia Partiia, Tsentral'nyi Ispolnitel'nyi Komitet, Sekretariat Glavnoi Redaktsii Istorii grazhdanskoi voiny v SSSR, *Sergei Lazo, Vospominaniia i dokumenty*, comp. G. Reikhberg, A. Romanov, and P. Krol' (Moscow: Gosizdat, 1938), p. 24.

[63] I have indicated here the range of figures which were differently reported by the British ambassador in Tokyo (memorandum from the British ambassador to the Japanese Foreign Ministry, March 8, 1918, *JGK, RKI, HK*, I), the British and French ministers in Peking (Yoshizawa to Motono, March 8, 1918, *ibid.*, I), the British and French military commanders in Tientsin (Japanese army commander in Tientsin to Uehara, March 9, 1918, *ibid.*, I), and the Russian military attaché in Peking (Saitō to Uehara, March 8, 1918, *ibid.*, I).

churian Railway, but Japan finally agreed to assume responsibility and by mid-March arms began to flow northward.

At about this time the Russian minister in Peking, Prince Kudashev, was reported to have ordered the commander of the Russian troops there to lead thirty-two Cossacks to the Trans-Baikal Territory, presumably to join the Semenov detachment.[64]

Cooperation from Horvat

This action by the Russian minister was concrete evidence of the support Semenov had won in some Russian quarters. On February 21, with Nakajima's plea that he form a government ringing in his ears, General Horvat had left Harbin for Peking,[65] ostensibly to confer on the election of a new board of directors for the Chinese Eastern Railway Company following the assumption of the presidency by the Kirin governor, Kuo Tsung-hsi. Actually, Horvat's purpose was to exchange views concerning Semenov with the Russian minister, Prince Kudashev, and with the president of the Russo-Asiatic Bank, A. Putilov.[66] Reassured that Britain and France did indeed mean to supply Semenov and to encourage the Far Eastern Committee for the Defense of the Fatherland and the Constituent Assembly, Kudashev, Putilov, and Horvat decided to try to seize control of the movement while it still appeared possible to do so. On March 1 they announced their resolve to support the "honest movement of revolt" against the Soviet power and the German and Austrian prisoners of war, which the Semenovists and the committee represented.[67] Prince Kudashev would assume the duty of coordinating this movement with the efforts of the Allies (mean-

[64] Saitō to Uehara, March 8, 1918, *ibid.,* I.
[65] Kurozawa to Tanaka, February 21, 1918, *ibid.,* I; and Japan, Sambō Hombu, *Shiberia Shuppei-shi,* III, 1066.
[66] Yoshizawa to Motono, February 28, 1918, *JGK, RKI, HK,* I.
[67] Announcement, signed by "Dm. Horvath," "Prince N. Koudacheff" and "A. Poutiloff," March 1, 1918, in Peking, transmitted in French with Japanese translation by Yoshizawa to Motono, March 7, 1918, *ibid.,* I. Yoshizawa reported that the announcement had been transmitted to all Allied ministers by the Russian minister.

ing the supply of money and munitions from Britain, France, and Japan and if possible an expeditionary force).[68] Putilov would seek the support of financial institutions, General Horvat would direct the organizations in Harbin.[69]

The Japanese army planners in Tokyo were pleased with the progress that had been made. The vice chief of the general staff, General Tanaka, wired: "Our government, I am sure, will extend its deepest sympathy to those Russians of firm resolve who are conscious of their patriotic responsibilities. As the situation develops hereafter, we shall supply them with munitions and take whatever other steps are necessary to assist them to achieve their ultimate objective." [70]

Tanaka's Siberia Planning Committee

At the same time that the Japanese army decided to give arms to Semenov through the Far Eastern Committee, it seems also to have decided that the Japanese troops which he and the committee wanted would eventually have to be sent. As has already been seen, as early as November, 1917, the army had drawn up a plan for sending one temporary detachment into the Maritime Territory and another, under the Kwantung governor general, into north Manchuria. In late January this plan had been revised to strengthen the Maritime Territory force. Now in February the army planners decided that these two forces should be supplemented by a third force, this one to penetrate the Trans-Baikal Territory in order to help the Semenovists drive out the socialist extremists and set up

[68] Horvat told a correspondent of the *Times* that 'Semenov's action "must be further aided by organizing a combined Allied force." Saitō to Uehara, February 24, 1918, *ibid.,* I. Prince Kudashev agreed heartily, as no doubt did Putilov.

[69] This apparently constituted his appointment as chairman of the Committee for the Defense of the Fatherland and the Constituent Assembly at Harbin, thus taking the leadership out of Popov's hands.

[70] Tanaka to Kurozawa and for information to Nakajima and the army chief of staff of the Kwantung government general, March 4, 1918, Japan, Sambō Hombu, *Shiberia Shuppei-shi,* III, 1052–53.

an independent government there.[71] Before such plans could be carried out, of course, the details of the various revisions would have to be coordinated and extensive preparations made. By the end of February the army felt that the time had come to make them.

From the beginning, the Japanese army's Siberian planning had been directed by the vice chief of General Staff Headquarters, Lieutenant General Tanaka Gi'ichi. Born in 1863, son of a samurai retainer of the Chōshū clan, Tanaka had graduated from the Military Academy and the Military Staff College and had served in the First Division in the Sino-Japanese War. Returning to Japan in 1902 after four years of study in Russia, he had risen rapidly in administrative and staff positions, gaining a wide reputation in the army as a Russian specialist and a military planner; in 1915 he was appointed to his post. In political circles Tanaka was known as a leading proponent of army expansion, and, among the public in general, as the founder (in 1910) of the Imperial Reserve Association and organizer and chairman of the greater Japan Young Men's Association in 1917. Later war minister in two cabinets, president of the Seiyūkai and finally premier, Tanaka was already in 1917 and 1918, at the age of fifty-four, one of Yamagata's most aggressive and most influential protégés. Now, in the wake of his agents' initial successes in Harbin, Tanaka was appointed on February 28, 1918, to the chairmanship of a joint Siberia Planning Committee, which was secretly created by the army general staff and the Ministry of War, to complete all preparations required for an expedition to Siberia.[72]

The joint committee set to work immediately. It soon agreed upon seven prerequisites: (1) a definite decision on the troops to be used and the preparation of materials needed by them; (2) a military agreement with China to secure the cooperation of its troops and its assistance in supply; (3) preparatory arrangements

---

[71] Text of an official summary of this plan is given below in English as Appendix D.

[72] Japan, Sambō Hombu, *Shiberia Shuppei-shi,* I, 35–38. This source refers to the committee simply as the "joint committee on military matters" (*gunji kyōdō i'in-kai*). I have referred to it by a title descriptive of its functions to enable the reader to identify it easily.

in Vladivostok and Harbin; (4) equipping and training the Semenov detachment under Japanese direction; (5) a change in the annual mobilization plans; (6) emergency preparations for sending troops to Vladivostok to support a preliminary naval landing; and (7) a revision in the organization and equipment of the Japanese army.[73]

The previous rough plans for the organization of temporary detachments in the Maritime Territory and north Manchuria were greatly expanded. According to the revised "Plan for Sending Troops to the Russian Far East," and its appended "Classification Table of Strength," [74] adopted by the joint committee in March, 1918, it was decided to organize two forces. The First Force would occupy Vladivostok, Nikol'sk-Ussuriisk, and Khabarovsk, and would then fan out to secure the Amur railroad and river; the Second Force would advance to Chita and secure the Trans-Baikal Territory.

Each force would be organized into two echelons, the second to be sent as a reinforcement if needed. The main strength of the first echelon of the First (or Maritime Territory) Force was to be the Twelfth Division, the main strength of the second echelon, the Fifth Division. The main strength of the first echelon of the Second (or Trans-Baikal Territory) Force was to be the Third, Fourteenth, and Seventh Divisions; its reinforcing echelon, chiefly the First and Fourth Divisions. The Chinese Eastern Railway Zone from Mu-tan-kiang in the east to Manchouli in the west was to be secured by the Fortieth Infantry Brigade and other forces under the command of the Kwantung governor general; this same headquarters would also be responsible for the Second Force's lines of communications. Thus, the plan envisaged an expeditionary force of more than seven divisions, organized under three headquarters, each to take over one sector of the Amur basin. Although it made no definite plans, the joint committee foresaw a fourth Japanese force to be sent to central Mongolia, thence, in cooperation with Chinese forces, to advance into the Trans-Baikal Territory. In any

[73] Text in English translation is given below as Appendix E.
[74] Text in English translation is given below as Appendix G.

event, after the basin was secured, the Chinese forces would be asked to cooperate.

The joint committee hoped to accomplish two fundamental objectives: first, "to maintain peace in the Far East by occupying various strategic points . . . and by assisting the Russian moderates"; and second, "to make necessary preparations of operations which may in the future develop against Russia and Germany." Thus, the Tanaka committee looked on the intervention as conceivably the first stage in a much larger operation, which it might be necessary for Japan to conduct jointly with China in order to save the Far East from an invasion by Russian and German forces.

Item five on the joint committee's agenda, the change in the annual mobilization plan, was also quickly accomplished. The plan for 1918 had been drawn up before any expeditionary force was contemplated and was now found inadequate. On March 9, Army General Staff Headquarters abrogated the mobilization plan instructions of 1918 and instituted a set of temporary instructions, more suited to the immediate purpose.[75]

Item six, the development of plans for joint preliminary operations with the navy at Vladivostok, was given immediate attention. Apparently the Versailles Hotel robbery on February 4, 1918, had convinced the navy that a marine landing might soon be needed. Shortly after this the naval leaders had begun conferring with the army authorities on a joint plan of operations in case the lives and property of Japanese nationals should be directly threatened there.[76] With the help of Tanaka's committee, an agreement was finally reached between the chiefs of the general staffs of the two armed forces that, if trouble should arise after the marines had effected a landing, the best policy would be for the army and navy jointly to occupy the city immediately. On March 6 and 7 the navy minister outlined the naval phase of the plan in his instructions to Vice Admiral Arima Ryokitsu, Third Fleet commander, and Vice Admiral Baron Yashiro Rokuro, commandant of the Sasebo Naval

[75] Japan, Sambō Hombu, *Shiberia Shuppei-shi,* IV, 1.
[76] Japan, Kaigun Gunreibu, *Taishō Yon-nen naishi Kyū-nen Kaigun Senshi* (1924), I, 146–48.

Station. The main strength of the Third Fleet was to be readied for action: the *Hizen* and the Ninth Destroyer Flotilla were ordered to stand by, outside Sasebo harbor; the *Katori, Hizen,* and Third Torpedo-boat Flotilla were to be equipped with cold-weather and mine-sweeping gear; and one marine company was to be organized for embarkation on the *Hizen.* The army would use its Seventy-fourth Regiment; to transport this from the Korean garrison at Hamhŭng, the navy agreed to loan its repair ship *Kantō.*[77]

On March 6, the very day on which these instructions were being given to the Third Fleet, the navy commander at Vladivostok reported to the navy minister that the Bolsheviks were becoming so threatening and the appeals to the Japanese consulate general so frequent that he was being forced to prepare for a landing. Navy Minister Katō, convinced of the probable necessity, replied on the following day that the commander should act on his own discretion after consulting with Consul General Kikuchi and the British and American naval commanders. Four days later Katō issued orders to the commander of the Third Fleet to embark the company of marines on the *Hizen* and "immediately upon completion of preparations lead the *Hizen, Katori* and Third Torpedo-boat Flotilla to Eiko Wan [a bay north of Wonsan (Genzan) on the east Korean coast] and await orders."

The Joint Siberia Planning Committee also took up item seven, the revision of the army's organization and equipment, and drew up a plan requiring changes in the organization of units and in communication instruments, artillery weapons, and equipment of mechanized and aerial warfare.[78] Items three and four promised to require some months to accomplish. The basic policy of aid to Semenov, item four, had already been adopted, but it would be at least two months before the weapons could arrive at Manchouli and before Japanese instructors could train the troops in their use.

Item three, the handling of preparatory agreements at Harbin and Vladivostok, had, as we have seen, been progressing well. The secret agents sent to the continent in late January and early Feb-

[77] Text of the Army's plan is given below in English translation as Appendix F.
[78] Text of "Plan for Revising Organization and Equipment" is to be found in Japan, Sambō Hombu, *Shiberia Shuppei-shi,* I, Appendix 7, 73–75.

ruary had already secured Japan's ascendancy over Semenov at Manchouli, over the Far Eastern Committee for the Defense of the Fatherland and the Constituent Assembly, over the Chinese Eastern Railway Company administration at Harbin, and over the Russo-Asiatic Bank and Russian diplomatic authorities at Peking. But much more remained to be done if the "situation" was to "develop" as the Tanaka committee desired. An anti-Bolshevik government capable of taking over power in the Amur basin would have to be set up; arrangements would have to be made with it at least for the use of facilities and for as much freedom of action as possible for Japanese troops within its area of jurisdiction. In this, Horvat, who had assumed direction of the Far Eastern Committee in Harbin, appeared to be the key figure.

Japanese Troops?

Early in March, 1918, Premier Terauchi sent Kawakami Toshihiko, a director of the South Manchurian Railway Company, to Harbin.[79] At the same time Tanaka ordered Nakajima from Vladivostok to Harbin; the latter was accompanied by Mori Mikage, chief of the industrial investigation section of the South Manchurian Railway Company. Upon their arrival, these three conferred with Consul General Satō, Lieutenant Colonel Araki, and Lieutenant Colonel Kurozawa. The five men joined in putting pressure on Horvat to organize and proclaim an autonomous government for the Amur region.

At a conference with Nakajima and Kawakami on March 15, Horvat is reported to have agreed, but then to have hesitated. He may have been sincerely concerned about the puppet role he was being asked to play. He must certainly have been concerned about the economic concessions which the Japanese negotiators were trying to extract from him. Exactly what concessions they were seeking is difficult to determine. The only direct evidence from Japanese official files is contained in a secret army report, dated April 21, 1918, which indicates Horvat's willingness at that date

[79] *Ibid.*, II, 1053–54.

to consider providing certain facilities for the use of Japanese troops in the event of an expedition and to open up various lumbering, mining and investment opportunities to private Japanese interests in the railway zone and the Amur Territory, provided adequate support from Japan was forthcoming.[80] On the other hand, United States Consul Moser reported from Harbin on April 4, 1918, that Nakajima was pressing Horvat to agree to the following: "(1) dismantling of all fortifications at Vladivostok, which would be an open port; (2) full fishing rights in all Siberia; (3) open navigation of the Amur River; (4) preferred forest and mining concessions similar to those demanded of China."[81] There were still other variants of the concessions that Japan was rumored to be seeking.[82] While none of these rumors can be wholly substantiated, no doubt the demands were greater than the promises listed by the army. They were certainly of a magnitude to convince Horvat that he could hold out for a high price: a prior guarantee of Japanese troop support.

Horvat was adamant. On March 17 he told Nakajima, Kawakami, and Satō plainly: "If he [Horvat] were guaranteed military assistance from Japan, he would immediately organize a provisional government, proclaim the autonomy of Siberia, and formally request the assistance of Japanese forces"; but first he wanted the guarantee.[83] The Japanese agents promptly conferred together and agreed to petition the government for such a guarantee.[84] Speaking for the group, Nakajima reported to Tanaka that, although Japan's policy of supplying money and arms to the anti-Bolshevik organiza-

---

[80] An unsigned, secret report on Japanese War Ministry paper, dated April 21, 1918, entitled "Horuwatto Seifu Sōshiki Enjo no Sekkyoku to narishi igo ni oite Teikoku no etaru Riken," *JGK, RKI, TT,* I, 0313–21.

[81] Moser to U.S. secretary of state, April 4, 1918, *USFR, 1918, Russia,* II, 98.

[82] Spargo confirms (1), (2), and (4) of Moser's list and adds three additional items: "(1) Japan to carry out intervention in Siberia alone; (2) Japan to receive the northern part of Sakhalin; (3) Japan to be given preferential commercial rights in eastern Siberia." John Spargo, *Russia as an American Problem* (New York: Harpers, 1920), p. 240. Mints states that on April 27, 1918, similar concessions were demanded as conditions for sending Japanese troops to Irkutsk, but cites no source. USSR, *Iaponskaia Interventsiia,* p. 206.

[83] Satō to Motono, March 17, 1918, *JGK, RKI, HK,* I.

[84] Japan, Sambō Hombu, *Shiberia Shuppei-shi,* III, 1054–55.

tions was encouraging them to rely on Japan, the timid "white Russian" leaders had neither the vision nor the energy to combat the rapid extension of Bolshevik power and the increasing activity of the German and Austrian prisoners of war. If a barrier against the Bolsheviks was to be built, Japanese troops would have to build it. He urged that a force of from 5,000 to 10,000 troops be sent immediately, one element to take Chita, the other element to take Vladivostok. Presumably, Satō wired a similar recommendation to Motono, and Kawakami to Terauchi.

A Barrier of Hopes

By mid-March, 1918, the Soviet tide had inundated most of the Siberian side of the Amur basin. The last feeble moderate socialist claimant to all-Siberian power, the provisional duma at Tomsk, had easily been dispersed by Red Guards on February 8.[85] The last territorial capital to fall was Blagoveshchensk, where the municipal duma had capitulated to the Bolshevik-controlled soviet on March 5, and irregular Russian, Cossack, Japanese, and Chinese volunteer troops had been overcome by Red Guards in a week's fighting, ending on March 13.[86]

Under the pattern gradually emerging in the winter and spring of 1918, local government was being administered by soviets or councils of deputies of workers, peasants, Cossacks, and soldiers.[87] These in turn, or as many as were able, participated in territorial or provincial conferences or congresses of soviets, called every few months at the capital cities to adopt policy and to select territorial or provincial executive committees, which in turn usually appointed councils of people's commissars to administer their areas. All of these, except the Far Eastern regional organization, probably rec-

[85] Maksakov and Turunov, *Khronika*, p. 56.
[86] "Oktiabr' v Sibiri, I: Blagoveshchensk," *Proletarskaia Revoliutsiia*, No. 10 (October, 1922), p. 362; Japan, Sambō Hombu, *Shiberia Shuppei-shi*, I, Appendix, pp. 1–6.
[87] For a more complete analysis of soviet political institutions in eastern Siberia during this period, see the author's "The Russian Revolution in the Amur Basin," soon to appear in *The American Slavic and East European Review*.

ognized the authority of the Central Executive Committee of Siberia (commonly referred to as Tsentrosibir'), which was elected by all-Siberian soviet congresses meeting at Irkutsk, and the Council of People's Commissars (called the Sovnarkom). These organs accepted the superiority of the central soviet authorities in Moscow. A Red Guard and a Red Army were ordered organized. The whole apparatus was given effective direction by the Bolshevik party and its left-wing Social Revolutionary supporters.

To roll back this Communist tide, the Japanese army had, by the middle of March, 1918, only a barrier of hopes, built out of the wreckage of Cossack armies, officers, and men who had been washed into the sanctuary of Manchuria. At the far western end of the Chinese Eastern Railway Zone was the erratic Semenov, who, by March 5, had been pushed back to the Chinese border by the Red Army and was being held in check at Hailar by the Chinese. Gathered at Harbin were the corps being organized by Colonel Nikitin, the remnants of the Amur Cossacks who had fled from Blagoveshchensk, and the nebulous political organization of the Far Eastern Committee and Horvat. At the far eastern end of the zone was the refugee Kalmykov, with a handful of his Ussuri Cossack followers. The Russian officials in Peking were giving doubtful support. Kolchak was holding aloof. The Japanese government faced serious questions. Should it land marines at Vladivostok? Should it aid Kalmykov? Should it promise Horvat troops?

These questions were complicated immensely by the attitudes taken by the other powers. The British and the French were backing Semenov; the British were also backing Kalmykov; the Americans seemed indifferent to all the Russian pretenders; while the Chinese were actively hostile toward them. This lack of agreement carried over also in the attitude of the powers toward the idea of a Japanese expedition. It is to the attempts of the Japanese government to reconcile these differences that we must now turn.

VI. INTERNATIONAL COMPLICATIONS

In their preparations for action on the continent, the Japanese army planners had so far found the British and French generally cooperative but were having trouble with the Chinese and the Americans. The Chinese were threatening to drive all foreigners, especially the Russians and Japanese, out of the Manchurian sanctuary. The Americans were believed to be acquiring special economic concessions in Siberia. Most alarming of all, the Americans were apparently preparing to take over the very railways regarded by the Japanese army as vital to the success of its future operations.

The Chinese Threat in Manchuria

From the end of December, 1917, the Chinese had been moving troops into northern Manchuria.[1] In March, 1918, they sent a mixed detachment of 4,000 men from Kirin and Heilungkiang provinces to Manchouli,[2] and other units followed in the ensuing months. In addition, special reinforcements were later dispatched to Outer Mongolia and Sinkiang, in particular, to Maimaichen, Urga, Uliassutai, Khobdo, and Kiakhta.[3]

China's effort to reassert its authority in the railway zone inevitably entailed conflicts with anti-Bolshevik Russians, such as Horvat and Semenov, who wanted to use the zone as a base of operations against soviet rule in Siberia. The Chinese feared these

[1] Saitō (in Peking) to Uehara, February 9, 1918, *JGK, RKI, HK,* I.
[2] Saitō to Uehara, March 12, 1918, reporting information told to him by the vice chief of the Chinese general staff, *ibid.,* I.
[3] Japan, Sambō Hombu, *Taishō Shichi-nen naishi Jūichi-nen Shiberia Shuppei-shi* (Tokyo, 1924), I, 85.

activities, not only because the forces that were being built up threatened China's control in the zone, but also because they might provoke an invasion of Manchurian territory by soviet forces based in Siberia. Accordingly, the Chinese tried to check the growth of anti-soviet detachments. They forbade Chinese to enlist in them and refused to permit any Chinese so enlisted to be transported to the front. They tried to seal the border by cutting off the transit of goods at the customs stations at Pogranichnaia and Manchouli. And in March, following Semenov's abortive offensive against Chita, they went so far as temporarily to intern him.

In late February and early March, as Semenov's detachment pulled back to the safety of Chinese territory, the Chinese were afraid that soviet forces would attempt to pursue him and would thereby extend the civil war to Manchuria. In order, if possible, to prevent this, the Chinese commander at Manchouli, Major General Lin Fu-man, reportedly sent a representative to Sergei Lazo, the soviet commander at Dauriia, on March 5 for a preliminary conference.[4] Lazo demanded that Semenov disarm and withdraw beyond Chalainoerh, the next Manchurian stop beyond Manchouli. The Chinese delegate apparently refused to commit himself, but three days later the Chinese commander announced that he would enforce an armistice for seven days, during which time neither soviet nor Semenovist forces would be permitted to cross the border, and he invited the soviet commander to discuss the situation with him further in Manchouli.[5]

On the same day Lazo moved his troops into Matsievskaia Station and the Chinese took up defensive positions at Railroad Siding 86. A seven-man soviet delegation, led by Lazo, conferred with Lin and his staff for three days. Lazo reports that he requested the Chinese to "have Semenov disarmed and expelled from Man-

<hr/>

[4] Kurozawa to Tanaka, March 12, 1918, transmitting a report from Manchouli, sent on March 7, *JGK, RKI, HK*, I.

[5] Vice Consul Sugino Hokotaro (at Irkutsk) to Motono, April 16, 1918, transmitting a translation of a report from commander of the Soviet forces in Dauriia to headquarters of the Irkutsk Soviet, dated March 10, and printed on March 16 in the official organ of the Irkutsk Soviet. The report does not include mention of any agreements reached. The Chinese commander's name is given as Major General Lin Fu-man. *JGK, RKI, HK*, II.

churia." [6] The Chinese seem to have agreed only to refer the matter to the central authorities; on the other hand, they "stated at length that they could not permit and they would not permit the interests of Chinese citizens to suffer, nor would they permit the fighting to spread over the border." To make sure of this, the soviet account claims, the Chinese agreed "to prevent the Semenov forces from advancing into Russia until April 5." [7] However, according to Premier Tuan the Chinese agreed only that if Semenov did advance into Siberia during that time and then, "meeting adversity," tried to seek refuge in Chinese territory, "China would have to have him disarmed." [8] The soviet forces, for their part, agreed to withdraw to Dauriia by March 23.[9] The Chinese then brought up another grievance: they accused the soviet authorities of interfering in the Trans-Baikal Territory with trains bound for Manchouli. In response the soviet delegates charged that the Semenovists were so destructive that unless China could guarantee the safety of Russian passengers, they could not permit regular traffic to be resumed.[10] After some discussion, both sides seem to have agreed to reopen the railroad and telegraph lines to regular traffic on April 17 and to try to prevent any interference with them.[11] The conference ended with the Chinese protesting against the arming of prisoners of war. Lazo replied that there need be no anxiety on this point. "I declare officially," he said, "that there is not a single prisoner of war in our forces"; but, having in mind no doubt the detachment serving at that moment in his own front lines, he refused permission to the Chinese to see for themselves.

[6] Bulletin from Commander Sergei Lazo at the front, dated March 11, 1918, quoted in Vse-soiuznaia Kommunisticheskaia Partiia, Tsentral'nyi Ispolnitel'nyi Komitet, Sekretariat Glavnoi Redaktsii Istorii Grazhdanskoi Voiny v SSSR, Sergei Lazo, Vospominaniia i Dokumenty, comp. G. Reikhberg, A. Romanov, and P. Krol' (Moscow: Gosizdat, 1938), pp. 80–81.

[7] Sugino via Satō to Motono, April 14, 1918, relaying a report of the chairman of the Irkutsk Soviet, Yanson. JGK, RKI, HK, II.

[8] Saitō to Uehara, March 28, 1918, reporting the substance of a conversation between Premier Tuan and Prince Kudashev as told him by Liu Ch'ung-chieh, ibid., I.

[9] Saitō to Uehara, March 26, 1918, summarizing a report sent on March 16 from the apparatus in Manchouli, ibid., I.

[10] Sugino to Motono, April 16, 1918, ibid., I.

[11] Sugino to Motono, April 14, 1918, ibid., I.

These acts of the Chinese in Manchuria were, of course, directed in the first instance against the Russians. It was the Russians who had exercised authority in the railway zone and it was the Russians whose troops they sought to replace and from whom they sought to take over control of the railroad. At the same time the Chinese were not unaware that the Japanese were eager to do exactly the same thing. In fact, according to the Chinese representative at the Manchouli conference on March 9, China's extreme awareness of that fact was the prime motive for instituting the powerful border patrol and railway guard in northern Manchuria.[12] Had China not done so, he said, "Japanese forces would occupy it." "Japan," he went on to say, "is extremely desirous of occupying the railroad, but China has not permitted it." Of course, he continued, if the disorder increased or if the fighting should spread into the zone, Japan might use it as an excuse to intervene anyway, and for that reason he was most anxious to reach some understanding with the soviet forces. The principle followed by China was that "it wanted no foreign intervention in Manchuria," which, when applied to Japan, meant "the principle of keeping Japan at a distance." [13]

The Army's Negotiations with China

To overcome this Chinese threat in Manchuria, the Japanese military planners adopted two policies: to press the negotiations, begun in November, 1917, for a Sino-Japanese military agreement; and to bring the cooperative Tuan Ch'i-jui back into power in Peking.

The negotiations with China had been proceeding slowly. Following the initial discussions in Tokyo on November 14 to 16, 1917, Japan's military representatives in Peking had been exerting pressure on leading Chinese officials. By the end of January, 1918,

[12] Sugino (at Irkutsk) to Motono, April 16, 1918, *ibid.,* I. It is not clear whether this attitude of the Chinese negotiators represented the views of the central government—in which case it shows that Tuan was not merely a puppet in Japan's hands—or whether it represented the views of local warlords in Manchuria and therefore illustrates Tuan's lack of control over them. Probably the latter explanation is closer to the truth.

[13] Kurozawa to Tanaka, March 12, 1918, *ibid.,* I.

the only concrete accomplishment had been an agreement reached between Major General Saitō, the Japanese military attaché in Peking, and the Chinese minister of war, Tuan Chih-kuei, providing for the establishment of a Sino-Japanese intelligence organization along the borders of Mongolia and Sinkiang, and for the exchange of intelligence about the eastward extension of German and Austrian influence.[14]

Dissatisfied that little progress was being made, General Uehara, chief of the Japanese army general staff, talked the problem over with Premier Terauchi on the morning of February 5.[15] Terauchi agreed that perhaps more talks between Vice Chief Tanaka and Chinese representatives in Tokyo would be useful. That afternoon Tanaka called on Minister Chang Tsung-hsiang, who, it will be remembered, was helpful in arranging the so-called "Nishihara loans."

Tanaka outlined the Japanese general staff's view that Germany was "making use of Russia" and might soon release "more than 100,000 German prisoners of war in Siberia" against the Far East.[16] In addition, he pointed to the rumors that Germany was instigating the "Mohammedans in Kansu and Chinese Turkestan to start an uprising." In the face of such an imminent German threat China and Japan would soon have to take common action. Minister Chang seems to have agreed with Tanaka's conclusion and so reported to his government, but his report found little sympathy in Peking. In November, 1917, the Anfu clique had been maneuvered out of power by an opposing war-lord coalition, and the new coalition was inclined to see Japan's proposals as a renewal of the aggressive

[14] Japan, Sambō Hombu, *Shiberia Shuppei-shi,* I, Appendix 5, p. 51.

[15] *Ibid.,* p. 50; and Araki Sadao, *Gensui Uehara Yūsaku Den* (Tokyo: Gensui Uehara Yūsaku Denki Hankō-kai, 1937), II, 143, extract from Uehara's diary, dated February 5, 1918.

[16] Chang to the Chinese Ministry of Foreign affairs, February 5, 1918, in Chinese Republic, Ministry of Foreign Affairs, *Diplomatic Documents* (hereinafter, *CRMFADD*), *Sino-Japanese Military Agreement* (Peking, 1921), pp. 1–2, Document 1 (English text). It appears that this and other documents in this publication were also published in Chinese by the Chinese ministry under the title, "Hung Pi Shu" (Red Paper), from which source they are cited by Wang Yun-sheng, *Liu Shih Nien Lai Chung Kuo Yu Jih Pen* (1932–34), VII, 126–237.

policy which had led to the "twenty-one demands." When Foreign Minister Lu Cheng-hsiang recounted the Chang-Tanaka conversations at the Chinese cabinet meeting on February 14, deep suspicion was voiced. The German threat had already been cited by Japan as an excuse for introducing its troops into Shantung. Was not the proposed military alliance merely a way to enable the Japanese army to seize northern Manchuria? After a bitter argument, the Chinese cabinet resolved on February 21 to make a strong reply: if Japan wanted China's military cooperation outside China's borders, namely, in Siberia, China was prepared to negotiate; but, it would have to insist that within China's borders, namely, in northern Manchuria, only Chinese troops could operate.

This stand would require the Japanese army to abandon its plans for building up a Russian administration and army in the railway zone and for basing its own expedition there. The Chinese counterproposal was clearly inacceptable. Something would have to be done, either by threats or persuasion, to bring about a change of view or to replace the Chinese government with one more amenable to Japan's desires. It was decided to try both lines of action.

From the point of view of the Japanese planners the most desirable policy was to bring their friend Tuan Ch'i-jui back into power in Peking as quickly as possible. His organization, the Anfu clique, agreed; on February 25, 1918, as the first step in his come-back, the clique persuaded President Feng to appoint Tuan commissioner of the War Participation Board.[17] At the same time, Nishihara's old friends, Lu Tsung-yu and Tsao Ju-lin, wired Minister Chang in Tokyo, requesting him to urge Nishihara to come to Peking immediately. Through Nishihara's agency, Japanese banks had already extended several large loans.[18] On January 6, 1918, for example, the second Kirin-Changchun railway-loan agreement was signed; on February 12, the Ssu-Cheng railway-loan agreement was

[17] Nishihara Kamezō, Yume no Shichi-jū-yo-nen, Nishihara Kamezō Jiden (Kumobara Mura, 1949), pp. 232–40.
[18] For useful discussions of these loans see Wang Yun-sheng, Liu Shih Nien Lai, VII, 126–237; Shōda Kazue, Kiku Bun Ne (privately published, 1918; Chinese translation, Kung Te-po, Hsi-yuan Chieh-Ruan Chen-hsiang, Shanghai: T'ai-p'ing Yang Shu-tien, 1929); and Nishihara, Yume no Shichi-jū-yo-nen.

signed; on February 21, 1918, a wireless-station loan was negotiated; others had been signed previously; and still others were being currently discussed. It seems likely, therefore, that the Anfu clique hoped that Nishihara might provide funds or at least promise loans that would help Tuan secure the premiership again. Nishihara was eager to go; and Terauchi and Shōda were eager to have him go.[19] Motono, on the other hand, strove to prevent the trip.

It was not that Motono objected to the Sino-Japanese coalition policy. Indeed, he was inclined to be even more threatening and uncompromising toward China than was the army. When Chang called on him on February 23 to explain the Chinese cabinet's position, Motono lectured him on the need to conclude a military agreement exactly as the Japanese army conceived it.[20] On the other hand, Motono was deeply chagrined to have Japan's policy toward China formulated and conducted by groups outside his own ministry. He particularly objected to Nishihara and for two weeks fought successfully to keep him home.

With or without Motono's obstructionism, bringing Tuan back into power in Peking might take considerable time; and the Japanese army's Joint Siberia Planning Committee, formed about this time, was not content to wait idly. The committee was apparently agreed that the conclusion of a Sino-Japanese military alliance was an immediate necessity; so much so, that an effort ought to be made to win the present Chinese government over by offering concessions. Accordingly, when Minister Chang called on Tanaka in Tokyo on February 26, he found Tanaka in a conciliatory mood.[21] Tanaka could not accept the Chinese government's position, he said; but he would be glad to relieve the Chinese of certain groundless fears. If they were worried about having Japanese troops operating freely on Chinese soil, then he would be pleased to insert an article in the agreement saying that, when joint operations no

[19] Nishihara, *Yume no Shichi-jū-yo-nen,* pp. 232–40.

[20] Chang to Chinese Ministry of Foreign Affairs, February 23, 1918, *CRM-FADD, Sino-Japanese Military Agreement,* Document 4, pp. 5–6.

[21] Chang to Chinese Ministry of Foreign Affairs, February 26, 1918, *CRMFADD, Sino-Japanese Military Agreement,* Document 6; and Japan, Sambō Hombu, *Shiberia Shuppei-shi,* I, Appendix 5, 51–52.

longer required their presence, Japanese troops would be immediately withdrawn from China. Chang appeared satisfied; thereupon Tanaka suggested that the two governments should proceed immediately to negotiate the agreement, offering China the freedom to select either of two procedures: to conclude a general agreement on the basis of which the military authorities could conclude a technical agreement, or, preferably, to have the military authorities conclude an agreement first and then to have the two governments sanction it.

The Chinese government's fears seem to have been allayed, for the cabinet, meeting on February 28, agreed to give up its original position and accept Tanaka's compromise. In so doing, it hoped to persuade Japan to make concessions on two other points, "the Shantung question and the pending cases in Manchuria," which Minister Chang was instructed to take up.[22] Possibly in the hope of avoiding any general military commitments, the Chinese government chose the second alternative, that is, to have an agreement first worked out by the military authorities.

On March 2, Chang was instructed to ask the Japanese government to send a military commission to Peking to open negotiations.[23] Chang immediately conveyed these decisions to Tanaka and Motono while Chin Yun-p'eng explained them to Major General Saitō in Peking. The project was then submitted to the Japanese cabinet for the first time on March 8, and agreement was won. Thus, thanks largely to Japan's overwhelming military superiority and to Tanaka's conciliatory behavior, a preliminary understanding was quickly reached.

Up to this time, the army had kept the negotiations with China largely in its own hands. Now Motono saw an opportunity to step in. Details of the discussions at the March 8 meeting of the Japanese cabinet are unavailable; but it appears that, while he approved the general project, Motono was anxious as always to recover

[22] Chinese Ministry of Foreign Affairs to Minister Chang, March 2, 1918, CRMFADD, Sino-Japanese Military Agreement, Document 8, pp. 12–14.

[23] Chinese Ministry of Foreign Affairs and cabinet to Minister Chang, March 2, 1918, ibid., Document 7, pp. 11–12 (English text); and Japan, Sambō Hombu, Shiberia Shuppei-shi, I, Appendix 5, 51–52.

what influence he could in the diplomacy with China. It is reasonable to assume that he was the one who insisted that actual discussions could hardly be held unless some diplomatic documents were exchanged beforehand. The cabinet agreed and Motono promptly assumed charge of the situation.

Motono called in Minister Chang and offered the Chinese government the choice of putting their general understanding in the form of an exchange of notes or of a diplomatic agreement like the various Russo-Japanese agreements. Whether embodied in a note or an agreement, the substance might well follow the lines of the March 2 note from the Chinese Ministry of Foreign Affairs and cabinet to Minister Chang, perhaps in the following language:

The situation having become increasingly threatened by Germany's political and military activity in Russia, an activity which has recently begun to damage the common objectives of the various allied countries, the Japanese government and the Chinese government together agree to the following:

1) Recognizing that the general peace and security are disturbed by the penetration of German power, the government of Japan and the government of China will consider in common the measures to be taken.

2) The methods and conditions agreed to by the army and navy of each country for giving effect to the measures which the government of Japan and the government of China may mutually agree upon shall be confirmed by the competent authorities of each country and these competent authorities will consult with each other fully and freely, concerning questions of mutual interest.[24]

While this draft purported to be based on the official Chinese instructions of March 2, it differed from them in two significant points: it made no mention of the withdrawal of Japanese troops when the German threat had ended and it opened the way in paragraph two for the political representatives of the two countries to discuss broader problems than the immediate issue of military action. This latter seems to have been provided in response to the

[24] Chang to Chinese Ministry of Foreign Affairs, March 8, 1918, *CRMFADD, Sino-Japanese Military Agreement*, Document 10, pp. 15–17; possibly more authentic text of the suggested note or agreement in Motono to Chang, March 8, 1918, Japan, Sambō Hombu, *Shiberia Shuppei-shi*, Appendix 5, pp. 52–54, from which the above has been translated.

Chinese government's suggestion that the Shantung and various Manchurian problems might also be considered.

The Chinese government replied that if a preliminary diplomatic exchange were necessary, it should take the form of notes, preferably in English or French, the proposal to come from the Japanese government and the reply to come from the Chinese government. In accord with Tanaka's promise, mention of a definite "period of validity" should be included in the preliminary draft in order to allay suspicions within China and abroad.[25] Minister Chang immediately conferred with Foreign Minister Motono. Again, as though to prove he could be tougher than the army, Motono refused any concessions: if the note form were followed, the correspondence must be initiated in China, not Japan; it must be drawn up in Chinese rather than in a European language; and no "period of validity" should be mentioned, since obviously the agreement would be valid only while the circumstances mentioned were in effect and any other suspicion did not accord with the underlying idea of "permanent friendship." [26]

By March 11 even Motono was forced to admit that the negotiations were not going well. Reluctantly, he conceded that it might be useful to have Nishihara return to Peking.[27] Nishihara left Tokyo immediately, whereupon Motono made a final desperate bid to retain control of the negotiations. Late in the evening of March 15 he made an unusual call on Minister Chang to speed action, warning him that "if any difficulty were to arise, it would only offend the friendly sentiment of Japan." [28] He warned him, too, of the impropriety of showing any documents to other powers. Chang was apparently frightened, for he immediately wired his government that there were some persons in Japan who were "in favor of Japan herself executing the right of self-protection" and

[25] Chinese Ministry of Foreign Affairs to Minister Chang, March 11, 1918, CRMFADD, Sino-Japanese Military Agreement, Document 11, pp. 18–19.
[26] Chang to Chinese Ministry of Foreign Affairs, March 12, 1918, ibid., Document 13, p. 21; and Chang to Chinese Ministry of Foreign Affairs, March 13, 1918, ibid., Document 16, pp. 24–25.
[27] Nishihara, Yume no Shichi-jū-yo-nen, pp. 232–40.
[28] Chang to Chinese Ministry of Foreign Affairs, March 16, 1918, CRMFADD, Sino-Japanese Military Agreement, Document 20, pp. 29–30.

who held that "in the dispatching of troops there is no need for Japan to cooperate with China." Chang pointed out that "if this should actually come to pass, the Russo-Japanese and German-Japanese war will again be staged at once in our territory. Then it will be impossible to repulse them and too late to join with Japan. It would be much better to plan for cooperation in the first place."

On March 18, three days after Motono had delivered his menacing lecture to Minister Chang in Tokyo, Nishihara arrived in Peking, calling immediately on Lu, Tsao, and Japanese Minister Hayashi.[29] On March 20 he talked with Tuan, urging him to resume the premiership and offering to provide the necessary money; he also urged that Liang be replaced by Tsao as minister of finance since Liang had not proved too sympathetic to economic cooperation with Japan. On March 23, Tuan accepted the premiership and appointed Tsao as requested. Before returning to Tokyo in mid-April, Nishihara negotiated a telegraph loan for 20,000,000 yen and with Finance Minister Tsao worked out a basic memorandum on ways of developing a Sino-Japanese economic partnership.

Neither in Nishihara's autobiography nor in other available records is there reference to any actions he may have taken at this time specifically on behalf of the proposed military agreement. On the other hand, during the early days of Nishihara's visit, the Chinese government capitulated on most points in dispute;[30] and on March 25, two days after Tuan became premier, official notes were exchanged between the two governments. It is true that in the end the Chinese were given certain concessions: a slight revision in wording of the original note and Motono's agreement to express Japan's intention to withdraw its troops when hostilities were over. On the other hand, it seems reasonable to suppose that these concessions were far less influential in bringing about agreement than was the pressure of Motono's threats; and, no doubt,

[29] Nishihara, *Yume no Shichi-jū-yo-nen*, pp. 232–40.

[30] Chinese Ministry of Foreign Affairs to Chang, March 17, 1918, *CRMFADD, Sino-Japanese Military Agreement*, Document 21, pp. 31–34; and Chang to Chinese Ministry of Foreign Affairs, March 19, 21, 23, 1918, *ibid.*, Documents 23–25, pp. 36–39.

the promises held out by Nishihara were far more convincing than Motono's threats.

The text of Chang's note to Motono on March 25 is as follows:

1. Having regard to the steady penetration of hostile influence into Russian territory, threatening the general peace and security of the Far East, the government of China and the government of Japan shall promptly consider in common the measures to be taken in order to meet the exigencies of the situation, and to do their share in the allied cause for the prosecution of the present war.

2. The methods and conditions of such cooperation between the Chinese and Japanese armed forces in the joint defensive movements against the enemy, for giving effect to the decision which may be arrived at by the two governments in common accord under the preceding clause, shall be arranged by the competent authorities of the two powers, who will from time to time consult each other fully and freely upon all questions of mutual interest. It is understood that the matters thus arranged by the competent authorities shall be confirmed by the two governments, and shall be put into operation at such time as may be deemed opportune.[31]

Motono replied with a brief note of agreement and in addition sent a second note, containing the desired assurance as follows:

On March 25 notes were exchanged between our two governments for the purpose of our joint defense. The imperial government would like to have the appropriate military authorities of both countries enter into discussions as indicated in the above notes. Once again the imperial government wishes to declare especially that the Japanese forces which are in China for the purpose of common defense, will, when the war is over, be entirely withdrawn from China.

Minister Chang replied with a brief note of gratitude for the declaration and expressed his agreement with the desire for a military conference.

---

[31] Text in Chinese in Chinese Ministry of Foreign Affairs, *Chung-Jih T'iao-yueh Hui-tsuan,* pp. 469–71; in English as released by the Japanese Ministry of Foreign Affairs, May 30, 1918, in J. V. A. MacMurray, *Treaties and Agreements with and concerning China, 1894–1919* (New York: Oxford, 1921), II, 1407–10; and in Japanese as gazetted on May 31, 1918, in Japan, Gaimushō, *Taishō Shichi Nen Hen-roku Jōyaku Isan* (Tokyo: compiler, 1918), pp. 413–17. The above is quoted from the English text in MacMurray.

The American Threat

While Motono's belligerent intervention in the negotiations can be explained in part by his chagrin at discovering that the prime minister, the army, and private cliques like Nishihara's had taken Chinese policy largely out of the hands of the foreign minister, it can only be understood fully in the context of the broader negotiations which Motono had initiated with the Western Allies.

The foreign minister was competing with the governing Chōshū clique for the control not only of Japan's Chinese policy, but of its Russian policy. With respect to Russia, Motono was as convinced as the army, Nishihara, and the others that a Japanese expedition to Siberia was needed, and he was no more prepared than they to wait idly for the Advisory Council on Foreign Relations to make up its mind. The diplomatic problem, as Motono saw it, was to persuade Britain, France, and the United States to invite the Japanese to undertake an independent expedition to the Amur basin. Such a joint request, he seems to have felt, the council would be unable to refuse, for there was general agreement in the Terauchi government that everything possible should be done to strengthen Japan's ties with the Western powers.

Agreement with the Western powers was felt to be important for Japan's postwar position in China proper. It was also essential for any military or political policy that Japan might pursue in Manchuria or in eastern Siberia. The British navy was in Vladivostok and British military and diplomatic agents were actively intervening on the side of certain anti-soviet elements in the Russian civil war. As long-time Russian allies and heavy investors in the Russo-Asiatic Bank, the French were likewise deeply interested in the course of the events. Fortunately for Japan, in this instance the primary interests of these two powers were not necessarily competitive with Japan's. They were interested in the Amur basin primarily as an avenue of approach to western Siberia and southern Russia. The Japanese were interested in it primarily for its own value. Moreover, the British and the French were both so hard pressed in the west that neither was in a position to take effective military action in the east.

The problem in Japan's relations with America was that, like Japan, the United States was interested in the Amur basin primarily for its own sake and also like Japan was able to fight in Asia if it chose. While the Americans had no territorial ambitions there, they were becoming increasingly interested in the economic possibilities of the region and were openly preparing to send American equipment and advisers to the railways. They were also being pressed by the Chinese to support China's effort to recover control of the Chinese Eastern Railway Zone.

The concern felt by Japan's military and diplomatic authorities over America's attitude toward the Amur basin is clearly seen in the extraordinary care taken by Japan's intelligence services from the summer of 1917 to collect and evaluate all rumors and reports from whatever source relating to America's activities in northeast Asia. The special diplomatic mission headed by Elihu Root, sent to Russia in June and July, 1917, to confer with the provisional government about assistance in prosecuting the war against Germany, gave rise to a series of disturbing rumors. In a confidential intelligence report dated October 10, 1917, the Japanese army general staff reported that, to the best of its knowledge, the provisional Russian government had agreed to open vast areas to American investment; in the Far East these were believed to include the oil fields on Sakhalin, and a number of gold mines, coal fields, railroads, and port facilities.[32] The American government was also thought to be negotiating for the purchase of Kamchatka Bay; it was rumored that American capitalists were planning to acquire rights for a New York to Petrograd railroad via Alaska and Siberia.

Japan's fears concerning the Russian railways were particularly sharpened by reports about the American Advisory Commission of Railway Experts sent to Russia in June, 1917, under the chairmanship of John F. Stevens to advise the provisional government on how to improve its rail facilities; and then by the activities of the

---

[32] Japan, Sambō Hombu, "Rokoku ni taisuru Beikoku no Kito," a confidential report, dated October 10, 1917, in JGK, RKI, SB, pp. 009–22.

Russian Railway Service Corps, a group of 288 American railroadmen under the direction of Colonel Emerson, who arrived in Vladivostok in November, 1917, to carry out the commission's wishes. Finding Vladivostok too disturbed to allow work to begin, the corps had retired temporarily to Nagasaki; but at the end of February, 1918, one hundred of its members moved to Harbin.

The Japanese government was officially informed of the purposes of these missions, but the information was not reassuring. In a letter dated March 5, 1918, for example, Stevens told Foreign Minister Motono that the Russian provisional government had agreed with the commission that the Russian railways could best be improved by revising certain of their procedures and some of their equipment to conform to American practice, that it would be helpful if the American government would extend credit to the provisional government to purchase American rolling stock and other needed equipment, and that the conversion could best be made under American instructors.[33] America's sole purpose, said Mr. Stevens, was "to aid, by advice, the Russian government and people in order that the war against the central powers may be conducted to a victorious close in favor of the allies."

Such an altruistic purpose was hard for the Japanese to believe. In the opinion of the army general staff, the Americans might well be seeking "the eventual control of all continental transportation." [34] A Japanese Foreign Ministry report, prepared shortly after the army report, warned that although the United States denied them, there were persistent rumors that the Americans had been offered control of all the railroads in the Amur basin, plus extensive Siberian mining concessions, and navigation rights on the Amur river in return for financial aid to the provisional government.[35] Other rumors were that America planned to flood the Russian railways with American equipment and was negotiating to buy not only Kamchatka bay, but all of the Kamchatka peninsula.

[33] Letter from John F. Stevens to Foreign Minister Motono, dated March 5, 1918, in *JGK, RKI, SB*, pp. 301–4.
[34] Japan, Sambō Hombu, "Rokoku ni taisuru Beikoku no Kito."
[35] Japan, Gaimushō, " 'Rūto' Kenro Shisetsu Ikkō no Hōro Ippan Moyō oyobi Sono Kekka," a confidential report, undated, in *JGK, RKI, SB*, pp. 530–44.

Whatever America's motives might be, obviously the Japanese could not launch an expedition into the Amur basin without coming to some understanding with Washington. Foreign Minister Motono set out to secure it, together with an understanding with Britain and France.

Motono's Suggestion for an Expedition

On February 5, 1918, Motono invited Ambassador Morris in Tokyo to discuss the Russian question with him.[36] After listening politely to Morris's explanation of America's "hands-off" policy, Motono cautiously outlined his own views. He began by saying that he did not want to enter into any "decisive discussions" but merely to "exchange views without reservation." "For my part," he said, "I think the Allies must reach a joint decision if we are to take any action to check the power of Germany from expanding through Siberia to Asia." He then unfolded a map of eastern Siberia and traced the eastward penetration of the Bolsheviks. The way to combat them was for the Allies to give considerable assistance to the "constructive elements" within Russia, meaning the anti-Bolsheviks who favored continuation of the war against Germany. When Ambassador Morris asked what sort of assistance this would be, the foreign minister replied: "I do not have a fixed plan, but if the railroad were to be controlled up to the intersection of the Siberian and the Amur railroads, I believe it would effectively prevent the spread of German power in the Far East."

The proposal is not entirely clear. Technically speaking, the Amur and the Siberian railway do not intersect, the Siberian being an inclusive name for the five separately administered national railways and their branches extending from western Siberia to Vladivostok, and the Amur being one of these five lines. Motono was probably recommending control up to the point where the Amur meets the Trans-Baikal Railway at the station of Kuenga; in other

[36] "Summary of conversation," JGK, RKI, SK, HMSK, pp. 279–82; also in Japan, Gaimushō, Shiberia Shuppei Mondai: Dai Ippen: Shiberia Shuppei ni itaru Kōshō Keika (November, 1922), pp. 7–8, and Morris's memorandum to secretary of state, February 5, 1918, in USFR, 1918, Russia, II, 42–3.

words, he was urging that the railways be controlled in both the Maritime and the Amur territories. If this interpretation is correct, it would seem that Motono was acting quite independently of the military leaders. In fact, the Army General Staff Headquarters had not yet considered sending troops beyond the Maritime Territory and in a few weeks was to consider a second and larger expedition not to the Amur, but to the Trans-Baikal Territory. It may be, of course, that Motono was referring to the eastern end of the Amur line where it joins the Ussuri railroad at Khabarovsk, in which case the area of proposed control would coincide roughly with that proposed in the general staff's secret plans of December and January; but, there is no evidence that Motono was exchanging views at that time with the military, so that this interpretation seems less likely to be correct. After the interview with Morris, Motono outlined the substance of his proposal to the Japanese ambassadors in Great Britain and France and instructed them to open similar negotiations with these governments.

Probably Motono's plan was kept vague on purpose. He did not want American and Allied approval of a Japanese proposal. He had no authority to make such a proposal. Rather, he hoped to induce discussions among the powers about the problem of the Russian Far East, in the course of which the United States and the Western Allies might be maneuvered into requesting the kind of Japanese action that Motono wanted to take. Such a request, he seems to have felt, the Advisory Council on Foreign Relations in Tokyo could not reject.

Anglo-French Policy

Motono's appeal to America was strongly supported in parallel action by Britain and France. As we have seen, by late December, 1917, the British were convinced that America could not be persuaded to intervene in Siberia, either alone or jointly with other powers and that the only way Japan could be persuaded to act was to give it a "free hand." The British were also by then convinced, as were the Japanese diplomatic and military planners, that friendly Russian elements should be aided in their attempt to build an anti-Bolshevik government in the Amur basin. France had been following a different policy, campaigning for an Allied expedition to protect the foreign nationals in Irkutsk, but we have already seen how, in the face of American and Japanese apathy toward the French proposal, Britain persuaded France to give it up and to entrust the Irkutsk mission to the Semenovists.

Britain seems to have been equally successful in persuading the French to leave any intervention to the Japanese.[37] The French were so persuaded of the wisdom of this course of action that they replied to Motono even before the British. On February 11, Colonel Nagai, Japanese military attaché in Paris, wired the chief of the army general staff that a high French officer had expressed the belief that the French would have "no objection to any action Japan might feel obliged to take."[38] The next day, in fulfillment of his instructions, Ambassador Matsui called on French Foreign Minister Pichon to ascertain his government's views toward Motono's informal proposal for control of the railroads in the Russian Far East. M. Pichon confirmed Colonel Nagai's intelligence and went on to explain that in the French view "the Russian situation gets progressively worse and if nothing is done, the power of the enemy will finally extend through all Russia to the Far East. I am convinced that the only way to prevent this is to rely on the strength of Japan."[39] He said that his government had been exchanging views with the British since mid-January on this question, that it was "now conferring about having Great Britain make a request of Japan in the name of the Allies; and that Great Britain has already agreed to it." The problem, of course, was the attitude of the American government, and this, said the French foreign minister, "We

[37] American Ambassador Roland Morris wired the State Department from Tokyo on February 8 that the French ambassador had told him that day that he had been instructed to join his British colleague in "acceding" to such a "request" from the Japanese government. *USFR, 1918, Russia,* II, 44.

[38] Nagai to chief, Japanese Army General Staff Headquarters, February 11, 1918, in *JGK, RKI, SK, HMSK,* pp. 15–16.

[39] Matsui to Motono, February 12, 1918, in Japan, Gaimushō, *Shiberia Shuppei Mondai,* I, 8–9.

do not know";[40] on the other hand, whatever objections might be made by the United States, joint representation by the Allies could be expected to overcome them. Even more emphatic was the note handed Viscount Motono by the French ambassador in Tokyo, which concluded:

The government of the Republic is completely agreed that Japan alone is in a position to act effectively and it declares itself ready to examine with the imperial government and the Allied powers the means and conditions of this intervention.[41]

These Anglo-French decisions, it should be noted, stemmed from the Chinda-Cecil talks in December and represent complete acceptance of the position then taken by Ambassador Chinda that any expedition would have to be purely Japanese. On the other hand, the British and the French seem not to have accepted as final the Japanese contention at the Paris conference that Japanese troops could not operate west of Irkutsk. Apparently, the European objectives of the Foch plan were still uppermost in the minds of the British and the French, but as a matter of diplomatic strategy they were temporarily deferred during the negotiation with Japan. When Ambassador Matsui replied to Pichon's declaration of French policy by outlining the proposal Viscount Motono had broached to the United States one week earlier—a limited proposal with purely Asian objectives—Pichon seems to have preferred not to argue. He expressed immediate agreement with Motono's proposal.

That France was actually no more reconciled than Great Britain to a Japanese intervention limited to the Russian Far East is clear from a paper, reported to have been submitted by the British War Office to the French general staff, dated February 15, 1918.[42] The paper reveals that Britain and France were agreed on the principle

---

[40] The substance of the American note of February 8 to the British embassy (see note 45, below), in which the British proposal of a mandated expedition was rejected, was not transmitted to the French embassy until February 14, 1918.

[41] Note from French ambassador to Japanese minister of foreign affairs, February 12, 1918 (in French), *JGK, RKI, SK, HMSK*, p. 17.

[42] Frazier, U.S. diplomatic liaison officer, Supreme War Council, to U.S. Department of State, February 19, 1918, enclosing memorandum he says had been shown him in confidence by a French general. *USFR, 1918, Russia*, II, 49.

of sole Japanese intervention in Siberia to take over the Trans-Siberian Railroad from Vladivostok to Cheliabinsk. The purposes of such an expedition were envisaged to be: to "reinforce the national element in Russia and Siberia," to "save Rumania," to prevent the Germans from withdrawing troops to the western front, and to prevent the formation of a German-Japanese coalition. In regard to this last point, the paper states: "If German domination over Russia and Siberia is a great danger, a German-Japanese domination over the entire world would be a still more formidable peril which could be eliminated by bringing Japan effectively and directly in opposition to Germany." The fundamental distrust that formed one basis of the Anglo-Japanese alliance as well as of the Inter-Allied expedition to Siberia was never more clearly illustrated. Pichon's agreement with the Motono proposal did not go very deep. It did not extend to the expedition's purposes or limits.

American Reluctance

Before replying to Motono's proposal, the British tried to win over the Americans as well as the French to their plan of a Japanese expedition. As early as January 28, a week before Motono had opened the subject with Ambassador Morris, the British government had begun its campaign in America. Strong local organizations in south and southeastern Russia, especially Cossack and Armenian groups, it argued, had recently been formed, and it was advisable for the Allies to assist them, in order "to prevent Russia from falling immediately and completely under the control of Germany." Such assistance could best be rendered by having the Allies invite the Japanese as their "mandatories" to extend support through the Trans-Siberian Railroad.[43] This was different from the Foch plan in that American troops were left out, but it was still intervention and the American government would have none of it. Ten days later the official reply was forwarded to the British embassy; information copies were also sent to the French, Italian,

[43] British embassy to U.S. Department of State, January 28, 1918, *ibid.*, II, 35.

Chinese, and Belgian diplomatic missions. The memorandum rejected the British proposal, declaring:

The American government is disposed at present to believe that any military expedition to Siberia or the occupation of the whole or of a part of the Trans-Siberian railway should be undertaken by international cooperation and not by any power acting as the mandatory of the others.[44]

In spite of the rejection, a little more than a week later France added its weight to the British proposal. On February 19 and 27, Pichon impressed on Ambassador Sharp in Paris that, if the Allies withheld prior consent, the Japanese would go in anyway but would then be impervious to Allied influence and might well form an alliance with Germany, "providing for the division of Russia." [45]

Under this constant pressure from its war partners, the Wilson administration began slowly to revise its stand. America had consistently felt that intervention was undesirable. But, in its attitude toward action by other powers, it had shifted from opposing, in December, 1917, intervention in any form to stating, in February, 1918, that only Inter-Allied intervention would be approved by the United States. In the note handed to Ambassador Tanaka in Washington on March 5,[46] a further step toward intervention was taken. Like the French reply, ostensibly a reply to Viscount Motono's proposal, the American note made no mention of the exact action proposed, but limited its attention to outlining, however reluctantly, the only conditions under which a solely Japanese expedition would be acceptable.

The wisdom of intervention still seemed questionable, but, "if it were undertaken, the government of the United States assumes

[44] United States memorandum to British embassy, February 8, 1918, *ibid.*, II, 41–42. Apparently no copy was sent to the Japanese government.

[45] Sharp to secretary of state, February 19, 1918, *ibid.*, II, 51, February 27, 1918, *ibid.*, II, 58–59.

[46] Tanaka to Motono, March 8, 1918, in Japan, Gaimushō Kiroku, "Rokoku Kakumei Ikken: Shuppei Kankei, Ei-Bei-Futsu no Kōshō" (hereinafter, *JGK, RKI, SK, EBFK*), I, identical with that transmitted by Ambassador Morris to Japanese minister of foreign affairs in Tokyo on March 7. Acting Secretary of State Polk to Ambassador Morris, March 5, 1918, *USFR, 1918, Russia,* II, 67–9; and Japan, Gaimushō Kiroku, "Rokoku Kakumei Ikken: Shuppei Kankei, Shiberia Shuppei Kōshō" (hereinafter, *JGK, RKI, SK, SSK*), pp. 100–102.

that the most explicit assurances would be given that it was under-taken by Japan as an ally of Russia, in Russia's interest, and with the sole view of holding it [Russia] safe against Germany and at the absolute disposal of the final peace conference." The note went on to say that, "even with such assurances given," the American government believed the expedition would be discredited, that the Russian people would be aroused to "a hot resentment," and that "the whole action might play into the hands of the enemies of Rus-sia and particularly of the enemies of the Russian revolution for which the government of the United States entertains the greatest sympathy." While not approving a Japanese expedition, the Amer-ican government was not absolutely opposing one, and was in fact stating under what conditions one could be tolerated. At least that seems to have been the hopeful construction placed by the British on the American attitude.

Britain's Appeal to Japan

The British were slow to reply to Motono's proposal since the re-jection of their effort on January 28 to secure American approval for a purely Japanese expedition acting in the name of the allies. In the latter part of February emergency meetings were reportedly held by the war cabinet on this subject.[47] British papers, including the *Daily Mail, Times, Chronicle,* and *Globe,* urged action by Japan,[48] but the government was hesitant to approach the Japanese again until there was some indication of a change in the American attitude.

The American note of March 5 to Japan, which had been shown two days earlier to the British ambassador at a dinner in Washing-ton, seems to have convinced the British government that the back of American opposition had finally been broken.[49] The very next

---

[47] Chinda to Motono, February 28, 1918, in *JGK, RKI, SK, HMSK,* p. 347; Colonel Tanaka to chief of Japanese army general staff, February 28, 1918, *ibid.,* pp. 383–84.

[48] Chinda to Motono, March 4, 1918, in *JGK, RKI, SK, EBFK,* I.

[49] Edward Mandell House, *Intimate Papers of Colonel House,* ed. Charles Sey-mour (Boston: Houghton Mifflin, 1926–28), III, 431.

day the British issued instructions to Ambassador Greene in Tokyo, the text of which was handed to Viscount Motono on March 11.[50] Like the American government, His Majesty's government seems not to have taken seriously the narrow scope of the expedition suggested by Motono; instead, it blithely returned to the proposal for Japanese action in western Siberia.

It is essential [the note stated] to prevent the food resources of Siberia as well as munitions of war, etc., stored at Vladivostok from falling into the hands of the central powers, who will be prepared before long to seize them. For this purpose an allied expedition is required which can occupy the Siberian railroad probably as far as Cheliabinsk and at least as far as Omsk, an expedition which, for reasons of geography, Japan alone is able to undertake.

His Majesty's government then proceeded to press on Japan its interpretation of the Wilsonian conditions. It argued that, were the Japanese to undertake such an expedition, its purposes might easily be misunderstood. Therefore, before sending troops, the government of Japan might well issue a declaration clearly distinguishing Japan's intervention in Russia from that of Germany. It suggested the points that might be made:

1. The central powers are intent on destroying Russia; the allies desire to come to its aid.

2. The central powers are taking advantage of the weakness of Russia to rob it of some important provinces; the allies promise to preserve the territory of Russia intact.

3. The central powers are making war not only on Russia itself, but also on any systems of government which it had established or which it might plan to establish; the allies have neither the desire nor the intention to intervene in its internal affairs.

4. The central powers have as their objective to destroy Russia both from the economic and the political points of view; the allies want to see it free and strong, both in their own interest and in that of the country as well.

[50] Greene to Motono, March 11, 1918. French text in Japan, Gaimushō, *Shiberia Shuppei Mondai,* I, 12–14 (excerpts which follow were translated from the French text). Japanese translation in *JGK, SK, EBFK,* I. Contents of the instructions were also related by Foreign Minister Balfour to Ambassador Chinda in London on March 6. Chinda to Motono, March 8, 1918, in *JGK, RKI, SK, SSK,* pp. 64–73.

In short, the British government felt that a declaration by Japan of respect for Russia's territorial integrity and of adherence to the principle of nonintervention in Russia's domestic affairs would secure America's approval for a nominally "Allied" but fairly independent Japanese expedition. Undoubtedly His Majesty's government was also not reluctant to keep Japan in leading strings if possible.

Allied Pressure on the United States

Britain was not at all sure that Japan could accept these conditions and seemed fully aware that, without clear American approval, Viscount Motono would face great difficulty. Indeed, on March 7, 1918, when Ambassador Greene first called on the Japanese foreign minister to ascertain how he might receive such a proposal, the foreign minister told him that, to undertake any action, the empire would need the material assistance of the United States and therefore must have its assent.[51] Thus, while awaiting Japan's reply to Britain's note, the European Allies determined to put greater pressure on America.

Their most effective argument, and one they no doubt sincerely believed, was that President Wilson could not have his cake and eat it too: he could not secure Japanese adherence to certain conditions unless he was willing to approve the action taken under those conditions. There could be no control without involvement; and the Allies well knew, from Wilson's statements, that he desired control.

On March 12, French Ambassador Jusserand spelled this out more specifically to the secretary of state in Washington.[52] Repeating the argument Pichon had made to Sharp, he said: "In a general way, Japan must and will intervene in Asia in defense of her present position and of her future. If she does so without our assent, she will do it against us and there is some likelihood of her later arriv-

[51] Summary of conversation between the British ambassador and Viscount Motono, March 7, 1918, in *JGK, RKI, SK, EBFK,* I.
[52] Jusserand to secretary of state, March 12, 1918, in *USFR, 1918, Russia,* II, 75–6.

ing at an understanding with Germany." Only through agreement
with Japan could the Allies assure themselves that Japan would:
act as an ally of Russia and respect its right to self-determination;
give "public guarantees of territorial disinterestedness"; and "clearly
define" and give "pledges" concerning the extent and effectiveness
of Japanese action. That the ambassador did not really share the fears
which he hoped to arouse in Wilson may be seen from his further
remarks. He indicated that by Japanese action the French hoped
to reinstate Siberian governments as far west at least as Tomsk.
These governments were then expected to serve as a "center of
resistance and attraction for the sound parts of Russia with which
relations may be entered into in southern Russia." It seems safe to
assume that France's eyes were really on the Ukraine and the
western front, and not on what Japan might do in Asia.

On March 15 the British prime minister opened a special two-day
conference of the Supreme War Council in London, attended by
the foreign ministers of Great Britain, France, and Italy. All three
reaffirmed their desire for Japanese intervention, and on the second
day of the conference it was agreed that Britain and France should
separately seek America's approval. On March 17 a note from
Foreign Secretary Balfour was delivered by the British ambassador
in Washington to President Wilson.[53] The note was clearly aimed
at removing the obstacle posed by Japan. Russia (like Turkey and
China before it) was pictured as a "sick" person, who "must be
helped by her friends" if she was to be saved from ravishment by
the Central Powers; and of her friends only Japan was in a position
to help—of course, "as a friend of Russia and the mandatory of
Russia and other Allies." Moreover, the ambassador added verbally,
if the Allies are at all to control the situation, they had best invite
Japan to act, for "in all probability Japanese intervention will take

[53] Foreign Office to British ambassador in Washington, March 16, 1918 (English text), *JGK, RKI, SK, EBFK*, I; conversation with Wilson reported by British
ambassador in U.S. to British Foreign Office, March 19, 1918 (English text),
ibid., I. Copies of both were transmitted to Vice Minister Shidehara by Ambassador Greene in Tokyo on March 26, 1918. The French are reported to have
sent a similar but separate note. Frederick Palmer, *Bliss, Peacemaker, the Life
and the Letters of General Tasker Howard Bliss* (New York: Dodd, Mead, 1934),
p. 293.

place with or without the assent of the Allies." The note went on to say that no action could be effective, for material and moral reasons, without the "active support of the United States." Although advanced with triple backing, these were old arguments which had not before, and did not this time, shake President Wilson's belief that the place to defeat Germany was not in Asia, but on the western front.

The Allies turned back to Japan; and Motono, unable to go any further alone, was forced at last to turn back to his colleagues.

VII. A CRISIS WEATHERED

By March, 1918, Motono's negotiations with the Western powers had reached a point necessitating a fundamental decision by his government. He could no longer put off the unpleasant business of facing the Advisory Council on Foreign Relations. Would the council support him or disavow him? It had not discussed the Russian question in any detail since the December meetings, when Motono had been unable to move it from a decision to "wait and see."[1] The council had not been consulted before ships were sent to Vladivostok; it was not even notified until three days after the *Iwami* had arrived in the harbor.[2] The meeting of January 27 is reported to have been perfunctory[3] and no further meetings were called.

The Advisory Council and Motono

About March 2, 1918, Motono circularized to the members of the advisory council a summary of the negotiations he had been conducting. This of course was before the American reply or the British proposal had been received and the foreign minister seems to have hoped that he might thus quietly enlist support for his efforts without a full-dress defense. "It would serve no purpose," Motono explained to Baron Makino on March 3, to bring up the negotiations at the advisory council; that "would simply stir up

[1] Hara Kei, *Hara Kei Nikki*, ed. Hara Kei'ichiro (Tokyo: Kengensha, 1950–52), VII, 311.
[2] *Ibid.*, VII, 311.
[3] *Ibid.*, VII, 317.

argument." [4] But the fires of argument had already been lighted by the circular.

Immediately upon receipt of the summary, Baron Makino called on the Seiyūkai president, Hara Kei. He telephoned him again on March 4. The two exchanged their fears about the foreign minister's independent actions,[5] and at the diet meeting later in the day Hara sought out Premier Terauchi to remonstrate with him, saying that, "according to the documents, it appears that if it were acceptable to the United States, we are committed to sending our troops to Siberia." Hara questioned whether Japan was either resolved or prepared for such action. In reply, Terauchi pleaded that he had not heard about the matter until the previous evening. He felt that Motono must have misunderstood Prince Yamagata's intentions. He assured Hara that "Motono would discuss it sincerely with each member" at the next meeting of the council.

In truth, the members of the Chōshū clique were as much startled by Motono's report as were Makino and Hara. The communications minister, Baron Den Kenjiro, for one, seems to have drafted a memorandum on the Siberian expedition, apparently primarily for the consideration of Yamagata and Terauchi;[6] and no doubt Count Itō Miyoji and Viscount Gotō Shimpei had much to say. Old Miura Goro wrote at length from Atami to the premier and then hurried to the capital to confer with Terauchi, Hara, Inukai, and probably with others.[7] The burden of Miura's concern seems to have been the "urgent necessity" to strengthen Japan's defenses in readiness for the German attack that Motono and the Allies regarded as imminent. Again Terauchi gave assurances, conceding that "the youngsters in the Ministry of Foreign Affairs are excited"; but, he promised "they will never rashly send an expedition."

Viscount Motono faced a hostile liberal faction and a worried Chōshū clique when the Advisory Council on Foreign Relations opened its meeting at 6 P.M. on the night of March 9, 1918, in

[4] *Ibid.*, VII, 340.
[5] *Ibid.*, VII, 338, 340.
[6] *Ibid.*, VII, 342.
[7] *Ibid.*, VII, 342–43.

the foreign minister's official residence.[8] Motono reviewed the course of the negotiations that had flowed from the expression of his "personal views" to the American ambassador on February 5. Emphasizing that these were "entirely his personal views," he sought to ward off criticism by conceding that "they did not at all limit any decision the government might take." He maintained vigorously that his suggestion of the advisability of Allied troops taking over the railroads in the Russian Far East had been misinterpreted. "He had never," he insisted, "made any proposal with the idea of seeking a [Japanese] expedition"; but the idea had come up and, while America opposed it and Britain had not yet replied, apparently Britain and France would give their support.

Motono's defense did not weaken the ire of his opponents. He might say that these were only his "personal views," retorted Hara, but "England and France at least took them as the views of the government . . . and it appears that the United States gave them serious consideration as the views of the Japanese government." After thus upbraiding Motono for presuming to act without specific authorization from the council, Hara made a bid for Miura's support. Refering to conditions in Russia and to what he felt to be the inadequacy of Japan's military strength, Hara warned, "This is no time to take such a decision." Priority should be given to "perfecting the national defense." Baron Makino announced his absolute hostility to an expedition.[9]

Navy Minister Katō strengthened Hara's contention that conditions did not demand an immediate decision, reporting that the situation at Vladivostok had not changed very much since the first of the year. Viscount Hirata joined in the attack, pointing out that any expedition to Russian territory was an act of war against Russia; yet "it is not known how England and France look on the Russian Bolshevik government." They should be questioned closely on this point. "Japan should know well what it is getting into," Hirata warned, and should "form a judgment in accord with its own interests" rather than permit itself to be stampeded into an action

[8] Ibid., VII, 345–56.
[9] Itō Miyoji, "Sui'uso Nikki, Gaikō Chōsakai Kaigi Hikki," pp. 1150–51.

which Britain and France were urging in *their* interests. Whether Viscount Itō Miyoji was present is not known, but in the face of such opposition, he seems to have been moving away from Motono and reconciling himself to postponing an expedition.[10] The premier, anxious to restore harmony, suggested that no decision be made until an actual request was received from England and France. Hara, however, pressed the government to declare its intentions, and at last Terauchi agreed to have Motono draft a decision for presentation to the council. Such a decision became more imperative two days later upon the receipt of the British note, expressing support for a Japanese expedition as far west as Cheliabinsk, providing certain guarantees were given. Terauchi professed to feel that this and the earlier French note were more "in the nature of feelers" than of concrete proposals; on the other hand, the American note demanded a detailed reply.[11]

Had the time really come for the army to act? Was the prize worth risking the government's future for? Could victory be won without American support? With the situation becoming daily more critical, all heads inclined toward the wizened sage at Odawara, Field Marshal Prince Yamagata. As the center of power of the Chōshū clique, he was the single most important influence on the determination of any important policy in those years. The cautious old man wielded more real power from his villa in Odawara than did the emperor from his palace in Tokyo. Finally he spoke. In a letter dated March 15 addressed to Terauchi, Motono, and Gotō, he warned the government that a Siberian expedition was "still premature." [12] Unless Japanese troops were requested by Russia, their landing would constitute "interference with Russia's authority." The result would be not to attract the support of the "constructive elements" in Russia, as Britain and France argued, but to drive most of them to turn for protection to the soviets. The Soviet government in turn would be driven to greater reliance on Germany. Japan would soon find itself fighting "Germany and most

[10] Hara, *Nikki,* VII, 370.
[11] Conversation between Terauchi and Hara, March 13, 1918. *Ibid.,* VII, 351.
[12] Tokutomi I'ichiro, comp. *Kōshaku Yamagata Aritomo Den* (Tokyo: Yamagata Aritomo Kō Kinen Jigyō-kai, 1933), III, 987–89,

of Russia." Such a major war the Japanese economy simply could not support alone. "Unfortunately," he said, "we should be forced to rely on England and America for help in munitions and funds. . . . Consequently, before the empire can come to a decision on its policy toward Russia, it is essential first to ascertain the Russian policies of England, France, and America." Although this letter does not mention it, Yamagata must also have discussed with his followers the desirability of taking no action until they had negotiated the proposed military agreement with China and reached a firm understanding with the Russian leaders in Manchuria.

As a consequence of Yamagata's decision, when the Advisory Council on Foreign Relations met again on March 17, the Chōshū clique joined with the liberal faction to reject Motono's repeated plea for an immediate expedition. Hara seems to have led the attack. No expedition would be justified except in self-defense. According to his diary, he told the council that, "if we should be requested by the powers and if such an expedition is not required for self-defense, we must be resolved immediately to tell them that we shall send no troops." [13] In this argument Terauchi certainly sided with Hara, for at a cabinet meeting later in the month he is reported to have insisted that troops should be sent only "when it is recognized that we are threatened to a dangerous degree by the eastward extension of German influence." [14] At any rate, Hara reports that at the council meeting on March 17 he won unanimous support for his view; and it was clearly embodied in the confidential memorandum adopted that day, transmitted to the United States on March 19, and shown confidentially to the governments of Great Britain, France, and Italy.[15] Thanks to Yamagata, Motono had lost again.

After expressing appreciation for "the absolute frankness with

[13] This reconstruction of Hara's position is based on the statements in his memorandum of "personal views," presented to the premier on April 2, 1918 (see below), and Hara, *Nikki*, VII, 3550.

[14] Tsurumi Yusuke, *Gotō Shimpei* (Tokyo: Gotō Shimpei Denki Hensankai, 1938), III, 879–80.

[15] English text of note in Motono to Morris, March 19, 1918, *USFR, 1918, Russia*, II, 81–82; Japanese text in Japan, Gaimushō, *Shiberia Shuppei Mondai, Dai Ippen, Shiberia Shuppei ni itaru Kōshō Keika* (November, 1922), pp. 15–16.

which the views of the American government" had been communicated in the note of March 7, the Japanese government maintained that "the intervention now proposed by the Allied governments to arrest the sinister activities of Germany in Siberia did not originate from any desire expressed, or any suggestion made by the Japanese government"; and it assured the United States it would not care to consider such action without "the whole-hearted support of all the great powers associated in the war against Germany." Japan would certainly "refrain from taking any action on which due understanding had not been reached between the United States and the other great powers of the entente," unless, of course, its security were threatened. "It will hardly be necessary to add," the note explained, "that should the hostile activities in Siberia develop to such a degree as to jeopardize the national security or vital interests of Japan, she may be compelled to resort to prompt and efficient measures of self-protection." Then, in an effort to quiet America's fears, but being careful not to commit itself so specifically as either the American or British governments had suggested, the Japanese note took pains to assure the government of the United States that "whatever action Japan might be called upon to take in the Russian territory will be wholly uninfluenced by any aggressive motives or tendencies and that it will remain unshaken in its profound sympathy toward the Russian people, with whom it has every desire to maintain the relations of cordial friendship."

On March 26, Motono reported in the same vein to the diet.[16] Reviewing the empire's Russian policy, he denied that Japan had either made or received a formal proposal for an expedition to Siberia. He then went on to declare that, if threatened, Japan would take "prompt and adequate measures of self-defense."

One of the reasons why the avowed interventionists in the Chō-shū clique were not ready to support Motono was their concern over America's opposition. They were also worried by Britain's insistence that Japanese troops should go as far as Cheliabinsk or Omsk. On March 18, the day following the council session, these

[16] Japan, Gaimushō, *Shiberia Shuppei Mondai*, I, 15–16.

questions were discussed by the cabinet. The ministers decided to tell the British government plainly how they felt. For Japan to undertake "military action in Siberia," they said in their note to Britain of that day, "the moral and material assistance of the United States government would be absolutely essential." [17] Even with American support Japan could not consider operating beyond the Amur basin. Acceptance of that fact was "an indispensable condition" of any Japanese expedition.

Alarming News from Vladivostok

The council's decision of March 17 provides the key for understanding the resolution of another crisis which attracted great attention around the world: the landing of Japanese troops at Vladivostok on April 4. The tense situation in Vladivostok was aggravated on March 25 when the local soviet of workers' and soldiers' deputies seized the post and telegraph office. The employees protested by going out on strike, with the result that communications were broken off.[18] The Allied consular corps conferred at once, agreeing to lodge another formal protest with the city authorities and to seek instructions from their home governments about the advisability of landing troops. In reporting these events to the central naval authorities of Japan, Admiral Katō indicated that he was prepared to act if the consular corps requested him to do so. The use of troops in these circumstances, he felt, "would mark the beginning of clear intervention in internal affairs," an act quite different from a landing to protect Allied lives and property, and he desired instructions.

[17] Ibid., I, 16 (Japanese text); JGK, RKI, SK, EBFK, I (French text). Excerpts below are translated from the Japanese text. Originally it was also decided to request information on the British government's attitude toward the Bolshevik government and toward assistance to the anti-Bolshevik groups, but the note received that day from the British ambassador concerning this point caused it to be deleted from the final version of the note sent. JGK, RKI, SK, SSK, p. 290.

[18] Urajiosutoku ni okeru Rikusentai Jōriku Temmatsu," a report dated April 23, 1918, in Japan, Gaimushō Kiroku, "Rokoku Kakumei Ikken: Sankō Chōsho" (hereafter, JGK, RKI, SC), I; and Japan, Kaigun Gunreibu, Taishō Yon-nen naishi Kyū-nen Kaigun Senshi (1924), I, 148–54.

Had Japan's naval authorities been ready to join Motono in demanding an expedition, here was an ideal opportunity; but they were not. No doubt a cabinet meeting was called and even Motono was forced to abide by the decision to minimize the developments in Vladivostok. On March 29 the navy vice minister wired Katō: "Should the consular corps make a formal request, there is no objection to the landing of marines after first consulting the British and American naval commanders; but, when they are no longer needed, you will withdraw them immediately." At the same time the foreign minister instructed the Japanese consul general to the effect that present conditions did not seem to warrant such a request, for the occupation by the soviet of "two or three government offices" did "not seem to be endangering immediately the lives and property of our residents." Of course, should a dangerous situation develop in the future, the ministry would reconsider its decision or, if an emergency arose, the consul general was empowered to act first and explain later.[19] For the time being he was instructed not to request the assistance of Katō's forces.

Katō, however, wanted to be prepared. The day he received his instructions, he conferred with the American and British commanders aboard the *Brooklyn*. The American commander, Admiral Knight, is reported to have taken the lead in expressing his deep concern lest the Bolsheviks seize political authority in the city and spread civil war in their wake. Only a few days earlier he had recommended that a temporary Siberian government be set up at Vladivostok under the protection of the Allied fleet. Now he urged that "a lull of two or three months" be bought by increasing the "silent pressure," namely, by bringing up fleet and troop reinforcements from Japan. His two counterparts readily agreed and Katō petitioned his superiors. Katō felt that the reinforcements would be useful either for direct intervention in support of the moderates or for the protection of the foreign nationals should the national policy be to permit the Bolsheviks to take over.

On March 30 the vice minister of the navy, Vice Admiral To-

---

[19] The exact date of these Japanese Foreign Ministry instructions is not given; but, a copy reached the Navy Ministry on March 31, 1918.

chinai Sojiro, rejected Katō's request, taking care to outline clearly the position, held jointly, no doubt, by both the army and navy authorities. In case of real necessity for protecting the foreign residents or in case the British and American naval commanders acted unexpectedly, of course the commander should act at once and the ministry would back him up with whatever reinforcements might be necessary. But, he explained, it was highly undersirable to "display more military strength there before such a situation develops"; to do so would be to "invite a misunderstanding in foreign relations" that would seriously damage Japan's position, "should operations be necessary later in Siberia." The truth is that the Japanese government knew Admiral Knight's proposal did not enjoy the full support of the authorities in Washington;[20] and the Advisory Council on Foreign Relations had just made plain that it would support no military action in Siberia except in self-defense or with the definite approval of the Western powers, including the United States. The navy had consistently shown itself anxious to operate strictly within the limits of national policy; and the army, although more prone to shape that policy, was not prepared lightly to jeopardize its plans for a major Siberian expedition merely to effect an occupation of Vladivostok.

While the "silent pressure" of the Allied naval forces had unquestionably given pause to the revolutionists in Vladivostok, it had not prevented incidents, nor had it prevented the Bolshevik-controlled soviet from increasing its authority. More significantly, the pressure of these events in Vladivostok, the ensuing conversations with Allied consular and naval authorities there and with their home governments, the continuous study of the problem independently and probably jointly by the Navy Ministry, the Army General Staff Headquarters, the Army Ministry, the Foreign Min-

[20] The United States government had consistently opposed intervention in Siberia. Moreover, on March 29, 1918, "a member of the American embassy staff in Japan told the vice minister of foreign affairs (Baron Shidehara Kijuro) in a confidential conversation that the views of Admiral Knight on the east Siberian question would probably not be supported by the American President and that the views of the admiral were not at all in agreement with those of the American ambassador in Russia and the United States government." Japan, Kaigun Gunreibu, *Senshi*, I, 153.

istry, and others, had by the end of March resulted in the navy's being militarily prepared, in cooperation with the army, to carry out an immediate occupation of the city. While it was agreed that this should be done only in self-defense or to prevent an exclusive occupation by American or British naval forces, the central authorities had, in case of emergency, given the consul general authority to join his colleagues in calling for a landing and they had given the naval commander the authority to effect it without specific prior approval.

As the Japanese commander later remarked, his original instructions had been as ambiguous as one of the equivocal problems which Buddhist masters sometimes give disciples to test their intuition. By the end of March, while his instructions still left room for his own judgment, it seems fair to say that in large part they had transferred real control over his actions from the central authorities to the American and British naval commanders, should they see fit to act, or to the soviet or any lawless element in the city of Vladivostok, should there be any attack on Allied nationals or their property.

To Motono the situation seemed a vindication of all his policies. Clearly it was time for Japan to strike and strike hard, whether complete agreement could be won from all the Western powers or not. Rebellious over his repudiation by the advisory council on March 17, he decided to stake his office on the issue. Drafting a complete statement of his "personal views on the question of sending an expedition to Siberia," and attaching to it a summary of his negotiations with the Allies, he presented both to Premier Terauchi on April 2.[21]

Although he did not go into the details of execution or the sphere of action, he outlined forcefully his contention that the civil war in Russia was enabling Germany to threaten the northern borders of China and that the opportunity should be seized to send an ex-

[21] Draft of summary of negotiations in Japan, Gaimushō Kiroku, "Rokoku Kakumei Ikken: Teikoku no Taidō" (hereinafter, *JGK, RKI, TT*), I, 0044–98, with clean hectographed copy on pp. 0099–138. "Personal Views" ("Shiberia Shuppei Mondai ni kansuru Hiken"), *ibid.*, I, 0139–54; excerpts have been published in Tsurumi, *Gotō*, III, 880–83.

pedition. By doing so, he argued, after full consultation with the Allies and after fully informing the United States, Japan could best strengthen its relations with the Allies and the United States, achieve closer relations with China, and occupy a position on the continent which would strengthen the empire's defenses, advance its continental policies, and lend weight to its voice at the coming peace conference.

The Japanese Landing

Before Terauchi could do any more than pass Motono's memoranda on to the genro, a wire was received on April 4 from Admiral Katō: "This morning in broad daylight robbers raided a Japanese shop in the city and attacked three Japanese, one of whom died immediately. It was soon like anarchy within the city. Order was completely destroyed, so that there did not exist ashore the means for protecting the lives and property of Japanese." [22] In this fashion the commander at Vladivostok reported the attack on three Japanese clerks in the store of the Ishidō Company in the downtown area of the city. The clerks had refused to hand over money demanded by a group of unidentified robbers, and in consequence were attacked.[23] The admiral immediately signaled the news to the commanders of the American and British warships, conferred with Consul General Kikuchi and the army general staff's special agent, Colonel Sakabe Tosuho, and decided that "self-defense" required a marine landing.[24] The units were readied.

At four the following morning the admiral notified the American and British commanders by letter of his action. At five o'clock the

[22] Commander Fifth Squadron to central naval authorities, forwarded by commander Third Fleet, April 4, 1918, Japan, Kaigun Gunreibu, *Senshi*, I, 155.

[23] The nationality of the robbers has never been determined, and their number is indefinite; Katō Kanji's biographers say there were three. Fukunami Sadao and Ishihara Kitao, *Katō Kanji Taishō Den* (Tokyo: Katō Kanji Taishō Denki Hensankai, 1941), p. 674. On the other hand, the American consul, Caldwell, reported five (Caldwell to secretary of state, April 4, 1918, in *USFR, 1918, Russia*, II, 99).

[24] Japan, Kaigun Gunreibu, *Senshi*, III, 27.

two companies of "Otsu" unit were mustered on the *Asahi,* given last-minute instructions, and a half hour later were landed at the commercial wharf. The Buddhist temple, Hontōji, and the Japanese consulate were used for billets. The next morning the four companies of "Kō" unit were landed and billeted in the Japanese movie house and elementary school.

While Katō had acted independently, he was warmly supported by the Allied officials in the city and harbor. One hour before landing "Otsu" unit, he had notified the American and British naval commanders and later in the morning he called on them individually to explain the reasons for his action. The American commander congratulated him: "You have done very well," he said. "If Americans had met the same harm, I should have taken the same action as you did." [25] Regretting that he could not take parallel action at the time, he explained that his instructions did not permit him to act on his own discretion unless his nationals were directly harmed or unless fighting were to break out in the city.[26] The British naval commander had earlier been instructed to act in cooperation with his Japanese counterpart,[27] so on the afternoon of the same day he landed fifty marines from the *Suffolk* and detailed them to the British consulate.[28] Two days later he explained to Admiral Katō that their mission was to guard the consulate, protect the lives and property of foreign nationals, and prevent the transfer of military stores to hostile hands, avoiding as far as possible hostilities with Russian forces. There were no French forces in the harbor; but the French consul publicly expressed his support by requesting that some of the Japanese marines be detailed to guard the French consulate.

Admiral Katō was equally careful to solicit understanding on the

[25] *Ibid.,* III, 28.

[26] It is interesting to compare Admiral Knight's reaction with that of American Ambassador Francis, who instructed Robins to assure the Bolsheviks that "the Allies did not sanction the Japanese landing." *USFR, 1918, Russia,* II, 107. Ambassador Francis more accurately represented sentiment in Washington, as the Japanese officials in Tokyo knew.

[27] "Urajiosutoku ni okeru Rikusentai," *JGK, RKI, SC,* I.

[28] Japan, Kaigun Gunreibu, *Senshi,* III, 27–28.

part of the Russians. On the day of the landing he issued a special notification to the city council, district zemstvo council, local soviet, the fortress command, and naval harbor command.[29] He explained that the Allies had been studiously avoiding any partisan intervention in Russian affairs and proclaimed his own and the other Allies' deep sympathy for "Russia in its present situation" and their ceaseless hope "that these national difficulties will quickly be overcome and the glorious revolution carried to completion." Nor was this landing, he declared, a partisan intervention. Disorder had recently increased to such a degree as to cause grave alarm "for the lives and property of Japanese and Allied residents." Finally the commander had been forced by the recent assault on his countrymen to land troops, "simply," he emphasized, "in order to protect Japanese nationals." He had "no other feeling than sincere friendship and sympathy for the Russian government and people." He hoped that the Russian people would "not be alarmed" and would "go about their business as usual."

Three days later Consul General Kikuchi, acting on instructions and accompanied by the consuls of the Allies, called on the chairman of the zemstvo committee and gave a similar explanation of the landing.[30]

Whatever hopes the Japanese commander and the local Allied officials might have had, they certainly were not realized. Frightened and angry, Russians of every political persuasion denounced the action. The local soviet at Khabarovsk belittled the robbery and murder as "the work of certain agitators from the seamier side of society," which by no means justified the landing of foreign troops:[31] "We must consider the action taken by the Japanese commander to be the first step in the occupation of Vladivostok." The regional Far Eastern Executive Committee at Khabarovsk added

[29] Japanese text, from which excerpts below have been translated, *ibid.*, III, 26, and in Fukunami and Ishihara, *Katō Kanji*, pp. 676–77. Russian text in USSR, Tsentral'nyi Arkhiv RSFSR, Arkhiv Oktiabr'skoi Revoliutsii, *Iaponskaia Interventsiia 1918–1922 gg. v Dokumentakh*, ed. I. Mints (Moscow, 1934), pp. 18–19.

[30] "Urajiosutoku ni okeru Rikusentai," *JGK, RKI, SC,* I.

[31] Japanese text of protest, undated, in Japan, Kaigun Gunreibu, *Senshi*, III, 33.

its protest.[32] The regional committee called the assault on the three Japanese nationals "clearly provocative" and the landing an unjustified, illegal "act of violence" of "a reactionary character." Brushing aside the Japanese government's protestations of good will, they placed their hope in "the workers and peasants of Japan" to press for a recall of the forces. At Irkutsk the Central Executive Committee of Siberian Soviets called on all "workers and peasants of Siberia" to support the soviets against the Japanese landing.[33] The highest governing organ of the republic, the Council of People's Commissars, issued a proclamation charging that for months the Japanese authorities had been looking "for a suitable pretext" to intervene at Vladivostok. Reviewing the events of April 4–5, the council declared:

The course of events leaves no doubt whatsoever that all this was pre-arranged and that the murder of the two [sic] Japanese was only a pretext for the imperialist attack from the east which had been contemplated for some time. The imperialists of Japan wish to strangle the Soviet revolution, to cut off Russia from the Pacific Ocean, to seize the rich territories of Siberia and to enslave the Siberian workers and peasants. The bourgeoisie of Japan advance as the deadly enemy of the Soviet Republic.[34]

The seriousness with which the Bolshevik leaders viewed the landing can be seen from the telegram sent by Lenin to the Vladivostok Soviet on April 7:

We consider the situation extremely serious and must categorically warn our comrades. Have no illusions: the Japanese will certainly ad-

---

[32] Telegram of protest to Japanese consul general, dated April 5, 1918: Russian text in USSR, *Iaponskaia Interventsiia*, pp. 20–21, and *Vlast' Truda*, No. 65 (April 12, 1918), quoted in V. V. Maksakow and A. Turunov, *Khronika Grazhdanskoi Voiny v Sibiri (1917–1918)* (Moscow: Gosizdat, 1926), Appendix 27, pp. 158–59; Japanese summary in Japan, Kaigun Gunreibu, *Senshi*, III, 34.

[33] Russian text of announcement, issued April 6, 1918, following the April 5 meeting of the executive committee, in Maksakov and Turunov, *Khronika*, Appendix 26, pp. 156–58.

[34] Proclamation of the Sovnarkom, dated April 5, 1918, published in *Rannee Utro*, No. 57 (April 6, 1918), p. 1, quoted in USSR, *Iaponskaia Interventsiia*, pp. 203–4; English translation in James Bunyan, ed., *Intervention, Civil War and Communism, April–December 1918; Documents and Materials*, (Baltimore: Johns Hopkins University Press, 1936), pp. 68–69.

vance. That is inevitable. All the Allies will assist them without exception. Therefore, you must begin to prepare yourselves, without the slightest delay, to prepare yourselves seriously, to prepare yourselves with all your power. Most of all you must give your attention to the best way out, the best retreat, the carrying off of stores and railroad material.[35]

In spite of the Japanese commander's proclamation that the landing was a purely local operation, conducted solely to protect foreign nationals, the Bolsheviks saw it against a larger background of events: the practice of the Allied consuls of dealing almost exclusively with the moderate-controlled municipal duma rather than with the soviet, the "silent" support given the anti-Bolsheviks by the anchoring of warships in the harbor, the anti-Bolshevik activities of Japanese agents, particularly military officers, at Blagoveshchensk, Harbin, and throughout eastern Siberia. Through eyes widened with fear, the Bolsheviks saw the landing at Vladivostok as the beginning of the widely rumored and deeply dreaded Allied intervention with the aim of crushing them.

There is no doubt that the landing had hit the central nerve of national feeling in the Russian people. The Vladivostok municipal duma and the mayor, while using less vigorous language, likewise protested that the landing violated Russian sovereignty.[36] The zemstvo council expressed its sympathy for the Japanese casualties, but went on to say: "It is our duty to protest such intervention in our internal affairs and, although we feel friendly relations between Japan and Russia are absolutely essential, we are convinced that such actions will somehow destroy these relations." The Social Democratic and Social Revolutionary parties, embracing the vast majority of the Russian people, also protested, as did a joint conference of various groups from the last national duma.[37] No doubt some moderate and reactionary Russian elements were encouraged

[35] V. I. Lenin, *Iz Epokhi Grazhdanskoi Voiny* (Partizdat, 1934), p. 32, quoted in G. I. Reikhberg, *Iaponskaia Interventsiia na Dal'nem Vostoke, 1918–1922 gg. Kratkii Ocherk* (Moscow: Gosudarstvennoe sotsial'no-ekonomicheskoe izdatel'stvo, 1935), p. 31.

[36] Japanese text, no date, in Japan, Kaigun Gunreibu, *Senshi*, III, 33.

[37] "Urajiosutoku ni okeru Rikusentai," *JGK, RKI, SC*, I.

by the landing; but clearly they were merely islands of dissent in a great sea of popular left-wing hostility.[38]

The Japanese commander seems to have anticipated serious trouble and again called for reinforcements. On the evening of April 4, before he had landed the first contingent, he reported the situation and his decision to his superiors. "I have ordered two companies of marines to land tomorrow morning, the fifth, at dawn," he wired. "It is difficult to tell what will follow. The dispatch of the *Hizen* and destroyer flotilla as reinforcements are urgently requested."[39] The Third Fleet commander, Vice Admiral Arima, who was waiting with the main strength of his command in Eikō Wan, off the Korean east coast port of Wonsan (Genzan), responded immediately. Word reached the authorities in Tokyo at 7 A.M., April 5, of his decision to send reinforcements to Vladivostok in readiness for any emergency: the *Hizen* and the Fifth and the Fourteenth Destroyer Flotilla (eight destroyers in all) would weigh anchor that evening for Vladivostok; the *Katori* and the Third Torpedo-boat Flotilla (probably the remaining four destroyers) would depart that morning for Rashin Ura, northen most Korean anchorage, to serve as a reserve.[40] Approval was requested. Immediate support was also given by the army general staff, in the conviction that the time had come to send the Seventy-fourth Infantry Regiment to occupy the city as previously agreed with the naval authorities.[41]

[38] It is interesting to note that, according to a Japanese navy intelligence report, the "Central Headquarters of the Korean People," representing refugees from Japanese rule in Korea, in Nikol'sk Ussuriisk, met on April 11 and decided in the face of the Japanese landing to cooperate with the soviet forces and to look to Russia and Germany for the deliverance of their homeland. Japan, Kaigun Gunreibu, Kaichō Rohō Dai 73 go: "Urajio Tsūshin" (April 19) in Japan, Gaimushō Kiroku, "Rokoku Kakumei Ikken: Han-Kagekiha Kankei" (hereinafter, *JKG, RKI, HK*), II.

[39] Fifth Squadron commander, to central naval authorities, forwarded by Third Fleet commander, 7:30 P.M., April 4, 1918, quoted in Japan, Kaigun Gunreibu, *Senshi*, I, 155.

[40] Report from commander Third Fleet to central naval authorities, via commander Fifth Squadron, received 7 A.M., April 5, 1918, quoted *ibid.*, I, 155–56. By Third Torpedo-boat Flotilla was apparently meant its remaining complement, the Twenty-fifth (or Ninth) Destroyer Flotilla.

[41] Japan, Sambō Hombu, *Taishō Shichi Nen naishi Jūichi Nen Shiberia Shuppei-shi* (1924), I, 38.

Katō Restrained

The news of the landing, coming on top of Motono's "ultimatum," shook the Japanese government to its foundations. The ruling coalition had only just decided on March 17 to postpone any decision about an expedition until Japan's security was threatened and preferably until the support of the Allies, including America, could be assured. Would Motono now be able to persuade the cabinet to ignore the advisory council? Would the navy force the army to send an expedition into Siberia before the army had completed its planning? Was Yamagata's will to be thwarted?

Terauchi wrestled with the problem, but it was too much for him. The once vigorous master of Korea had been weakened by months of sickness. Exhausted by worry and care for his wife, who had contracted myelitis in September, 1917, he had himself fallen ill in December with diabetes.[42] Complications set in. In February, 1918, important conferences had to be held at his bedside in Oiso. At the time of the crisis in late March and early April, the chief of the Red Cross hospital was diagnosing his trouble as diabetes, nephritis, and a developing arterio-sclerosis, and was confining him to his home as much as possible.

Exhausted by illness, mortified by Motono's revolt, and alarmed by the navy's landing at Vladivostok, Terauchi could see no alternative but to resign. Late on April 4 he dragged himself painfully to Odawara to offer his resignation to Yamagata, but the astute old prince would have none of it. Although it is only surmise on our part, he must have read Motono's memoranda already and decided that Motono would have to go. As for the landing at Vladivostok, he seems to have felt it was premature and would have to be curtailed. Moreover, Terauchi was the man to do it. Appealing to the premier's samurai spirit, Yamagata directed him to continue in office at whatever cost. In a scene reminiscent of feudal days, the old Chōshū lord said, "You must sacrifice yourself to the nation and

[42] Katakura Tōjiro, *Fushi Terauchi Gensui* (Tokyo: Ajia Seinen-sha, 1944), pp. 198–200; and Hara, *Nikki*, VII, 323 (entry of February 3, 1918) and p. 329 (entry of February 14, 1918).

exert yourself with unflagging spirit." [43] One can almost see
Terauchi, the loyal retainer, incline his body stiffly forward in silent
obedience.

Upon his return to Tokyo, Terauchi set to work feverishly to
carry out the prince's directive. He demanded that Navy Minister
Katō have the landing forces withdrawn immediately.[44] The navy
minister, in his turn, while insisting that the landing had been
justified in order to protect Japanese nationals and while insisting
on authorizing the forces in Vladivostok to land the rest of the
marine complement if needed, immediately stopped all reinforcements. They would be "premature and likely to result in provoking
the Russians," he told Admiral Katō at Vladivostok.[45] And he
quickly ordered the commander of the Third Fleet to move the
Hizen and the two destroyer flotillas no farther than Rashin Ura,
and return the other units to Wonsan (Genzan).[46]

A few hours later, upon receipt of another plea from the Vladivostok commander, the navy minister revised his order, instructing
the Third Fleet commander to proceed with all his ships (except
Kantō) to Rashin Ura and await further orders there. Then, lest
Rear Admiral Katō misinterpret this move, the navy vice minister
reminded him on April 6 that "the movement of the marines has
no other object than to protect the residents" and warned him "it
is necessary not to go beyond this sphere of activity.[47] Avoid a col-
lision as much as possible. You must be careful not to be drawn
into so-called positive action by intriguers. This is an order." And
the following day the rear admiral was further instructed to limit
his actions to those previously agreed on with the consul general.

While the Navy Ministry restrained its Third Fleet and Fifth
Squadron commanders, the War Ministry held back the army general staff. The *Kantō* lay at anchor at Wonsan and the staff was
ready to embark the Seventy-fourth Regiment. At a confidential

[43] Katakura, *Fushi Terauchi*, pp. 198–200; Den Kenjiro Denki Hensankai,
comp., *Den Kenjiro Denki* (Tokyo: Den Kenjiro Denki Hensankai, 1932), pp.
344–45.
[44] Fukunami and Ishihara, *Katō Kanji*, pp. 678–79.
[45] Japan, Kaigun Gunreibu, *Senshi*, I, 156–57.
[46] *Ibid.*, III, 30.
[47] *Ibid.*, I, 158–59.

conference between the staff and the ministry, the latter insisted
that, in view of the government's Russian policy, this was no time
to send an occupation force to Vladivostok.[48] The staff temporarily
dropped its plans. Three days later the navy yielded to the army
staff's argument that, even though the troops were not embarked,
rifle ammunition and food ought to be loaded so as to be ready
for any sudden change in the situation; and 150,000 yen in gold
notes were transferred aboard from the Bank of Korea. Lest this
appear to indicate a change in policy, the navy vice minister took
pains to inform the chief of staff of the Third Fleet that "the above
loading was to be prepared for an emergency and not because it had
been decided to despatch troops." [49] And on April 9, in order to investigate the possibilities for an early withdrawal, the navy ordered
its councilor, Yamagawa Hashio, to Vladivostok.[50]

Terauchi's sense of failure was shared by others in high office.
In the week following the landing at Vladivostok, the continuation
of his government became a subject of serious concern among the
genro and their confidants. Yamagata's close friend, Miura Goro,
felt that Terauchi was fumbling both the Russia and China questions and should soon have to accept responsibility.[51] Various elements in the diet were maneuvering for a coalition to back a new
"cabinet of national unity." [52] Clique politicians began considering
alternative leaders. Yamagata spoke to Saionji about recommending
another senior member of the Chōshū clique, the conservative privy
councilor, Viscount Hirata Tosuke. And Gotō sounded out Hara
on the possibilities of party support for another such "transcendant
cabinet," led either by Hirata or Itō.[53] However, Terauchi's agreement to continue for the time made an immediate decision unnecessary. Not so with Foreign Minister Motono.

[48] Japan, Sambō Hombu, *Shiberia Shuppei-shi,* I, 38.
[49] Japan, Kaigun Gunreibu, *Senshi,* I, 158; and *ibid.,* III, 30–31.
[50] Text of his report, dated April 25, 1918, *ibid.,* I, 162–63.
[51] Miura to Hara, diary entry April 6, 1918, Hara, *Nikki,* VII, 362; and diary
entry of April 12, 1918, *ibid.,* VII, 372.
[52] Diary entry of April 11, 1918, *ibid.,* VII, 371.
[53] Diary entry of April 17, 1918, *ibid.,* VII, 378–81.

Motono Replaced

During the month of the Motono negotiations, the genro, other than Yamagata, seem to have taken no active part in the formulation of Russian policy. Indeed, Matsukata and Saionji, not being members of the prevailing wing of the Chōshū clique (Matsukata was the leader of the Satsuma clique and Saionji the leader of a subordinate wing of the Chōshū clique, formerly headed by Prince Ito Hirobumi), may have received their first briefing on the Motono *démarche* in the viscount's memoranda of April 2. Upon their receipt of these papers or possibly at the request of the prime minister, the three elders hurried up from their villas to the capital to consider what was to be done. Saionji conferred on April 11 with the chief of his old party, Hara Kei, and after hearing Hara's views that no expedition should be undertaken unless it proved "inescapable for reasons of self-defense," he expressed his complete agreement.[54] Two days later Marquis Matsukata also called on Hara and said that he, too, was opposed to an expedition; but the truth is that the junior members of the Chōshū clique had only recently brought him around to this. Matsukata is reported to have at first been inclined to go along with the foreign minister until dissuaded by the action of the Advisory Council on Foreign Relations and the opinions of various members of the cabinet.[55]

The road to "Kokian," Yamagata's suburban villa, must have been particularly busy those days. The old master showed himself to be the ablest politician of them all. Without modifying his decision that an expedition should not be undertaken without the full support of England and America, he stressed one phase of his position to one conferee, showed another phase to another. Some com-

[54] *Ibid.*, VII, 369–70. Diary entry of April 11, 1918.
[55] Itō Miyoji's explanation to Den Kenjiro, recorded in Den's diary, April 24, 1918, quoted in Den Kenjiro Denki Hensankai, *Den Kenjiro Denki*, p. 345. Gotō Shimpei explains the origin of Yamagata's attitude similarly to Hara, according to Hara's diary, April 17, 1918 (Hara, *Nikki*, VII, 377–78), but Yamagata's letter to Terauchi on March 15 shows that Yamagata had made up his mind earlier.

plained later that his words were difficult to understand, but each
came away reasurred that Yamagata agreed with *him*. Gotō and
Itō, for example, were convinced that Yamagata was basically in
favor of intervention. On the other hand, Saionji quoted Yamagata
as saying that "an expedition is impossible" although "later" it might
be necessary to send "some troops to Manchuria." [56] This was essentially what he had told Hara earlier.[57] Terauchi was already
well informed about Yamagata's views, but, lest he falter, he was
reminded in a letter: "If we are going to send troops, we must inquire the views of various countries. They must be united and we
must be truly justified." [58]

Motono seemed unable to understand these arguments; nor was
he able to assess the political currents about him. He only knew that
he had gone so far in his negotiations with the Allies that the Japanese government would have to give him a greater measure of support or he could not go on. He demanded a decision and on April
10 it was given to him. Meeting at the palace, the genro rejected his
views completely.[59] Motono, pleading illness, offered his resignation
immediately thereafter.[60] It was accepted on April 23 and Gotō
Shimpei, the home minister, was appointed Motono's successor.

Vladivostok Given to the Soviet

In Vladivostok, the crisis was resolved on April 25 by permitting
the soviet to take over the city. The Japanese government's decision
not to send reinforcements and not to exploit the landing had been
made quickly and independently on April 4; but the decision was

[56] Saionji to Hara, reported in diary entry, April 11, 1918. Hara, *Nikki*, VII,
370.
[57] Yamagata called on Hara, March 30, and told him that "in order to create a
militant spirit in the nation, it would be necessary to send some troops," *ibid.*,
VII, 360 (diary entry March 31, 1918).
[58] Excerpt shown by Terauchi to Hara. Diary entry, April 22, 1918, *ibid.*, VII,
389.
[59] The existence and general trend of opinion of the conference were reported
by Saionji to Hara, diary entry of April 11, 1918, *ibid.*, VII, 370. Marquis Okuma
is reported to have been present also, but if he expressed any opinion, there seems
to be no record of it.
[60] Yamagata-Hara conversation, April 15, 1918. Hara, *Nikki*, VII, 374–75.

strengthened by support from abroad. Contrary to the approval expressed by their representatives on the spot, Britain and America were actually far from pleased with the landing.

From the beginning, the British had never given up the possibility of working out an accommodation with the Bolshevik regime. Treating it as a local government in control of northern Russia, they had clung to the hope that it might be won over to a pro-Allied policy. Following the signing of the separate peace with Germany at Brest-Litovsk on March 3, 1918, the Moscow authorities had played on this hope by inviting British, French, Italian, and American military officers to help them organize a Red army. In the course of the negotiations, the British and French had become intrigued with the possibility of persuading the Soviet rulers to invite an Allied expedition into Russia to help them against the Germans.[61]

On April 16, for example, the British ambassador to the United States told Secretary Lansing that the war cabinet had instructed Lockhart, and would like the American government to instruct Robins, to try to work out "an agreement in general principles" between Russia and the Allies. Under its terms, Russia would: raise a national army and guerrilla forces against Germany; prevent supplies and war matériel from going to Germany and Austria; keep control of Transcaucasia and the Black Sea; and request "naval and military assistance from the Allies," at least via Vladivostok and, if needed, via Murmansk as well.

Just at this time, when the Allied consuls in Moscow had become convinced that Bolshevik agreement was in sight, the Japanese landed at Vladivostok, thereby reawakening in the mind of the Soviet leaders the very lively fear of a hostile Japanese expedition to Siberia. The whole plan of accommodation with the Soviet government and of an unopposed Allied expedition was threatened. On

[61] See, for example, the British note sent to President Wilson, April 25, 1918, in R. H. B. Lockhart, *Memoirs of a British Agent* (London, 1932), pp. 135–37; and Sadoul to Thomas, March 30, 1918, quoted in Jacques Sadoul, *Notes sur la Révolution Bolchevique (October 1917–Janvier 1919)* (Paris: Editions de la Sirène, 1919), p. 272, and thence quoted in Bunyan, *Intervention, Civil War, and Communism,* p. 63.

April 6, as the British commander, acting on previous instructions, landed a covering unit, the British, French, and American diplomatic representatives in Moscow called on Foreign Commissar Chicherin to assure him the landing had been made solely to protect Japanese nationals.[62]

On April 11 the British ambassador called on Japan's vice minister of foreign affairs, Shidehara, and handed him a note in which the British government deplored the landing, or rather the misunderstanding engendered by it, stating that, "if this misunderstanding did not exist or if it could be peacefully resolved, Trotsky would probably agree to invite Allied intervention in the interests of Russia." [63] His Majesty's government was very anxious, therefore, to have the misunderstanding cleared up; and to that end it had instructed the commander of the *Suffolk* to confer with his Japanese and American colleagues about ways "to bring about a peaceful understanding with the local authorities concerning the local disturbances which have necessitated the landing of the marines and to have the marines withdraw." The note pointed out that the American government had been notified, and the British consul in Moscow had been instructed to assure the Bolshevik government, "This landing has no connection with any intervention in Siberia, it being only to protect the lives and property of foreign Allied nationals in Vladivostok." It asked that Admiral Katō be given similar instructions. The Ministry of Foreign Affairs promptly transmitted a copy of the memorandum to the Navy Ministry, and the latter sent a summary to Admiral Katō at Vladivostok.

On April 17 the United States government also made a direct appeal to Japan. The Japanese chargé in Washington was assured the United States understood that the landing had no connection with a Siberian expedition and hoped that the troops would be withdrawn as soon as the matter was settled.

No doubt few Japanese placed any reliance on the possibility that the Bolsheviks would ever request an Allied expedition. The Western powers, reported Lieutenant Colonel Furuya, military

---

[62] "Urajiosutoku ni okeru Rikusentai," *JGK, RKI, SC*, I.
[63] *Ibid.*; and Japan, Kaigun Gunreibu, *Senshi*, I, 160–61.

attaché at Moscow, "can hardly be expected to achieve their objective. They are basing their actions on wishful thinking and on the selfish protection of their own interests." [64] What was of great moment to the Japanese government was its strong desire not only to maintain, but if possible to strengthen, its understanding with the Western powers.

Similar advice was also received from the Soviet Republic. On April 17, in accordance with instructions, Secretary Ueda Sentaro in Moscow called on Karakhan, vice commissar for foreign affairs, to express his "personal views" that the landing at Vladivostok had been made solely to police the city and not to interfere in Russia's internal affairs in any way. Karakhan retorted that the landing had been completely unjustified and demanded the withdrawal of the troops. Ueda then called on Voznesensky, chief of the Oriental Section of the Foreign Commissariat, with the same results. On April 22 he talked again with Karakhan, this time with greater success, for he was advised that if Japan really wished to settle the trouble, it should deal with the local soviet authorities in Vladivostok and should withdraw its forces.

Almost identical advice was received on April 25 from Navy Councilor Yamagawa.[65] His report shows a significant change in the thinking of at least some of the navy officials. He fully supported the observation of the consul general and the naval commander that the moderate-controlled duma and zemstvo organs, with which the Allies had been dealing, were unable to maintain order; indeed, it could be said that "local political authority has not been established." "It is," he argued, "inevitable sooner or later that the Bolsheviks will seize power." This being true, Yamagawa proposed that the best way to protect foreign nationals was to withdraw the marines and to permit the Bolsheviks to take over political power. They should then be held responsible for "maintaining local order." He recognized that such an action would excite the Japanese residents and would confuse the Russians, who up to that time gen-

[64] Lieutenant Colonel Furuya to vice chief of army general staff, April 11, 1918. *JGK, RKI, SK, EBFK,* II, 606–10.
[65] Text of his report, dated April 25, 1918, in Japan, Kaigun Gunreibu, *Senshi,* I, 162–63.

erally believed that Japan was supporting the moderates. Therefore, lest such confusion embarrass Japan in any future expedition, he urged that, when the marines were withdrawn, the statement of Kikuchi and Katō be reemphasized: Japan had no intention of intervening in Russia's internal affairs. Of course, when the Bolsheviks took over, "we must be ready to send westward the munitions which are piled up in the vicinity of Vladivostok."

In view of the original decisions and subsequent advice, it is not surprising that on April 25 the soviet was allowed to take over Vladivostok. On that day Krasnoshchekov, the chairman of the Soviet Far Eastern Executive Committee at Khabarovsk, with four other committee members marched into a meeting of the zemstvo council in Vladivostok and demanded that it hand over its business to the committee.[66] When the zemstvo council refused, the soviet representatives called in six Red Guards who were waiting outside. The council was forced to withdraw. Although it refused to cede its authority to the soviet committee, it made no effort to resist. Five days later the acting chairman of the zemstvo council called on each consul in the city, informing him that the council was no longer able to perform its functions and asking that hereafter he take up with city hall all negotiations concerning the maintenance of order. This the consular corps had already decided to do on the day following the soviet putsch. The soviet take-over was completed on May 2, when the executive committee of the city soviet decided to abolish the city duma and assigned its duties to one of its members, Comrade Nikiforov. Every major city in far eastern Siberia was now in Soviet hands.

[66] "Urajiosutoku ni okeru Rikusentai Jōriku Temmatsu" (as of May 8, 1918), *JGK, RKI, SC,* I.

VIII. THE ARMY'S PROBLEMS

During March and April, 1918, the Japanese army urged the government to restrain the navy in its action at Vladivostok and worked to force the foreign minister out of office, not from opposition to an expedition to Siberia but in obedience to Yamagata and because more time was needed for its own necessary preparations. The army leaders were particularly convinced that, first, defense agreements must be signed with China and some kind of Russian government must be organized in Manchuria. All during the crisis in Tokyo, the army worked feverishly and with high hopes to complete these preliminaries. Would it not, after all, be dealing with its own hand-picked protégés: Tuan in Peking, Kalmykov in the Ussuri valley, Horvat in Harbin, and Semenov in Manchouli?

Delay of the Defense Agreements

With Tuan Ch'i-jui's return to the Chinese premiership on March 23, the Japanese military leaders were sure the desired military and naval agreements could now be secured. In accord with the notes exchanged on March 25, 1918, the Japanese sent delegations to Peking to carry on the negotiations. The Japanese army delegates immediately offered a draft agreement, which the central authorities in Tokyo had drawn up to serve as a guide.

DRAFT MILITARY AGREEMENT
BETWEEN THE CHINESE AND JAPANESE ARMIES
FOR JOINT DEFENSE[1]

Basic Principles of the Agreement

It is agreed that the military agreement between the Japanese and Chinese armies will be based on the following principles:

1. In order to fulfill the aim of joint action, the armies of both countries will endeavor in this agreement to accept as their usual practice the principle of military cooperation.

2. The fundamental intention of the armies of both countries will be to achieve joint action by each operating in its own special area and not in combination with the other.

3. So as to avoid injuring the honor and self-respect of either country, each country is treated in this agreement on equal and reciprocal terms.

Draft of a Military Agreement between the Japanese and Chinese Armies

Article I. The representatives of the armies of both countries, with the mutual consent of the governments of China and Japan, agree to the following:

Article II. First of all, to strengthen their defenses against the eastward movement of the power of Germany and Austria, the Japanese and Chinese armies will undertake joint military action in accordance with the following policy:

1) The Japanese imperial army will operate mainly in the area from northern Manchuria, eastern Mongolia and the Russian far east to eastern Siberia.

Elements of the Chinese republican army, police and other agencies in this area will coordinate their movements under the direction of the Japanese imperial army authorities.

2) The Chinese republican army will operate mainly in the area from central Mongolia to eastern Siberia and part of it will defend the western Mongolian and Sinkiang area.

Elements of the Japanese imperial army in this area will coordinate their activities under the direction of the Chinese republican army authorities.

Article III. In accordance with the final items under (1) and (2),

---

[1] Japan, Sambō Hombu, *Taishō Shichi-nen naishi Jūichi-nen Shiberia Shuppei-shi* (1924), I, Appendix 5, 58–61.

that country's forces which have their main strength in the area will be responsible for transporting and distributing men, horses, and supplies to the cooperating military units of the other country and to the various military agencies attached to them.

Article IV. When operations are begun, both Japan and China will order and instruct their military units and other officials, especially those in the areas of military operations, to seek to achieve the common objective by working together in mutual friendship.

Article V. In accordance with (1) and (2) of Article II, when the Japanese imperial army, disposed within the territory of the Chinese republic, has completed its operations, it will be immediately withdrawn.

Article VI. In order to insure the perfect conduct of joint action, when operations are begun or when it becomes necessary, the army authorities of both China and Japan will carry out the following items:

1) In order to facilitate cooperation in the movement and supply of the forces, each country will send competent officials to the necessary military agencies of the other country and will be responsible for negotiating with them.

2) In order to insure that the movement and supply of the forces will be quick and certain, various transportation and communications facilities will be used in common and, where necessary, new installations will be built.

3) If necessary, the Japanese empire will supply weapons and other munitions to the Chinese republic and the Chinese republic will supply the raw materails for the weapons and other munitions to the Japanese empire.

4) If it is necessary to supplement each other's lacks in order to carry on successful operations, one country will send command, supply, and other expert military advisers to assist the other.

5) Intelligence agencies will be set up in strategic places and maps and reports of military value will be mutually exchanged; the activity of intelligence agencies will be planned so as to be mutually convenient for communications.

6) A military code to be used in common will be decided upon.

Article VII. The details necessary to put this agreement into practice will be agreed to by persons appointed by the military authorities of both countries.

Article VIII. As the military operations outlined in Article II develop or as world conditions, particularly the situation in east Asia, changes, the Japanese and Chinese supreme military authorities and various other agencies will cooperate in determining what policy is to be followed.

Article IX. In order to achieve definitely the object of the above articles, the Japanese and Chinese army authorities, always working together harmoniously, will assist each other unhesitatingly even in planning tactics and organizing units.

Article X. This agreement and the stipulations appended to it will be treated with strict secrecy by both China and Japan.

Article XI. This agreement will become effective after it has been signed by the representatives of the Japanese and Chinese armies and ratified by each government. To abrogate this agreement, at least six months' notice will be required.

So sweeping were these proposals that even the government of Tuan Ch'i-jui objected. General Chin, of the Chinese delegation, would not accept responsibility and referred the draft to the cabinet for a decision. The cabinet hesitated. Foreign Minister Lu Cheng-hsiang in particular opposed the draft. Meanwhile, the provincial military governors were informed; and somehow news of the negotiations leaked to the general public, who were already inflamed by the "twenty-one demands." So great was the furor that the life of the government seemed threatened.

Although details of the negotiations are lacking, a comparison of the agreements as signed with the draft submitted by the Japanese military delegation suggests that during the March–April crisis in Tokyo, the Chinese fought desperately for a revision of at least five important provisions.[2] One of these was the Japanese demand for military control of northern Manchuria and eastern Mongolia (Article II). The Chinese themselves hoped to regain control of this area and had already sent many fresh troops into the railway zone for precisely this reason. In the end, the Japanese were willing to concede that the question of "military areas" and "military operations" could be postponed until "necessary" and that the decision could then be made "in accordance with the military strength of each country."[3]

---

[2] The text, in English, of the Sino-Japanese joint-defense military agreement signed on May 16, 1918, is presented as Appendix N, of the present volume and that of the joint defensive naval agreement, signed May 19, 1918, as Appendix O.

[3] See Article 6, Appendix N.

The Chinese were fearful that draft Article III might provide an excuse for the Japanese army to take over the Chinese Eastern Railway. To block this, they insisted that in place of the disputed article the provision be explicitly stated that the "management and protection" of the railway would not be affected by the military agreement.[4] They were also troubled by the provision in draft Article VI, item 4, that, "if necessary," Japan would send "expert military advisers." Apparently fearful lest such advisers come when they were not wanted, the Chinese demanded they be sent not simply "if necessary," but only "if one country requests" their services.[5] There was concern about several of the more general articles, especially those which seemed to go beyond the necessities of the immediate agreement; namely, that the two countries should "accept as their usual practice the principle of military cooperation" (draft Basic Principle 1), and also that "as the situation in east Asia changes, the Japanese and Chinese supreme military authorities and various other agencies will cooperate in determining what policy is to be followed" (draft Article VIII). Lastly, the Chinese seem to have been concerned lest the Japanese begin operations at their own convenience and insist on prolonging the agreement to the prejudice of Chinese interests. To conciliate the Chinese, the Japanese negotiators agreed to revise this provision to read that "the time for commencing actual military operations shall be decided by the highest military organs of the two countries," and that the agreement itself would "become null and void as soon as the military operations of China and Japan against the enemy countries of Germany and Austria come to an end." [6] Still the Chinese would not sign, and that is where matters stood when Motono resigned from office on April 23.

---

[4] See Article 8, Appendix N. This principle was adhered to in the supplementary military agreement, signed on September 6, 1918, and stating that while Japan should assume "responsibility" for transporting Japanese and Chinese forces on the South Manchurian Railway, arrangements for the transportation of these and Czechoslovak forces on the Chinese Eastern Railway should be negotiated by a joint Sino-Japanese organ (including Allied delegates, if Allied forces operated in the area) with the Chinese Eastern Railway authorities.

[5] See Article 7 (f), Appendix N.

[6] See Article 11, Appendix N.

The Failure of Kalmykov

Meanwhile, the Japanese military authorities had intensified their preparations in Vladivostok and Harbin. In late March, Tanaka's Siberia Planning Committee decided to strengthen Lieutenant Colonel Sakabe's organization in Vladivostok by detailing to him Engineering Major Samura Masao and five other officers.[7] The army thus hoped to put itself in a better position should the growing crisis occasion a landing of troops. It could also keep a closer check on Ivan Kalmykov and Peter Derber.

Kalmykov's situation was desperate. He had gone to Iman on March 9, promising to mobilize the Ussuri Cossacks. The British had been so hopeful that, on March 11, Ambassador Greene had broached to Foreign Minister Motono the question of sending Kalmykov supplies.[8] But Kalmykov's brave words came to naught. The Ussuri Cossacks refused to respond to his call. On March 27 the British considered strengthening Kalmykov's appeal by having their consul at Harbin purchase seed corn to supply the Ussuri Cossacks and inquired of the Japanese government what its attitude might be.[9]

It soon became clear that more than seed corn was needed. Not only did Kalmykov fail to attract any Cossack support, but he was forced to flee to the border town of Grodekovo, and, finally, to seek refuge across the border in Pogranichnaia. On April 2 the Japanese government gave the British government its answer.[10] It had "no objection whatsoever" if the British wished to procure seed corn for the Ussuri Cossacks and would, itself, be interested in helping them if success could be "reasonably assured." But "the Ussuri Cossacks are not sufficiently consolidated to present a united front in any issues of national or international importance.

---

[7] Japan, Sambō Hombu, *Shiberia Shuppei-shi,* III, Appendix VI, 22–23.

[8] Confidential memorandum from the British embassy, Tokyo, to the Japanese Ministry of Foreign Affairs, March 11, 1918 (English text), *JGK, RKI, HK,* I.

[9] Confidential memorandum from the British embassy, Tokyo, to the Japanese Ministry of Foreign Affairs, March 27, 1918 (English text), *ibid.,* I.

[10] Motono to British embassy in Japan, April 2, 1918, *ibid.,* II.

Nor has their authority been definitely established in any part of the Russian territory to the exclusion of alien or opposing influences." Accordingly, supplies intended for the Cossacks would very probably fall into Bolshevik hands.

On April 16, 1918, the British government informed the Japanese government that it had decided to give up the seed-corn idea. Thereafter, events would be allowed "to take their natural course." [11]

Rejection of Derber

While Kalmykov's movement was fizzling in the hinterland, another movement was gaining ground in Vladivostok: that of Peter Derber. Following the dispersal of the provisional Siberian duma at Tomsk on February 8, 1918, some duma leaders had remained there, while others scattered to various cities across Siberia. A particularly energetic group of Social Revolutionaries set up a west Siberia emissariat of the Siberian government, with a central military staff at Novonikolaevsk and related military organizations in other cities.[12] Another group of those who had escaped issued a public proclamation that the duma was still the legal authority in Siberia and met secretly to elect a twenty-member Provisional Government of Autonomous Siberia, with Peter Derber as minister-president. Derber and others of this group fled east to Irkutsk, whence, after failing in an effort to set up a similar emissariat for east Siberia, they went quickly to Harbin and sought the support of the Allies. Derber and Moravskii remained for a month or so in Harbin and then moved on to Vladivostok, leaving behind L. A. Ustrugov, who had been assistant minister of communications under the provisional government, and Staal, chief public procurator of the Moscow court of appeals under the same government.

[11] Memorandum from the British embassy in Tokyo to the Japanese Ministry of Foreign Affairs, April 16, 1918, enclosed in a letter from Ambassador Greene to Vice Minister Shidehara, April 17, 1918, *ibid.*, II.

[12] V. V. Maksakov and A. Turunov, eds., *Khronika grazhdanskoi voiny v Sibiri (1917–1918)* (Moscow: Gosizdat, 1926), p. 58; and P. S. Parfenov, *Uroki proshlogo, grazhdanskaia voina v Sibiri 1918, 1919, 1920 gg.* (Harbin, 1921), p. 23.

Neither the British, the French, nor the Russian officials in Peking were attracted to the Derber group. The French government had been studying the situation of the provisional government since February 16, 1918, when the French commercial agent at Irkutsk reported adversely on an appeal by Peter Derber for a loan.[13] After extensive talks in Harbin and Peking, French representatives told the Derber group it could give them no aid unless they put themselves under Horvat's leadership.[14] Apparently the British agreed, for when Ustrugov came to Peking on March 28, Sir John Jordan made no move even to meet him.[15] And the Russian minister, Prince Kudashev, urged that support should be given to Horvat alone.[16]

In reporting these views, the Japanese representatives added their wholehearted agreement. Consul General Satō in Harbin told Horvat on March 17 that, "since the [provisional Siberian] government had been organized by socialists, it was not sound," and that the best course would be for him to form a new provisional government under his own leadership, getting "suitable members of the former one to participate in it." [17] In a dispatch on March 26, the consul general expressed aversion to the Derber group at greater length:

It is clear from their declaration, printed in the newspapers here on March 23 that they are extreme socialists, for, before the assembly meets, they would seize authority in the Siberian government, would set about making the land common property and nationalizing mining

[13] V. V. Maksakov, "K istorii interventsii v Sibiri," *Krasnyi arkhiv* (Moscow), No. 34, 1929, p. 158, cited in John Albert White, *The Siberian Intervention* (Princeton: Princeton University Press, 1950), p. 105.

[14] According to the French military attaché in Peking, Saitō to Uehara, March 28, 1918, *JGK, RKI, HK*, I; and according to the French minister, Saitō to Tanaka, March 29, 1918, *ibid.*, II.

[15] Saitō to Tanaka, March 29, 1918, *ibid.*, II.

[16] Hayashi to Motono, March 28, 1918, *ibid.*, I. Ustrugov seems to have held conversations also with the American minister in Peking, and Derber may have talked with the American consul general in Harbin, but their reaction is not known. V. D. Vilenskii (-Sibiriakov), *Chernaia godina sibirskoi reaktsii* (*interventsiia v Sibiri*) (Moscow: V. Ta. I. K. Sovetov R.S.K. Deputatov, 1919), p. 8, on the basis of the documents found by the Soviet authorities in the possession of M. A. Kolobov, April 21, 1918.

[17] Satō to Motono, March 17, 1918, *JGK, RKI, HK*, II.

and industry. Therefore, there is no difference between their principles and those of the Bolsheviks. Not only do they not represent the views of the majority of the Russian people, but there can be no doubt that the empire would be foolish to aid persons who support such dangerous thoughts.[18]

The advice was unanimous: Derber's request for aid should be turned down. Japanese interventionists in the cabinet must also have had their own reasons for accepting this advice. Doubtless they considered Derber ideologically inacceptable. At the same time, support was already on its way for Semenov and the Horvat clique, so that now to support the Derber group separately would simply encourage civil strife among the anti-Bolsheviks and increase the difficulties of forming a united organization against the Soviet regime. They could, of course, have urged Horvat to subordinate his own to Derber's organization. But, so far as they could be sure, Derber had no organization and certainly no seat of power and no troops; and the forces then being built up at Harbin and Manchouli were not likely to follow Derber. Moreover, the Japanese interventionists had no reason to believe that Derber would be any more willing an agent of their designs than was Horvat. On March 30, 1918, the Army General Staff Headquarters and the Ministry of Foreign Affairs in Tokyo each issued instructions to refuse separate aid to the provisional Siberian government.[19] If its adherents wished support, they should accept Horvat's leadership.

Derber seems to have anticipated this decision, for he had already moved his headquarters to Vladivostok. There the guns of the Allied fleet were creating another privileged sanctuary, from which anti-Bolshevik refugees could lay plans for a return to power and in which the prevailing mood was anti-Horvat, democratic, and socialist. The influential moderate elements, Admiral Katō reported, regarded Horvat as "a holdover from the monarchist party" and were convinced that "a government erected with the aid of foreign troops could not command the confidence of the general public."[20] Mayor Agarev confirmed Katō's report, telling Lieu-

[18] Satō to Motono, March 26, 1918, *ibid.*, II.
[19] Motono to Hayashi, March 30, 1918, *ibid.*, II.
[20] Katō Kanji to Tochinai and Yamaya, April 3, 1918, *ibid.*, II.

tenant Colonel Sakabe the following day that "a Horvat government would not represent any local organs and would be nothing more than a private gathering of like-minded men." [21]

The Derber group with its promise of a representative Siberian government seemed to attract most of the anti-Bolshevik leaders in Vladivostok. In early April its ascendancy was strengthened by the support of a number of businessmen and industrialists under the leadership of the president of the chamber of commerce.[22] The Japanese and British landing at Vladivostok on April 5 stimulated Derber to step up his activities. His Provisional Government of Autonomous Siberia added to its cabinet the former commissar for the Far East, N. A. Rusanov, and three other members from Amur, Maritime, and Kamchatka territories.[23] As it grew in strength, it continued to seek the cooperation of the anti-Bolshevik Russian leaders in Harbin and Peking and the recognition and support of the Allies abroad. Three emissaries were sent from Vladivostok to establish liaison with Horvat, and apparently various coalition arrangements were proposed, but no agreement could be reached.[24]

Continued appeals were made to Japan in spite of the army's earlier lack of interest. Members of the Derber group in Vladivostok approached Lieutenant Colonel Sakabe and Rear Admiral Katō.[25] On April 6, "Prime Minister Derber" and "Secretary Moravsky" wired Foreign Minister Motono in Tokyo directly, outlining the Siberian government's aims:

Immediate Siberian government's aims are, first, establishing legal order, securing personal property, inviolability [sic] and second, active opposition to Bolsheviks in order to establish legal power all-Russian

[21] Sakabe to Tanaka, April 4, 1918, *ibid.*, II.

[22] Sakabe to Tanaka, March 17, 1918, *ibid.*, II, and Japan, Sambō Hombu, *Shiberia Shuppei-shi*, III, 1060.

[23] Sakabe to Tanaka, April 8, 1918, *JGK, RKI, HK,* II.

[24] Sakabe to Tanaka, April 8, 1918, *ibid.*, II. One proposed coalition government which seems to have been discussed, but was rejected by Horvat, would have made him chief executive of a government including Putilov, Ustrugov, Vostrotin, Taskin, Erakov, and Kolchak. This proposal suggests that not all supporters of the Siberian government were unwilling to accept Horvat's leadership. Japan, Kaigun Gunreibu, "Kaichō Rohō, Dai 73 Go: Urajio Tsūshin" (as of April 19, 1918), dated May 2, 1918, *ibid.*, II.

[25] Japan, Sambō Hombu, *Shiberia Shuppei-shi*, III, 1083–84.

constituent assembly; third, defense of political, economical independence, territorial integrity of Siberia; fourth, meeting all-Siberian constituent assembly; fifth, active resistance to Bolshevik-German peace; sixth, reestablishment of good relations which Allied friendly powers, based on existing treaties, agreements; seventh, taking all measures to prevent further German advance in Russian territory.[26]

This was a program believed by its authors to "coincide" with Japan's "interests" and therefore meriting Japan's "active assistance." Personal appeals were being made in Peking by Ustrugov and Staal. In mid-April several emissaries were sent to negotiate in Tokyo.[27]

Japan's representatives in Vladivostok were favorably impressed. Rear Admiral Katō and Lieutenant Colonel Sakabe seem to have felt that Japan would do well to hedge its bet on Horvat by backing the Derber government also; from Harbin, however, Satō and Horvat continued to denounce the Derberites as socialists in disguise and hardly less dangerous than the Bolsheviks.[28] The central military authorities in Tokyo decided to follow their original decision: to refuse all aid to the Derberites unless they subordinated themselves to Horvat. No doubt the army's rejection of Derber was one of the strong reasons for its agreeing to limit the landing operations at Vladivostok.

Derber may also have appealed to the American government and possibly to the other Allied governments, but the appeal, if listened to, cannot have been generously answered.[29] The rejection of Derber is instructive, for it illustrates the process of elimination by which the Japanese military leaders selected Horvat.

The Japanese were not impressed by Horvat's abilities. After looking over the field, Nakajima reported to General Tanaka that

[26] Telegram (in English) to foreign minister in Tokyo, from Harbin, signed by "Prime Minister Derber, member council imperial, Secretary Moravsky," dated April 6, 1918, *JGK, RKI, HK,* II.

[27] Satō to Motono, April 13, 1918, *ibid.,* II. The names of the emissaries are given as "Peter Iakovlevich" (which suggests Peter Iakovlevich Derber) and "David Gorbunov."

[28] Satō to Motono, April 13, 1918, *ibid.,* II.

[29] Katō to Tochinai and Yamaya, April 24, 1918, *ibid.,* II; and Z. Karpenko, *Grazhdanskaia voina v Dal'nevostochnom Krae (1918–1922)* (Khabarovsk, 1934), cited in White, *Siberian Intervention,* p. 104.

there was "no really able man in the Far East." [30] They were all, he judged, "old and crafty, lacking in resolution and courage." What continued to recommend General Horvat to Japan's attention was not that he was a leader around whom all anti-Bolsheviks could be expected to rally nor that he was an able civil administrator or military commander, but simply that he could be expected to obey Japanese orders. He did not share Ustrugov's vice of being pro-American, nor Kolchak's vice of being pro-British, nor Putilov's vice of being pro-French.[31] He seemed to be "a subservient individual" who would "bow to whatever decision" Japan might take.[32]

Horvat's Delay

The difficulty with this estimate of Horvat is that he did not bow very readily. Throughout March, 1918, as we have seen, the Japanese representatives had been pressing him steadily to form a government, and he had just as steadily refused to do so until Japan would agree to send troops to his aid. Nakajima and his associates had become convinced that he meant it, and on March 17 they had urged the central military authorities to send troops to northern Manchuria immediately. The authorities in Tokyo were not ready to take that final step.

For one reason, they believed that the small forces recommended by Nakajima and the other Japanese representatives at Harbin would be totally inadequate to establish Horvat in Siberia. For another, many of the prerequisites to a successful expedition on a sufficiently large scale had not yet been met, especially the completion of the communications and supply arrangements in the railway zone, the modernization of the army, the equipping and training of the Semenov detachment, and the conclusion of a joint

[30] Nakajima to Tanaka, March 1, 1918, *JGK, RKI, HK,* I.

[31] Mutō to Tanaka, May 8, 1918, *ibid.,* II; Hayashi to Motono, April 6, 1918, *ibid.,* II.

[32] Nakajima to Japanese Army General Staff Headquarters, May 19, 1918, *ibid.,* II.

military agreement with China. A third reason was a genuine fear
lest an uninvited expedition would arouse the mass of the Russian
people against Japan and the very government it hoped to support.

Following Yamagata's argument, Tanaka told Nakajima in his
reply of March 23: the Imperial government could not publicly
encourage the establishment of a new government "by using its
military forces beforehand, for that would give rise to a suspicion
that Japan has territorial ambition. That is false, but it would result
in unnecessarily arousing the hatred of the Russians and would
drive them into the hands of the Germans, which would contradict
our main purpose." [33] Although Tanaka did not say so, it was
equally true that such a suspicion would undoubtedly arouse the
hostility of the Americans as well and would thus destroy the understanding which the empire was laboring so hard to build. Moreover,
the Siberia Planning Committee must have been very conscious of
the fact that an expedition proposed for no better reason than to
encourage a refugee Russian clique to declare itself a government
would get little hearing from the Imperial government and would
surely be rejected by the Advisory Council on Foreign Relations,
where there was vigorous opposition to any expedition except one
undertaken in strict self-defense or possibly in response to a united
Allied request.

Following a conference with Premier Terauchi, General Tanaka
told Nakajima that the anti-Bolsheviks would have to help themselves before Japan could help them. The leaders must redouble
their efforts to seek out "those persons who oppose the extreme
communism of the Bolsheviks and who are trying to encourage
moderate action"; they must organize these people into autonomous
bodies and unite them under a "firm temporary government."
Nakajima and the other Japanese representatives were to tell Horvat: Japan will send troops, but you must set up your own government first.

Partly to emphasize this fact, the army, at the end of March,
sent to Harbin one of its most competent staff officers, General

[33] Japan, Sambō Hombu, *Shiberia Shuppei-shi*, III, 1056–58.

Mutō Nobuyoshi.[34] At the same time Captain Kuroki Shinkei was sent to work with Semenov.[35] Mutō joined Nakajima and the others in urging Horvat to organize a government, but Horvat continued to delay. His first response was simply to reshuffle his military organization.

Sometime toward the end of March, 1918, Horvat appointed a newly arrived officer from the Ussuri region, General Pleshkov, to be commander in chief of the Chinese Eastern Railway troops.[36] Pleshkov announced his determination not only to try to unify the direction of the Semenov, Kalmykov, and Orlov detachments, but also to recruit a basic corps of his own.

Recognizing that "the number-one necessity of the day" was "to unify the military groups and to maintain an inseparable connection between them and Japan" or "by giving these forces definite protection and assistance to gather the actual authority into the hands of Japan," [37] the army gave Pleshkov its immediate support. Nakajima promptly supplied him with 100,000 rubles and 20,000 rifles;[38] and Pleshkov set to work vigorously, but his success was nothing more than slight. He was able to recruit only a small motley corps composed of "Chinese soldiers, mounted bandits, Koreans, and Mongolians."

Captain Orlov also showed promise at this time and, to encourage him, some of the ordnance sent to the Society for the Protection of the Fatherland and the Constituent Assembly was transferred to his detachment. In addition, eight instructors returning from Manchouli were detailed to give instruction to his troops in the use of machine guns.

The military structure he proposed to build was as follows.

[34] *Ibid.*, III, Appendix VI, 22–23. Mutō (1868–1933) was later to distinguish himself as commander of the Third Division in the Siberian expedition in 1921, vice chief of the Army General Staff Headquarters in 1922, commander of the Kwantung army and inspector general of military education in 1926, and ambassador plenipotentiary to Manchukuo in 1932. He died in 1933, a baron and a field marshal.

[35] *Ibid.*, III, 1079.

[36] Japan, Sambō Hombu, *Shiberia Shuppei-shi*, III, 1059; and Spencer to Lansing, March 29, 1918, *USFR, 1918, Russia*, II, 93.

[37] Japan, Sambō Hombu, "Sanchō Tokugō, Rokoku Dai 4 Gō" (as of the last ten days of April, 1918), *JGK, RKI, HK*, II.

[38] Japan, Sambō Hombu, *Shiberia Shuppei-shi*, III, 1059.

CHINESE EASTERN RAILWAY ADMINISTRATION CHAIN OF COMMAND
(late April, 1918)

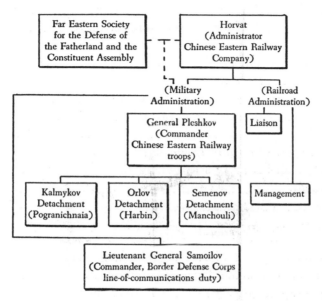

Sources: Japan, Sambō Hombu, "Sanchō Tokugō, Rokoku Tokugo, Rokoku Dai 4 Gō" (as of the last ten days of April, 1918), *JGK, RKI, HK,* II; Japan, Rikugunshō, "Jikyoku ni Renkei seru Tōshin Ensen no Genjo" (undated, but appears from the contents to be a description of conditions in late April, 1918), *JGK, RKI, TT,* I, 0260–98.

Nevertheless, the Japanese support was small, its effects were meager, and friction was growing. Finally, Horvat began to wonder if his strategy would work, if he could secure a troop commitment without taking more decisive action himself. He decided to feel out official opinion in Japan itself.

Early in April, Secretary Crabbe was sent from the Russian legation in Peking to Tokyo.[39] On April 13 he conferred with the vice minister of foreign affairs, Shidehara Kijuro, and with the vice chief of Army General Staff Headquarters, General Tanaka. Shidehara would say no more than that Japan could only act in accord with the Allies. Tanaka went further to assure Crabbe that Japanese troops would be forthcoming, but only after Horvat had established

[39] *Ibid.,* III, 1060.

his government. Other representatives followed Crabbe. In a few weeks, a three-man mission left Harbin, consisting of Vostrotin (a member of the third and fourth dumas from Yenisei Territory and for a time minister of food in the Kerensky government), Nikolaevich (a member of the Vladivostok chamber of commerce), and Chechikov (an influential mine operator from Trans-Baikal Territory).[40] From both these missions the report was the same: for the time at least, Japan would send money and arms but not men.

Convinced by this news and, no doubt, worried lest the Japanese shift their support to Derber in Vladivostok, Horvat decided to delay no longer. On April 18 he left Harbin to confer, as he announced, with his backers in Peking "about the organization of a government." [41]

Concessions Withheld

Besides insisting that Horvat organize a government before they would send troops, the Japanese military planners wanted other concessions. The primary facilities in the Amur basin were the railways and the telegraph. To secure use of these, Major General Mutō was instructed to confer with Nakajima and then to open confidential negotiations with General Horvat.[42] As the basis of his discussions,[43] he was given a "draft agreement" applying to the Chinese Eastern, Ussuri, Amur, and Trans-Baikal railways. The agreement provided that, if Japanese troops should move into the eastern Siberian area, the Russian railways would provide the essential military transportation and telegraph lines for the exclusive use of Japanese forces. The Japanese army, in its turn, would not only pay for these services, but would transfer as much soft

[40] Satō to Motono, April 19, 1918, *JGK, RKI, HK,* II.
[41] Japan, Sambō Hombu, *Shiberia Shuppei-shi,* III, 1062; and Satō to Motono, April 19, 1918, *JGK, RKI, HK,* II. The date of Horvat's departure is given as April 17, 1918, in Baron Aleksei Budberg, "Dnevnik," *Arkhiv russkoi revoliutsii,* XIII, 201; but the Japanese had better access to such information and I have followed the Japanese account.
[42] Japan, Sambō Hombu, *Shiberia Shuppei-shi,* IV, 692.
[43] For an English translation of the text of this "draft agreement" see Appendix K, below.

coal as possible, provide tools and repair materials, and be responsible for maintenance of the lines. In addition, railroad and communications technicians, together with commissioned officers under the command of a representative of the Japanese Imperial forces, were to be assigned to each railroad administrative department, transport office, important railroad station, and communications administrative department.

But Mutō was too late. On March 27, the day following the issuance of his instructions, Colonel Stevens of the American Advisory Commission of Railway Experts, had succeeded in concluding an agreement with Horvat before Mutō could even open negotiations. The agreement provided for the installation of "a few of the American railway operatives at Harbin on the Chinese Eastern Railway only, to instruct railway operatives." [44] Over 100 members of the Stevens Railway Service Corps were reported already in Harbin.[45] As the American railwaymen moved into the machine shops and out to the dispatch offices along the lines to east and west and particularly to the south of Harbin, the Japanese military agents, Railway Board, and diplomatic representatives became more and more concerned.

Nakajima advised Horvat on March 30 that he ought to postpone introducing American technicians to the lines east of Harbin.[46] A month later Minister Baron Hayashi pointed out from Peking that the American railroad activity was in fact, if not in name, an act of intervention against the Bolsheviks and that, by it, America was building up a strong position in north Manchuria vis-à-vis Japan.[47] In a detailed report on April 30, the councilor of the Japanese Railway Board, Kanai Kiyoshi, expressed this apprehension even more clearly.[48] Reviewing the originally announced objective of the corps as a friendly effort to help Russia against the

[44] U.S. Consul C. K. Moser, at Harbin, to Foreign Minister Motono (English text), April 1, 1918, *JGK, RKI, SB,* pp. 417–20.
[45] Kanai to Gotō, president of the (Japanese) Railway Board, March 25, 1918, *ibid.,* pp. 325–27.
[46] Mutō to Tanaka, March 30, 1918, *ibid.,* p. 405.
[47] Hayashi to Gotō, April 28, 1918, *ibid.,* pp. 428–30.
[48] Kanai Kiyoshi, councilor of the Railway Board, "Beikoku Tetsudōtai ni kansuru Hōkoku," dated April 30, 1918, *ibid.,* pp. 493–516.

common enemy, he pointed out that in view of the Brest-Litovsk treaty "this original objective obviously cannot be achieved now." The truth is, he declared, America is seeking a base in north Manchuria.

When Japan began to operate the South Manchurian Railway, there was a question of joint Japanese-American control. Later, America proposed making this railroad independent and after that sought a base from which to operate in Manchuria. Japan always refused, but now America seems to have a suitable base. America, which is supplying great quantities of munitions and railroad materiel, has a commanding position toward Siberia and north Manchuria when compared with Japan, which cannot supply any railroad material. [America] will be strong enough to try to establish a base either in railroads or in mining. From now on, Japan must not neglect giving as much study and attention as possible to these actions.

Major General Mutō did his best to get Horvat to conclude an agreement with him along the lines of the army's draft, but Horvat was adamant. In fact, despite all Japan's efforts to arrange transportation and communication preliminaries for an expedition to Siberia, by the time the expedition was begun, the use of only two facilities had been secured and neither of these was provided by General Horvat. One was granted by General Pleshkov: the use of the wireless station at Harbin. After the capture of the telegraph office at Vladivostok by the soviet, the Japanese at Harbin had no direct means of communication with the naval forces at Vladivostok. The wireless station at Harbin, then under the control of General Pleshkov, offered a solution. Major General Mutō approached Pleshkov and on April 7 secured permission for Japanese technicians to take over the station.[49]

The other concession was granted by the South Manchurian Railway Company: the use of a telegraph line between Harbin and Changchun. When Horvat refused to turn over a line for the exclusive use of the Japanese army or to permit it to build one, the

[49] Japan, Sambō Hombu, *Shiberia Shuppei-shi*, IV, 968–69. Two communications technicians and an engineer were sent up from the Kwantung government general temporarily; in June they were replaced by a nine-man outfit, detailed by the army authorities in Tokyo under Engineering First Lieutenant Takehazama Osamu and attached to Major General Mutō's office in Harbin.

central military authorities finally turned to the South Manchurian Railway Company, which had borrowed a line from the Chinese Eastern Railway for business use. Working through the Kwantung government general army headquarters, they secured permission by the end of May for joint use by the army of the borrowed line; operations were begun on July 1.[50]

There were three probable reasons for Horvat's reluctance to sign with the Japanese. One, of course, was that he had already introduced American technicians all along the railroad and would certainly have been concerned about the effects of introducing rival Japanese experts and military men, even if not actually under official American pressure not to do so. Another reason may have been his feeling that the draft agreement gave Japan too much control. At any rate, the agreement as finally signed was much less sweeping and related only to the Chinese Eastern Railway, cutting down the number of trains to be reserved for Japanese military use, and defining and thereby reducing the scope of transport agencies and telegraph lines affected by its terms. A third and perhaps the most important reason was, no doubt, simply that Horvat was determined to hold out until Japan sent troops, in the hope of thereby hastening the Japanese decision.

These same reasons may also explain why Horvat persisted in refusing further concessions sought by the army. As already explained, a full list of these demands is unavailable, but a secret army report of April 21 indicates what concessions, in addition to the use of railway and telegraph facilities, Horvat was willing to promise in return for "positive assistance." [51] Horvat would "prepare barracks and look for materials in case Japan should advance." He had already agreed to furnish 17 ships, 26 barges, and wharves on the Amur and Sungari rivers, and he could be expected to provide additional facilities if Japan's attitude became more favorable. Lumbering and mining operations would be permitted in various specified areas in the railway zone and in the Amur Territory. Hous-

[50] Ibid., IV, 969.
[51] An unsigned, "secret" report on Japanese War Ministry paper, dated April 21, 1918, entitled "Horuwatto Seifu Sōshiki Enjo no Sekkyoku to narishi igo ni oite Teikoku no etaru Riken," JGK, RKI, TT, I, 0313–21.

ing would be provided for Japanese troops at Harbin, Manchouli, Tsitsihar, Hailar, Ashengho, Hailin, and other locations. "Various manufacturing plants," such as the Harbin municipal electric company, would be turned over to the Japanese. In addition, Horvat would supply "many intelligence reports" and would be willing to grant many other "informal rights and rights for private investment"; it would be easy, for example, to secure visas for Japanese surveying groups. By holding out these attractive prospects, Horvat tried to coax the Japanese army into giving him the troop support he needed.

Semenov's Bid for Leadership

Meanwhile, at the western end of the Chinese Eastern Railway zone the Cossack captain, Gregorii Semenov, was growing restive under Horvat's indecisive leadership. Semenov's first campaign against Chita, begun so energetically on January 16, had ended in defeat at Sharasun on March 5. The Chinese had promptly interned him and had come to an agreement with the Soviets to prevent him and his forces from again crossing the border, at least until April 5. While Semenov objected strenuously to this restriction, he did not really suffer from it. He had not been disarmed, and he was, in effect, being protected by Chinese troops while building up his forces. The Allied aid promised in February began to pour in during March and April (for a summary of the aid given, see Appendix I). Most of the aid was passed on to Semenov.

Since many of the weapons sent were new to Semenov's troops, instruction in their use was needed. Accordingly, the Japanese army detailed 6 officers and 43 enlisted instructors from the Seventh Division to disguise themselves in Russian uniforms and proceed to Manchouli.[52] They were directed by Lieutenant Colonel Kurozawa to teach the battle use of the ordnance but not to participate directly in battle, to complete their assignment quickly and return. General instruction did end on April 3. However, due to the late

[52] Japan, Sambō Hombu, *Shiberia Shuppei-shi*, III, Appendix VI, 21–24. After March 26, 1918, the ordnance instructors were placed under the supervision of Major General Mutō.

arrival of certain pieces of equipment, some instruction continued, for example, in the use of pack harnesses, so that while some instructors returned to their original units, others became involved in Semenov's Onon river offensive. They seem to have helped in the training of Semenovist and, later, of Japanese volunteer troops, right up until the Inter-Allied expedition began.

With this support, mainly Japanese, Semenov began to reorganize, train, and arm his "Special Manchurian Detachment," known popularly, by its Russian initials, as the O.M.O.[53] By April he had built up a force consisting of three cavalry regiments of 400 men each: a Mongol-Buriat cavalry regiment, consisting of Kazakhs, officer-volunteers, and Buriats, and two cavalry regiments of Mongol-Karachens.[54] In addition, he had two groups of infantry, the First Semenov Regiment and the Second Manchurian Regiment; two officer companies, which served as reserve cadres and as command staffs; and two Serbian companies, organized at first as the Third Battalion of the First Semenov Regiment, later reorganized as a separate cavalry division under Lieutenant Colonel Dragovich. For artillery, Semenov had a two-gun heavy battery, two field batteries of four guns each, and a four-gun battery of French mountain guns. In addition, he had four armored trains.

Semenov has left no record of the actual strength of the detachment at this time, but, according to Japanese Army General Staff Headquarters, which had direct contact with it, by the end of April the detachment numbered about two thousand men,[55] comprised approximately as follows:

Officers	350	Buriats	50
Cossacks	350	Mongols	600
Russians	300	Chinese	50
Serbs	250	Koreans	50

[53] O.M.O. stands for the Russian name of the detachment, Osoboi Man'chzhurskii Otriad.

[54] Grigorii Semenov, *O Sebe* (Harbin: Zaria, 1938), pp. 96–98.

[55] Japan, Sambō Hombu, "Sanchō Tokugō, Rokoku Dai 8 Gō (May 11, 1918): Semenov Shitai no Onon Kakan ni mukatte suru Zenshin," *JGK, RKI, HK,* III. Parfenov's assertion that Semenov commanded a "bandit army" of 10,000 men would seem to be based largely on soviet fears at the time. V. Parfenov, *The Intervention in Siberia in 1918–1922* (New York: The Worker's Library Publishers, 1941), pp. 13–14.

The unit was probably not as strong as these figures might suggest, for, with so many different nationalities represented, each kept more or less separate to avoid friction with the others, an integrated command was virtually impossible. Nevertheless, small as it was, Semenov's Special Manchurian Detachment was the strongest indigenous anti-Bolshevik force in the Amur basin.

As Semenov's forces grew, so did his ambitions. Although he had never really accepted Horvat's authority, Semenov had all along been expected by the Japanese to coordinate his activities with those of the other pro-Japanese forces in the railway zone and to recognize a Horvat government if one could be organized. Now he began to talk differently. At Manchouli, speaking to Captain Kuroki Shinkei, and at Harbin to Lieutenant General Araki Sadao, Semenov began to point out that Horvat was a man of "weak and indecisive character" who had "not yet won the confidence of the Cossacks, Buriats, and peasants of Trans-Baikal." [56] The Japanese would do well not to rely solely on him, but instead to act now on their own initiative to "send troops into the Far East." The "band of cutthroats" who "call themselves Bolsheviks" are "aiming to destroy the peace and order of society in general," said Semenov. Having sold out to the Germans in European Russia, they are now moving into the Far East, "arming or preparing to arm the prisoners of war there" and threatening to "Germanize" the area. Their actions, if unchecked, would wreck the hopes of the Russian people for self-government, would "seriously cripple the joint operations of the Allied powers," and would present "a serious postwar threat to Japan's military and economic foundations." Only Japan could destroy this threat. "The best plan now," Semenov concluded, "would be for Japan first to send troops on its own initiative and then, after restoring order in the Far East, to erect a just government, elected by the citizens of the various territories under its control; and meanwhile to appoint a military dictator and entrust

[56] "Semenofu no Horwatto Seifu Jūritsu narabi ni Nihon Shuppei ni kansuru Ikken," by Captain Kuroki Shinkei, with a foreword by Lieutenant General Araki Sadao, dated April 15, 1918, *JGK, RKI, TT,* I, 0289–312.

to him the complete administration until a government is set up."

No doubt there were those among Japan's representatives who favored this bold plan, but the military authorities had decided it was best for a Russian government to be organized before sending Japanese troops, and they well knew that no such rash expedition as Semenov proposed would be approved by the Advisory Council on Foreign Relations; in fact, the Japanese government was no more ready to put troops in the field than Horvat was to organize a government. Semenov now decided to seize the initiative. He would not wait for the Japanese, but would immediately lead his newly organized forces across the border, mobilize the friendly Cossacks, advance on Chita, and there set himself up as a temporary dictator.

In his scheme Semenov must have been greatly encouraged by the action of the Chinese. In spite of any verbal agreement they may have made with the soviet forces on March 5, the Chinese had not reopened the railroad or telegraph facilities across the border; and as the armistice period drew to a close, they sought another conference with the soviet representatives. The soviet commander accepted the invitation and, after moving a force of 1,200 men, said to have included 800 prisoners of war, up to Dauriia on April 5,[57] he led a Russian delegation of eight men to Matsievskaia the following day.[58] Information concerning this conference is even more sparse than for the one in March, but apparently the Chinese refused to open the railroad or telegraph lines in the near future. Lazo renewed his demand that the Chinese treat Semenov as a "political criminal" and that, "in cooperation with Russia, they disarm him or hand him over to Russia or at least in the future not

[57] Mutō (in Manchouli) to Tanaka, April 9, 1918, *JGK, RKI, HK,* I.

[58] Sugino (in Irkutsk) via Satō to Motono, April 14, 1918, *ibid.,* I, transmitting a report of the chairman of the Irkutsk soviet, Yanson. The soviet delegation was made up of Yanson, the commander and chief of staff of the Semenov suppression forces, the chief of staff of the forces at Chita, two representatives of the Trans-Baikal Railway, an officer from the staff in Moscow, and the commander of the Omsk international brigade. The Chinese delegation consisted of the vice chief of staff of the military governor of Heilungkiang province and his aide. Webster and Hicks, the American and British officers then touring Siberia to report on the prisoner-of-war situation, were about to accompany Yanson when the Chinese disapproved.

let him reenter Chinese territory." According to Yanson, who was one of the soviet delegates, "the Chinese refused under any circumstances to permit the Red forces to cross the border"; they also refused to commit themselves concerning Semenov, saying that China's future attitude would have to be decided by the central Chinese authorities in accord with the Allies. Thus, at the expiration of the month-long armistice, the Chinese were ready to permit Semenov to cross into Trans-Baikal Territory if he so chose. Semenov was also convinced by his intelligence reports on soviet activities that he would need to act soon unless he were to face overwhelming odds.

At the end of February, 1918, the second All-Siberian Congress of Soviets had ordered each echelon of the soviet structure to organize a Red Guard or a Red Army unit, and Tsentrosibir' had appointed the young Krasnoiarsk Social Revolutionary–Internationalist, Sergei Lazo, in charge of the front against Semenov.[59] West Siberian, central Siberian, east Siberian, Far Eastern, and all-Siberian military commissariats were set up, but for various reasons local soviet executive committees were slow to organize subordinate sections and did not respond uniformly to Lazo's call for help. Since Trans-Baikalia was most immediately threatened by Semenov, naturally the soviet appeal found its greatest response in this territory. Various territorial conferences and congresses of Social Democratic–Internationalists, village populations, workers, Cossacks, peasants, and Buriat deputies were held to enlist support.[60] Finally, on April 1 the territorial central executive committee called the population to arms. Martial law was declared in Chita and along the Trans-Baikal railroad. In the territory full authority was turned over to a military revolutionary staff, consisting of D. Shilov,

[59] Lazo did not join the Bolshevik party until June, 1918, when he received his card through the Chita organization. O. Lazo, "Komanduiushchii frontom," Vsesoiuznaia Kommunisticheskaia Partiia, Tsentral'nyi Ispolnitel'nyi Komitet, Sekretariat Glavnoi Redaktsii Istorii Grazhdanskoi Voiny v SSSR, *Sergei Lazo, vospominaniia i dokumenty* (Moscow: Gosizdat, 1938), p. 59.

[60] Vsesoiuznaia Kommunisticheskaia Partiia (bol'shevikov). Chita Okruzhnyi Komitet, *Partizany* (Chita, 1929), p. 203; Maksakov and Turunov, *Khronika grazhdanskoi voiny*, p. 61.

I. A. Butin, and N. M. Matveev.[61] A plea for help was sent to
various soviets from Moscow to Vladivostok.[62]

On April 9 the soviet forces resumed skirmishing near the border;
and on April 21 they closed in on Semenov's two Cossack bands
seeking refuge in the upper reaches of the Onon river around
Aksha and Kulusutai.[63] Since these 750 cavalrymen were the largest
organized body of Semenov supporters in the territory and since
their destruction would have had disastrous effects on his prestige
among the Trans-Baikal Cossacks, Semenov decided to respond to
their call for help without waiting for training to be completed. An
advance force of about three hundred Cossacks was sent northward
immediately.

Semenov had not been encouraged by the Japanese to launch
his offensive, but he undoubtedly expected his bold action to gal-
vanize Japanese intervention at last. However, like Horvat, Semenov had underestimated the difficulty of the decision for Japan.
The truth is that his independent action placed Japan's military
planners in a very embarrassing position. If the action failed, it
would greatly weaken the armed forces Japan was trying to build
up. If it succeeded, it would threaten the leadership of Horvat,
whom Japan was supporting. Thus, success or failure would jeopardize Japan's understanding with Great Britain.

In the beginning the British had urged the Japanese to support
Semenov, and had persuaded the French to abandon in his favor
their own Irkutsk expedition. In late February or early March the
British and French had agreed to supply Semenov with a few
weapons and a small supply of ammunition from their stocks

[61] On May 16, the danger past, the executive committee of the soviet took back
full authority and on May 29 the military revolutionary staff was abolished and
military functions were entrusted to a military commissar.

[62] P. Pozdeev, "Sovetizatsiia Zabaikalia v usloviiakh interventsii 1918 g.," *Proletarskaia revoliutsiia*, No. 34 (November, 1924), pp. 187–88.

[63] Main sources for the following account of Semenov's Onon river offensive
are: Japan, Sambō Hombu, "Sanchō Tokugō, Rokoku Dai 8 Gō (May 11, 1918),
JGK, RKI, HK, III; Japan, Sambō Hombu, *Shiberia Shuppei-shi*, I, 22–23; *ibid.*,
III, 1080–81; Semenov, *O Sebe*, pp. 106–17; V. Borodavkin, "Vospominaniia
komandira," Vsesoiuznaia Kommunisticheskaia Partiia, *Sergei Lazo*, pp. 44–45;
and N. M. Matveev, "Bor'ba za sovety v Zabaikal'e," *ibid.*, pp. 31–36.

in China. The British in particular had agreed to defray his clothing and ammunition costs to the extent of perhaps £10,000, monthly. In addition, both the British and the French had sent observers to the detachment as well as several officers and men to accompany the shipments. This operation was to be kept secret, in accordance with the policy of the two governments of supporting local anti-German organizations wherever they might be. At the same time they had been endeavoring to treat the Soviet government in Moscow as a local regime in north Russia. Without officially recognizing its claim to be the only government of Russia, the Allies hoped to convert it to a pro-Allied and anti-German policy and to persuade it to invite an inter-Allied expedition to Siberia. To realize this hope, they would have to placate it by restraining Semenov, and they would have to win American and Japanese support for the plan.

Early in April, as Semenov stepped up his preparations for an offensive, the British government urged him, through Sir John Jordan, "to hold his hand for the present and confine himself to organizing his force, and to refrain from military operations until the question of possible allied intervention in Siberia had made further progress." [64] When Semenov refused to accept this advice, the British proceeded to cut off the promised aid,[65] and then protested to the Japanese and French, asking them to join in restraining him.[66]

[64] Confidential letter from Sir Connyngham Greene to Vice Minister Shidehara, April 12, 1918, JGK, RKI, HK, II, reporting the substance of the instructions Sir John Jordan had received from the foreign minister; Satō to Motono, April 16, 1918, ibid., II, reporting conversation with Porter, former British consul in Harbin, recently returned from Manchouli; and Colonel Tanaka (in London) to Vice Chief of Staff Tanaka, received May 17, 1918, JGK, RKI, SK, EBFK, I, reporting conversation on May 16 with Major General Macdonough.

[65] Japan, Sambō Hombu, Shiberia Shuppei-shi, III, 1079–80; Moser to U.S. secretary of state, May 23, 1918, USFR, 1918, Russia, II, 169, reporting advice from the British consul. Mints's assertion that the British decided on May 16, 1918, to contribute £50,000 a month to Semenov is difficult to accept since it does not accord with British policy as revealed in the official Japanese and American sources consulted. USSR, Tsentral'nyi Arkhiv RSFSR, Arkhiv oktiabr'skoi revoliutsii, Iaponskaia interventsiia 1918–1922 gg. v dokumentakh, ed. I. Mints (Moscow: 1934), p. 206.

[66] Unsigned letter from the British embassy in Tokyo, apparently sent to either

The months of March and April, 1918, were difficult ones for the Japanese army planners. Nothing seemed to go well. In Tokyo, Motono tried to force their hands prematurely. In Vladivostok, the navy forced the pace. In Peking, their own man, Tuan, had proved intractable. In Harbin, Horvat stalled, while in Manchouli their other instrument, Semenov, threatened to wreck their plans not only for a Russian "barrier," but also for an Allied understanding. Hopes had become headaches. Protégés had become problems.

---

the Foreign Ministry, the Army General Staff Headquarters, or the Army Ministry, dated May 4, 1918, Japan, Sambō Hombu, *Shiberia Shuppei-shi*, III, 1079–80.

IX. UNRULY PROTÉGÉS

In late April, 1918, it was obvious that much remained to be done before the Japanese army would feel prepared to recommend an expedition to Siberia. The Chinese government must be persuaded to sign joint-defense agreements. Horvat must be persuaded to carry out his announced intention to form a government. Semenov must somehow be persuaded not to waste his forces on a premature offensive. Of course, the Allies had still to be won over.

Pressure upon China

In Peking, after a month of bargaining the Japanese military delegation was at the end of its rope. It had conceded all it was empowered to yield, and still the Chinese refused to agree. Pressure would have to be applied. In late April members of the Japanese delegation called personally on General Chin, War Minister Tuan Chih-kuei, Foreign Minister Lu, and others.[1] On April 30, Minister Hayashi Gonsuke called on Premier Tuan. At last, on May 3 in Tokyo, Vice Chief Tanaka pulled the final string. He called on Minister Chang and told him that until an agreement was reached, no more loans or weapons would be supplied by Japan.[2] This made the issue clear: the Tuan government would either sign the agree-

[1] Japan, Sambō Hombu, *Taishō Shichi-nen naishi Jūichi-nen Shiberia Shuppei-shi* (1924), Appendix 5, pp. 49–67, "Account of the Conclusion of the Sino-Japanese Joint Defensive Military Agreement."
[2] Tanaka was referring no doubt to the telegraph loan of 20 million yen and others projected by Nishihara on his fifth visit to Peking, March 11 to April 19. Nishihara says that he advised Tanaka and talked with Chinese officials about the military agreements. Nishihara Kamezō, *Yume no Shichi-jū yo nen, Nishihara Kamezō Jiden* (Kumobara Mura, 1949), pp. 241–42.

ment or take its chances without the support of Japanese money and munitions. It chose the former, and on May 14 the two delegations agreed on a draft. Two days later a formal conference was opened and the documents were signed. A joint naval agreement was also signed on May 19.[3]

The agreements apparently met with general approval in Tokyo. They were reported to the Advisory Council on Foreign Relations on May 27 and presented to the Privy Council the following day,[4] and there is no evidence that they aroused any opposition or even prolonged discussion. At last the military authorities had completed one important phase of their preparations for a Siberian expedition: the negotiation of agreements with China which might be used to permit Japanese troop operations in the Chinese area of the Amur basin and possibly to bring Chinese troops there under Japanese command.

Kolchak to the Rescue

Meanwhile, from April 18 to May 3, 1918, another important conference was being held in Peking between General Horvat and his backers in the Russian legation, the Russo-Asiatic Bank, the Chinese Eastern Railway offices, and other quarters. The question was: should Horvat proclaim a government as requested by the Japanese representatives in Harbin? Before coming to Peking he was apparently convinced he would have to do so to secure Japanese military support. At Peking, however, the Chinese warned him they would tolerate no such action on Chinese soil.

The view of the Chinese government had been clearly stated on April 5 by Kuo Tsung-hsi, governor general of Kirin province, in a conversation with Baron Hayashi.[5] Kuo told Hayashi that the Chinese government was sympathetic to the anti-Bolsheviks and had

---

[3] For texts in English of these two agreements, see Appendixes N and O.

[4] Hara Kei, *Hara Kei Nikki* (Tokyo: Kengensha, 1950–52), VII, 406–7, diary entry for May 27, 1918. The cabinet's approval was probably secured a few days earlier.

[5] Hayashi to Motono, April 6, 1918, JGK, RKI, HK, II, reporting his conversation with Kuo Tsung-hsi on April 5, 1918.

always hoped they would be successful. However, "they do not yet have a superiority in actual strength over the Bolsheviks and, therefore, were a government proclaimed, the Bolsheviks in Siberia would be greatly aroused and would press hard on the border. It would be difficult to prevent the Bolsheviks in Manchuria, who are even now awaiting such an event, from responding and disturbing the public order." For this reason it would be best for the anti-Bolsheviks to build up superior strength before proclaiming a government. Since Kuo had doubtless been conferring with Chinese government officials on the problem, it seems likely that he was speaking for the government in this instance.

As Chinese troops controlled the railway zone and its exits to Russian territory, China's attitude had to be taken into account, even by the Japanese. Major General Saitō, to whom Kuo had expressed similar ideas, wired Tanaka on April 5 that in view of the weakness of Chinese forces in northern Manchuria, "the empire is forced to refuse" to permit the Russians to organize a government in Harbin. Kuo certainly convinced the Russian minister, Prince Kudashev, for at the conference with Horvat at the end of the month the prince maintained that it would be "improper" to proclaim a Russian government on Chinese soil. This point of view, of course, fitted in well with General Horvat's thinking; he had always wanted the support of Japanese expeditionary forces before proclaiming a government.

What then could be done? Could Horvat move immediately to Russian soil and proclaim a government there? He was obviously too weak to do so successfully. It was therefore decided at the Peking conference to set up a kind of shadow government in the guise of a reorganized board of directors of the Chinese Eastern Railway and then to exert every energy to building up its armed forces.[6]

At a meeting of the stockholders of the Russo-Asiatic Bank, the board of directors of the railway was completely reorganized.[7] As

[6] Saitō to Tanaka, April 22, 1918, *ibid.*, II.

[7] Japan, Sambō Hombu, "Sambō Tokugō, Shina Dai 4 Gō, May 3, 1918," *JGK, RKI, SB*, pp. 432–39; Reinsch to Lansing, April 27, 1918, *USFR, 1918,*

usual, a Chinese was elected president: this time the Kirin governor, Kuo Tsung-hsi. Yeo Shih-ching was elected director of Chinese affairs. The other officials, elected to serve in the office at Harbin, clearly betrayed the true character of the board as a shadow government for the Amur basin. General Horvat took over the office of vice president (formerly filled by appointment in Petrograd) as well as that of administrator; Putilov was placed in charge of finance; Kolchak, of military matters; Ustrugov, of technical railway affairs; Count Jezierski, Konovalov, and others headed other special departments. The company made its claim to independent authority even clearer by severing connections with the Russian government.[8] The Chinese government, anxious to eliminate Russian influence over the road, readily approved these changes.

The second decision, to build up an anti-Bolshevik Russian armed force, was taken in a burst of enthusiasm generated by the appearance of a new face on the Peking scene, that of Admiral Kolchak. Only a month before, following the signing of the Treaty of Brest-Litovsk, Kolchak had apparently decided to leave the Far East. The Russian ambassador to Japan, Krupenskii, had introduced him to British military authorities in Tokyo and had arranged for him to serve with the British army.[9] The British decided at first to send him to the Mesopotamian front. When news of Kolchak's imminent departure from the Far East reached Peking, the admiral's supporters, led by the Russian minister in China, Prince Kudashev, immediately requested that his orders be canceled and

---

Russia, II, 155–56. Several Soviet sources date this reorganization differently: April 14, according to USSR, Tsentral'nyi Arkhiv RSFSR, Arkhiv oktiabr'skoi revoliutsii, *Iaponskaia interventsiia 1918–1922 gg. v dokumentakh* (Moscow, 1934), p. 205 (apparently a confusion of old and new style); April 16, according to George Chicherin, *Dva goda sovetskoi vneshnei politiki* (Moscow, 1920), p. 11, quoted in Louis Fischer, *The Soviets in World Affairs* (London: Cape and Smith, 1930), I, 106; May, according to "Khronika sobytii na tikhom okeane 1914–1918 gg.," *Tikhii okean,* III, No. 9 (July–September, 1936), 255, but these Soviet sources would seem to be in error.

[8] Moser to Lansing, May 8, 1918, *USFR, 1918, Russia,* II, 155–56.

[9] M. I. Smirnov, "Admiral Kolchak," *Slavonic and East European Review,* XI, No. 32 (January, 1933), 373–85; George K. Guins, *Sibir', Soiuzniki i Kolchak, 1918–1920* (Peking: Tipolitografiia Russkoi Dukhovnoi Missii, 1921), I, 5; Gotō to Satō, May 31, 1918, *JGK, RKI, HK,* II.

that he be permitted to proceed instead to Peking in order to take an active part in strengthening the anti-Bolshevik movement in Siberia. The British agreed. In view of the British army's original orders, it seems hardly likely that the admiral was regarded as the potential dictator of a "white" government in Siberia. Moreover, Kudashev's backing of Horvat strongly suggests that Kolchak's British and Russian supporters thought of him at this stage primarily as a man around whom military forces could be rallied to carry a Horvat-led government into Siberia. At any rate, this is the role Kolchak said he was prepared to play.

Apparently Horvat was willing to accept Kolchak, but how would the Japanese and the Chinese authorities regard him? Japanese approval was necessary if Kolchak was to get any aid, and every effort was now made to win Japan's support, even to the extent of agreeing to rely on it exclusively. To a query by Lieutenant Colonel Tanaka, Kolchak and Horvat replied: "Since it would be difficult to unify the views of each country if aid were received from different ones, we should like to rely on the assistance of Japan alone." [10] Even if the support were to be an Allied venture, they would prefer that the Allies work through Nakajima.[11]

The Japanese were pleased with the vigor of the admiral's planning. After months of nagging Horvat to little effect, now, as soon as Kolchak appeared on the scene, they were presented with a concrete plan of action. As outlined to Major General Saitō and Minister Baron Hayashi, the Kolchak plan was very similar to Japan's own: to envelop the region east of Lake Baikal by advancing immediately on Vladivostok in the east and Chita in the west, crushing the Bolsheviks between the two forces moving along the trans-Siberian railway.[12] The operation would require about 4 infantry regiments, 5 special garrison infantry battalions, 2 cavalry regiments, and machine-gun units, totaling 1,000 officers, 16,100 non-commissioned officers and men, and 2,400 horses (including reserves); of these, 4,000 men would be needed for the initial ad-

[10] Saitō to Tanaka, April 23, 1918, *ibid.*, II.
[11] Saitō to Tanaka, April 27, 1918, *ibid.*, II.
[12] Saitō to Tanaka, April 24, 1918, *ibid.*, II; Saitō to Tanaka, April 27, 1918, *ibid.*, II; Hayashi to Gotō, April 27, 1918, *ibid.*, II.

vance, the rest later. If Chinese were used for one quarter of the requirement and artillery instructors were sent from Japan, a force of this size could be organized in about six weeks. Of course, weapons and money would have to be supplied by Japan. Including the weapons already supplied to Semenov, Kolchak estimated the requirement to be as follows:

Rifles	11,900	8-inch heavy guns	4
Carbines	2,250	Cavalry swords	1,200
Machine guns	224	Telescopes	500
Field guns	24	Rangefinders	30
5-inch howitzers	16	Airplanes	12
	Ammo and bombs		

For expenses, 2,500,000 to 2,600,000 rubles would be needed initially; after the muster of troops, 3,500,000 rubles (c.1,000,000 yen) would be needed each month. "I think we ought to accept Horvat's proposal," wired Minister Baron Hayashi. He added, "We ought to tell the English and French governments clearly that the Imperial government does not refuse to bear this responsibility alone." [13]

Semenov's Onon River Offensive

These promising developments in Peking made the Japanese extremely anxious to get Semenov back out of danger and also into the good graces of the Allies, China, and the new Harbin regime. But the headstrong Semenov was even more unruly than Tuan or Horvat. After crossing the border on April 21, Semenov had pushed rapidly northward, taking Dauriia in the morning of April 23 and Halainor that night.[14] On April 28, Borzia fell. The soviet forces fled northward, crossing the Onon river on April 30. After blowing up the railroad bridge, they halted temporarily at Oloviannaia on

---

[13] Hayashi to Gotō, April 27, 1918, *ibid.*, II. American Minister Reinsch reported that Japanese support was promised when the board was reorganized "on acceptance of harsh conditions"; but he does not specify these conditions. Reinsch to Lansing, April 25, 1918, *USFR, 1918, Russia*, II, 137–38.

[14] Japan, Sambō Hombu, "Sanchō Tokugō, Rokoku Dai 8 gō (May 11, 1918), Semenov Shitai no Onon Kakan ni mukatte suru Zenshin," *JGK, RKI, HK*, III.

the north bank. Semenov's advance units followed in hot pursuit. Crossing the Onon, they broke up the temporary camp and drove the main Red strength back to Karymskaia, less than fifty miles from Chita, and occupied Aga Station on May 9.

At that point Semenov was forced to call a halt. He had outrun his supplies and could not risk plunging with unprotected flanks into the main strength of an enemy now gathering in overwhelming numbers. He decided to consolidate his forces on the south bank of the Onon while rallying the territory to his support. Severing all ties with Horvat and the other Russian groups in the railway zone, he proclaimed himself head of the Temporary Government of the Trans-Baikal Territory.[15] At the outset of the campaign he had assumed the Cossack title of ataman in order to give himself proper military authority over his forces and had organized a military staff for the detachment with Colonel Natsvalov as its chief.[16] Now he proclaimed himself supreme authority in the territory, appointed Cossack General Shil'nikov in charge of Cossack affairs and Taskin, former commissar of Trans-Baikal Territory under the provisional government, in charge of civil administration.

The new temporary government, he announced, would wield "all military power," using it to lead the "Siberian people" toward "self-government." This it proposed to accomplish by gradually restoring "the laws relating to justice which were established under the provisional government," giving special attention to the restoration of banking facilities and the readjustment of agriculture, and,

[15] For an English translation of the proclamation, see Appendix L. The exact date of the proclamation was not given in the sources consulted. The American consul at Harbin, Charles Moser, reported that the government was established on May 4. Moser to Lansing, May 8, 1918, USFR, 1918, Russia, II, 156. Semenov does not give a date. Gregorii Semenov, O Sebe (Harbin, 1938), pp. 104–6. Budberg records that news of Semenov's action reached Harbin on May 19. Baron Aleksei Budberg, "Dnevnik," Arkhiv russkoi revoliutsii, VII (1923), No. 13, 213–14. The earliest reference in the reports from Japanese army agents in the Japanese Foreign Ministry files is in Nakajima to Tanaka, May 20, 1918, JGK, RKI, HK, II, but this refers to the "government" without explanation, indicating earlier relevant reports no longer extant.

[16] Semenov, O Sebe, pp. 104–6. Semenov states that his assumed title of ataman was later legalized by his election as "campaign ataman" (pokhodnyi ataman) of the Ussuri, Amur, and Trans-Baikal troops, and, upon the death of Ataman Dutov, of the Ural and Siberian Cossacks as well.

by degrees, restoring "the organs of republican self-government which existed before the invasion of Bolshevik authority." He promised, as conditions became suitable, to call a Siberian legislative assembly to establish a permanent government. In short, this was the program Semenov had offered unsuccessfully to the Japanese in return for immediate troop commitments: a temporary Semenovist dictatorship until a popularly elected government could be organized. The Japanese had not been prepared to commit troops, but they had indicated many times in the past to Horvat that, if he would first set up a government in Siberia, they would be prepared to give him whatever support he needed. So, although not acting directly at Japanese suggestion, Semenov was certainly acting in the belief that the proclamation of a government would bring increased Japanese support.[17] He also believed that the people of the territory, or at least the Cossacks, would flock to his standard. Some in fact did join his troops on the Onon, possibly as many as 2,000. Unfortunately for Semenov, he had no time to train them and integrate them into his detachment before overwhelming Red forces swarmed down upon him.[18]

In his surprise advance on April 21, Semenov struck before soviet reinforcements could arrive, but, during his halt on the Onon, they began pouring in. Quickly checked for reliability at Chita,[19] the new troops were directed to Adrianovka, where headquarters for the Trans-Baikal front had been set up with Ensign Sergei Lazo as commander in chief and Lieutenant General Taube, formerly of the staff of the Irkutsk military district, as his chief of staff.[20] Lazo's

[17] As he told Lieutenant General Mutō, he hoped that Japan would help him secure the independence of the Trans-Baikal, Amur, and Maritime territories and set himself up as governor general of military administration. Mutō to Uehara, May 29, 1918, *JGK, RKI, HK,* II.

[18] The number of new recruits is not conclusively stated in the sources available; but Mutō, on his tour of the front, May 19–21, 1918, reported that Semenov's forces totaled about 4,000, which would suggest that roughly 2,000 had been added since the campaign began. Mutō to Tanaka, May 24, 1918, *ibid.,* II.

[19] The main problem was to weed out as many anarchists as possible.

[20] P. S. Parfenov, *Uroki proshlogo, grazhdanskaia voina v Sibiri 1918, 1919, 1920 gg.* (Harbin, 1921), p. 31. Parfenov identifies Taube as a lieutenant general while Semenov identifies him as Major General Baron Taube, German general staff, formerly director of communications of the staff of the Irkutsk military district (Semenov, *O Sebe,* p. 105).

forces eventually consisted of three kinds of troops: territorial, extra-territorial, and prisoner of war. Their backbone was the Chita Red Guard, the Trans-Baikal Railway Red Guard, and elements of the sovietized regular regiments back from the front, like the First Verkhneudinsk, Second Chita, and Second Nerchinsk, which had established soviet rule in Chita, as well as the First Argun.[21] These organized territorial units were supplemented by partisan detachments from various Cossack villages. From beyond the territory, Red Guard and other detachments came from the soviet organizations in most of the large cities as far west as Omsk. From the Far East, the regional committee of the party sent a socialist detachment, consisting of units from Vladivostok, Khabarovsk, and Blagoveshchensk, under the military command of V. Borodavkin and the political direction of the Bolshevik commissar, Gubel'man. The assignment of such a commissar was not at all unusual; the party endeavored to place "political fighters" in each unit in order to Bolshevize it in so far as this was possible. The third major source of manpower were the prisoner-of-war stockades. Although the number of Austrian and German prisoners actually armed for service against Semenov was greatly exaggerated by Semenov and by some of the Allied leaders, an international detachment was formed, numbering from 1,000 to 1,500 men.[22] Estimates, made by the anti-Bolshevik leaders, of the total size of Lazo's forces varied considerably. Apparently, by the middle of May he actually commanded about 4,000 men at the front, roughly twice as many as Semenov

[21] This description of the soviet forces on the Trans-Baikal front is derived chiefly from P. Pozdeev, "Sovetizatsiia Zabaikalia v usloviiakh interventsii 1918 g," *Proletarskaia revoliutsiia,* No. 34 (November, 1924), pp. 185–95; V. Borodavkin, "Vospominaniia komandira," Vsesoiuznaia Kommunisticheskaia Partiia, Tsentral'nyi Ispolnitel'nyi Komitet, Sekretariat Glavnoi Redaktsii Istorii Grazhdanskoi Voiny v SSSR, *Sergei Lazo, vospominaniia i dokumenty* (Moscow: Gosizdat, 1938), pp. 43–47; O. Lazo, "Komanduiushchii Frontom," *ibid.,* pp. 53–80; and N. M. Matveev, "Bor'ba za sovety Zabaikal'e," *ibid.,* pp. 24–36. Borodavkin was commander of the Far Eastern socialist detachment; O. Lazo was a "political fighter" in the first Tomsk fighting detachment; and Matveev was a member of the military revolutionary staff.

[22] Satō to Gotō, August 2, 1918, *JGK, RKI, HK,* III. A Japanese military agent, Sasaki, reported to Consul General Satō that one third of the Red forces opposing Semenov were prisoners of war. As explained below, these Red forces probably totaled about 4,000 men.

could muster effectively, and could call on perhaps 5,000 more, scattered over the basin, as a last reserve.[23]

The soviet counterattack began on May 14, with the Far East socialist detachment spearheading the drive down the railroad. Four days later Lazo's armored train rolled into Oloviannaia. For more than a week the two armies faced each other across the river, but on the night of May 27 elements of the Far East detachment swam the Onon and attacked Semenov in the rear, forcing him to pull back to Borzia. Partizan bands raided his flanks and again Semenov had to evacuate, giving up Borzia on June 11. By the end of the month the Special Mongolian Detachment and the temporary government it had borne into Trans-Baikal Territory were backed up against the Chinese border.

Reasons for Semenov's Failure

The failure of Semenov's Onon river offensive can be explained in part by the fact that he had failed to stir the imagination of the anti-Bolshevik majority in the Trans-Baikal Territory or at least had failed to organize that support effectively. Most of the people there were basically socialist and nationalist in feeling. Semenov was anti-socialist and brought a poorly disciplined, international, mercenary army into the territory. His failure can also be explained partly by the rapidity and effectiveness, relatively speaking, of the soviet mobilization. He must also have suffered from Britain's withdrawal of support.

[23] Semenov's estimate of 30,000 seems to come from a faulty memory or a calculated effort to justify his defeat (Semenov, *O Sebe*, p. 97). N. M. Matveev, a member of the military revolutionary staff at Chita, gives the figure of "about 9,000" (Matveev, "Bor'ba za Sovety Zabaikal'e," *ibid.*, p. 31). This is roughly corroborated by, and may have been derived from, the public report of the Siberian military commissariat on May 21, 1918, which listed 8,450 Red Guards and Red Army troops in the Amur basin as of May 18. Sugino to Gotō, May 21, 1918, Ō Ju 924, Japan, Rikugunshō, *Ō Ju Dai Nikki* (June, 1918). This figure would seem to include Red troops whether actually on the Zabaikal front or scattered in other localities in the Amur basin. Captain Kuroki, who was with Semenov, and Major General Mutō, who toured the front, May 19–21, reported no more than 4,000 Red troops actually in the field against Semenov. Mutō to Tanaka, April 22, 1918, *JGK, RKI, HK,* II; and Mutō to Tanaka, May 24, 1918, *ibid.,* II.

There are in addition, three other reasons for the failure: the hostility of Kolchak and to a lesser extent of Orlov; the obstructionism of the Chinese; and the restraining influence of the Japanese. The hostility of Kolchak and Orlov was important because it virtually cut Semenov off from troop reinforcements and supplies from the Horvat organization in Harbin. Horvat had apparently given prior approval to Semenov's offensive; at least, he had approved an advance as far as Karymskaia;[24] on April 23, Pleshkov, then still commander in chief of the Chinese Eastern Railway forces, hurried with his staff to confer with Semenov at Manchouli.[25] Shortly thereafter, an advance body of perhaps 400 men from Orlov's detachment in Harbin was sent as a reinforcement.[26]

Then the situation changed. With the reorganization of the Chinese Eastern Railway board of directors in Peking in late April and early May, Pleshkov was replaced by Admiral Kolchak, who immediately set about reducing Semenov to subordination. In mid-May Kolchak left Harbin for Manchouli to inspect Semenov's Special Mongolian Detachment and bring it under his authority. What actually transpired at Manchouli remains in doubt. Kolchak seems to have asked Semenov to come to Manchouli for a conference, while Semenov, who was conducting an offensive on the Onon river, seems to have insisted that Kolchak should visit him in the field. Finally Semenov did come to Manchouli and Kolchak managed to see him.[27] Semenov and the Japanese report that the admiral violently opposed the so-called "Japanese orientation," on the ground that "only England and France were prepared to render disinterested and exhaustive assistance to the Russian nation." [28] As for Japan and the United States, "they were striving to use our

---

[24] Saitō to Uehara, April 24, 1918, *ibid.*, II.

[25] Satō to Gotō, April 25, 1918, *ibid.*, II.

[26] Moser to secretary of state, May 23, 1918, *USFR, 1918, Russia*, II, 169. These included one infantry battalion and two cavalry companies. Unnamed source in Peking to Japanese Army General Staff Headquarters, May 10, 1918, *JGK, RKI, HK*, II.

[27] K. A. Popov, ed., *Dopros Kolchaka* (Leningrad: Gos. izd., 1925), p. 149.

[28] Semenov, *O Sebe*, pp. 111–12. This conversation is reported in substantially the same terms in Mutō to Tanaka May 21, 1918, *JGK, RKI, HK*, II, passing on a report from Kuroki on May 19; and in Japan, Sambō Hombu, *Shiberia Shuppei-shi*, III, Appendix VII, 25–26.

difficult situation for their own interests, which actually dictated
the greatest possible weakening of Russia in the Far East." Kolchak
demanded that Semenov give up his pro-Japanese policy and subject himself to Harbin. This, Semenov says, he refused to do, warning that he would brook no interference in his policies or in the
command of his detachment and that he would answer only "to the
legal and generally recognized all-Russian government."

Following his break with Kolchak, Semenov proclaimed his independence as military dictator of the Temporary Government of
Trans-Baikal Territory. Thereafter, despite repeated pleas by Semenov for the promised reinforcements and arms, none were forthcoming. Kolchak even arrested one of Semenov's emissaries in Harbin.[29]
Finally, about May 29, Semenov came to Harbin in one of his
armored trains to negotiate; met by Kolchak's machine guns, he was
forced to return empty handed.[30]

Another reason for Semenov's failure was that the Chinese ob-
structed his offensive as much as did Kolchak. In spite of the Sino-
Japanese military agreement the Chinese were not at all friendly
toward Japan's protégé, Semenov. His detachment prevented their
own troops from recovering undisputed military control of the western end of the railway zone, and his activities, they feared, would
provoke an invasion by soviet forces. The Chinese threatened to
disarm him if he returned to the zone, and, until Allied pressure
caused them to lift the ban on June 20, they did not permit any
goods for Semenov to pass through the Manchouli customs station.[31]
Even then the Chinese commander in Harbin forbade the transportation to the front of Chinese who had joined the Semenov forces.[32]
Between Kolchak and the Chinese, once Semenov crossed the
border, he was cut off from supplies and reinforcements.

Lastly, Semenov was restrained by a crucial decision of the Japanese army. Had the army been willing and able to send an expedition to support him, Semenov might well have been carried into

[29] Budberg, "Dnevnik," *Arkhiv russkoi revoliutsii*, VII (1923), No. 13, 216.
[30] Popov, ed., *Dopros Kolchaka*, p. 124.
[31] Lieutenant Commander Sugizaka (in Harbin) to vice chief of the Japanese
naval board, June 21, 1918, *JGK, RKI, HK*, III.
[32] Mutō to Tanaka, June 24, 1918, *ibid.*, III.

Chita and beyond. But the military leaders were by no means prepared to take such a decision at that time. On the other hand, they
were not prepared to abandon Semenov as the British were urging.

Japan's representatives in the field argued for continuing the
"Asia first" policy. Despite Semenov's exposed position and his
break with Kolchak, despite the hostility of the Chinese and the
British pressure for a reversal of policy, they urged continued support for him.[33] Major General Mutō wired, for example, that, even
if the British secured an invitation from the Soviet government to
intervene in Siberia, an expedition under such auspices "would
cause great losses to the empire." [34] On April 17, Consul General
Satō sent a long report from Harbin, attacking vigorously the British and French negotiations in Moscow and declaring that Japan
certainly should do nothing to strengthen the "Bolshevik government." "This very act," he said, "would convert all Russia to extreme socialism and endanger the social structure of the empire." [35]
He urged the government to ignore the efforts of the Western Allies
and to go ahead in assisting "the development of the anti-Bolshevik
influence of Horvat and Semenov, in accord with our already established policy, and endeavor to make all Siberia independent." Major
General Saitō agreed emphatically.[36]

In Tokyo the central military authorities appear also to have
agreed, but they were worried lest Semenov be cut to pieces in his
drive northward. On May 9, Tanaka told Nakajima that the empire's policy concerning Semenov and Horvat remained unchanged:
they were to be supported and built into a spearhead for a future
Japanese expeditionary force, but, at a time when the empire was
not yet prepared to support them with troops, they should be

[33] As Shidehara later recalled, "When the Russian Ataman Semenov raised a
standard in Siberia in opposition to the Red government of the time, [the inter-
ventionists] were beside themselves with joy and supported him. And so, pock-
marks came to look like dimples and, treating him like an Oriental-style hero, they
came to feel that as a matter of honor he had to be backed up." Shidehara Kijuro,
Gaikō Go-jū-nen (Tokyo: Yomiuri Shimbun-sha, 1951), p. 87.
[34] Mutō to Tanaka, April 13, 1918, JGK, RKI, HK, II.
[35] Satō to Motonō, April 17, 1918, ibid., II.
[36] Saitō to Uehara, May 8, 1918, ibid., II.

"secretly held in check" in order to "preserve their strength." [37] In accordance with this decision, Japanese agents cautioned Semenov at the height of his offensive to hold up at the Onon river and to consolidate his position;[38] when he broke with Kolchak and proclaimed himself independent dictator of Trans-Baikal Territory, Major General Mutō warned him to keep some kind of liaison with Horvat lest Horvat cut him off from his supplies.[39]

Increased Aid to Horvat and Semenov

While restraining Semenov, on the one hand, the Japanese army became convinced, on the other, of the necessity to give both him and Horvat greater support. In the secret army report of April 21, 1918, there were outlined not only the concessions which Horvat might be persuaded to give, but also the "positive assistance" which the army felt Japan should offer immediately:

1. In response to the demands of General Horvat, to send men and capital, actually taking over the operation of the railroad, etc.
2. By aiding Semenov, Pleshkov, etc., to save for us the military power of the Chinese Eastern Railway.
To accomplish this, it is urgent for us to send a railway telegraph unit, supply communications equipment, increase officer inspectors, send more instructors, supply capital, etc.
3. In order to organize troops, pacify the local residents and in addition acquire actual rights, we ought to send an average of ¥1,000,-000 a month and later we can get the rights in return.
4. To have businessmen and industrialists lay out money and make direct investments.
5. To promote an advantageous economic and political development by aiding Russian businessmen and politicians who are in difficulty. To supply them with money and help them make a living, thereby expanding the influence of the pro-Japanese group.
6. To send military police officers and intelligence agents to investigate from within the various political parties and groups.

[37] Tanaka to Nakajima, May 9, 1918, quoted in Japan, Sambō Hombu, *Shiberia Shuppei-shi*, III, 1070–71, the substance having been approved by the prime minister, the foreign minister, and the war minister.

[38] Japan, Sambō Hombu, *Shiberia Shuppei-shi*, III, 1080–81.

[39] Mutō to Uehara, May 24, 1918, *JGK, RKI, HK*, II, reporting on his tour of inspection of the Trans-Baikal front.

7. To buy up the Russian-language newspapers and make use of them.

8. To allot about ¥20,000 monthly for operational preparations and intelligence reports.

9. To strengthen the liaison between Tokyo and Peking, so that reports eminating from these places will ease the minds of Horvat and the public at large.

10. To fix the qualifications for military officers to be sent (special duty personnel, etc.) and organize a headquarters (Russia is offering headquarters housing; at present, what about non-commissioned paymasters, paymasters, clerks, and orderlies?).

11. In case of emergency, military currency (consideration should be given now to small coins).

[The report concluded]:

We must go forward on the basis of further developing the present excellent conditions in the far east, and above all along the Chinese Eastern Railway. Being prepared to respond to the present situation in Russia and in accordance with those pro-Japanese or various elements which have faith in Japan, we should promote various enterprises to strengthen the basis for future military operations against Germany; and by strengthening our economic bases within this sphere of influence we should make preparations for long-term military operations against Germany and for the postwar period.

We have always hoped to move forward in unity with our allies for this purpose, but, if we give too much consideration to the inclinations of the powers, we shall in the end be despised by the world and the Russian people and lose the Russian people's trust in the empire. . . . And now when the flags and agencies of various countries are appearing, it is time to begin immediately to put into effect an open policy.[40]

There is no evidence as to who drafted this report, though it was probably one of the younger officers in the Army General Staff Headquarters, possibly someone on General Tanaka's Joint Siberia Planning Committee. However, it indicates clearly certain phases of the army's negotiations at Harbin and suggests the climate of mili-

[40] An unsigned, secret report on Japanese War Ministry paper, dated April 21, 1918, entitled, "Horuwatto Seifu Sōshiki Enjo no Sekkyoku to narishi igo ni oite Teikoku no etaru Riken," *JGK, RKI, TT,* I, 0313–21.

tary opinion in which General Baron Uehara reached his conclusion that a decision by the government was unfortunately necessary.

Uehara's final proposal, which he had the war minister, Lieutenant General Ōshima Ken'ichi, present at a cabinet meeting on May 14, was briefer and more general. It stuck to preparations for military operations. It was absolutely essential for future military operations and for Japan's self-defense, Ōshima argued, that Japan control the Chinese Eastern Railway. After outlining the past efforts of the army to build up an anti-Bolshevik barrier, he went on to say that it was now necessary to secure the government's commitment to the army's program. He proposed specifically that the government:

1. Together with organizing forces required by Horvat, lend munitions and money (quantities to be recommended in a later report) and actually place under our power the authorities of the railroad and others.
2. Fulfill the previous agreements with the Semenov detachment and continue aid.
3. Under the pretext of providing what is necessary for supplying the Semenov detachment, send railroad and telegraph personnel as instructors to the Chinese Eastern Railway.
4. Send representatives of the government to render military and financial assistance.

The army had already secured the government's commitment to the program of aid to Semenov, so that this part of the proposal was not new in principle: an additional 1,000,000 rubles (c.300,000 yen) was approved. The new element in the proposal was the request that the government give all-out support to Horvat in order to secure control of the Chinese Eastern Railway. What debates there may have been in the cabinet meeting is not known; at any rate, the proposal was adopted, thus committing the government to the army's Manchurian policy. Four days later, the vice chief wired Nakajima to increase his pressure on Horvat to invite or at least express his willingness to accept a Japanese railroad and telegraph mission, especially for the lines south of Harbin.[41]

[41] Tanaka to Nakajima, May 18, 1918, *JGK, RKI, HK,* II.

The Kolchak Fiasco

The stage appeared set for the new Horvat-Kolchak team to build
an effective force at Harbin, but the high hopes of Kolchak's supporters were soon dashed. He failed to secure the necessary assistance from Japan or to win the allegiance of the atamans who
were already operating in the railway zone. Five weeks after his
appointment Kolchak was removed from his post, leaving behind
a disillusioned Japanese staff and a core of embittered Russian
leaders who later helped destroy the admiral's own regime at Omsk.

At Peking it had been clearly stated that the new railway government intended, as far as possible, to rely completely on Japan
for aid and to follow Japan's strategic plans for the seizure of the
Amur basin. In view of Kolchak's connections with the British
army, the Japanese army authorities were understandably skeptical
of his sincerity in giving these pledges. They were, moreover, concerned about his relations with the other detachment commanders.
Kolchak had assured the Japanese in Peking that "Pleshkov,
Samoilov, Semenov and the others will bring troops to my support." [42] In the middle of May representatives of Kolchak and
Prince Krupenskii reassured Tanaka in Tokyo that Kolchak and
Semenov have a "complete understanding." [43] The vice chief preferred to rely on the judgment of Nakajima and on May 15 wired
for his advice as to whether or not to support Kolchak.[44]

It was just at this time that Kolchak returned from Manchouli.
He was violently irate about Japan's support for Semenov and
complained bitterly and insultingly to Nakajima.[45] A complete
break with the Japanese mission resulted. On May 19 Nakajima
reported to Tanaka:

I must admire his [Kolchak's] gallant spirit, but how unfortunate!
He does not understand the situation; he lacks knowledge about the
army, consideration, and tolerance, and is quick-tempered. . . . I am

[42] Saitō to Tanaka, April 23, 1918, ibid., II.
[43] Tanaka to Nakajima, May 15, 1918, ibid., II.
[44] Japan, Sambō Hombu, Shiberia Shuppei-shi, III, 1072.
[45] Popov, ed., Dopros Kolchaka, pp. 121–22.

worried about his being able to handle such complicated affairs as the mustering of forces, organization, command, supply, and civilian administration.[46]

Two days later Nakajima went further: Kolchak was pro-British; if Japan were not to lose all, it must immediately throw greater weight behind "the pro-Japanese faction." [47] He urged that "arsenals be set up here, necessary artillery officers and non-coms be sent and given custody of them, and a company of infantry be sent in disguise as a guard" in order to strengthen Horvat, Semenov, and Kalmykov.[48]

On May 26, Consul General Satō strongly supported Nakajima's recommendation. He urged that the empire deal only with Horvat and Pleshkov, if it did not want to hand over the Amur basin to the British.[49] Kolchak, he explained, had "no respect for the empire":

Being violently opposed to an imperial expedition, he is overconfident that he can drive out the Bolsheviks by himself. On this point his views are entirely different from those of Horvat and Pleshkov. At present, the latter firmly hold the opinion that nothing can be done without a Japanese expedition. Up to now Kolchak's idea has been not to work with Japanese troops, but simply to try to get money and weapons supplied. . . . It is not clear what relations he now has with Britain. At any rate, he seems personally to have a great sympathy for Britain, so that, when Japan is about to give material aid, it will be difficult to say whether, no matter how generously he may give concessions to the British, he may not refuse absolutely to consider them for the Japanese. . . . I am afraid that in the end Japan will get nothing.

In view of the hostility of Japan's representatives, it is not surprising that the admiral failed to secure the allegiance of the pro-Japanese Russian commanders in the railway zone. Pleshkov naturally resented Kolchak's appointment, for it signaled his own demotion from the top command to the rank of military aide to Horvat.[50] Semenov, as has been seen, was even more hostile.

[46] Nakajima to Tanaka, May 19, 1918, *JGK, RKI, HK,* II.
[47] Nakajima to Tanaka, May 21, 1918, *ibid.,* II.
[48] Nakajima to Tanaka, May 23, 1918, *ibid.,* II.
[49] Satō to Gotō, May 26, 1918, *ibid.,* II.
[50] Mutō to Tanaka, May 12, 1918, *ibid.,* II.

The exact sequence of events during the next few weeks is not clear. By the end of May, Nakajima had come to the conclusion that Kolchak would have to go.[51] Horvat seems to have reached the same conclusion;[52] in late May he is reported to have drawn up the order relieving the admiral of his post and demoting him to command of the Orlov unit in Harbin, the one detachment loyal to Kolchak, simultaneously restoring Pleshkov to his former post as commander in chief.[53] It was an extremely awkward situation and Horvat was no man for decisive action. Instead of telling Kolchak personally, he apparently gave the order to Pleshkov to transmit while he himself slipped away to Peking to appeal to the board of directors for support.[54]

Kolchak, of course, had no intention of being shouldered to one side. Instead of accepting the order, he recalled those of Orlov's men who were fighting with Semenov,[55] took personal command of at least part of the Orlov detachment in Harbin, and set out on a campaign of his own, moving eastward along the Chinese Eastern Railway to set up an advance headquarters at Muling in preparation for a descent on Vladivostok.

It was a bold step, but one which was doomed to failure, for Ivan Kalmykov, the Japanese puppet in command of the anti-Bolshevik Cossacks at Pogranichnaia, refused to follow Kolchak's lead and thereby effectively blocked his path.[56] Meanwhile, on June 10 and 17, Pleshkov had talked with Consul General Satō, seeking Japanese aid in forcing Kolchak to recognize his demotion;[57] and Horvat was talking with the board in Peking. The board seems to have been somewhat reluctant to oust Kolchak, for Horvat immediately appealed to Major General Saitō to have the

---

[51] Japan, Sambō Hombu, *Shiberia Shuppei-shi,* III, 1073.

[52] Saitō to Tanaka, June 12, 1918, *JGK, RKI, HK,* III.

[53] Japan, Kaigun Gunreibu, "Kaichō Rohō Dai 93 Gō, Harbin Dempō" (May 30, 1918), *ibid.,* II.

[54] Satō to Gotō, June 11, 1918, *ibid.,* III; Budberg, "Dnevnik," *Arkhiv russkoi revoliutsii* VII (1923), No. 13, 219–20 (diary entries of June 8–9, 1918).

[55] Budberg, "Dnevnik," *ibid.,* XIII, 216.

[56] Japan, Kaigun Gunreibu, "Kaichō Rohō Dai 93 Gō, Harbin Dempō" (May 30, 1918), *JGK, RKI, HK,* II.

[57] Satō to Gotō, June 11, 1918, *ibid.,* III; and Satō to Gotō, June 13, 1918, *ibid.,* III.

Japanese government inform the Russian ambassador in Tokyo and the minister in Peking that it would give no support to Kolchak. Were this done, he felt sure the board would come around.[58] General Mutō supported his plea.[59]

Finally, opposed by the commanders in the railway zone, by General Horvat and by the Japanese, Admiral Kolchak gave up. On June 30 he set out for Tokyo, primarily, it seems, to protest to the Japanese and to consult his Russian and British friends.[60] He left behind a legacy of hate and a Horvat organization, more devoted to Japan, but even more torn by rivalries than before.

The Rescue of Semenov

While Kolchak, in Harbin, was upsetting the Japanese army's plans, Semenov was threatened with the loss of all his forces in the Trans-Baikal Territory. By the end of May, 1918, he had been forced back to the border.[61] Seven months earlier he had escaped across that same border. This time the soviet forces were determined to hunt him down to the end.

Late in May the Soviet government appealed to the Peking government not to permit Semenov's detachment to retire to a base in China "or, if the Peking government is not sufficiently strong, to agree to have troops of the Soviet government cooperate with independent or regular Chinese troops to suppress the Semenov troops on Chinese territory." [62] On June 10 an agent of the Red forces in the field made similar demands on Commander Chang in Manchouli and asked further that the soviet troops be allowed to purchase provisions at Chalainoerh. To invite another foreign

---

[58] Saitō to Tanaka, June 12, 1918, *ibid.*, III.

[59] Mutō to Tanaka, June 14, 1918, *ibid.*, III.

[60] Mutō to Tanaka, July 3, 1918, *ibid.*, III; Popov, ed. *Dopros Kolchaka*, pp. 125–26, 140.

[61] The Czechoslovak uprising on May 25, 1918, was confined largely to western and central Siberia in the beginning and consequently for a month had no appreciable effect on the Trans-Baikal front.

[62] Acting Minister Maruno to Gotō, May 28, 1918, *JGK, RKI, HK*, II, containing a Japanese translation of a telegram Chicherin is said to have sent to U.S. Ambassador Francis, May 26, in which Chicherin asked Francis' reaction to the request made by the Soviet government to the government of China.

force into the railway zone was the last thing the Chinese wanted
to do, and they warned the soviet commander under no circumstances to cross the border.[63] On the other hand, they realized that
if they did not do something about Semenov, the Red forces might
pursue him into the zone whether the Chinese liked it or not. The
solution that appealed to them most was to permit the Semenov
detachment to cross the border, but only on condition that it sur-
render its arms. Military Governor Pao of Heilungkiang Province
so instructed the border guard on June 17.[64]

As Semenov's position deteriorated and it became clear that
Britain and France had abandoned him and China opposed him,
the Japanese military planners could conceivably have decided that
the hopes placed in him had been misplaced and that he should
be left to his fate. In fact, however, the greater his difficulties became, the more they were determined to support him. They had
previously supplied Semenov with weapons and a team of instructors and had put pressure on the Chinese government to permit
goods to pass through the Manchouli customs station. In May,
June, and July, the Japanese extended further aid in at least three
ways. One was to furnish money. Major General Mutō reported
the transfer of 500,000 rubles via Horvat to Semenov on June 25,
and a further sum on July 15.[65] He gave a separate grant of
100,000 rubles to the destitute Buriat Mongols, who had fled to
Manchouli before the soviet advance.[66]

The Japanese also aided Semenov through organizing and supporting a volunteer Japanese force. Early in June, when Semenov
was being pushed back against the Chinese border, Mutō came
to the conclusion that there was "no alternative but to organize a
volunteer force immediately in order to rescue him." [67] After first

----

[63] Saitō to Uehara, June 17, 1918, ibid., III; and Saitō to Uehara, June 17,
1918, ibid., III, reporting a conversation with Tuan Ch'i-jui.

[64] Mutō to Tanaka, June 19, 1918, ibid., III, as reported by Kuroki.

[65] Mutō to Nakajima, June 25, 1918, ibid., III; and Mutō to Nakajima, July
15, 1918, ibid., III. These may have been the funds approved by the cabinet
on May 14.

[66] Mutō to Nakajima, June 25, 1918, ibid., III; this appears to have been on
Mutō's own authority.

[67] Mutō to Nakajima, June 19, 1918, ibid., II.

securing the secret approval of the Kwantung Government General and of the central military authorities in Tokyo,[68] Mutō assigned nominal leadership in the program to the chairman of the Japanese residents' association at Manchouli, Ansho Jun'ichi, and to a Japanese mining operator in Siberia, Seo Eitaro. Beginning on June 13, these two toured the major cities in south Manchuria, offering 60 yen to 130 yen a month, depending on rank, plus food, clothing, and ammunition to Japanese reservists between the ages of 24 and 40 who would agree to serve with the Semenov forces on the Trans-Baikal front.[69] Agents were even sent to recruit volunteers in Tokyo.[70] By July 7 the first battalion had been organized [71] under the command of Reserve Infantry Captain Okumura Naonari. Semenov had high praise for Captain Okumura and his battalion,[72] but, in fact, the unit seems to have been quite ineffective. Only some 484 men were recruited in all; of these only 301 stuck it out even until August 23, when the battalion was disbanded. Moreover, it had to be rushed into the lines without proper training.[73] The total cost of this experiment was 200,000 yen.[74]

A third form of Japanese aid was pressure upon the Chinese government to give Semenov's Special Manchurian Detachment sanctuary in China. Araki was sent to Manchouli. Saitō hurried up to Tsitsihar, and on June 7 he and Nakajima called on Military Governor Pao.[75] Saitō made it clear to Pao that, "if it happened

[68] The cabinet was not consulted; but, when Foreign Minister Gotō learned of it from the consular reports from posts in south Manchuria, he instructed the ministry's representatives not to interfere. Gotō to Miyake (Yingkow) and Tamura (Mukden), July 2, 1918, *ibid.*, III. Japan, Sambō Hombu, *Shiberia Shuppei-shi*, III, 1081–82.

[69] Miyake to Gotō, July 1, 1918, *ibid.*, III, Kwantung Tōtokufu Rikugun Sambōbu, Tokuhō (Rokoku), Dai 6 Gō (July 12, 1918): "Semiyonofu Shitai no Nihon Giyūhei Bōshū."

[70] Kwantung chief of staff to Tanaka, July 17, 1918, *JGK, RKI, HK*, III.

[71] Mutō to Tanaka, July 9, 1918, *ibid.*, III.

[72] Semenov, *O Sebe*, p. 111.

[73] Table in Japan, Sambō Hombu, *Shiberia Shuppei-shi*, III, 1082.

[74] *Ibid.*, III, 1082. It is not clear whether this sum is identical with that referred to above as having been transferred via Horvat to Semenov in June and July, 1918. Probably it was additional.

[75] Japanese consulate at Tsitsihar to Foreign Ministry, June 8, 1918, *JGK, RKI, HK*, III.

that Semenov withdrew to the Chinese Eastern Railway, he hoped that [the Chinese] would not have him disarmed, but would make suitable arrangements and give the detachment positive assistance." Hurrying back to Peking, Saitō called on Premier Tuan Ch'i-jui[76] and asked him to "consider carefully" before having Semenov disarmed, because "the powers were feeling that intervention in Siberia was necessary." Japan and China would soon be forced to take "joint military action." In these circumstances, Semenov was an ally. Tuan explained that his government had regarded disarmament of Semenov's forces as the only means of keeping Red forces out of Manchuria, but that, since "the situation had changed," he would confer immediately with the council of state. The very next day the premier obediently wired Military Governor Pao that henceforth the Red forces should be considered as enemy elements and the Semenov detachment as a potential ally.[77] "If the Semenov forces cross our borders," he instructed, "ostensibly they should be disarmed, but actually no force should be used to compel them." Pao seems to have raised no objection at Tsitsihar.[78] At Manchouli Commander Chang was reported to have made appropriate arrangements with the front-line forces.[79]

For the increasing aid to Semenov, it was widely rumored that Japan in turn was exacting rights and concessions in Siberia. American Minister Reinsch reported on June 5: "Semenov compensation to Japan believed to comprise exclusive mining, fishery rights, Amur province and dismantling Vladivostok fortifications."[80] The available official Japanese records do not confirm these suspicions, and Semenov states emphatically that "the assistance rendered to me by the Japanese government never depended on the fulfillment of any obligations on my part which could be interpreted as attempts to take advantage of our grievous situation in their own interests."

[76] Saitō to Uehara, June 17, 1918, ibid., III.
[77] Saitō to Uehara, June 18, 1918, ibid., III.
[78] Japanese consul at Tsitsihar (Furusawa?) via Satō to Gotō, June 24, 1918, ibid., III.
[79] Mutō to Tanaka, June 26, 1918, ibid., III.
[80] Reinsch to Lansing, June 5, 1918, USFR, 1918, Russia, II, 189.

The one request to which Semenov is known to have acceded concerns the Trans-Baikal Railway, and Semenov probably did not regard this as a concession. Major General Mutō seems to have feared that the American Railway Corps might move in behind Semenov. After some negotiation, on May 21 he reported that he had reached "a firm, confidential agreement" with Semenov not to admit the American engineers to the Trans-Baikal Railway.

Some officers, like Captain Kuroki, felt Japan should go farther. In their retreat in late April and early May, the soviet troops had destroyed the Trans-Baikal Railway at several places, particularly where it spanned the Onon river. Captain Kuroki saw in this an excellent opportunity to expand Japan's influence, and he talked to Semenov about Japan's undertaking repair and operation of the railroad.[81] Semenov had "no objection," but there is no evidence that he requested Japan to send a railway unit or that Japan pressed him to accept one. As Lieutenant Colonel Kurozawa pointed out, were such specific concessions to have any meaning, Japan would need to guarantee them by taking basic policy decisions concerning intervention in Siberia.[82] Once these decisions were taken, there would be no trouble about concessions. Consul General Satō probably reflected accurately the views of the military planners when he said, in connection with the expense of sending troops to Siberia, "even if it does take vast wealth, it must be remembered that the situation will arise where it will be possible to redeem [the cost] . . . directly from the natural wealth of Siberia." [83]

Semenov was undoubtedly informed of the arrangements made by the Japanese for his withdrawal into China, but for more than a month he hesitated to take advantage of them. One reason was that he and perhaps his Japanese advisers did not trust the Chinese. Would they actually try to disarm the Semenov forces as they had promised the soviet representatives, or would they only pretend to

[81] Kurozawa to Araki, May 13, 1918, *JGK, RKI, HK,* II, reporting Kuroki's negotiations with Semenov.
[82] Kurozawa to Araki, May 15, 1918, *ibid.,* II.
[83] Satō to Motono, April 17, 1918, *ibid.,* II.

do so as they had assured the Japanese? It grew increasingly clear
that they would do whatever they were compelled to do by superior forces on the spot, and at the time superiority was on the
soviet side. Tuan explained his predicament to Minister Hayashi
in Peking, warning him, only one week after he had agreed to
befriend Semenov, that the Chinese government could not go
through with the fake disarmament unless a Sino-Japanese expedition could actually be organized to support it.[84]

Once again the army's continental policy required an expedition but the army was still held back by two essential preliminaries.
The one was the obligation it had assumed of persuading Horvat
to set up a government and of rallying the anti-soviet Russian
forces to it. The other was the obligation it had assigned to the
Foreign Ministry to secure an agreement between America and the
powers that Japan should either intervene alone or else head up
a joint intervention in support of an anti-soviet Russian government.

[84] Hayashi to Gotō, June 26, 1918, *ibid.*, I; Hayashi to Gotō, June 27, 1918,
ibid., III.

X. UNACCOMMODATING ALLIES

While the military authorities were having great difficulties in building a pro-Japanese center in the Russian Far East, the new foreign minister, Viscount Gotō, was having an equally difficult time in his efforts to harmonize the conflicting views of the great powers abroad and of the various factions in the Advisory Council on Foreign Relations at home.

Gotō's Policy of "Aggressive Defense"

The selection of a new foreign minister to replace Motono had been made with care. The liberals, including Saionji and Hara, had favored an anti-interventionist, like the returning ambassador from Russia, Viscount Uchida Kōsai,[1] or the ambassador to Great Britain, Viscount Chinda Sutemi, but Yamagata refused to consider either of them. He wanted a man he could trust to do his bidding. His first choice went to the legalistic, loyal Itō Miyoji, but Itō declined on the ground that the position would be too difficult with the cabinet's life so dependent on Terauchi's health. Instead, he recommended the home minister, Gotō Shimpei.[2]

Gotō was a strong advocate of intervention. In a policy paper presumably dating from this time, he outlined the necessity for the empire to draw up a "long-range" plan.[3] The power of the

[1] Hara Kei, *Hara Kei Nikki* (Tokyo: Kengensha, 1950–52), VII, 370.

[2] According to the diary of Communications Minister Den, as quoted in Den Kenjiro Denki Hensankai, *Den Kenjiro Denki* (Tokyo: Den Kenjiro Denki Hensankai, 1932), pp. 346–47, and partly substantiated by Hara, *Hara Kei Nikki*, VII, 381–82.

[3] Tsurumi Yūsuke, *Gotō Shimpei* (Tokyo: Gotō Shimpei Denki Hensan-kai, 1938), III, 883–88.

Western Allies, he argued, was "declining like that of a spent bow." The future belonged to the United States, on the one hand, and to Germany and the Central Powers, on the other. This was of considerable moment to Japan because the Bolsheviks were pawns of German power, so that their movement eastward meant that soon "enemy attacks would be threatening neighboring territory in the Pacific." At the same time the United States was threatening to take over Russian rail transportation by sending vast amounts of rolling stock to Vladivostok and on to Irkutsk.

To protect its own interests, Gotō argued, Japan would need to adopt a five-point "policy of aggressive defense." (1) It should negotiate with America to secure the right to administer the rolling stock America was sending and to help protect it. (2) It should negotiate with England, France, and the United States to secure their complete agreement with Japan's policies. (3) It should plan an expedition to Siberia, either to occupy the Amur basin east of Irkutsk or to guard the Trans-Siberian Railroad all the way to Moscow. (4) In preparation for these operations, it should modernize the weapons and expand the budgets of the army and navy. (5) It should negotiate with China to secure for Japan the exclusive right to maintain peace and order in northern Manchuria.

A Siberian expedition was not simply an integral part of Gotō's program; it was the heart of it. The more Gotō examined the question of an expedition, the more he felt that nothing but good results could be expected to follow.[4] In Japan's relations with the Allies, a Japanese expedition could bring nothing but a closer understanding. Were not the Bolsheviks agents of Germany? Would not an expedition against them be in effect an offensive against the Germans and therefore a welcome contribution to the Allied war effort? An expedition would be highly desirable also for Japan's interests in Russia; it would assure Japan a "voice in the peace conference," where many Russian questions were sure to be discussed. An expedition would be equally helpful for Japan's

[4] Tsurumi, *Gotō Shimpei,* III, 895–98. Part I of this three-part document, quoted by Tsurumi, is identical with an undated, unsigned memorandum, written on foreign ministry paper and marked "secret," entitled, "Shiberia shuppei mondai ni kansuru iken" in *JGK, RKI, SK, EBFK,* I.

Chinese policy. It would save China from the Germans and also, if it were conducted jointly with the Chinese, might so impress the Allies with the solidarity of the Sino-Japanese coalition that it might serve to deter them from taking too great an interest in China after the war. This concern for Chinese policy was directly related to what Gotō felt was the most important consideration of all: the value of an expedition for checking America's economic penetration in the Far East.

Before the outbreak of the Russian Revolution, Gotō was convinced, as was the Chōshū clique, that the most serious threat to Japan's future development was the possible seizure of the Chinese market by Western, particularly American, businessmen returning to China after the war. Following the outbreak of the revolution, he became convinced that, while America might have no territorial ambitions in Siberia, it was certainly planning to expand its economic activities there just as in China. Whether the empire desired to cooperate or to compete with American capital, it would first have to secure a strong position in Siberia. By a strong position, Gotō meant not only militarily, but especially economically.

For months the Japanese government had been concerned about America's railroad interests and about the increasing number of reports of American financial and commercial activity in the Amur basin.[5] There were numerous reports about Americans: they were energetically hunting concessions, especially for lumbering, gold mining, and fishing; they were buying up Russian newspapers and subsidizing Russian publicists; they were opening up new consulates and staffing them with businessmen and "Red Cross" personnel expert in local conditions; they were developing connections with the Siberian Foreign Trade Conference in Irkutsk; they were offering loans, secured by concessions, to such organizations as the Vladivostok city council and the Krasnoiarsk soviet; they

[5] *JGK, RKI, SB, passim;* Japan, Gaimushō, "Shiberia ni okeru Beikoku no katsudō ni kansuru choshō" (as of June 15, 1918), *ibid.*, pp. 103–29; and Japan, Gaimushō, "Shiberia ni okeru Beikoku no katsudō ni kansuru chōsa" (as of July 10, 1918), *ibid.*, pp. 130–31; Japan, Sambō Hombu, *Kaigai Tokuhō,* No. 62 (for the last ten days in September, 1917); and Japan, Sambō Hombu, *Shiberia Shuppei-shi,* III, 1170–74.

were promoting the organization of large trading combines, especially a Russo-American association at Vladivostok and a Russo-
American Far Eastern trading association at Harbin; and funds
would soon be forthcoming from a newly organized Asia banking
corporation, with its home office in New York and with branch
offices in San Francisco and Shanghai, and later other branch
offices in Hankow, Peking, Tientsin, Harbin, and Vladivostok.

That the United States government was not only deeply interested in such ventures, but in fact intended to promote their
expansion, seemed clear. Ambassador Ishii reported from Washington President Wilson's announcement that the American government would "extend aid to Russia as well as to France," an
idea which referred, he thought, to the rumored United States
plan to spend several tens of billions of dollars to provide agricultural machinery for use in Siberia.[6] Two days previously Secretary
Lansing told him "the United States intends to assist the development of Siberia's agriculture and commerce." A month later, on
June 26, he learned from Lansing that the American government
was considering sending an economic commission to Siberia to
supply some goods to the Russians on the basis of charity and to
exchange some "for Siberian agricultural produce."[7] Lansing
maintained that any such commission would act purely from hu-
manitarian motives and from a desire to strengthen the Russian
people against the Germans, but he insisted that the commission
would have to be a wholly independent American venture: "If it
were made up of Japanese, the Russians would suspect it of political designs; and if it were made up of Englishmen, they would
suspect it of commercial ambitions." As Admiral Katō Kanji had
remarked earlier, it began to appear that, unless the Japanese
government took some positive action, it all might end "in Japan's
being employed in policing activity while England and America
are getting the gravy."[8]

[6] Ishii to Gotō, May 26, 1918, *JGK, RKI, SB*, pp. 91–93.
[7] Ishii to Gotō, June 30, 1918, *ibid.*, pp. 149–52.
[8] Letter from Armiral Katō Kanji to Amano Genjiro in Osaka, March 5, 1918,
Fukunami Sadao and Ishihara Sadao, *Katō Kanji Taishō Den* (Tokyo: Katō
Kanji Taishō Denki Hensankai, 1941), p. 680.

While the Japanese supporters of intervention were worried by this threat, the Ministry of Foreign Affairs under Baron Gotō took the initiative in formulating plans to meet it. As in the case of Motono, Gotō's own inclinations were reinforced and given detailed form by various policy recommendations submitted to him by an eager group of subordinates in the ministry. The key junior officials most interested in developing an active economic policy toward Siberia and northern Manchuria included Arita Hachiro, former chief of the first (Asian) section of the Political Affairs Bureau, who had been brought back from the Honolulu consulate in June; Hirota Kōki, chief of the first (Asian) section of the Commercial Affairs Bureau; Marquis Kimura Ei'ichi, assigned to the second (European and American) section of the Political Affairs Bureau; and Matsuoka Yōsuke, secretary to both the foreign minister and the prime minister and one of the key influences on Motono in the latter's effort in April to set an expedition on foot.

The earliest extant concrete proposal is in the handwriting of Arita, dated June 7, 1918, and entitled, "Shiberia Haken Keizai Shisatsu An, I'in no Ken" (Proposal for an Economic Mission to Siberia. The Committee).[9] In it, he recommended that a private or preferably an official mission be organized by the Foreign Ministry, including technical mining, forestry, and chemical engineering specialists, Osaka-Kobe merchants experienced in Amur basin trade, representative industrialists, translators, and interpreters. This mission would proceed to the Amur basin for a period of three to six months "(1) to investigate enterprises suitable for Japanese investment; (2) to investigate materials lacking in Siberia and markets for Japanese goods; and (3) to collect research data relating to Siberian natural resources." At the same time, Arita recommended that a special research organ be established within the temporary investigation department of the Foreign Ministry to coordinate the findings of the mission with all relevant official and

[9] Handwriting identified by former diplomat, Okamoto Suemasa, on September 30, 1951. Japan, Gaimushō Kiroku, "Shiberia Keizai Enjo Kankei Zakken: I'inkai no Seiritsu ni kansuru Ken" (hereinafter, *JGK, SKE, IS*); and Japan, Gaimushō, *Shiberia Keizai Enjo no Gaiyō* (1919), pp. 1–10.

private information and to embody the results in a series of studies
and reports.

As a diplomatic and economic planner, Gotō was a useful ad-
junct of the military planners. Even more important to the Chōshū
clique at the moment, he was an able politician. As a man with
wide financial and political connections and a trusted confident of
the clique, Gotō understood what Motono never had: namely, that
the government depended on coalition support. He knew he could
remain in office only so long as he fulfilled the wishes of the
Chōshū clique, but that, to do so, his diplomacy must command
the support of the liberal party politicians as well as the military
planners. By his "policy of aggressive defense" he showed himself
prepared to seek that support through negotiating with America
while working closely with the army. At last the Chōshū clique
had in the Foreign Ministry a man it could trust.

Gotō's problem was to adjust his "long-range" thinking to the
apparent impasse which faced him when he assumed office on
April 23. The Allies were deeply split over the question of an
expedition: Britain and France wanted one, America did not. The
governing coalition in Japan was similarly divided: the Chōshū
clique wanted an expedition; Hara, Makino, and others did not.
And the groups at home and abroad which did favor an expedition could not agree on the kind: Britain and France wanted one
sent to western Siberia or possibly to European Russia at the invitation of the Soviet government; the military planners within
Japan were in favor of one to the Amur basin only, made up
solely of Japanese troops and sent in support of Horvat and
Semenov.

Gotō, probably after conferring with the military planners, the
cabinet, and the elders of the Chōshū clique, seems to have determined on a three-point program to break the deadlock. First of
all, he would try to convert the American government by offering
to accept the principle of an Inter-Allied expedition; he would, on
the other hand, reserve to Japan the right to run it. Secondly, he
would try to persuade the entente to give up their negotiations
with the Soviet regime for a west Siberian expedition and in its

place to support one to eastern Siberia in behalf of Horvat and Semenov. Finally, he would attempt to induce Britain, France, and America to propose such an expedition to Japan. Such an invitation, he felt confident, would be accepted by his government.

Negotiations with America

Gotō's program represented a new departure. From the beginning the Japanese government had never deviated from its insistence that the only expedition acceptable to it would be an independent Japanese expedition. But it had also insisted that it would need America's "moral and material support." Now the history of Motono's negotiations seems to have convinced the cabinet and the military planners that their project could never be achieved and that they could never secure America's support for a purely Japanese operation. On the other hand, they seem to have been encouraged, perhaps by America's note to the British government of February 8 and no doubt by more recent suggestions from the British,[10] in the belief that they might secure American backing for an Inter-Allied undertaking. At least, they came to think it might be worth while to offer acceptance of an Inter-Allied expedition in principle, providing of course that no one questioned Japan's right to command it in fact.

Viscount Ishii, who was already in Washington to seek a closer understanding with the United States, opened the negotiations on April 28, when he had his first interview with Secretary Lansing. Two days later he called on President Wilson to present his credentials. His first move was to ingratiate himself and his government by assuring America of Japan's complete accord. He was so successful in the interview of April 28 that Lansing reported enthusiastically to President Wilson:

[10] It would appear to be hardly a coincidence that, when Viscount Ishii brought up the question of a Siberian expedition with Lansing on April 28 (see below), the American secretary of state revealed that he also was now thinking in terms of a nominally Inter-Allied, but predominantly Japanese, expedition.

The Japanese government agree fully with our point of view and . . . they do not see at present the military compensation for the danger of uniting the Russian factions to resist intervention and of throwing them in the hands of Germany. . . . Viscount Ishii said that the menace to Japan was a Germanized Russia and that intervention might increase rather than decrease it.[11]

Then, having dispelled his listeners' fears, Ishii proceeded adroitly to lead them to discuss the kind of expedition they might be induced to support.[12]

Since the British had only just recommended an Inter-Allied expedition to Wilson, it is not surprising that this was the idea Lansing broached to Ishii. Ishii gathered that the Americans were prepared to think, first of all, in terms of a joint expedition made up largely of Japanese, but including American troops as well. Ishii opined that his government would agree to a joint expedition of this type and on May 6 he was able to report specific instructions from Gotō to that effect.[13] He pointed out, however, the basic conviction of the Japanese government that in view of the need for unifying the command and in view of Japan's geographic position in the Far East, a solely Japanese expedition would be preferable. Lansing then sought to meet him halfway by stating that in his personal opinion,

the proposal to add allied forces alongside the Japanese units was simply made with the thought that it would enlist the sympathy of the Russian people; and that when the expedition was actually undertaken, it would seem quite natural, in order to unify the command, for the right of command to be exercised by Japan, which would send the largest number of men.

Secondly, in the American view the expedition would proceed to the interior of Siberia to divert German forces from the western European front. Japan, as Ishii pointed out, had repeatedly rejected such an expedition; the only operation his country could consider

[11] Lansing to President Wilson, April 29, 1918, USFR, 1918, Russia, II, 144.
[12] Ishii's account of this interview is found in the report from Ishii to Gotō, April 28 and April 30, 1918. Japan, Gaimushō, Shiberia Shuppei Mondai, Dai Ippen Shiberia Shuppei ni itaru Kōshō Keika (1922), p. 21.
[13] Gotō to Ishii, May 1, 1918, Japan, Gaimushō, Shiberia Shuppei Mondai, I, 21.

was one to the Amur basin, to build a barrier against the extension of German power into northeast Asia.

Thus, Viscount Gotō succeeded in reopening with the United States government the subject of intervention and made the strongest concession he could for its support: the offer to accept the participation of Allied units. He immediately informed Britain, France, and Italy of his action. Upon receiving sympathetic responses and their assurances that Allied participation would be only a formality,[14] he apparently asked them to renew their efforts to secure America's approval, although such a request was now hardly needed.[15]

Negotiations with Britain

Gotō then proceeded to the second phase of his campaign: the effort to win over the entente to support the kind of expedition the Japanese military wanted. The British, and to a less extent the French and Americans, had not yet lost hope that the Allies might be able to deal with the Soviet government. Throughout March and April the British in particular, having failed otherwise to induce America and Japan to intervene in Russia, had been seeking to win them over by persuading the Soviet government itself to extend them an invitation. To prove their sincerity, the British had even gone so far as to cut off aid to Semenov and to ignore the opportunities which Japan's landing in Vladivostok in April had presented.

Viscount Gotō had no sympathy with this policy and sought to reverse it. On May 18 he instructed Ambassador Chinda to reopen the subject by asking the British whether good results were expected soon from Lockhart's endeavors to secure from the Soviet government an invitation for an Allied expedition.[16] He was then

[14] *Ibid.*, I, 22.
[15] French Ambassador Regnault (in Japan) to Vice Minister Shidehara, May 9, 1918, *JGK, RKI, SK, EBFK*, II.
[16] Gotō to Chinda, May 18, 1918, *ibid.*, I; and Japan, Gaimushō, *Shiberia Shuppei Mondai*, I, 22–23. It appears that similar conversations were held at about this same time with the French government. Sharp to Lansing, May 29, 1918, *USFR, 1918, Russia*, II, 180.

to go on tactfully to suggest that, even were an invitation forth-coming, an Allied expedition could hardly be satisfactory. Its pre-sumed object must be to aid soviet resistance to an armed German invasion. On the other hand, if that invasion did not extend to Siberia, how could a Siberian expedition be justified? Moreover, would not any such intervention "result indirectly in strengthening the position of the workers' and peasants' government," thereby arousing the hostility of the anti-Bolsheviks toward the Allies? Lastly, since it involved discontinuing support to Semenov, would not this example of Allied inconstancy drive the Semenovists and, indeed, "the Russian people in general" to the Soviet-German side?

On May 22, Chinda raised these questions with Lord Robert Cecil,[17] who, of course, could only reply that he would refer them to his government. But Cecil reiterated that, regardless of the atti-tude of the Soviet government, if Japan were to launch an expedi-tion to the Urals he was sure that the "allies generally would wel-come it enthusiastically." Chinda reminded him that in the Jap-anese view a Urals expedition and a Siberian expedition were two different things and went on to ask him what he thought concern-ing America's attitude. In Cecil's view, America appeared to sym-pathize with the Soviet government as a kind of sister republic and to fear lest any move against it might arouse the Russian peo-ple; and in any case the actions of the Germans would soon in-spire a popular Russian uprising in retaliation. Of course, said Cecil, the British government did not share these mistaken ideas.

Eight days later, on May 30, Ambassador Chinda had an ex-tended interview in which Lord Balfour replied to the questions raised by Gotō. Chinda quotes Balfour as saying: "As for the first point about the possibility of the Allies being invited by the work-ers' and peasants' government to intervene, while such an invitation was at first expected, Germany is exerting such ever increasing pressure on Russia that it is no longer anticipated."[18] Did Britain still support a Siberian expedition? Most certainly, it did. "Even

[17] Chinda to Gotō, May 25, 1918, *JGK, RKI, SK, EBFK,* I; and Japan, Gai-mushō, *Shiberia Shuppei Mondai,* I, 26–27.

[18] Chinda to Gotō, June 2, 1918, *JGK, RKI, SK, EBFK,* I; and Japan, Gai-mushō, *Shiberia Shuppei Mondai,* I, 23–24.

though Germany has not carried out a military invasion of Siberia, since the Siberian expedition which Britain hoped for was based on an estimate of the general war situation, it is still viewed as important to carry it out at this time." As for the effect of an expedition on the Soviet government, the British cared not a whit. The Soviet government would not last long anyway; moreover, His Majesty's government "is not concerned about whether a Siberian intervention would influence the power of the parties within Russia or not." Lastly, Semenov had been cut off because he had "acted counter to British policy" in advancing when the British had told him to hold fast. If Semenov were prepared now to act in accord with British policy, "he would continue to be supplied financial means, weapons, etc."; and "in case of the beginning of Allied operations, the British intended to use him, but it was not believed he would be of great value."

In short, the British honeymoon with the Bolsheviks was over. Britain like Japan was ready for a new departure. After trying for two months without success to elicit a Soviet invitation to intervene, the British government had decided to abandon the effort and to return to the policy of supporting all "anti-German," which meant also anti-Soviet, elements in Russia and of trying to bring about an intervention through Siberia regardless of Soviet opposition.

Balfour's Hypothetical Question

Britain's new policy was made perfectly clear on May 30, not only by Lord Balfour's reply to the question submitted by the Japanese government, but also by the questions he asked in his turn.[19] Balfour explained to Ambassador Chinda that on the following day he was leaving with the prime minister and the war minister for a meeting of the Supreme War Council in Paris and that he was sure the question of an expedition would come up. He was, he

[19] Chinda to Gotō, June 2, 1918, Japan Gaimushō, *Shiberia Shuppei Mondai,* I, 25; JGK, RKI, SK, EBFK, I; Japan, Kaigun Gunreibu, *Taishō Yon-nen naishi Kyū-nen Kaigun Senshi* (1924), I, 181–82; and Japan, Sambō Hombu, *Taishō Shichi-nen naishi Jūichi-nen, Shiberia Shuppei-shi* (1924), I, 41.

said, "extremely anxious for intervention in Siberia." If only Allied forces would penetrate western Siberia, they could economically rob Germany of the Ukraine and give the Allies control of north Russia as well; militarily, they could force Germany to divert critical divisions from the western front. He was sure France would agree and hoped that at last America might be persuaded. Before approaching either government, he wished to know what Japan's reaction would be to an invitation by all three powers to join them in "a Siberian expedition with Japanese troops as its main strength."

To secure some such invitation was precisely the Japanese foreign minister's goal. But he did not want to answer on his own responsibility lest something he might say should reawaken America's fears and deter it from joining in a concrete invitation. In addition, he was sure that few persons, certainly not the military authorities, would be willing to commit themselves to any expedition so vaguely defined. His predecessor had ignored such difficulties and had met disaster. Gotō was determined to proceed cautiously with the powers abroad—and also with the Advisory Council on Foreign Relations in Tokyo.

On June 5, at the prime minister's official residence, Gotō laid Balfour's question before the council and suggested that Japan counter with a proposal for Allied help to the "constructive elements" in Siberia in establishing "an independent government." [20] As was to be expected, Gotō's proposal was immediately attacked by Hara Kei, who doubted that any such elements were available and asked what the entente's attitude might be toward them or toward the Soviet regime. Prime Minister Terauchi agreed that it was difficult to proceed until the attitude of Britain and France toward the various factions in Russia was made clear. Finally, Itō Miyoji drew up a compromise draft which the council could accept. It was sent to the ambassador on the following day.[21]

[20] Hara Kei, *Hara Kei Nikki* (Tokyo: Kengensha, 1950–52), VII, 409–10.

[21] Gotō to Chinda, June 6, 1918, in Japan, Gaimushō, *Shiberia Shuppei Mondai*, I, 26–27; *JGK, RKI, SK, EBFK,* I; Japan, Kaigun Gunreibu, *Senshi,* I, 182–84.

To reassure the Hara faction that the government meant to take no action without America's approval, and also to reemphasize that fact to the entente, Chinda was instructed to reply:

In so far as there is mutual understanding among the Allied powers and America concerning the question of intervention in Siberia, the Imperial government is resolved to give the matter its sincere consideration. And in this decision, which was communicated to America on March 19 and was also confidentially told the Allied powers, there is still no change.

Chinda was then instructed to argue most forcefully that in the Japanese government's view the Soviet regime not only could not be relied on to oppose the Germans but was in fact their tool, and to express the Japanese government's deep concern over their penetration into the Far Eastern region. He was to call for Allied aid to be given "to the sincere plans of those Russians who are trying to establish self-governing or independent bodies in that area, with the object of enabling Siberia to throw off the yoke of the Bolshevik government or of any succeeding government which likewise submits to the power of Germany." It was the British who had urged the first step of securing the military stores at Vladivostok. Now the Japanese government felt it was time to take a second step, "to decide which Russians are to be recognized as the central personnel of the body politic which the allies are to assist." Specifically, Japan considered it appropriate "to plan to unite General Horvat and Captain Semenov and to maintain connection with them."

The Allied Supreme War Council's Request

Then, before the reply could be delivered, a new report arrived from Chinda.[22] On June 7, Foreign Minister Balfour handed the

[22] Chinda to Gotō, June 7, 1918, Japan, Gaimushō, *Shiberia Shuppei Mondai*, I, 27–28; *JGK, RKI, SK, EBFK*, I; Japan, Kaigun Gunreibu, *Senshi*, I, 185–86; Japan, Sambō Hombu, *Shiberia Shuppei-shi*, I, 41–42; and briefly mentioned in Makino Nobuaki, *Kaiko-roku* (Tokyo: Bungei Shunshu Shinsha, 1949), III, 132–33, and in Araki Sadao, *Gensui Uehara Yūsaku Den* (Tokyo: Gensui Uehara Yūsaku Denki Hankō kai, 1937), II, 143.

Japanese ambassador a formal request from the Supreme War Council of the Allies. On June 3, without waiting for Japan's reply to Balfour's inquiry, the council had discussed the Russian question. Apparently it had buried irrevocably the plan of persuading Japan and America to send an expedition after securing a Soviet invitation. Its strategy now was to persuade Japan to agree to the kind of expedition that America might be persuaded to accept, and then to have the Allies approach America *en bloc.* The council had decided, Chinda was informed, that "the governments of Great Britain, France, and Italy should formally inquire of the Imperial Japanese government whether the latter was prepared to take common action in Siberia, with such help from the other co-belligerents as the military exigencies of the situation would allow." The three Allied governments were of the opinion that in order to make Allied intervention in Siberia acceptable to the Russian people and to public opinion in the three Allied countries and in America, the following conditions should be fulfilled:

First, The allies should promise to respect the territorial integrity of Russia;

Second, The allies should declare that they will take no side in the internal politics of Russia;

Third, The allied expedition should advance as far west as possible, with the avowed object of meeting and defeating German influence and compelling the central powers to reverse their own policy of sending all their forces to the western front.

In response to an inquiry from Chinda, Balfour explained that the phrase "as far west as possible," meant at least as far as Omsk and if possible to Cheliabinsk, so that the Allies might keep the cereals of western Siberia out of German hands and keep Germany from concentrating all its forces on the western front.[23]

In spite of Japan's repeated objections, the Western Allies still wanted an expedition to the Urals as an indirect way to save the western front. Once again they failed to understand how deeply "Asia-minded" was the Japanese administration.

[23] Chinda to Gotō, June 7, Japan, Gaimushō, *Shiberia Shuppei Mondai,* I, 29–31.

Debates in the Advisory Council on Foreign Relations

The inquiry of the Allied Supreme War Council was presented by Gotō and discussed at the meetings of the Advisory Council on Foreign Relations on June 17, 19, and 20. Although the available reports of these meetings are too inadequate to give a complete picture, there is little doubt that the army representatives raised serious objections to the expedition proposed by the war council.

In a special report circulated at this time[24] the Army General Staff Headquarters vigorously charged that an expedition to western Siberia would commit all of Japan's permanent divisions and some special ones in addition, might take more than three years to reach Cheliabinsk, would require 107,000 railroad guards and workmen, and would necessitate increasing the rolling stock of the Chinese Eastern Railway ten times over. If Japan were to make such an effort, the army asked, what would happen to its interests in east Asia? They would be left unprotected. "The reason the empire cannot use its national strength now to send an expedition to western Siberia is simply that as the leader of east Asia the empire must have strength to respond immediately to emergencies in order to protect the allied areas in east Asia." It would be a far better policy for Japan gradually to reconstruct the Siberian railway and occupy the Trans-Baikal Territory, from which position Japan's forces could "protect the Russian Far East, insure China's northwestern borders, and indirectly be able to suppress disturbances within India."

As for the proposal that the expedition be inter-Allied, the Japanese military planners, having already apparently resigned themselves to this necessity, do not appear to have raised the issue. They were, of course, determined that Japan should not lose thereby the right of command.

These views of the army were ones with which even Hara

[24] Japan, Sambō Hombu, "Study of an Expedition to Western Siberia" (dated the first ten days of June, 1918) in Japan, Sambō Hombu, *Shiberia Shuppei-shi*, I, Appendix VIII, 77–85.

could agree. He told the council that Japan should make it emphatically clear to the Allies that "the sphere within which troops are sent must be limited to eastern Siberia"; and he insisted that "the united command must be ours." [25]

The question then arose: with these two reservations, should Japan express willingness now to undertake an expedition? Views here were sharply divided. Although the draft reply presented by Gotō to the council does not appear to be extant, he is reported to have favored telling the Allies that Japan was ready and willing to act. At the other extreme, Baron Makino protested that the expedition talk had been allowed to go entirely too far. He urged the council to end it once and for all by taking a definite decision that an expedition was "clearly impossible." [26] Hirata and Inukai supported Gotō, but Terauchi, the military representatives, and Hara refused to enter into the argument. On this question, for the first time Hara parted company with Baron Makino. He wanted no decision of any kind at the moment and insisted that there be no departure from the position expressed in the reply of March 19 to the United States and in the reply of June 6 to Great Britain: that Japan would maintain its "freedom of action," [27] that it would promise the Allies not to accept, but only to consider, any invitation which might be extended.

Henceforth Hara was no longer fighting a delaying action against the proposal for an expedition. If self-defense required one, he would unquestionably support it. More than that, he confided to Itō Miyoji on June 22: "If America were to agree with the English and the French proposal and request us to send an expedition, there would probably be no question about sending one"; in that case, however, it would be important to ascertain how strong was America's approval.[28]

<hr/>

[25] Hara's speech before the Advisory Council on Foreign Relations, June 19, 1918, as summarized in Hara, *Hara Kei Nikki*, VII, 421–24.

[26] Makino's speech before the Advisory Council on Foreign Relations, June 20, 1918, as noted in Hara, *Hara Kei Nikki*, VII, 425.

[27] Hara's speech, June 19, 1918, *ibid.*, VII, 421–24.

[28] *Ibid.*, VII, 427.

If America were to agree unwillingly, [before accepting] we should propose suitable conditions and only then need we consider it. If however America were to turn out to be the determined leader and were to
urge us sincerely to send an expedition, we should consider it, for it
would no doubt lead to a coalition between Japan and America in the
future.

In short, Hara urged the council to take no action that might
threaten the vitally important understanding with the United
States. No doubt Hara made this view clear to other members of
the council.[29]

After three days of debate Hara carried his point, and Itō Miyoji
incorporated it in the final version of the reply sent to Ambassador
Chinda on June 21 for transmission to the British government.

Japan's Reply to the European Allies

In replying to the Allied Supreme War Council's inquiry, the
Japanese government reminded the British foreign minister of
Japan's firm conviction that no military action should be undertaken in Siberia without "the moral and material support of the
United States." [30] Consequently, "in view of the Imperial government's declaration to the United States government, on March
19, until perfect harmony has been established between these three
governments and the United States government, it asks the three
governments to understand that it is morally bound not to give its
decision." In any event, it would be impossible to engage in the
kind of expedition suggested unless it were under Japan's supreme
command and its operations were limited to eastern Siberia.

Such was the official reply presented by Ambassador Chinda to
Lord Balfour on June 24 and also confidentially communicated to
the French, Italian, and American governments. The reply had,

[29] Gotō repeated the same argument to the British ambassador on July 1.
Japan, Gaimushō, *Shiberia Shuppei Mondai*, I, 42–44; and Tsurumi, *Gotō Shimpei*, III, 906–9.

[30] Gotō to Chinda, June 21, 1918, Japan, Gaimushō, *Shiberia Shuppei Mondai*,
I, 33–35; *JGK, RKI, SK, EBFK*, I.

of course, been framed largely with the American position in mind, and it seems to have had the desired effect. When the American ambassador was informed about it on June 26, he assured Gotō that the United States would be gratified by the statement, as evidence that Japan's view "agreed with its own." [31] Lest the reply antagonize Britain, France, and Italy, however, Gotō instructed the ambassadors, much as they had done in communicating the Japanese reply to America of March 19, to explain orally that his government was really sympathetic to their proposal, but felt it best not to announce a decision since it might arouse the fear held by "some Americans" "that the desire of the Imperial government for an expedition is based on some egoistic ambition." [32] In addition, since Ambassador Chinda had not yet had an opportunity to deliver the June 6 reply to the British government, he was instructed to express as his personal view the plea therein developed for Allied aid in establishing the Horvat and Semenov forces as a successor government for the Far Eastern region.

Although the Allies were naturally disappointed at Japan's failure to join them in an appeal to the American government, apparently they deemed it unwise to contest the decision, but they could not help remonstrating with the stubborn Japanese refusal to consider moving west of Irkutsk. Lord Balfour questioned Ambassador Chinda closely on this point and requested him to ask his government whether its contention was based solely on the matter of practicality.[33] On June 30, Chinda was instructed to reemphasize that, while, as a matter of principle, opinions in Japan did differ, there was "absolutely no disagreement" about Japan's inability to advance beyond eastern Siberia as a matter of "practical diffi-

[31] Interview with Foreign Minister Gotō, June 26, 1918, *ibid.*, I, 36. It should be pointed out that the only paper relating to Japan's reply which has been published by the U.S. State Department, Frazier to Lansing, June 27, 1918 (USFR, 1918, Russia, II, 233), incorrectly reports Japan's action. On the other hand, General Bliss was better informed. Frederick Palmer, *Bliss, Peacemaker* (New York: Dodd, Mead, 1934), p. 301.

[32] Gotō to Chinda, June 21, 1918, Japan, Gaimushō, *Shiberia Shuppei Mondai,* I, 33–35.

[33] Chinda to Gotō, June 24, 1918, *ibid.*, I, 37.

culty." [34] Lord Robert Cecil, who received this clarification on July 2, said that if this were true, then of course Japan's decision would have to be respected.[35] No doubt, the British shared Pichon's confidence that, after troops had actually been landed, the Japanese would find Russian support so widespread and the advance westward so easy as to make them reconsider.[36]

Thus, after two months of negotiations, Gotō had succeeded partly in point one of his three-point program: he had offered to accept an Inter-Allied expedition on the assumption that Japan would command it; and even America had agreed to this in case it approved any expedition at all. In point two, he had been assured that the entente would cease trying to curry favor with the Soviet regime, and he had won their reluctant acceptance of Japan's determination to limit its activities to the Amur basin. However, he had not secured from America and the Allies a joint proposal for such an expedition, and he had been strongly reminded by the Advisory Council on Foreign Relations that America's invitation would be necessary. Nor had he succeeded in winning Allied agreement to support Horvat and Semenov as the logical Russian instruments of control.

When the question of aid to them was raised by Ambassador Chinda on June 2, Cecil replied that Britain would be willing to help and to use Semenov if an Allied expedition were begun,[37] but his government took no action. On June 24 Ambassador Chinda made a new appeal. He succeeded two weeks later only in eliciting the reply that the British government agreed there might be some merit in keeping Semenov's movement "alive" and would be willing "to consider, together with their allies, any proposals which may be put forward provisionally for financing him." [38] The British did send a certain Captain Stepany to establish liaison with him, but that was all.

---

[34] Gotō to Chinda, June 30, 1918, *ibid.*, I, 41.
[35] Chinda to Gotō, July 2, 1918, *ibid.*, I, 42.
[36] Matsui to Gotō, June 25, 1918, *ibid.*, I, 38.
[37] Chinda to Gotō, June 2, 1918, *ibid.*, I, 23–24.
[38] Confidential memorandum (in English) from the British embassy, Tokyo, dated July 4, 1918, *JGK, RKI, HK,* III.

Neither Foreign Minister Gotō's policy of "aggressive defense," nor the army's efforts to erect an anti-Bolshevik barrier with Semenov and Horvat, could be called a success. In Tokyo the Japanese interventionists had again reached an impasse when the situation was drastically altered by a sudden event deep in western Siberia. On May 25, 1918, some 50,000 Czechoslovak troops began to take over the Trans-Siberian Railroad.

XI. THE IMPASSE BROKEN

The role of chance in history is perhaps nowhere better illustrated than in the impact of the Czechoslovak anabasis on the history of the intervention. The Czechoslovak corps had been recruited from among Czechs and Slovaks resident in Russia, or captured on the eastern front, to fight for independence from Austria-Hungary. The Russian provisional government permitted them to form a volunteer corps to fight for the Allies on the Russian southwestern front. At the same time they were under the political direction of the Czechoslovak National Council in Paris which, with Thomas G. Masaryk as president, was leading the movement for establishing an independent Czechoslovak state.

The Czechoslovak Uprising

With the withdrawal of Soviet Russia from the war, Masaryk, on January 25, 1918, declared the corps in Russia to be a part of the Czechoslovak army in France. He hoped to secure Allied assistance in transporting these forces to France, where they could join with other units to form a national army fighting on the western front. A concrete military contribution to the Allied cause, Masaryk felt, was the surest way for the aspiring nation to win the support of the powers.

Masaryk's estimate proved correct. The French government showed an immediate interest in this plan. In return for the assignment of National Council forces to operate under the French high command, France recognized the forces as a national army and agreed to support the independence of Czechoslovakia at the peace conference. Negotiations with the British government were left to Edvard Beneš, chairman of the council, while Masaryk turned his attention to securing the support of Russia, Japan, and the United States.

The most critical negotiations were those with the Soviet Republic. The Czechoslovak leaders said publicly that their only desire was to pass quietly and quickly to the western front, taking no part in Russia's internal affairs. However, the passage of some 50,000 well-armed, well-disciplined, veteran troops through a country engaged in civil war could hardly be viewed with unconcern by either side in the struggle. For a while it appeared that the Bolshevik leaders in European Russia wanted the Czechoslovaks to stay in order to reinforce the regime in Russia or to spread the revolution to Austria-Hungary. Agitators were sent among the Czechoslovak soldiers in the big cities and the camps. On January 14, 1918, a meeting of Czechoslovak "workers' organizations," held in Moscow, "recognized the Russian Revolution as the forerunner of the triumph of socialism throughout the world." [1] A month later, a similar meeting was induced to call for a congress of representatives of Czechoslovak societies to elect new members to the Russian section of the Czech National Council. *Izvestiia* reported that Czechoslovaks in Kiev had organized their own soviet of workers' and soldiers' deputies. These were preliminary steps in a campaign to take over control of the political organization of the Czechoslovaks in Russia, a campaign which was stepped up in succeeding months by the Bolshevik government. The Soviet Prisoner-of-War Bureau and the Commissariat of Foreign Affairs established special Czechoslovak sections, and the Russian Communist Party permitted its Czechoslovak branch to issue its own organ, the *Prokopnik*.

Apparently, these Bolshevik efforts were not without some success. At the congress of Czechoslovak Socialist-Internationalists held in Moscow on May 27, the Communist delegates claimed to represent a membership of 5,600 and the supporters of the National Council to represent some 1,850 sympathizers. But there is no

---

[1] *Pravda*, February 7, 1918, quoted in R. Khabas, "K istorii bor'by s Chekhoslovatskim," *Proletarskaia revoliutsiia*, No. 76 (May, 1928), pp. 58–63.

record that these converts held commanding positions either in the
National Council administration or in the fighting corps, and the
soviet leaders soon concluded it would be best to get the Czechoslovak corps out of Russia. On March 26 the Soviet government gave
permission to French and Czechoslovak representatives at Penza
for the Czechoslovak troops to leave Russia over the Trans-Siberian
Railroad, providing they went as private citizens and with a certain
number of small arms only. The troops were thereupon organized
into 60 trains, each made up of some 700 to 1,000 men; arms, ammunition, and horses were left at Penza; and the first echelon began
to move out across Siberia. On April 14 the forward element passed
through Irkutsk, reaching Vladivostok on April 25.

To send the Czechs through Siberia was to roll a powder keg
through a forest fire. An explosion was inevitable. It was obvious
to everyone that the corps was strong enough to make or break any
government in Siberia. As one Omsk Bolshevik later remarked,
"We did not understand why they were permitted to cross Siberia
to their fatherland. The Czechoslovak echelons were for us a
superfluous luxury." [2] On March 22 the presidium of Tsentrosibir'
had gone so far as to petition the authorities in Moscow not to permit the Czechs to come through, lest they precipitate an uprising
against soviet authority.[3] The central authorities themselves began
to waver, and when Japanese and British units landed at Vladivostok they tried to persuade the Czechs to evacuate via Archan-
gel'sk and Murmansk, without success.[4]

Fears mounted in Moscow that the Czechs had not surrendered
their weapons to the extent required by the Penza agreement. Finally, on April 24, N. Aralov, chief of the Operations Section of the
Soviet Commissariat for Military and Naval Affairs, reportedly gave
secret directions to the executive committees at Penza and Cheliabinsk to disarm the Czechoslovak troops when they entered their

[2] L. Germanov (Frumkin), "K istorii Chekho-Slovatskogo nastupleniia i sverzheniia sovetskoi vlast' v Sibiri," *Proletarskaia revoliutsiia*, No. 4 (1922), p. 16.
[3] V. V. Maksakov and A. Turunov, *Khronika grazhdanskoi voiny v Sibiri*
(1917–1918) (Moscow: Gosizdat, 1926), p. 60. Excerpts from protocol of the
March 22 session. *Ibid.*, Appendix XXI, p. 146.
[4] Khabas, "K istorii bor'by," p. 61.

areas.[5] On May 14 a dispute broke out between Czechoslovak troops passing through the station at Cheliabinsk and liberated Hungarian prisoners who had joined the Red Guards. Three days later the soviet authorities intervened to arrest several Czechoslovak officers and men suspected of relations with counterrevolutionaries; on May 25 the Czechs, led by Voitsekhovskii, a colonel of the Russian army who had transferred to the Czech service, occupied the railroad station and forced their release.[6] Trotsky, as people's commissar for military affairs, immediately countered with an order to stop the Czechs along the Penza-Omsk line and to disarm them completely.[7]

News of these events spread almost instantaneously to the various units of the corps, who were stretched out over the network of the Trans-Siberian Railroad. It evoked a violent response. Under the command of the Russian major general, M. K. Dietrichs, some 14,000 Czechoslovaks had reached the comparative safety of Vladivostok, but the other two thirds were still spread across soviet-held territory. If the soviet authorities could cut the line at Cheliabinsk, they would be able to split the rest of the corps roughly in two halves, isolating some 16,000 men between Penza and Cheliabinsk and another 13,000 between Cheliabinsk and Irkutsk.[8] Whether or not they received orders to seize the stations en route, individual Czech commanders could hardly have failed to fear that the soviet order to disarm them meant that Moscow had decided to break up and possibly to destroy the corps. They decided to use what arms they had to seize control of the railroad, their sole lifeline to supplies, military support, and eventual safety. Anti-soviet Russian military units sprang immediately to their support.

Between May 25 and the end of June, with the exception of Irkutsk the cities along the Trans-Siberian Railroad from Penza eastward came into the hands of the Czechoslovaks, now eagerly assisted by groups of anti-Bolshevik Russians. The soviet authorities

[5] Maksakov and Turunov, *Khronika*, p. 64.

[6] According to the account of the incident given in P.S. Parfenov, *Uroki proshlogo, grazhdanskaia voina v Sibiri 1918, 1919, 1920 gg.* (Harbin, 1921), pp. 35–36.

[7] Text of the order in Maksakov and Turunov, *Khronika*, Appendix XXXVII, p. 168.

[8] Parfenov, *Uroki proshlogo*, p. 34.

had resisted where they could, but to little avail, for they had no base in popular support and their motley troops, ill-trained, undisciplined, and poorly led, were no match in numbers, equipment, or skill for their opponents. They could only withdraw north or south of the railroad into the hinterland or to European Russia behind the Kama, Volga, and Samara rivers, where on June 14 a shaky northern Urals-Siberian front was hastily formed.[9]

As the Bolshevik–left-wing Social Revolutionary representatives withdrew, the moderate socialist and rightist groups immediately sought to take over. Independent governments, claiming sovereignty over all Siberia, sprang up across western and central Siberia and the Volga region. Three in particular were important. One was set up at Samara, led by a five-man committee of members of the constituent assembly, known popularly as the "Komuch." A second was organized at Omsk by supporters of the former provisional Siberian government, now calling themselves the "western commissariat of the provisional Siberian government." This group was especially vigorous in organizing a west Siberian army under the command of a Social Revolutionary officer, Colonel Grishin-Almazov, formed of Russian volunteers and of Czech elements under Captain Gaida, Lieutenant Syrovy, and Lieutenant Colonel Voitsekhovskii. At Tomsk, a gathering of members of the provisional Siberian duma selected a new provisional Siberian council of ministers, consisting of two of the council's original members, G. B. Patushinskii and M. B. Shatilov, and three new members, V. M. Kurtovskii, I. A. Mikhailov, and P. Vologodskii, president,[10] to replace those who were absent.

Negotiations were immediately begun to unite these various local authorities in order to form a generally accepted government for all Siberia and possibly for all Russia. A union between the Omsk and Tomsk groups, basing their claims as they did on the authority of election to the Constituent Assembly, was quickly effected: on June 30 the western Siberian commissariat recognized

[9] Maksakov and Turunov, *Khronika,* p. 69.
[10] Parfenov, *Uroki proshlogo,* pp. 38–45; and Maksakov and Turunov, *Khronika,* pp. 65–78.

the authority of the new council and dissolved itself. Thereupon claiming "complete state authority over all the territory of Siberia," the provisional government decreed the abolition of the soviet authority, the denationalization of business, the restoration of property, the organization of nonpolitical trade unions, and the conscription of all youths aged twenty and twenty-one. The government could proceed thus with some confidence since, as might have been expected from its general popularity before the October Revolution, it received early pledges of support from the cooperative unions, the peasants, and the Siberian Cossack army. Although negotiations with other rival governments, such as those at Samara, Ufa, and Ekaterinburg, achieved no immediate results, the groundwork had been laid for the creation of the Directory, which was formed in the fall.

In one month the entire situation in Siberia had changed. Thanks to the Czechoslovaks, the moderate socialist and constitutional monarchists who had led the February Revolution and who had been on their way to forming a locally autonomous, democratic socialist regime for Siberia, until suddenly ousted by the Bolsheviks, were once more back in power, politically more precarious perhaps, but militarily much stronger. And the Czechs, once so eager to get to the western front to fight the Germans, had seemingly reversed themselves by opening an eastern front against the Soviet regime in Russia.

Responsibility for the Uprising

Soviet writers charge that the Czechoslovak uprising was no accident, that the Czechs were in fact the tools of a giant Anglo-French-Russian conspiracy to overthrow the Soviet regime and that they cooperated in it in order to win the support of the entente for their independence. As evidence, one writer claims that a certain Čerensky, a Czech, was secretly approached as early as February at Jassy by representatives of the entente, who asked him whether the

Czechoslovaks were "ready for an armed uprising against the Bolsheviks." [11] As early as late February or early March, entente statesmen are asserted to have reached an agreement with Masaryk to recognize his movement in return for an uprising against the soviets.[12] Following this alleged agreement, the British are charged with having supplied to the Czechs, through the council in Moscow, the sum of £80,000 (about 750,000 gold rubles); and between March 7 and April 3 the French are alleged to have supplied the National Council with an additional 11,188,000 rubles.[13] The Soviet case might seem to be roughly supported by the assertion of Paul Miliukov, former Russian foreign minister, that in early April the British proposed to Beneš that Russian agreement be sought to have the Czechoslovak contingents remain in Russia;[14] since at this time the British were seeking a soviet invitation for an Allied intervention, it appears likely that the idea was for the Czechs to reinforce the soviet forces rather than to oppose them. As for the granting of money, it should be recognized that the Czechs would need large sums of money to evacuate Russia and concentrate on the western front, so even if the grants were made, this does not prove the existence of a conspiracy or a plan for an uprising.

In order to provide for a Russian government to replace the soviets, entente agents supposedly negotiated with various anti-soviet elements and in particular encouraged the organization early in April of the Union for the Regeneration of Russia, an anti-Bolshevik league of right-wing Social Revolutionaries, Popular

---

[11] Khabas, "K istorii bor'by," p. 57, quoting B. Shmeral', *Chekhoslovaki i Esery* (Glavpolitprosveta, 1922), p. 9.

[12] *Prokopnik Svobody* (Czech communist organ), June 27, 1918, cited in F. Chuchin, "Imperialisticheskaia interventsiia na dal'nem vostoke i v Sibiri (1917–1919 gg.)," *Proletarskaia revoliutsiia*, No. 106 (November, 1930), p. 31.

[13] *Ibid.* These figures are open to serious question. According to Ambassador Jusserand, the French government as of July 28 had paid to the Czechs in Siberia only 3,500,000 rubles and had spent only 250,000 rubles to recruit soldiers of other nationalities to join them. Jusserand to Lansing, July 28, 1918, *USFR, 1918, Russia*, II, 308.

[14] P. Miliukov, *La Politique Extérieure des Soviets* (Paris: Marcel Girard, 1934), pp. 42–43.

Socialists, and left-wing Kadets.[15] Two key meetings are said to have been held at which the uprising was planned. The first was on April 14 in Moscow, where French Ambassador Noulens, Colonel Corbeil, representing the French general staff, General Lavergne, chief of the French military mission, the British representative Bruce Lockhart, Colonel Syromiatnikov and General Inostrantsev of the former Russian general staff met with a certain Captain Konshin, representing the central staff of the Union, and reached an agreement to use the Czechoslovaks.[16] The signal for the uprising was to be an attempt by the soviets to disarm the Czechs. Shortly thereafter Social Revolutionary Lieutenant Colonel V. I. Lebedev, is said to have explained to a fellow party member that the party was preparing for an early uprising and that they "placed their hope on the Czechoslovaks." [17] According to one source, Czech Staff Captain Gaida wired the party leader, Markov, in Mariinsk, telling him that the uprising was set for May 25.[18]

A second key conspiratorial conference is reported a month after the first, on May 14, at Cheliabinsk.[19] On this occasion, representatives of the Czechoslovaks, the British, the French, the central staff of a Siberian officers corps, and the military section of the Komuch

[15] Maksakov and Turunov, *Khronika,* p. 62. Nabokov reports that Kerensky told him during his July visit that the union was "formally bound by promises" to organize a government for Russia. K. D. Nabokov, *The Ordeal of a Diplomat* (London, 1921), p. 250. Leaders of the union were A. V. Sazonov, president of the All-Russian Bureau of Cooperatives, V. V. Kulikov, president of the Union of West Siberian Cooperative Unions, and A. A. Balakshin, president of the Union of Butter Makers. Sections were organized in various cities and a newspaper, *Zaria,* was published at Omsk. Parfenov, *Uroki Proshlogo,* pp. 52–54.

[16] Parfenov, *Uroki proshlogo,* pp. 29–30; USSR Tsentral'nyi Arkhiv RSFSR, Arkhiv Oktiabr'skoi Revoliutsii, *Iaponskaia Interventsiia 1918–1922 gg. v Dokumentakh,* ed. I. Mints (Moscow, 1934), pp. 204–5, which appears to recount Parfenov's story although no source is cited; and Chuchin, "Imperialisticheskaia interventsiia," p. 31.

[17] This remark is said to have been made by Lebedev to B. Solodovnikov in the quarters of a certain lawyer, named Vilenkin, early in May, 1918, according to Chuchin, "Imperialisticheskaia interventsiia," p. 32, citing Solodovnikov, *Sibirskie avantiury i General Gaida* (Praga), p. 3.

[18] Khabas, "K istorii bor'by," p. 64.

[19] Parfenov, *Uroki proshlogo,* pp. 34–35; and Khabas, "K istorii bor'by," pp. 63–64 (the meeting at Cheliabinsk appears to be the one recorded by Parfenov on the same date).

conferred on final details and of the position to be taken by the various Czech echelons. Meanwhile, the corps was reputedly infiltrated by Russian anti-Bolshevik officers and officers of the French army, who had established connections with the Siberian cooperatives.[20] On the appointed day, May 25, the Czechs moved against Cheliabinsk.

Since the dispute had actually begun at Cheliabinsk on May 14, it seems entirely likely that some kind of conference of responsible officials would necessarily have been held at that time and place, but there is no evidence that it concerned anything more than the immediate dispute. The case would seem to rest primarily on the alleged meeting of April 14 in Moscow, but for this, too, no confirming official sources or memoirs of participants have so far been brought to light.

There is, then, no adequate evidence to support the charge of conspiracy. And yet it is entirely possible and indeed very likely that some representatives of the entente were working to have the Czechs evacuated from Russia and moved to the western front, while others may have been working at the same time to have them rise in Siberia to sweep out the Bolsheviks and restablish an eastern front. It is also difficult to believe that the anti-soviet elements in Siberia could have acted in such close coordination with the Czechs if at least some Russian Social Revolutionaries and others had not had an understanding with some Czechoslovaks.

The Western Allies, of course, vigorously denied all these allegations and demanded that Trotsky's order for disarming the Czechoslovaks be rescinded. The Japanese did not participate in the protests to the Soviet government, but they expressed their sympathy with the Allied position and seem to have given no serious thought to the soviet charges. They were generally convinced that the Soviet government was a puppet of Germany; although they were not sure exactly what had happened at Cheliabinsk, it was not difficult for them to believe that the order to disarm the Czechs and to stop their progress through Siberia had come directly from Trotskii's

[20] Parfenov, *Uroki proshlogo,* p. 29.

German masters.[21] This theory also has plausible elements, for the Germans certainly would not have wanted the Czechs to escape to the western front; however, no reliable evidence has yet been presented in support of it, and it is questionable whether Germany had such power over the Soviet regime even at that time.

Effect on British and French Plans

Whether or not the entente had instigated the Czechoslovak uprising, the British government, in particular, was not slow to realize and to accept the opportunity it presented for organizing intervention in Siberia. It was immediately apparent that there was now no possibility of securing an invitation from the Soviet government. No doubt the British and French decision to abandon the negotiations with the soviet leaders was prompted in part by their discouragement over the explorations thus far and in part by their hope that Japan's offer to accept an Inter-Allied expedition might now bring America around, regardless of the soviet position. In any case, so long as the soviet forces were fighting the Czechoslovaks, they could hardly be expected to invite any friends of the Czechs to intervene in Russia. On the other hand, such an invitation seemed much less necessary than before. The increasing success of the uprising and the almost instantaneous reappearance all along the Trans-Siberian Railroad of moderate socialist regimes persuaded the Allies that the soviet regime had very little support; hence, it could not be expected to oppose an intervention effectively or perhaps even to maintain itself in power much longer.

Secondly, the startling success of the Czechoslovaks, in contrast to Semenov's abortive offensive to the Onon and Horvat's failure to

[21] Colonel Nagai (in Russia) to chief of Army General Staff Headquarters, June 4, 1918, in Japan, Gaimushō Kiroku, "Rokoku Kakumei Ikken: Chiekku Gundan 'Minzoku Undō,' Rengō-koku-gawa no Enjō" (hereinafter, *JGK, RKI, CGMU*), I; Acting Consul General Kumazaki (in Moscow) to Gotō, June 18, 1918, *ibid.*, I; Chinda (in London) to Gotō, July 6, 1918, Japan, Gaimushō Kiroku, "Rokoku Kakumei Ikken: Shuppei Kankei: Chiekku Kyūen Hahei" (hereinafter, *JGK, RKI, SK, CKH*); and Japan, Gaimushō Seimukyoku Dai 2 Ka (Europe and America), *Rokoku ni okeru "Chiekkosurovakkii" Guntai*, dated June 27, 1918.

move from Harbin, convinced the British that they could dispense with "Japanese puppets." Instead, they could use troops to restore to power persons like Admiral Kolchak or possibly Peter Derber, who had shown themselves more amenable to French and especially British suggestions. It also aroused in them the hope of arranging for an expedition to western Siberia on the plea of supporting the Czechs.

Britain's first move was to seek French support. On May 26, Lord Cecil told Ambassador Chinda that "negotiations are in progress with the French government concerning the advisability of using the Czechoslovak forces concentrated at Vladivostok in case of action in Siberia." [22] Chinda explained Cecil's attitude:

At a time like this it would be useless to leave these troops concentrated in Vladivostok, waiting in vain for transportation to the western front. Since the need for allied military operations in Siberia becomes daily greater, it might be desirable to make use of these forces; that is, should Japan send a military expedition, it might be desirable to attach them to it.

The French fell in with this scheme immediately. On June 1 the French military attaché in Russia, General Lavergne, advised the French Ministry of War that "the presence of Czech forces at strategic points along the Trans-Siberian Railroad could well be utilized for purposes of intervention." [23] On June 6 the councilor of the French embassy in Russia was telling the Japanese chargé Marumo Naotoshi, how convenient it would be to use the Czechs to support a Japanese intervention in Siberia.[24] On June 20 the French minister of war issued instructions to the Czechs to hold their positions along the Trans-Siberian Railroad.[25] The next move was for the entente to approach Japan formally.

Japan had been considering the Czech problem for more than a month. When the decision was taken to evacuate the Czechs via

[22] Chinda to Gotō, May 26, 1918, in *JGK, RKI, SK, EBFK,* I; and *JGK, RKI, CGMU,* I.

[23] Beneš, *Souvenirs,* II, 250–51, quoted in James Bunyan, *Intervention, Civil War, and Communism, April–December, 1918, Documents and Materials* (Baltimore: Johns Hopkins University Press, 1936), pp. 101–2.

[24] Marumo to Gotō via Matsui, June 7, 1918. *JGK, RKI, CGMU,* I.

[25] Bunyan, *Intervention,* pp. 104–5.

Siberia, it became immediately apparent that only Japan was in a position to supply the necessary matériel and shipping. The Czechs recognized this. Masaryk himself made a first appeal to Tokyo in April. Traveling on a British passport made out to "T. G. Marsden," he arrived in Tokyo on April 8 in quest of supplies and shipping to move the corps in Russia to France by way of Panama.[26] Masaryk made contacts with certain liberal political leaders, like Makino, Hara, and Katō; he was written up favorably in the *Tokyo Asahi Shimbun,* a leading liberal daily, and was even given space in that paper for a series of three articles on the importance of Bohemia as a principal object of German aggression toward the east.[27] He was also permitted to state his case to the Foreign Ministry, where he was accorded interviews with an acting vice minister on April 10 and April 19. There is no record of encouragement by any responsible official. With empty hands Masaryk boarded the *Empress of China* on April 20 for America.

In the weeks to follow, representatives of the Czechoslovaks followed up Masaryk's appeal. The Allies too, as they were won over to the Czech cause, added their pleas. On May 2, May 28, and June 1 the Supreme War Council joined the campaign.[28] On May 29, Secretary Lansing expressed the sympathy of the United States Government for the national aspirations of the Czechoslovaks.[29]

Only the Japanese government had taken no position. It had heard no mention of payment for its services. Without substantial compensation it could hardly have been expected to look with favor on the introduction of foreign military elements into the Amur basin. How could the entente persuade Japan to accept the Czechs as partners in intervention? The best chance of success was not to

[26] *JGK, RKI, CGMU,* I; and Takeyama Yasutaro, *Shiberia Jihen to Kokusai Kankei no Shinsō* (Tokyo: Nittō Shuppansha, 1934), I, 8–9. Masaryk's movements were reported by the police to the Foreign Ministry and other interested agencies.

[27] *JGK, RKI, CGMU,* I, and Makino Nobuaki, *Kaikoroku* (Toyko: Bungei Shunshu Shinsha, 1949), III, 146. The three articles appeared in the editions of April 19, 20, and 21 under the title, "Doitsu no Tōhō Shinryaku" (Germany's Eastward Invasion).

[28] Colonel Tanaka (in London) to vice chief, Army General Staff Headquarters, June 15, 1918, in *JGK, RKI, CGMU,* I.

[29] Ishii to Gotō, May 31, 1918, *ibid.,* I.

press for an immediate policy decision, but rather to involve Japan gradually in the Czech predicament at Vladivostok.

The Czechoslovaks' Request for Aid

The French had ordered the Czechs to hold the line, although this was no easy order for them to carry out. One third of the corps had already reached Vladivostok. The rest was stretched over the line from Penza to Nizhneudinsk; between Nizhneudinsk and Vladivostok the line was still securely held by the soviet forces. Two thirds of the corps was thus cut off, without avenue of help or retreat. In order to save the troops and also to prevent the Soviet government in Vladivostok from sending westward the munitions stockpiled there, Major General Dietrichs, commanding the 14,000 men of the Second Division who had already reached Vladivostok, decided to launch a westward offensive to seize the lines through the Amur basin. The British and French realized that nothing short of this would serve, at the least, to rescue the Czechs and, at the best, to spearhead an Allied intervention. They heartily approved. The Czechs were grateful, but pointed out their need in addition to moral support—more weapons and ammunition. To this the British and French were agreed, and since only the Japanese were able to furnish the supplies, they promptly renewed their appeals in that direction, this time not for shipping to evacuate the Czechs, but for materials of war to support the movement westward.

The proposal was put first to Rear Admiral Katō at Vladivostok, who was known to favor action. French Military Attaché Paris called on him on June 19.[30] British, French, and Czech representatives called on him the following day.[31] The French Consul called on him on the twenty-second.[32] Katō immediately wired his support for the request to the naval authorities in Tokyo.[33] Consul General

[30] Japan, Sambō Hombu, *Taishō Shichi-nen naishi Jūichi-nen Shiberia Shuppei-shi*, III (1924), 1086.
[31] Japan, Kaigun Gunreibu, *Taishō Yon-nen naishi Kyū-nen Kaigun Senshi*, III (1924), 44–45.
[32] *Ibid.*, I, 166–67.
[33] Katō to commander in chief Third Fleet, navy vice minister, and vice chief of the Naval Board, June 22, 1918, *ibid.*, III, 95.

Kikuchi was next. On June 25 a Czech representative asked him, as dean of the consular corps, to call the corps for a discussion of the predicament of the Czechs. Each of the consuls, including Kikuchi, agreed to request his home government not only to send weapons and provisions but also to assign forces in aid of the Czechoslovaks.[34] Having won over Japan's local naval and diplomatic officials, on June 26 Major General Dietrichs sought the army's approval through Lieutenant Colonel Sakabe. "If we could get weapons from Japan," Dietrichs promised, "we should rise up as soon as possible." [35] Meanwhile, the French ambassador called at the Foreign Ministry on June 29, in Tokyo.

The estimated quantity of necessary munitions varied with each speaker.[36] But the burden of their argument was the same: the Bolsheviks and their cohorts, the "German spies" and the armed "German and Austrian prisoners of war," were becoming increasingly dangerous. Currently they threatened to transport westward or to destroy the munitions at Vladivostok, so that the Czechoslovak troops had been forced since June 20 to establish a patrol of the city. Soon they could be expected to go farther in the effort to prevent the eastward passage of the remaining Czech forces from west of Irkutsk. In this case, the Czechs in Vladivostok would be forced westward to their rescue.

Specifically, the Czech representative is reported to have proposed the following:

[34] Japan, Sambō Hombu, *Shiberia Shuppei-shi*, III, 1086. An English text of the document presented by Czech representatives to the Allied consuls, explaining the Czech position in Russia, is enclosed in Caldwell to Lansing, July 8, 1918, *USFR, 1918, Russia*, II, 265–67.

[35] Sakabe's reaction is not recorded.

[36] Katō was told on June 20 by British, French and Czech representatives that the following were needed: 12 mountain guns (with 300 shells for each), 100 pom-poms, 13,000 pistols, 1,000,000 rounds of ammunition for them, and 6 airplanes. Sakabe was told by Dietrichs on June 26 that his needs included: "rifles —13,000, shells—1,000,000, mountain guns—18, machine guns—100, hand grenades—60,000, materials for building bridges, communications equipment, medical supplies, etc.," and on June 29, the French ambassador pared this down to 3 mountain guns, 100 machine guns, and necessary ammunition. U.S. Ambassador Morris was under the impression that only 30 machine guns, a number of mortar guns, and some ammunition were being sought. Morris to State Department, July, 1918, *USFR, 1918, Russia*, II, 239.

After getting a supply of arms, the Czechoslovak forces would immediately rise up, first sweeping the Bolsheviks out of Vladivostok and
Nikol'sk; then, one force would occupy Khabarovsk while the main
force would go directly by the Chinese Eastern Railway to Oloviannaia
and advance to Chita; then if an Allied expedition were decided upon,
the two forces would combine and secure the main Trans-Siberian rail
line, facilitate the westward transportation of the Allied forces, and
jointly with the Allies enter the anti-German front in Russia. If, on
the other hand, the Allies decided not to send expeditionary forces, the
Czechs would withdraw from the rear and leave from Vladivostok or
Dairen for the battlefront in France.[37]

The Seizure of Vladivostok

Suddenly, before the Japanese had time to reach a decision, the
Czechs and no doubt their backers, the French and British, seem
to have decided either that they could act without Japanese assistance or that Japan's hand could be forced.[38] In the evening of
June 28, Major General Dietrichs informed the Allied consuls at
Vladivostok that at 10 o'clock the next morning he intended to
present the Vladivostok soviet with a 30-minute ultimatum to disarm.[39] The word was immediately passed to Rear Admiral Katō.
Following the April 5 landing, Katō had been given permission
by the navy minister to land the rest of his marine complement if
he thought the situation required it. Apparently pleased with the
news from Dietrichs and acting on this authority, he promptly conferred with his British counterpart. Together they agreed to alert
their respective units for action, and in the morning to have the
Japanese detail their force already ashore (the "Otsu" landing

[37] Ōtsu Jun'ichiro, *Dai Nihon Kenseishi* (Tokyo: Hōbunkan, 1927), VIII,
328–29.
[38] There is no apparent evidence in the Foreign Ministry's archives of any
decision by the ministry to approve the Czech plan, but some officials seem to
have believed that such a decision was reached and was conveyed to the Czechs.
An entry in the diary of Chief of Staff Field Marshal Baron Uehara on June 29
carries this implication: "Today the foreign minister must answer to his own
country and to the Allies for agreeing in principle to great difficulties." Uehara
goes on to outline the practical difficulties of a military operation directed at
Blagoveshchensk and Chita. Araki Sadao, *Gensui Uehara Yūsaku Den* (Tokyo:
Gensui Uehara Denki Hanko-kai, 1937), II, 1934.
[39] Japan, Kaigun Gunreibu, *Senshi*, III, 37–42.

unit) to protect Allied residents in the established defense zones, jointly to detach several platoons to secure the small arms warehouse and gunpowder shed, and to have the Japanese prepare to land other elements (the machine-gun units of the "Kō" landing unit) if needed. Admiral Knight had expressed strong approval of Katō's landing of April 5, but he had not taken any supporting action and had not been backed up by the American government, so that Katō could hardly have anticipated much cooperation from that quarter. At 9 o'clock the next morning, the Japanese and British commanders called on Admiral Knight. They learned, as they had probably expected, that the Americans preferred to take no action unless their nationals were directly endangered. The Chinese commander does not appear to have been consulted.

At the very hour when the British and Japanese commanders were conferring with Admiral Knight, a Czechoslovak company was drawn up before the soviet headquarters. Promptly at 10, the ultimatum was delivered. When no reply had been received by 10:30, the Czechs broke into the building and confiscated the weapons found there. The telegraph office was occupied at noon, and by 5:50 the fortress headquarters, to which the soviet leaders had fled, was in Czech hands. Meanwhile, the Japanese and British naval commanders had executed their plans, and in the afternoon the Chinese landed about eighty men and the Americans about twenty to insure the protection of resident nationals. The city was so secure by 6:30 that the British and Japanese promptly withdrew their special units. This did not complete their part in the coup, however, for Admiral Katō assented to the Czech, British, and French request that he disarm the four Russian destroyers and one auxiliary ship in the harbor on June 30 and that he turn them over to the new regime on July 3.

Although the Czechs had been the chief agents, the overthrow of soviet authority in Vladivostok was obviously a combined British-French-Japanese-Czech affair. The local naval and diplomatic officials of the three powers had given the Czechs their fullest cooperation in carrying out the seizure. They had stood by approvingly while the Czechs arrested the executive committee of the

Vladivostok soviet and rounded up all the members they could find of the regional committee of the Bolshevik faction; very few escaped.[40] The three powers immediately recognized the executive committee of the territorial zemstvo and the city council restored by the Czechs. When, at 3 P.M. on the same day, Peter Derber claimed all authority for his provisional government of autonomous Siberia, which these organs acknowledged,[41] the powers seem to have decided to work with that, too.

Had Peter Derber also been one of the planners of the coup? The Japanese records do not say. It is possible that, from the beginning, he and his provisional government had been secretly supported and groomed by the British and the French. All that is known with certainty is that Japan's two service representatives, Sakabe and Katō, had been favorably impressed by Derber's wide popularity among the moderate socialists of Vladivostok; when the coup occurred, his organization was the only one in the city able to muster even two companies of non-soviet Russian troops.[42] These facts might explain why the police power was immediately entrusted to him and might even explain how it was that the moderate Russians, once back in power, immediately accepted him. Whether Derber was an original conspirator or not, he emerged a victor. Basing his authority on the dispersed provisional Siberian duma that had also fathered the Omsk and Tomsk regimes in western Siberia, he claimed for his organization the "central governmental power over the territory of Siberia." [43] Faced with this *fait accompli*, the local Allied officials in their turn may simply have decided to deal with the Derber government as the only effective, immediate alternative to the soviet. The American government declined to give it official recognition. So far as the Japanese were concerned,

[40] T. Sviderskii-Politovskii, "V gostiakh u chekhov," *Katorga i ssylka*, CVIII (1933), 20–35; "Oktiabr' v Sibiri: Vladivostok," *Proletarskaia revoliutsiia*, No. 10 (October, 1922), p. 371; and Japan, Sambō Hombu, *Shiberia Shuppei-shi*, III, 1089.

[41] Declaration, enclosed in Caldwell to Lansing, July 19, 1918, *USFR, 1918, Russia*, II, 294.

[42] Japan, Sambō Hombu, *Shiberia Shuppei-shi*, I, 18.

[43] Caldwell (in Vladivostok) to U.S. secretary of state, July 19, 1918, in *USFR, 1918, Russia*, II, 293–96.

their government had not been consulted and had always been cold to Derber's claims, so that Katō and Kikuchi must simply have acted on their own.

Support from the Japanese Navy

On the afternoon of the day of the coup, Major General Dietrichs conferred with the British, French, and Japanese military and consular representatives aboard the British warship *HMS Suffolk*.[44] The same group, joined by Admiral Knight, seems to have met again on July 2.[45] The seizure of Vladivostok had gone well. However, it would do little good, said Dietrichs, unless he could move immediately into the second phase of the operation he had outlined to the consular corps, the seizure of Nikol'sk. This was essential, he declared, to protect the approach to Vladivostok and also to open the way for a two-pronged drive northward to Khabarovsk and westward via the Chinese Eastern to Chita. Of course, if he moved his forces out of the city, other friendly units must move in to protect it. Could the Allies provide, say, a thousand men to do this job? The American representative surprised everyone by offering naval support and by asking what "weapons and ammunition" would be needed.[46] The British representative immediately offered the support of his naval forces. To the Czechs, all this indicated that Allied help would be forthcoming, and they set out on the same day for Nikol'sk.

Since Admiral Katō's instructions did not cover this turn of affairs, he referred Dietrichs' request to the central authorities in Tokyo, accompanying it with a strong recommendation that it be granted. He called attention to the recognition recently accorded

[44] Japan, Kaigun Gunreibu, *Senshi*, III, 36.

[45] Admiral Katō to central naval authorities, July 3, 1918, *ibid.*, I, 167–68; and Balfour to British ambassador in Paris, July 11, 1918, paraphrased in the message from British Ambassador Reading to the U.S. secretary of state, July 12, 1918, in *USFR, 1918, Russia*, II, 275.

[46] Published records indicate that Knight was not authorized until July 7 (Vladivostok time) to use his forces to help hold the city. Lansing to Morris, July 6, 1918, *ibid.*, II, 263–64.

to the Czechs as an Allied army and to the change in American attitude. Instead of referring the question to the cabinet, the naval authorities decided on their own to authorize Katō immediately "to take such action as you deem appropriate after consulting the British and American commanders." [47] The result was that, on July 6, Japan found itself party to a proclamation issued by the commanders of all "the Allied and associated forces at Vladivostok" (including the Americans, the British, the French, the Chinese, and the Czechoslovaks). The proclamation announced that they had taken over the city and vicinity in order to protect it and the Allied forces from inimical acts by the Austro-German prisoners of war.[48]

It would appear that representatives of some of the other powers had also acted on their own in agreeing to a protectorate over Vladivostok. At any rate, it was not until July 10, or four days after the protectorate had been proclaimed, that the British war cabinet ordered Colonel Ward to bring up to Vladivostok the 400 or 500 men of the battalion of the Middlesex Regiment, then garrisoned at Hong Kong.[49] The French followed suit, ordering up some 300 troops from Indo-China.[50] Of course, none of this had anything to do with intervention, the British asserted to Japan and the United States. They were sending troops only "with the object of restoring order in Vladivostok, securing the stores of the allies at that town, and ensuring the safety of the communications of the Czech forces." [51]

---

[47] Navy vice minister to Katō, July 3, 1918, Japan, Kaigun Gunreibu, *Senshi*, I, 168.

[48] *Ibid.*, III, 43; Caldwell (at Vladivostok) to Lansing, July 9, 1918, *USFR, 1918, Russia*, II, 271.

[49] Colonel John Ward, *With the "Die-hards" in Siberia* (London: Cassell, 1920), p. 2; Chinda to Gotō (reporting talk that day with Balfour), July 10, 1918. Japan, Gaimushō, *Shiberia Shuppei Mondai, Dai Ippen, Shiberia Shuppei ni itaru Kōshō Keika*, I (1922), 65–66; memorandum from Ambassador Greene to Japanese government, July 12, 1918, *ibid.*, I, 67–68; and Greene to Shidehara, July 13, 1918, in *JGK, RKI, SK, EBFK*, I.

[50] Matsui to Gotō (reporting talk that day with Pichon), July 13, 1918. Japan, Gaimushō, *Shiberia Shuppei Mondai*, I, 67.

[51] Greene to Japanese government, July 12, 1918, *ibid.*, I, 67–68.

After a few skirmishes Nikol'sk fell to the Czechs on July 5.[52] That same day their representatives in Vladivostok and the British pressed Admiral Katō again for ammunition and weapons to sustain the northward drive.[53] Katō apparently ordered 304,478 rounds of rifle and pom-pom ammunition transferred to the Czechs from the stores of the Fifth Squadron. In doing so, he acted at his own discretion, but he judged the temper of his government correctly. On the day before, the Japanese cabinet had finally come to a fundamental decision "to treat the Czechs as an Allied army"[54] and to accede to their repeated requests for aid.[55] It would send the navy transport, *Aoshima*, with 6 mountain guns, 1,000 mountain-gun shells, 20 machine guns, and 3,000,000 rounds of small arms ammunition. Along with this ordnance, one officer and six men under other guise would go to instruct the Czechs in its use. The *Aoshima* arrived at Vladivostok on July 12; the Japanese army promptly transferred the cargo to the Czechoslovak corps for shipment to the front at Nikol'sk.

Barely had this request been granted, when the Japanese government was presented with another. On July 8, three days after the victory at Nikol'sk, Major General Dietrichs returned to Vladivostok to report to the representatives of the Allied and associated powers aboard the USS *Brooklyn*.[56] After describing the battle, he revealed that the Czechs had sustained numerous casualties, so many in fact that their medical facilities were inadequate to handle them. Would the Allies send some medical squads in a hurry? Of course, only Japan or America could meet the emergency. The American representative, Admiral Knight, showed America's new eagerness to assist. He was sure, he said, that Japan and America

[52] Japan, Kaigun Gunreibu, *Senshi*, III, 46; Japan, Sambō Hombu, *Shiberia Shuppei-shi*, III, 1088. Soviet sources give July 6. Parfenov, *Uroki proshlogo*, p. 40; Maksakov and Turunov, *Khronika*, pp. 74, 77.

[53] Japan, Kaigun Gunreibu, *Senshi*, III, 46.

[54] *Ibid.*, I, 168–69.

[55] Japan, Sambō Hombu, *Shiberia Shuppei-shi*, III, 1088. There is no mention here that the decision was contingent upon U.S. approval as reportedly stated by Ambassador Ishii to Secretary Lansing, in memorandum of Lansing-Ishii conference, July 8, 1918, *USFR, 1918, Russia*, II, 267–68.

[56] Japan, Kaigun Gunreibu, *Senshi*, III, 47.

would soon come to an agreement to render vigorous assistance. For immediate help, he had, on the day before, ordered the Red Cross unit in Tokyo and doctors in Yokohama and Cavite to form a first-aid squad to rescue the immediate Czech casualties. The British commander pressed the Japanese to do the same thing. Katō promptly forwarded this request with his approval,[57] and the Japanese navy at once sent to the Fifth Squadron an emergency squad of sixteen men. The squad left Maizuru on July 10 aboard the destroyer *Asakage* and arrived at Vladivostok two days later.

Strongly encouraged by these actions, the British government on July 16 asked Japan to strengthen its naval forces in the harbor.[58] Meanwhile, Japan's Minister Hayashi, together with the British and French ministers in Peking, requested the Russian legation to arrange with the Chinese Eastern Railway authorities for transportation of the Czech forces westward over that line.[59]

Horvat's Proclamation of a Government

The entente's plan for involving Japan in a west Siberian expedition in cooperation with the Czechoslovaks was progressing very smoothly and rapidly, so much so as to give the impression that the Japanese government must have changed its course. The truth seems to be that, beyond agreeing to give a limited amount of arms and ammunition to the Czechoslovaks, as it had also agreed to do for the Semenovists, the government in Tokyo had not yet set a course. Events in Vladivostok seem not yet to have been seriously reviewed by the government as a whole. Action was being taken there mainly by the navy and the Foreign Ministry. Apparently the Japanese army was not consulted and indeed it and its protégés in northern Manchuria seem not to have concerned themselves with the Czech movement until Dietrichs advanced to Nikol'sk and then announced his intention to push along the Chinese Eastern Railway to Chita.

[57] *Ibid.*, I, 169–70.
[58] Reading to U.S. secretary of state (memorandum), July 16, 1918, *USFR, 1918, Russia*, II, 284.
[59] MacMurray to Lansing, July 9, 1918, *ibid.*, II, 271–72.

The Japanese army had never shared the British view that the Czechs would make a dependable vanguard for an expedition to Siberia. The Czechs had neither the strength nor the inclination to realize the Japanese army's objective. Major General Saitō summarized the army view in a report to General Uehara:

For the time being, the Czechs are successful, but their foundation is extremely weak. If the Allies were to strengthen their foundation by giving military assistance, they would be able to restore order; however, if the Allies do not, the Czechs will one day be expelled by the Bolsheviks or some other influence supported by Germany. Therefore, it will, I believe, be just as absolutely essential as before to crush the Bolsheviks in Siberia.[60]

The entente and the Czechs agreed; but, whereas they argued that Czech weakness made support imperative, Saitō contended that this very weakness made it unnecessary. Moreover, it was undesirable. After all, "being socialist," he said, "the Czechs will not finally agree when the Allies try to restore the imperial government." Saitō therefore proposed that the Czech uprising be used merely as an opportunity for putting the Japanese protégés in power.

We must have Horvat strengthen the Semenov detachment as much as possible and have it immediately destroy the Bolsheviks east of Irkutsk. For this purpose, it would be best, first, to have the Kalmykov detachment crush the Bolsheviks between Grodekovo and Vladivostok, link up with the Czech forces in Vladivostok, and send reinforcements to Semenov.

Until this time, Horvat had obstinately refused to cross the border. He insisted that Japan would have to send reinforcements first. The reason was obvious: he had been able to rally very few men of his own. By early July he could count on a total strength of only some 100 men who were being organized into the Maklenko detachment and 450 of the Orlov detachment at Yeh-ho (modern Ai-ho), about 600 of the Makovkin detachment at I-mien-p'o and Harbin,[61] a handful of Amur Cossacks being recruited by Ataman

[60] Saitō (in Peking) to Uehara, July 6, 1918, *JGK, RKI, HK,* III.
[61] Japan, Sambō Hombu, *Shiberia Shuppei-shi,* I, 26.

Gamov along the Amur,[62] and a few scattered railway guards along the Chinese Eastern Railway. Now the Czech uprising suddenly convinced Horvat that he had better take the Japanese army's advice. By driving the Bolsheviks out of the lower end of the Maritime Territory, the Czechs presented him with an opportunity to move despite his weakness. Moreover, if he did not move soon, he would have no place to move to and perhaps no place to move from. After all, the Czechs had permitted the Derber regime to take over Vladivostok while they themselves were preparing to come down the Chinese Eastern Railway.

Accompanied by his Japanese advisers, including Major Takeda Kakuzo and possibly Colonel Araki Sadao,[63] Horvat set out at once for Nikol'sk, at the head of his forces. As Nikol'sk was the junction of the Chinese Eastern with the Ussuri Railway, Horvat hoped there to block off the Czechs and to reestablish immediately a government for all Russia.[64] Kalmykov, waiting impatiently with perhaps 250 men on the border at Pogranichnaia,[65] dashed across in advance.[66]

The action was bold but belated. Dietrichs had already taken Nikol'sk on the fifth. Two days later he asked for and received the consent of the Allied consular corps in Vladivostok to his plan to move along the Chinese Eastern Railway, ignoring completely the

[62] Gamov, the Amur Cossack ataman, had escaped from Blagoveshensk to Harbin following the March incident and offered his services to Horvat. On June 21, Horvat instructed him to return to the Amur river and set about organizing an Amur detachment of anti-Bolshevik volunteers. By early September, he is reported to have recruited about 200 men for the detachment and to have organized another 1,000 from the Cossack villages into seven guerrilla units. *Ibid.*, III, 1050, and I, 25.

[63] *Ibid.*, III, 1090.

[64] *Ibid.*, III, 1073; U.S. consul in Harbin to U.S. secretary of state via MacMurray, July 9, 1918, *USFR, 1918, Russia*, II, 273–74.

[65] This was his strength in mid-August after the intervention had begun and probably is an overestimate as of early July. Japan, Sambō Hombu, *Shiberia Shuppei-shi*, III, Appendix, Table 18 (1).

[66] Whether Kalmykov did so in cooperation or in competition with Horvat is not clear from the record. Budberg notes in his diary on July 7 that on reaching Pogranichnaia station, Kalmykov declared "he would not serve Pleshkov [Horvat's commander in chief] and would not act in cooperation with Orlov." Baron Aleksei Budberg, "Dnevnik," *Arkhiv russkoi revoliutsii*, XIII (1923), 228. It should be noted, however, that Budberg was extremely hostile to the Horvat movement and recorded many unverified rumors to discredit it.

claims of the various political organizations along the line and especially in Harbin.[67] Thus, when Kalmykov's Cossacks plunged
into the Maritime Territory, they encountered, not the scattered
remnants of the fleeing soviet units, but the solid front of the
Czech Second Division. The Czechs refused to let them pass. In
accord with the decision of the consular corps, said Dietrichs, the
Czechs could not cooperate with any elements having political connections. He ordered Kalmykov either to allow his detachment to
be disarmed or to withdraw again across the border. Two days later
Peter Derber persuaded the British consul to ask the consular corps
to appoint an Inter-Allied committee representing Japan, Great
Britain, the United States, and China, to investigate Kalmykov's
activities.[68]

At the suggestion of his Japanese advisers, Horvat reined up his
forces at Grodekovo, but decided to go ahead with his plans. On
July 9 he proclaimed a new all-Russian government.[69] It was a
coalition government, to which he hoped by his appointments to
rally all those in Siberia who were hostile to soviet rule, from constitutional monarchists to moderate socialists. In particular, he
wooed those Social Revolutionaries in the Russian Far East, the
adherents of the provisional Siberian government, the officers'
union, and the Semenovists. Under himself, a constitutional monarchist, as provisional head and commander in chief, he appointed
a provisional cabinet: S. Vostrotin, a Kadet, former minister of food
in the Kerensky government, who had been working to unite the
anti-soviet movements in Vladivostok and Harbin; S. Taskin, a
Kadet, former commissar of Trans-Baikal Territory under the provisional government, whom Semenov had appointed chief of civil
administration in his abortive Trans-Baikal government; M. Kur-

[67] Japan, Sambō Hombu, *Shiberia Shuppei-shi*, II, 1089–90.
[68] *Ibid.*, II, 1092.
[69] *Ibid.*, II, 1073; Maksakov and Turnov, *Khronika*, p. 75; U.S. Consul at
Harbin to U.S. secretary of state via MacMurray, July 9, 1918, *USFR, 1918,
Russia*, II, 273–74. The names of A. Putilov and B. Glukharev, included in the
provisional cabinet by Maksakov and Turunov, are not included by the U.S.
consul. Horvat's all-Russian government maintained its claims until September
23, 1918, when it subordinated itself to the government at Omsk.

skii, a socialist; A. Okorokov, a socialist member of the dispersed provisional Siberian government; L. Ustrugov, independent democrat, former railway administrator and lately diplomatic emissary in Peking of the Derber rump of the provisional Siberian government; A. Putilov, president of the Russo-Asiatic Bank; General V. Pflug, independent democrat, former military governor in Vladivostok, recently returned from European Russia as a representative of General Alexeev and his anti-soviet movement in South Russia; and B. Glukharev, an associate of Pflug's in the officers' union.

It was not the kind of government Horvat wanted. He had in fact rejected the idea of just such a coalition when it was proposed in April by emissaries of the provisional Siberian government. But on July 9, facing the hostile Czech Second Division at Nikol'sk, an unsympathetic consular corps, and the rival Derber government in Vladivostok, Horvat decided to make as wide an appeal as he could.[70]

Thus, after six months of inviting, cajoling, and threatening, the Japanese army, thanks largely to the action of the Czechoslovaks, had finally persuaded Horvat to move to Russian soil and set up a government. At last it could point to a Russian regime, hostile to the soviets and subservient to Japan. True, the regime was in an exposed position at Grodekovo and its 1,050 men were completely outnumbered by the Czech Second Division. But the Japanese army was determined to support it. On July 10, General Tanaka sent instructions to Japanese officers in Manchuria:

Since the advance of the Horvat group into the Maritime Territory is essential to protect our influence there, you will support the Kalmykov detachment in that area, where, I hope, Russian military power will be built up around the Ussuri Cossacks.[71]

[70] Horvat is reported to have said that Grand Duke Michael Alexandrovich was en route to Vladivostok from Murmansk via Japan on the *Askold*. U.S. Consul Moser was led to suspect that Horvat planned eventually to place the grand duke on the throne of a constitutional monarchy, but there seems to be no sure evidence. Moser to Lansing via MacMurray, July 11, 1918, *USFR, 1918, Russia*, II, 279–80.

[71] Tanaka to officers in Manchuria, July 10, 1918. Japan, Sambu, *Shiberia Shuppei-shi*, III, 1091–92.

Tanaka went on to emphasize again the value of Horvat's operations as the vanguard of a Japanese expedition. Then, to see what could be done about the Czechoslovaks, Major Takeda and Colonel Araki immediately set out with General Pflug to talk things over in Vladivostok.[72]

Respite for Semenov

Meanwhile, the Czechoslovak action was also changing the fortunes of Japan's other protégé, Captain Semenov. Backed up against the Chinese border after the collapse of his Onon river offensive, Semenov and his detachment had almost been forced to give themselves up to the Chinese when the Czechoslovak uprising brought an abatement in the soviet pressure. The seizure of Vladivostok on June 25 heralded the beginning of a Czech pincer movement against the Amur basin. From Vladivostok the Second Division pushed northward and westward. At the same time from central Siberia other Czech forces began to move eastward, and Irkutsk fell on July 11.[73] Gamov, Kalmykov, and Horvat had already crossed the border in the south. In desperation the soviet forces threw up new fronts; a Baikal front against the Czechoslovaks near Irkutsk, a Chinese front against Gamov near Blagoveshchensk, and a Maritime front against the Czechoslovaks and the detachments led by Horvat and Kalmykov above Nikol'sk.[74] Frantically, local soviet leaders recalled their volunteer units from the Trans-Baikal front.[75]

Semenov might yet live to fight another day. Now that Horvat

---

[72] *Ibid.*, III, 1090.

[73] Parfenov, *Uroki proshlogo,* p. 40; and Harris to Lansing, July 29, 1918, *USFR, 1918, Russia,* II, 309–14.

[74] V. Vilenskii-Sibiriakov, "Bor'ba za sovetskii Sibir'," *Severnaia Aziia,* II, No. 3 (1926), 60–61. The association of Kalmykov with the Chinese front in this source is an obvious mistake for Gamov.

[75] V. Borodavkin, "Vospominaniia komandira," in Vsesoiuznaia Kommunistichiskaia Partiia, Tsentral'nyi Ispolnitel'nyi Komitet, Sekretariat Glavnoi Redaktsii "Istorii Grazhdanskoi Voiny v SSSR," *Sergei Lazo, vospominiia i dokumenty* (Moscow: Gosizdat, 1938), p. 45.

had formed a government, the Japanese army might bring off its expedition. Only one important task remained: the achievement of an understanding with the United States and the Allied powers. Who could have predicted that in this, too, the Czechoslovaks were to play a decisive role?

XII. A DECISION FORCED

Whoever or whatever may have prompted the uprising of the Czechoslovak corps in Siberia, the effect of its success was felt around the world. Already it had helped to win the British and the French away from their flirtation with Moscow. It was beginning to make the Japanese think that perhaps the Czech forces could be used to further Japanese objectives in the Amur basin. Now it was to influence the United States government not only to abandon its opposition to an expedition in Siberia, but actually to propose one.

The American Invitation

For months the Americans had refused to consider intervention in Siberia. They had maintained adamantly that intervention there would contribute little to winning the war in Europe. They had argued that the war would be won on the western front and that no effort to revive Russia or reestablish an eastern front could do aught but dissipate their strength and that of their allies. Now they suddenly reversed themselves. On July 8, Secretary Lansing informed Ambassador Ishii that the United States government would like to invite Japan to join it on an equal basis in an immediate program to furnish arms and ammunition to the Czechoslovaks, land available forces from their naval vessels to guard Vladivostok, and send a limited expedition of approximately 7,000 men each to guard the lines of communications of the Czechoslovaks as they proceeded toward Irkutsk.[1] If such action were agreeable to the

[1] Ishii to Gotō, July 8, 1918. Japan, Sambō Hombu, *Taishō Shichi-nen naishi Jūichi-nen Shiberia Shuppei-shi*, 1924, I, 46–48; Japan, Kaigun Gunreibu, *Tai-*

government of Japan, said Lansing, the United States hoped that Japan would join it in making a preliminary public declaration to the effect that

the purpose of landing troops is to aid Czechoslovaks against German and Austrian prisoners, that there is no purpose to interfere with internal affairs of Russia, and that they guarantee not to impair the political or territorial sovereignty of Russia.

The government in Tokyo may have suspected something was in the offing, for on July 2 and 8, at Vladivostok, Admiral Knight had agreed on behalf of his government to extend material aid to the Czechoslovaks, and the Japanese had responded on July 4 with a pledge of their own to send arms and ammunition. But the Japanese could hardly have known that a proposal for an expedition was to follow. Indeed, historians ever since have been trying to account for this surprising turn of events.[2] It has been widely asserted that America decided to propose a joint expedition chiefly for preventive purposes, because it feared that otherwise Japan would send an independent one of its own on a much larger scale. Certainly there were many reasons why American policy makers should have been concerned on this score: the record of American-Japanese rivalry in Manchuria, Japanese aid to potential Russian puppets in the Chinese Eastern Railway Zone, reported military movements in the home islands and in Korea and South Manchuria, rumors of the secret military and naval agreements between Japan and China, Chinese requests for support against Japan, cur-

---

shō Yon-nen naishi Kyū-nen Kaigun Senshi, I (1924), 189–90; Tsurumi Yūsuke, Gotō Shimpei (Tokyo: Gotō Shimpei Denki Hensankai, 1938), III, 916–17. Secretary Lansing's account of the interview, substantially the same as Viscount Ishii's, is given in his memorandum of the secretary of state's conference of July 8, in USFR, 1918, Russia, II, 267–68; memorandum of secretary of state of a conference at the White House in reference to the Siberian situation, July 6, 1918, USFR, 1918, Russia, II, 262–63.

[2] There have been several recent studies of America's role in the Siberian expedition, including those published by White, Tompkins, and Williams, and the unpublished dissertations of Bock and Unterberger. These scholars have made excellent use of the U.S. State Department and private sources; but, unfortunately, no private scholar has yet been given access to the archives of the U.S. Navy and War departments relating to the expedition, so that any estimate of America's motives, including that below, must perforce be tentative.

rent news that Japan was preparing to move into the Amur basin, and the repeated warnings of the Allies that, if America hesitated much longer, Japan would undoubtedly act alone. On the other hand, there is little substantial, direct evidence that such fears and strategic considerations actually did play a leading role in the American decision.

The bulk of the contemporary evidence points to two other factors of overriding importance. One was a growing concern over the misunderstanding that America's opposition to any Siberian expedition was creating in the minds of its war partners. Some American leaders were coming to feel that, if not cleared up, the misunderstanding might seriously damage the united war effort. It was in the frame of mind of wanting to agree with the Allies if he possibly could that President Wilson received a final and formal request from the Supreme War Council on July 3.

Having tried nearly every conceivable way to secure American cooperation in an expedition, including unsuccessfully soliciting an invitation from the Soviet government, the British and French had decided once again to make a direct appeal. They had hoped that the Japanese would support them, but Tokyo had refused. In a secret meeting of the seventh session of the Supreme War Council, on July 2, they decided then to dress up their request by making it in the name of that council.[3] They asked the United States government to participate in an Allied force to be sent to Siberia. The force was to be about 100,000 men strong, with the Japanese contributing most of the troops and, therefore, appointing the commander. It would have three objectives: to enable the Russians "to throw off their German oppressors"; to weaken Germany by denying it Russian supplies and engaging its troops on a reconstituted eastern front; and "to bring assistance to the Czechoslovak forces." The Japanese, said the council, were ready to move, awaiting only the approval of the United States.

[3] Frazier to Wilson, July 3, 1918, *USFR, 1918, Russia,* II, 245–46; and Supreme War Council document 260, quoted in Frederick Palmer, *Bliss, Peacemaker; the Life and Letters of General Tasker Howard Bliss* (New York: Dodd, Mead, 1934), 298–99. The premiers and foreign ministers of the three states were present.

The high officials who gathered at the White House on July 5 to confer with President Wilson were no more moved by the first two objectives than they had ever been.[4] They still agreed that an expedition to western Siberia was out of the question. However, the final purpose, "to bring assistance to the Czechoslovak forces," suggested the possibility of a much more limited operation, which might pacify the Allies and at the same time relieve a second concern from the American mind—the unhappy situation of the Czechoslovaks.

The Czechoslovak movement for national independence had appealed strongly to the American people. For this reason and also because the United States wished to encourage similar movements among other Slavic groups within the Austro-Hungarian empire, the American government could not ignore the Czechoslovak difficulties in Siberia. On June 25, Consul General Caldwell reported the plea for help made by Major General Dietrichs to the consular corps at Vladivostok, and strongly recommended that the United States respond with arms, ammunition, and even troops.[5] The next day, Admiral Knight transmitted a direct request by the Czechoslovak representatives for Allied aid:

In view of many difficulties involved for the Czech forces in making their way to Irkutsk, holding the road open behind them, and finally cooperating efficiently with their western detachments, they ask to be informed whether help can be expected from the other allied powers whose ally they consider themselves to be and in whose interest as well as in their own they consider that they are acting against the many thousands of armed Austro-German prisoners in Siberia.[6]

It was primarily with the dual objective of responding to the call of the Czechs and thereby appeasing if possible the demand of the Allies for action in Siberia that the group of policy makers at the White House on July 5 seems to have taken the fateful decision to propose that Japan join the United States in a limited operation to rescue the Czechoslovaks. The Allies, of course, could

---

[4] The conferees included the secretary of state, the secretary of war, the secretary of the navy, General March, and Admiral Benson.
[5] Caldwell to Lansing, June 25, USFR, 1918, Russia, II, 226.
[6] Knight to Daniels, June 26, 1918, ibid., II, 230–31.

not be expected to rejoice over so small an action as this, but they might find it better than nothing. Anyway, as they had not proposed to shoulder much of the burden themselves, they would be forced to comply if America and Japan were to agree.

The more serious question was: would Japan agree? The American leaders must have known that two issues were bound to come up. One concerned the command. Japan had already indicated its desire to command any expedition sent into Siberia. The Allies apparently accepted this principle. America, on the other hand, was not disposed to do so. In western Europe it had insisted on maintaining the independence of its command; it was determined to insist on the same in Siberia. The principle preferred by the United States, Secretary Lansing told the ambassadors of the Western Allies, was that of "joint equal military action." [7] Would Japan give in?

The second question, of course, concerned the purpose of an expedition. The Japanese had repeatedly insisted that it could not operate effectively beyond the Amur basin. But would Japan be willing to operate even there if the purpose were restricted solely to aiding the Czechoslovaks? What the American officials did not know was that their proposal was to force Japan to a decision about the long-developing plans of the military interventionists for a large-scale independent expedition to Siberia.

The Chōshū Clique's Reaction

Ishii's report of his July 8 meeting with Secretary Lansing reached Foreign Minister Gotō two days later. Tanigawa sent through a report at the same time to Chief of Staff Uehara.[8] Gotō saw at once that the American proposal differed from his own "long-range plan" not only in the above respects, but also in two others: it did not envisage Japan's taking over the administration of Russia's railroads, nor did it suggest that Japan might send an independent

[7] Lansing to President Wilson, reporting his conference with the British, French, and Italian ambassadors, July 9, 1918, *ibid.*, II, 269–70.

[8] Araki Sadao, *Gensui Uehara Yūsaku Den* (Tokyo: Gensui Uehara Yūsaku Denki Hankōkai, 1937), II, 144. Diary entry of July 10, 1918.

expedition either into the Amur basin or possibly along the rail lines from Vladivostok to Moscow. The military planners, including Chief of Staff Uehara, Vice Chief of Staff Tanaka, and War Minister Ōshima, with whom Gotō conferred immediately, saw that its objectives did not include support for a friendly, anti-soviet regime in the Amur basin.[9] And Premier Terauchi pointed out that the American note completely ignored the empire's special interests on the continent and consequently failed to acknowledge its need to take special measures to defend these interests.[10] Clearly the American proposal was not the kind the interventionists had hoped for.

On the other hand, all other preliminaries considered necessary by the Siberia Planning Committee had been completed. Military mobilization plans had been drawn up. Secret military and naval agreements had been signed with China. Horvat had finally been prevailed upon to proclaim a government on Russian soil. All that remained was for the Foreign Ministry to secure the "understanding" of the United States and the Western Allies. The present American proposal was the first sign that such an "understanding" might be possible. Gotō, Terauchi, and the military authorities agreed that no time should be lost. The American proposal should be accepted and expanded to suit Japan's purposes. The Japanese government would say that it was pleased to cooperate with the United States in rescuing the Czechoslovaks, but that "self-defense" as well as the difficulties of the Czechoslovaks would require Japan to send more troops than America had suggested and to operate not only at Vladivostok but throughout the Amur basin. To this end, Japan must send a second, independent expedition through northern Manchuria into the Trans-Baikal Territory, as cherished for so many months by the Siberia Planning Committee. It would need also, of course, to insist on the right of supreme command.[11]

[9] Japan, Sambō Hombu, *Shiberia Shuppei-shi*, I, 48–49.
[10] Itō Miyoji, "Sui'usō Nikki," p. 1158.
[11] These decisions are inferred from subsequent statements and actions of the participants, especially from Gotō's conversation with Itō later that day. Itō, "Sui'usō Nikki," pp. 1148–56.

Having decided on a course of action, Gotō and perhaps others of this inner group immediately solicited the support of their mentor, Prince Yamagata.[12] Until July 10, Yamagata appears carefully to have reserved his final decision. Perhaps he had always believed that some kind of expedition would one day be necessary, but he had not wished to launch one rashly until the conditions were right. As he is reported to have told one of the project's earliest and most ardent advocates, "When drawing the sword, one does not grasp the handle until he has considered first how it can be sheathed." [13] Now, when the new situation was outlined to him, he agreed that the handle should be grasped. And a veteran liberal, Ozaki Yukio, was probably not far wrong when he said, "With Prince Yamagata's conversion, a Siberian expedition was immediately decided upon."

The next move of the interventionists was to enlist Itō Miyoji. Gotō called on him the same day and explained what he and the Yamagata men had in mind. Itō readily agreed that the American proposal should be accepted and he thought two divisions, or in an emergency, four, would be a reasonable force for Japan to send. As for an independent expedition to Siberia "such as the military specialists had previously planned," he did not think conditions in the Amur basin warranted it, nor that the political parties at home or the powers abroad would permit it. It would be best, he thought, for the government to limit itself to accepting the joint expedition to Vladivostok. But, when Gotō informed him that the Yamagata clique had already taken the decision, Itō, like a loyal samurai, pledged himself to the cause.

The next step was to secure the official approval of the cabinet. Championed by Terauchi and Gotō and supported by a special communication from the chief of the army general staff,[14] the

---

[12] Probably several persons talked with Yamagata. Ozaki Yukio says that it was Tanaka who won him over "by treating him as a grandson would his grandfather." Ozaki, Yukio, *Nihon Kensei-shi wo Kataru* (Tokyo: Monasu, 1938), II, 234. Itō Miyoji reports that on July 12 Gotō also conferred with the prince. Itō, "Sui'usō Nikki," pp. 1159–64.

[13] Reported by Mochizuki Kotaro to Ozaki Yukio. Ozaki, *Nihon Kensei-shi,* II, 234.

[14] Japan, Sambō Hombu, *Shiberia Shuppei-shi,* I, 48–49.

plan of the interventionists received speedy approval at the meeting on July 12.[15]

The army set about implementing the cabinet's decision. At home, it reviewed the Siberia Planning Committee's work and decided to use the proposed Maritime Territory Expeditionary Force for the Vladivostok mission. As these plans provided, the Twelfth Division would form the nucleus of an organization of 8,910 men and 1,560 horses.[16] On July 16 the division was mobilized on a peacetime basis; the next day, the order for mobilization was increased to wartime strength.[17]

For the independent action in "Siberia," by which the army meant the parts of the Amur basin beyond Vladivostok, the military authorities turned to the committee's plans for a Trans-Baikal Expeditionary Force. These plans called for an initial echelon built around three divisions, two of which were to proceed to Chita and thence move out along the Siberian railway, while the other, supported by the Fortieth Infantry Brigade, was to back them up and secure the Chinese Eastern Railway in northern Manchuria. The army heads decided to modify these plans. On July 16 and 17 the initial echelon was reduced from three to two divisions. The Seventh Division and the Fortieth Infantry Brigade would be sent up from the Kwantung Leased Territory and Korea to secure northern Manchuria and the Third Division and additional forces would then move into the Trans-Baikal Territory.[18] Inas-

---

[15] The records of the meetings are unavailable, but cabinet approval is attested to by many sources; for example, *ibid.*, I, 49; Japan, Kaigun Gunreibu, *Senshi*, I, 174; Hara's conversations with various government officials, Hara Kei, *Hara Kei Nikki* (Tokyo: Kengensha, 1950–52), VII, 435; and Ito, "Sui'usō Nikki," pp. 1173–84.

[16] "Summary table of organization of the Maritime Territory Expeditionary Force, reviewed July 12, 1918," is given in English translation below as Appendix H.

[17] Japan, Sambō Hombu, *Shiberia Shuppei-shi*, I, 52–53. The mobilization of July 17 provided that to the Twelfth Division should be attached a medium artillery battalion, the Twelfth Cavalry Regiment, the First Air unit, the First Field Telegraph unit, the First Radio unit, the First Railway unit and some line of communications forces, generally as provided in the revised plan for the force of July 12.

[18] *Ibid.*, I, 52–53. The total echelon would include the Third Division, Seventh Division (emergency organization) then in Manchuria, the Fortieth Infantry

much as military operations in northern Manchuria had already been provided for in the secret agreements with China, there was no need to discuss these with the United States. All the Foreign Ministry needed to do was to secure the supreme command for Japan and to impress on the American government the need felt by the Japanese government to send at least one division immediately into Trans-Baikal. Of course, provision would also have to be made for reinforcements to be sent later.

Meanwhile, in view of the decision to work with the Czecho-slovaks, it was imperative for the army leaders to find a speedy solution to the differences between the Czechs and Horvat. The Czech Second Division had brought Horvat's movement to a standstill at Grodekovo, and, while Horvat had bravely declared the Chinese Eastern Railway closed to them, he was obviously in danger of annihilation. Moreover, when Major Takeda and Colonel Araki arrived in Vladivostok with General Pflug, they found that the Japanese diplomatic representatives were on the side of the Czechs. The consular corps in Vladivostok had already appealed to the Allied ministers in Peking and, on July 12, Minister Hayashi agreed with the British, French, and Russian ministers that Russian Ambassador Krupenskii should appeal to Horvat to cancel the proclamation of his government, withdraw to Harbin, and open the Chinese Eastern Railway to the Czech forces.[19] On the eve of its own expedition to support him, the Japanese army now became extremely anxious for Horvat to reach some working agreement with the Czechs, without sacrificing his own government. Kalmykov was already seeking his peace with them, announcing that all he had ever wanted was to cooperate with them.[20]

Brigade (emergency organization) then in Korea, the Seventh Cavalry Regiment (emergency organization) then in Manchuria, the Fourth Medium Artillery Regiment, the Second Air unit, the Second Field Telegraph unit, the Second Radio unit, the Second Railway unit and some line of communications forces.

[19] *Ibid.*, III, 1090; and MacMurray to Lansing, July 12, 1918, *USFR, 1918, Russia,* II, 277–78. Although it is not clear, it seems most likely that Kikuchi and Hayashi were acting on their own authority since Gotō would hardly have authorized them to abandon the Horvat government.

[20] Japan, Sambō Hombu, *Shiberia Shuppei-shi,* I, 19–20.

On July 15 the Japanese mediators and the French military attaché, Paris, prevailed on Major General Dietrichs to talk things over with Horvat in Grodekovo. The Japanese officers made it plain that the price for use of the Chinese Eastern Railway and for support by Horvat's forces in the railway zone was acknowledgment by the Czechs of the right of Horvat's all-Russian government to maintain itself at Grodekovo. On this basis a compromise was struck.[21] Horvat addressed himself to the problem of building up his troops, offering 1,500 rubles monthly to volunteers and sending General Pleshkov to Vladivostok to win some of his wartime colleagues from the Derber forces there.[22]

Hara's Opposition to the Government

The army was proceeding on the basis of the cabinet decision of July 12. But before Ambassador Ishii could try to secure an understanding with the American government in Washington, the cabinet decision had still to pass muster before the genro, who were to meet on July 15, and the Advisory Council on Foreign Relations, scheduled to meet on July 16. The major difficulties were bound to be with the advisory council. The votes of Terauchi, Gotō, Ōshima, and Itō were certain. Hirata could also be counted on, for, as Gotō said, he would be sure to obey "the order of Prince Yamagata."[23] Inukai, on the other hand, might require a little special attention. On the eleventh, Gotō talked the problem over with Itō, who agreed to invite Inukai to his home the next morning to try to bring him around.[24] The task proved to be an easy one. Inukai readily listened to the plan of the interventionists and agreed that "there was no other way than for the government to carry it out."

[21] *Ibid.*, III, 1092. Warner, an American representative with Horvat's train, reported that the Japanese were prepared to disarm the Czechs if they did not recognize Horvat. Warner to Lansing, July 12, 1918, *USFR, 1918, Russia*, II, 280.

[22] Baron Aleksei Budberg, "Dnevnik," *Arkhiv russkoi revoliutsii*, VII (1923), 234–35.

[23] Gotō, in conversation with Itō, July 12, 1918, in Itō, "Sui'usō Nikki," p. 1172.

[24] *Ibid.*, pp. 1157–59.

Thus, a majority was assured; but a majority without Hara was useless. Were the government to persist in opposition to Hara, he could eventually, by rallying his Seiyukai party in the diet, not only thwart the plan, but even break up the government as well. It was decided to summon Hara to the capital from his home in Morioka for the advisory council meeting. At the same time his mentor, Marquis Saionji, was requested to come up from Kyōto for the meeting of the genro. Upon Hara's arrival, the interventionists planned to have Foreign Minister Gotō call on him at his home. Yamagata would then invite him in for a conference on the fourteenth. Meanwhile they would try to win over Saionji, since Hara was sure to seek advice from him. Finally, they would cap the campaign with the genro conference, hoping to influence Hara by securing its official approval. The stage would then be set for the meeting of the Advisory Council on Foreign Relations the following day.

Having returned to Tokyo on July 12, Hara first called on Marquis Saionji to learn what was afoot.[25] Saionji had probably already talked with Yamagata, as he was able to warn Hara of the American proposal and of the government's intended response. Hara then arranged for a visit in the afternoon to Viscount Itō, who outlined the government's plans and spoke for them at length.[26] Hara listened intently to Itō's assurances that, while the military authorities wanted two expeditions, they had only very limited operations in mind; but he remained suspicious.

Hara wanted to know more about the details from the foreign minister and he intended to study them with care. He warned Itō:

Examples are too numerous to mention of the fact that military diplomacy has been a deep-rooted abuse in the government for many years and has always given the nation trouble. . . . In this matter itself, you cannot tell whether or not the army has adopted the procedure of presenting an apparently small plan in the beginning and of gradually enlarging the plan later. We must be very much on our guard in this matter.

[25] Hara, *Hara Kei Nikki,* VII, 434–35.
[26] Brief reference *ibid.;* a more extended account in Itō, "Sui'usō Nikki," pp. 1173–84.

That evening, when Foreign Minister Gotō called, Hara quizzed him in detail. Hara did not state his own views categorically, but Gotō came away convinced that he was determined to support the Vladivostok expedition, but to oppose the independent Siberian operation vehemently.[27] The next round was up to Yamagata.

The relationship between the prince and "the commoner" was an unusual one. In spite of their profound differences over the issue of party versus clan government, Yamagata had for years taken a special interest in Hara; and Hara in turn, partly no doubt out of respect for the older man's great ability and judgment, but even more in recognition of the enormous political influence wielded by him, had come to admire Yamagata and frequently sought his counsel. On July 14, Hara made the pilgrimage to Odawara. The prince reviewed the situation and told him that, in view of the American proposal, he felt it "essential" for Japan to send its troops.[28] He then showed Hara copies of the American note and of the draft reply which the government proposed to send, including passages referring to an independent Siberian expedition. As usual in their relations, the conversation proceeded smoothly, but Hara did not give in. He expressed his concern about Japan's postwar position and his conviction that Japan should take no steps which would interfere with establishing a closer understanding with the United States. Yamagata agreed, but felt that the government's program involved no such danger. Hara was dubious whether Japan was militarily strong enough to take on a major enemy. Yamagata replied, contrary to his views in March, that, "since the present expedition is not to fight with Germany, there is no need for that inadequacy to give anxiety." Hara returned to Tokyo, unpersuaded.

On that afternoon and evening a triumvirate of resistance was formed. Marquis Saionji called and agreed with Hara that for the sake of building a coalition with America the American proposal for a joint expedition should be accepted, but Japan's proposal for

[27] Hara, *Hara Kei Nikki*, VII, 435; and Itō, "Sui'usō Nikki," pp. 1184–85, reporting Gotō's account of the conversation.
[28] Hara, *Hara Kei Nikki*, VII, 436–37.

an independent expedition should be fought.[29] In the evening Hara outlined this view to Baron Makino, who agreed that the independent expedition should be resisted. He was inclined to go even further and argue that even sending an expedition to Vladivostok was excessive. Better not let the military get started. The marines already there were enough. Encouraged by the attitude of Hara and Saionji, Makino sent a messenger down to Kamakura early the next morning in an effort to enlist the support of Marquis Matsukata, who would be coming up for the meeting of the genro at 10 A.M.

If Makino and Hara had thought Saionji and Matsukata would hold out in the genro conference against the arguments of Gotō, Terauchi, and Yamagata, they must have been disappointed. Some liberals felt sure that the two elders had resisted, but the government proclaimed the meeting a success. Whatever reservations the two genro expressed about the necessity of keeping the Western powers fully informed and about seeking an adequate understanding among the people, they appear to have been reluctant to force a break with their old colleague Yamagata. In the end, they seem to have agreed not to oppose the government's plan, so long as the approval of the Advisory Council on Foreign Relations could be secured.[30] Hara and Makino were left to fight alone.

An emergency cabinet meeting was held in the afternoon,[31] following which, at Yamagata's suggestion, Terauchi invited Hara to his residence at 5 P.M.[32] Again he outlined for Hara the government's proposal and emphasized that "he wanted this matter really settled." Unless it were settled then as the government planned, he argued, a much greater expedition would have to be sent later. Japan could not tolerate indefinitely the extension of German power eastward and the increasing occupation of the rail-

[29] Ibid., VII, 438.

[30] An anonymous article in the Tokyo Asahi, July 20, 1918, p. 2, cited in Takeuchi Tatsuji, War and Diplomacy in the Japanese Empire (Garden City: Doubleday, Doran, 1935), p. 207; and Tsurumi, Gotō Shimpei, p. 919. Itō records that "generally speaking, they approved his [Gotō's] proposal and . . . there was no argument." Itō, "Sui'usō Nikki," pp. 1186–87.

[31] Tsurumi, Gotō Shimpei, III, 921.

[32] Hara, Hara Kei Nikki, VII, 439–40, 453.

roads by America. But Hara remained unmoved. "The question of Vladivostok," he agreed, "was comparatively simple. As for the question of Siberia, that required sincere consideration." On the same day that old political intriguer of the Yamagata clique, Miura Goro, called on Hara to dangle before him the ultimate inducement, the possibility of Yamagata's support for the premiership.[33] Hara knew that Terauchi was not well and that he had several times said he wished to resign. Now Miura had come to report that Terauchi was "dangerously ill" and would resign as soon as Yamagata gave him the word. But "Yamagata told him there was the matter of the Siberian question and it would be difficult to permit him to resign until he had resolved it." Of course, if the Seiyūkai could be counted on to follow Yamagata's wishes . . . Take this matter of the Siberian expedition. Yamagata had maintained all spring that Hara agreed with him. Now if Hara . . . Hara replied that it was true, he had agreed with Yamagata, because all spring Yamagata had urged caution. But to say that Hara continued to agree with him when Yamagata had suddenly changed his mind, well, "That is Yamagata's way." Miura joined Hara in a chuckle and departed.

At 10 that evening, Hara held a long conference with the directors of his party.[34] He wanted to be sure of their support before opposing the government in the advisory council the next day. He outlined the situation to them, describing the American note, the government's proposed reply, the Kokumintō's inevitable approval of it and the Kenseikai's inevitable opposition.[35] As for his own attitude, the American proposal for a joint expedition to Vladivostok should be accepted, the government's proposal for a second, independent expedition to Siberia should be fought. And if the council ignored his views, he was prepared to withdraw from it and join forces with the Kenseikai in the diet. Secretary General

---

[33] *Ibid.*, VII, 439.

[34] *Ibid.*, VII, 441; Maeda Renzan, *Hara Kei Den* (Tokyo: Takayama Shoin, 1943), II, 323–26; *Tokonami Takejiro Den*, pp. 420–21.

[35] Director Tokonami Takejiro had already talked with Kenseikai President Katō Kōmei and was assured that he would "never agree" to a Siberian expedition. Hara, *Hara Kei Nikki*, VII, 449.

Yokota Sennosuke, who seems to have been in touch politically with the premier and Baron Den,[36] disagreed: the party should continue to go along with the government. But, by the time the meeting broke up at 1 A.M., Hara had won the directors to his views. He would challenge the government with the ultimate threat.

The Advisory Council Meeting, July 16

At 10:10 the next morning, Premier Terauchi opened the scheduled meeting of the Advisory Council on Foreign Relations in the San-no-ma room of the palace. He reviewed briefly the diplomatic negotiations which led up to the American note and then presented the draft reply proposed by the government. Foreign Minister Gotō was invited to explain it. No complete copy of the original draft appears to be available, but a reasonably accurate version has been reconstructed from a variety of sources. Those portions that were later revised are italicized.

In regard to the first point of the secretary of state's remarks, namely, that of sending weapons to the Czechoslovak forces, the Imperial government is pleased to learn that the views of the American government agree completely with its own and to state that it has already shipped the weapons.

As for the second point, namely, the United States government's proposal that Japanese and American forces be sent to Vladivostok and *police the area* with the object of supporting the Czechoslovak forces, although we have not yet had an opportunity to ascertain the views of the European Allies, it is not believed that there will be any objection in principle to this proposal by the Allied countries in view of the attitudes hitherto expressed by them toward the question of intervention in Siberia and the question of support for the Czechoslovak forces; therefore, on the basis of this understanding, the Imperial government is pleased to express its agreement in the matter of sending troops to Vladivostok as proposed by the United States government and at the same time would like to make plain its position.

[36] *Ibid.,* VII, 442.

1. The secretary of state has proposed that Japan and the United States should each send the same number of troops at the present time; and the United States, being inclined to send two regiments to Vladivostok, hopes that Japan will send the same number of troops; however, to put *any* limit *beforehand* on the number of troops Japan is to use would inevitably arouse the suspicion of the Japanese people that the Allies suspect Japan of wild ambition and want to restrain it. Therefore although the Japanese government might try to explain it, *it believes that* this misunderstanding would cool the nation's ardor to achieve the joint objectives of the Allies and, forming a source of lengthy controversy, would exert an extremely bad effect on the sensibilities of the nation; *but, in view of the United States government's declaration in its message of March 7 to the effect that, if intervention were deemed wise, it would be entirely willing to entrust the enterprise to the Japanese government, the Imperial government would like to believe that, in proposing the present expedition to Vladivostok, the United States does not necessarily view the equality in numbers of Japanese and American troops as a condition.* The number of troops needed by Japan and the United States and the other Allies in order to achieve their objectives will have to be decided *in the future* in accordance with necessity. Therefore, it considers it improper to limit the number beforehand.

2. From various sources, the Imperial government has learned that the number of Bolshevik troops and of German and Austrian prisoners of war opposing the Czechoslovaks at the present time is not to be despised. The Imperial government is deeply concerned lest the Czechoslovak forces be unable to bear up well against them and to maintain their present positions very long; and if it should happen that this force unhappily were to be defeated and of course even if the workers' and peasants' government and the German government were completely to change their previous attitudes so as to permit the Czechoslovak forces to proceed to the western front, it can only be expected that the pressure of German and Austrian power in Siberia will become increasingly severe hereafter; and *as a result of that, geographically speaking, the Allies and Japan in particular would suffer an extremely serious threat to their vital interests.* Consequently, together with the policy of supporting the Czechoslovak forces, we shall be forced to meet the situation by sending troops to Siberia. *Not only is this unavoidable for reasons of the self-defense of the Empire, but we believe it will serve the purpose of maintaining order locally where representatives of various Russian groups have recently been appealing to the Imperial government. It has been decided to dispatch warships to*

Vladivostok and to send troops immediately to other places deemed necessary.[37]

In discussing the draft, Foreign Minister Gotō emphasized especially that the government was ready to join the United States in a joint expedition to Vladivostok, but that the increasing threat of the German and Austrian prisoners of war and the repeated requests from moderate Russian groups for "aid from abroad" deserved more consideration than the American government had given them.[38] Moreover, the pride of the Japanese people could not be lightly ignored. He urged the council members to realize that, "as soon as we take military action to assist the Czechs, new dangers are bound to arise." The government would be remiss in its duty to the empire, he argued, if it did not insist, when accepting America's invitation, that the size of Japan's participation and the area of its operations be left to "necessity."

When Gotō had finished, Inukai raised several questions.[39] Did the government intend to wait for an answer from the United States? Not necessarily, replied Gotō. The troops were so urgently needed that they should be sent at once. But, interposed Hara and Makino, was it not desirable at least to arange with America beforehand about the Siberian railroads? What if the United States did not agree to Japan's extending its operations along these lines? Well, certainly, replied Gotō, Japan would need to work

[37] This version is a reconstruction of the revised version submitted to the Advisory Council on Foreign Affairs on July 17 (see below). The italicized portions comprise material that, according to Itō Miyoji in "Sui'usō Nikki," pp. 1299–1302, was revised or deleted by Itō and Gotō to meet the objections raised by the council the previous day. It should be noted that Itō does not make clear whether the part beginning with "as a result" in the second sentence of the last paragraph and ending with "Czechoslovak forces" in the next sentence was in this or a slightly different form in the original draft (*ibid.*, p. 1310). In addition, the phrase in the final sentence, "to detach warships to Vladivostok and," may or may not have been in the original draft. Itō records Hara as mentioning it at the council meeting on July 17 (*ibid.*, p. 1311) and Hara refers to it as part of the government's proposal, in his diary entry of July 16 (Hara, *Hara Kei Nikki*, VII, 446). Neither of these passages would appear to affect the substance of the draft.

[38] Itō, "Sui'usō Nikki," pp. 1193–1205; summary of government's (presumably Gotō's) statement in Tsurumi, *Gotō Shimpei*, III, 919–20.

[39] Itō, "Sui'usō Nikki," pp. 1205–15.

out some arrangement on the spot about the use of the railroads, but, since "America had changed its attitude," he saw no reason to anticipate that this would be difficult. Even so, persisted Hara, you cannot ignore America completely. The United States had asked Japan to issue a specific declaration of intentions before launching its troops; and "it would be wrong to send troops before an announcement is made." [40] Several others agreed.

Inukai then asked why there had been no mention of the supreme command. Gotō assured him there was no need to raise the issue. The command would be Japan's by right of sending the most troops. The discussion then focused on troop strength. If the government was unwilling to accept the limit set by the United States, exactly what strength would be needed and why? Gotō started out by repeating his previous explanation and went on to point out that the American equation of 7,000 Japanese troops with 7,000 American troops was highly deceptive. After all, "America looks on the Czech forces as its own army. It is a fact that there was formerly a plan to organize a 500,000-man Czech force in America." Therefore, any reckoning of American strength in Siberia must include the Czechoslovaks. As for the exact number that Japan should send, Gotō called on War Minister Ōshima to explain.

Ōshima began by emphasizing how totally inadequate 7,000 men would be. According to the army's best estimates, a Japanese expedition would face 110,000 German and Austrian prisoners of war, more than 11,000 of whom were already armed. Others would be armed shortly and reinforcements from the central powers could be expected. In view of this threatening situation, the army was convinced that Japan must send no less than seven divisions, two (numbering about 43,000 men and 12,000 horses) to the Maritime Territory to operate in conjunction with the American and Czech forces, and five (numbering about 108,000 men and 23,000 horses) to the Siberian area east of Irkutsk.[41] In addition,

---

[40] Hara, *Hara Kei Nikki*, VII, 446.

[41] This was in accord with the plans of the Siberia Planning Committee, worked out in March and slightly revised in June.

six more divisions would have to be kept in readiness as reinforcements.

When Ōshima had finished speaking, the council erupted. All the earlier talk about sending one or two divisions appeared now as camouflage! What the army intended was nothing less than to use the American proposal as an excuse for launching the all-inclusive expedition it had so long been planning and to do so immediately regardless of American reaction! The debate became so excited that finally Terauchi stepped in. He tried to reassure the council members that "what Ōshima was saying referred to a distant emergency." [42] After all, "in devising the best plan, the military specialists must consider the maximum effort that may be required in case of emergency. War Minister Ōshima was speaking only in that sense and has no intention of sending a large number of troops immediately." What Ōshima meant to say, said Terauchi was that "if we are going to succeed in rescuing the Czechs, we must not confine ourselves to the Vladivostok district, but must go on to begin operations in Siberia and of course must assume the burden of protecting the railroads so as to get out the Czechs in the rear." And for these purposes, the government contemplated, for the present, one division to Vladivostok and one to the interior of Siberia. [43] The atmosphere remained tense as the council recessed for lunch.

When the meeting was reconvened at 1:30 P.M., Hara Kei led off the attack on the government's proposal by distinguishing clearly between a small "Vladivostok expedition" and a large "Siberian expedition." The former he could accept, although it was not in any sense necessary. "Since Vladivostok is now peaceful, I do not fear that it will again fall into the grasp of the Bolsheviks." [44] But, after all, "America has made the proposal and in consideration of future relations between Japan and America, I

[42] Itō, "Sui'usō Nikki," pp. 1220–23.

[43] The premier was quite truthful in insisting that the army intended to send only one division into each area at first; but, he certainly knew that the army did not believe the "emergency" requiring the others to follow would be so "distant."

[44] Itō, "Sui'usō Nikki," pp. 1228–34.

think it would be best to accept. . . . Especially since we have
learned that England has already sent troops from Hong Kong,
we cannot refuse." [45] Certainly 1,000 or 2,000 men would be
sufficient. As for sending a separate expedition into Siberia to secure the railroads, that had best be deferred; and even though the
"necessity" should "arise at another time," the government "should
first notify the powers that we are sending troops for such and
such a necessity," so that the government could proceed with
united support.

Hirata then spoke up to stem the Hara attack.[46] The government members settled back; they had already talked with Hirata
and felt sure of his support. The old Chōshū bureaucrat began
strongly by agreeing with the government that both expeditions
would be needed. Of course, if a joint declaration could be negotiated before the Vladivostok expedition was begun, that would
be fine; on the other hand, if it could not, well, then perhaps
separate declarations would be all right. As for sending an expedition to Siberia only after the one to Vladivostok was under way,
perhaps the government should not wait so long. . . . On and on
he droned, his scarcely audible voice wandering from one point
to another with such a mixture of rashness and hesitancy that,
although he seemed to be approving the government's draft, when
he had finished, no one was quite sure where he stood. While the
others strained to catch his meaning, the face of the premier flushed
with anger.

Baron Makino thereupon pressed the attack which Hara had
launched.[47] He argued vigorously that the government's draft
should be drastically revised. It was obviously contrary to America's
intention and could only lead to a dangerous estrangement between the two countries. The United States government apparently believes that its proposal does not constitute "intervention,"
he said; but, the Imperial government's draft reply is nothing more
than a notice that Japan intends exactly that. "If our empire plans

[45] Hara, *Hara Kei Nikki*, VII, 447.
[46] *Ibid.*, VII, 447–48; and Itō, "Sui'usō Nikki," pp. 1235–42.
[47] Itō, "Sui'usō Nikki," pp. 1242–48.

to take the grave decision alone to send troops to Siberia, at a time when no general decision has yet been reached in the negotiations which the powers have hitherto been conducting in regard to operations in Siberia, then America, when it receives this reply, is going to be extremely disturbed." He warned that if Japan antagonized America the consequences would be serious.

Our empire [has] already proclaimed two or three times that, if we should by chance act in Siberia, we shall expect America's spiritual and material assistance. America would not dream that, without its approval, our empire would decide on operations in Siberia like this. The empire has announced previously that it would take independent action in self-defense should danger arise; and therefore, logically speaking, we are simply saying that such is now really the case. However, I cannot in fact believe that the conditions today can be properly so described. There are very many things which our empire expects of America in the future and consequently we must work out a good understanding with America.

On the other hand, Makino pointed out, it would be dangerous for the government simply to accept the American proposal as it stood. The proposal was quite unrealistic. Obviously, any "expedition to Vladivostok" could "not avoid having a truly interventionist character." America seemed to be proposing an operation whose consequences were not well thought out. Before engaging in such a venture, the empire should seek further agreement "between the Allied powers and America." Meanwhile, in order to avoid "the reality" as well as the name of "intervention," which America still seemed to oppose, "I should prefer our empire to stop at simply landing some marines from our warships." Were Japan to go farther than that at the present time, he concluded, it would inevitably be drawn into a misunderstanding with America and might face a major war in Siberia for which the army was ill-prepared. "From what I hear on all sides, the truth is that there seem to be hundreds of weaknesses in our army which are greatly in need of attention." With this parting shot at the war minister, Makino turned the floor over to Inukai.

The Kokumintō party president spoke briefly to the effect that he, too, did not want to see Japan involved in a major war. Nevertheless, in the situation Japan faced, the government had no alternative but to take the stand it had adopted.

Last to speak was the legalist Itō Miyoji, on whom fell the task of making the government's rebuttal.[48] Viscount Itō turned first to Makino's contention that American and Japanese views were dangerously divergent.[49] He agreed that the Western powers' Russian policy had not consistently followed that of Japan. In fact, it had been exceedingly difficult to determine what their policy really was: it had been very contradictory, now "looking hostilely on the Bolshevik government behind its back," now "casting loving glances at its face." Now, at last, this "contradiction in Allied policy" had been "resolved," and, like Japan, America and the Allies seemed ready to treat the Bolsheviks as an enemy. In view of this common attitude it was highly desirable for Japan to express general agreement with America's proposal. It was not that Japan had any obligation toward the Czechs, but that as an ally in the European war Japan should cooperate in any effort its partners believed would advance their success in the war. Moreover, this was an excellent opportunity "to strengthen the relations between Japan and the United States and to increase America's trust in Japan," which all council members would agree was highly desirable. Under the circumstances, if Japan were to insist that America should go it alone, Japan would thereby abandon its "vital position in the Orient" and would receive less consideration in future world affairs.

But, in expressing general agreement with the American proposal, was it reasonable for Japan to accept the limitations as to the area of operations and the number of troops designated by the United States? He thought not. He agreed with Baron Makino that the American proposal meant intervention, whether the Americans thought so or not. "Can you say it is not intervention when you send troops forcibly inside another country's territory

[48] While Navy Minister Admiral Katō is recorded as having been present at the meeting, neither the diaries of Hara and Itō nor other records examined indicate that he expressed any views.
[49] Japan, Sambō Hombu, *Shiberia Shuppei-shi,* I, Appendix 9, 87–96; Itō, "Sui'usō Nikki," pp. 1250–77.

without waiting for the permission of the sovereign, when you send troops to support forces which are combatting the existing government of that country?" Even so, it was the act of sending troops and not the number of troops sent that constituted intervention, and Makino could no more avoid it by sending "a small naval landing force" than could the Americans by sending their limited detachments. To agree at all with the American proposal was to agree to intervention.

The question for the Japanese government was, then: what kind of intervention would be most in Japan's interests? The purposes of the Americans and the British, who had already ordered up troops from Hong Kong, were limited to aiding the Czechs as joint participants in the European war. Japan, on the other hand, was in a very different position. That was simply a "self-evident truth." As "leader of the east," with "the responsibility of maintaining peace in the Far East," it had direct and heavy obligations in Korea and the Kwantung leased territory; and now that the military and naval agreements had been concluded, it had increasing obligations in China. If, in the name of "self-defense," which is the "sovereign right of the empire," we insist on having "sufficient room to exercise our national rights," how can the Allies or the United States object? For the same reason, they must surely accept the fact that it would be unwise for Japan to commit itself beforehand to the number of troops needed simply because the United States could spare only that number.

Therefore, he summed up, in agreeing with the American proposal we should make clear three reservations: Japan needs to retain its freedom of action in respect to the objectives of the expedition; the empire will send additional troops; and we cannot "restrict our action in Siberia to Vladivostok." As for the declaration, it was not an important matter; but, if it must be joint, let the appropriate authorities work it out.

Itō's speech was the best defense of the government's position made, but Hara refused to capitulate. He insisted that the objective should clearly be stated as limited to "rescuing the Czechs" and that the area of operations should be accepted as Vladivostok.[50]

[50] Hara, *Hara Kei Nikki*, VII, 448.

After further discussion, Terauchi conceded that perhaps the objective of "self-defense" might be eliminated from the draft, but the reply must provide for Japanese troops to protect the Siberian railroad. Hara seems to have conceded the point. At the close of the meeting, Itō was asked to revise the draft in accordance with the decisions that had been reached, in order that the matter could be considered again when the council reconvened at 2 P.M. the next day.

Agreement on a Reply, July 17

Immediately after the council session, Foreign Minister Gotō set to work with Viscount Itō to revise the draft.[51] Together they decided that it might be well not to outline so specifically their understanding of the ideas of the American government. They would not say they understood that the function of an expedition to Vladivostok was simply to "police the area" and they would not refer at all to the stand taken by the United States on March 5. These sections were deleted. In addition, they tried to revise the note to read as if they were meeting Hara's demands that Japan agree to limit its objective to rescuing the Czechoslovaks and to limit the number of troops. Their problem was to achieve this without really tying the hands of the government. The result of their efforts was the following change in the last two sentences of the original draft:

ORIGINAL DRAFT	REVISED DRAFT
Consequently, together with the policy of supporting the Czechoslovak forces, we shall be forced to meet the situation by sending troops to Siberia. Not only is this unavoidable for reasons of the self-defense of the empire, but we believe it will serve the purpose of maintaining order locally where representatives of various Russian groups have recently been appealing to the Imperial government. It has been decided to detach warships to Vladivostok and to send troops immediately to other places deemed necessary.	Consequently, together with the policy of supporting the Czechoslovak forces, the situation may arise which will require the sending of troops to Siberia. Warships will be detached and troops will be sent.

[51] Itō, "Sui'usō Nikki," pp. 1299–1302.

When the revised draft was presented, Hara was generally pleased with the changes made; but, in view of Ōshima's talk about thirteen divisions, he was still not convinced that the government did not really intend to send "a large expedition at this time." Both Terauchi and Gotō vehemently denied that Ōshima had been talking about anything but an extreme emergency. Finally, to break up the argument after it had continued for more than an hour, Itō drafted a brief statement of the government's position and offered it to the council:

If it is necessary to send troops quickly, we shall be forced to send an unmobilized division. If in negotiating with America we have time, we shall send a mobilized division. But, whether mobilized or not, we shall send no more than a total of two divisions to Vladivostok and Siberia.[52]

Allowing themselves to think only of the army's plans for the immediate future, the government representatives readily confirmed Itō's formulation. Now that he had it in writing, Hara felt better; but, he insisted, if the government was really sincere in the matter, it should not mind committing itself in its reply to the United States. Itō agreed, as did the others, to the following revision of the key sentence:

ORIGINAL AND REVISED DRAFTS	REVISED DRAFT AS AMENDED
Therefore, [the Imperial government] considers it improper to limit the number beforehand.	Therefore, although the Imperial government has no intention of sending large numbers of troops, it considers it improper to limit the number beforehand.

Hara then turned to the last paragraph in the revised draft, which still expressed the government's intention to send troops to Siberia in defense of the "vital interests" arising from Japan's geographical position. To Hara, it betrayed the government's desire to slip over the Siberian expedition on the excuse of self-defense, whether America liked it or not. Terauchi vigorously denied that this was the case. Of course, geography did impose special "vital

[52] Ibid., p. 1308; and Hara, Hara Kei Nikki, VII, 450–51.

interests" on Japan, and for that reason Japan might be required to act in Siberia. He did not see how that could be denied. On the other hand, he was ready to reassure Hara categorically on the following points:

1) The question of sending troops in self-defense is not included in this draft.

2) The expedition to Siberia will be limited now to protecting the railroad.

3) If there are additional proposals from America, we shall consult with them.

4) After a decision has been reached today, we shall not send troops arbitrarily on the plea of necessity and shall not fail to confer with the Advisory Council on Foreign Relations in case troops are sent.

5) We shall not send troops to Vladivostok except in accord with the declarations of Japan and America (whether a joint declaration or a separate declaration is made).

6) If we arrange to confer about a Siberian expedition, it will be after Vladivostok.[53]

Well, said Hara, if this was the case, he would withdraw his objection to the sentence concerning Japan's "special interests" and the possibility of sending troops to Siberia. But then, he thought the government in turn could have no objection to changing the repetitious last line[54] in the reply as follows:

REVISED DRAFT	AMENDED BY HARA
Warships will be detached and troops will be sent.	Action shall be taken in accord with the proposal of the United States government.

The government members agreed and finally, after a few other stylistic changes were made, the revised draft as amended was turned over to Foreign Minister Gotō to wire that evening to Ambassador Ishii in Washington.[55]

[53] Hara, *Hara Kei Nikki*, VII, 450–51.

[54] Itō, "Sui'usō Nikki," p. 1311. Sometime before the reply was sent, the last line appears to have been deleted entirely, but exactly when it was done or by whom does not appear in the records examined.

[55] Japan, Gaimushō *Shiberia Shuppei Mondai, Dai Ippen, Shiberia Shuppei ni itaru Kōshō Keika,* I (1922), 53–56; Japan, Kaigun Gunreibu, *Senshi,* I, 190–91.

The Declaration and Gotō's Quandary

Just at this critical time the government committed a blunder which, like the Ōshima speech on July 16, threatened completely to destroy the agreement won with such difficulty. Having worked out the reply to Washington, Premier Terauchi now turned to a discussion of the proposed declaration.[56] Since the council had agreed that the sphere of the Japanese expedition would be a little broader than the American one, the Imperial government deemed it best for each government to issue its own declaration separately, and he passed around a draft declaration for comment.[57]

As the council members read it, their interest turned to surprise, and surprise to shock. It was replete with references to a Siberian expedition undertaken in self-defense and with "hardly a single line about rescuing the Czechoslovak forces." Baron Makino was the first to recover his voice. He could take no more. "I can see," he exploded, "that the true intent of the government is not to respond to the American proposal, but rather to contrive to intervene in Siberia. This is an extremely grave matter for the nation. I regret to say that I cannot go on in this council, following at your heels!" [58]

The premier interposed quickly to soothe the irate baron, he assuring him that there was some mistake, that he himself was reading the draft declaration for the first time. He could "see absolutely that it must not be published in response to the present American proposal." By all means, it would have to be thoroughly revised in accord with the "council's desires." If only the baron would give the government time to make the necessary revisions . . . With these assurances, Makino agreed to reserve judgment. At Itō's suggestion, the foreign minister was requested to bring in a revised version for the council to consider the next day.

That evening Viscount Itō was so concerned lest the redraft not

[56] Itō, "Sui'usō Nikki," pp. 1312–19.
[57] No text of this draft declaration has been brought to light.
[58] Opposition of Makino and Hara confirmed in Hara, *Hara Kei Nikki*, VII, 450.

satisfy the council, that at 9 o'clock he called Gotō and asked him to come over so that they work it out together. Gotō agreed, but said he would be detained for a while since he had felt so poorly all day that he had asked a doctor to come to see him.[59] Finally, at 12:30 A.M. the foreign minister arrived in an extremely over-wrought state. He confided to Itō that he simply did not know how to proceed. He was sure the original author of the declaration would never accept the changes which the council would require.

Itō did not record in his diary who the original drafter was, if indeed he knew, but Gotō's extraordinary concern strongly suggests that the draft declaration had been written or at least approved by one or more persons of very high status outside the government. The most likely explanation is that it was drawn up originally by the Siberia Planning Committee, possibly in the spring when the Siberian expedition was being discussed and before the Czechoslovak question had arisen, and that it had perhaps been modified slightly at some time between July 10 and July 16 by the four who first considered the American note: Uehara, Ōshima, Tanaka, and Gotō. Possibly also it had been shown to Terauchi and Yamagata.

Gotō had been so busy on July 16, attending the council meetings in the day time and revising the draft reply in the evening, that apparently he was unable to consult his military friends or to consider the problem of the declaration. He was forced to assume that the Yamagata clique had supported the concessions authorized by Terauchi. In any case, these concessions were not substantial; the text, as he and Itō revised it that evening, still did not limit the number of troops to be used by Japan or specify the area of operations.

After the meeting of July 17, however, Gotō was in a quandary. It was not so much what Terauchi had conceded in the draft reply as the solemn assurances he had given the opposition members of the council that the army intended to send only two divisions and that, without prior consultation with the advisory council, it would not use the plea of self-defense to reinforce them

[59] Itō, "Sui'usō Nikki," pp. 1319–27.

and convert them into the Siberian expedition that the army desired. Terauchi's assurances, if carried out, would, Gotō knew,
seriously handicap the operations drawn up by the army. And on
the very day that Terauchi made them, Gotō received a firm letter
from the chairman of the Siberia Planning Committee, Lieutenant General Tanaka, again emphasizing the army's position.[60] The
latest reports from Lieutenant Colonel Sakabe in Vladivostok,
wrote Tanaka, revealed such an alarming accumulation of prisoner-
of-war strength that it was absolutely essential to mobilize the
Vladivostok expeditionary force without delay, prepared "immediately to engage in battle, not simply in defense patrol." There
was "no sense at all in limiting the number of troops," for it was
absolutely essential to conduct operations in Manchuria not after,
but simultaneously with, those in Vladivostok.

Had the premier made concessions in the advisory council far
beyond any the military authorities would accept? Was the premier violating Yamagata's commands, or were the military authorities doing so? Gotō could feel developing within the Yamagata
clique the tremors of an earthquake that threatened to shake the
government to its foundations and perhaps the entire bureaucratic
political structure as well, and he did not know where to find
refuge. His close friend, Viscount Itō, talked with him until 1
A.M. that morning, but could not calm him. Itō apparently was
convinced that Terauchi must be acting with the full support of
Yamagata. Finally, he suggested that Gotō leave the draft declaration with him and he would revise it. Gotō could look at it in the
morning. Following Gotō's departure, Itō labored until 3 A.M. to
bring the draft declaration into line with the final revision of the
reply to the United States.

Four hours later the viscount was awakened by Gotō, who asked
to see the revised declaration. Gotō then promptly called the
premier on the telephone to make sure that he at least would accept it. Learning that Terauchi had already left his home to confer
with Yamagata, Gotō hurried over to the prince's residence, where

---

[60] Letter from Tanaka to Gotō, July 17, 1918, printed in Hoshino Tatsuo,
comp. *Zuroku Nihon Gaikō Taikan* (Tokyo: Asahi Shimbun-sha, 1936), p. 205.

he showed both men the revised form. To his great relief, he found them both resigned to accepting it. Itō had been right.

At the brief council meeting on the afternoon of July 18 the revised declaration was approved.[61] At 4:10 P.M., Foreign Minister Gotō took it to the palace, where it received the Imperial sanction.[62] The next day Gotō wired it to Ambassador Ishii, instructing him to show it confidentially to the United States government with the explanation that the Japanese government would prefer to issue it as a separate declaration at the appropriate time.[63] The official English text follows:

The Japanese government, actuated by the sentiment of sincere friendship towards the Russian people, have always entertained the most sanguine hopes of the speedy reestablishment of order in Russia and a healthy and untrammeled development of her national life. Abundant proof, however, is now afforded to show that the central European empires, taking advantage of the chaotic and defenseless condition in which Russia has momentarily been placed, are consolidating their hold on that country and are steadily extending their activities to the Russian far eastern possessions. They have persistently interfered with the passage of the Czechoslovak troops through Siberia. In the forces now opposing these valiant troops, the German and Austro-Hungarian prisoners are freely enlisted and they practically assume the position of command. The Czechoslovak troops, aspiring to secure a free and independent existence for their race and loyally espousing the common cause of the allies, justly command every sympathy and consideration from the co-belligerents to whom their destiny is a matter of deep and abiding concern. In the presence of [the] danger to which the Czechoslovak troops are actually exposed in Siberia at the hand of the Germans and Austro-Hungarians, the allies have naturally felt themselves unable to view with indifference the untoward course of events and a certain number of their troops have already been ordered to proceed to Vladivostok. The government of the United States, equally sensible of the gravity of the situation, recently approached the Japanese government with proposals for an early dispatch of troops to

[61] Itō, "Sui'usō Nikki," pp. 1327–38; and Hara, *Hara Kei Nikki*, VII, 452–53.

[62] Tsurumi, *Gotō Shimpei*, III, 923–24.

[63] *Ibid.*, III, 923–24, and Japan, Gaimushō, *Shiberia Shuppei Mondai*, I, 55–56. Formal cabinet and privy council approval for the advisory council's decisions was given on July 19. Takeuchi, *War and Diplomacy*, p. 207; Hara, *Hara Kei Nikki*, VII, 457.

relieve [the] pressure now weighing upon the Czechoslovak forces. The Japanese government, being anxious to fall in with the desires of the American government and also to act in harmony with the allies and having regard at the same time to the special position of Japan, have decided to proceed at once to dispatch suitable forces for the proposed mission. A certain number of these troops will be sent forthwith to Vladivostok and, if called for by the further exigencies of the situation, another detachment will eventually be ordered to operate and to maintain order along the Siberian railway.

In adopting this course, the Japanese government remain unshaken in their constant desire to promote relations of enduring friendship with Russia and the Russian people and reaffirm their avowed policy of respecting the territorial integrity of Russia and of abstaining from all interference in her internal politics. They further declare that upon the realization of the objects above indicated they will immediately withdraw all Japanese troops from Russian territory and will leave wholly unimpaired the sovereignty of Russia in all its phases whether political or military.[64]

[64] Enclosed in Polk to Wilson, July 24, 1918, *USFR, 1918, Russia*, II, 301–2; and Ishii to acting secretary of state, August 2, 1918, *ibid.*, II, 324–25. Translation confirmed by comparison with Japanese text in Japan, Gaimushō, *Shiberia Shuppei Mondai*, I, 56–57; Itō, "Sui'usō Nikki," pp. 1328–32; and Tsurumi, *Gotō Shimpei*, III, 923–24.

XIII. HIDDEN MEANINGS

During ten anxious days while the Terauchi government was awaiting the reply from Washington, the storm which had assailed it from the Hara quarter abated. Now it was braced against the threat of an earthquake from the opposite quarter, the army. As Gotō had foreseen, the military authorities, who had worked so hard and so long to foster a "big war" in Siberia "to decide the fate of the nation,"[1] were enraged by the concessions made by the government in its reply to the United States, particularly by the proposal to limit the expedition to a single division. They despised the "weak and indecisive expedition" proposed by the United States and denounced the government for daring to interfere in military plans, their prerogative, alone. Of the three key figures in the army project, Field Marshal Uehara reacted so strongly that he apparently refused to take any part in revising the plans and threatened, in protest, to resign as chief of staff.[2]

Terauchi versus the Army

Fortunately for the government, Uehara took no overt action, and Premier Terauchi was able to come to an agreement with Ōshima

[1] Memorandum, prepared in the Japanese Army General Staff Headquarters, following the advisory council meetings of July 16–18, 1918. Japan, Sambō Hombu, *Taishō Shichi-nen naishi Jūichi-nen Shiberia Shuppei-shi*, I (1924), 641.

[2] Hara Kei, *Hara Kei Nikki* (Tokyo: Kengensha, 1950–52), VII, 460, 474. It seems likely that this was the decision discussed by Uehara with Ōshima, Yamada and other close friends on July 18, 19, 22, and 23, with Terauchi on July 26, and possibly with Yamagata on July 28. Extracts from Uehara's diary, printed in Araki Sadao, *Gensui Uehara Yūsaku Den* (Tokyo: Gensui Uehara Yūsaku Denki Hankō-kai, 1937), II, 144. He did not actually resign until March 17, 1923.

and Tanaka. On July 20 the premier, the war minister, and the vice chief of staff together went over the political and military situation in detail.[3] They agreed that the army would have to abandon any idea of sending troops in advance of the main body of the Twelfth Division, whose movement was being discussed with the United States; when the Twelfth was sent, its function would be limited to guarding the rear of the Czechoslovak forces, though its deployment for this purpose would not be limited to Vladivostok.

The matter of instructions to the military commander was next discussed. Terauchi persuaded Tanaka and Ōshima that these should be drafted in accordance with the foreign policy recommendations of the government. In any event, Japan's forces could not operate independently from those of the Allies, although it was understood, of course, that Japan would insist on exercising the supreme command.

The question of the ultimate size of the expedition was also considered. The premier assured Ōshima and Tanaka that in the decision of the advisory council and in the draft declaration the government had specifically provided not only for sending the stipulated division to Vladivostok, but also for later moving another division (it was agreed that this should be the Third) into the Trans-Baikal Territory. Lastly, they turned to the question of northern Manchuria and the Chinese Eastern Railway. Terauchi seems to have assured them that the government, in signing the secret military and naval agreements with China, had approved the army's plans there and that nothing in the recent negotiations need occasion any change. The premier approved their decision to send the Fortieth Infantry Brigade and the Seventh Division into northern Manchuria to support the Third Division and to patrol the Chinese Eastern Railway. Lastly, the question of Chinese participation was discussed. All three agreed that the time had come to implement the provisions of the secret military and naval agreements of May 16 and 18.

The foreign minister promptly notified Minister Hayashi in

[3] Japan, Sambō Hombu, *Shiberia Shuppei-shi*, I, 55–56.

Peking, and Chief of Staff Uehara sent instructions to Japan's military attaché, Major General Saitō Kijiro.[4] The Chinese government was more than anxious to participate in any military action which the Allies might take along its borders and expressed its desire to both the Japanese and the American governments on that same day.[5] Again, on July 27 the Chinese government re-emphasized its readiness to act under the agreements as soon as the Japanese government indicated its intention to begin the expedition.[6]

In view of the imminence of the expedition, the army now quickly drew up plans for communications and maritime transport.[7] As for land transport, Major General Mutō having so far failed to negotiate an agreement with Horvat at Harbin, Major General Nakajima was ordered to Vladivostok to see what could be done with the Chinese Eastern Railway office there.[8] The hope was to set up an Inter-Allied committee under the direction of a Japanese army officer, but Allied personnel were not available or prepared to enter into such a commitment. Lest Japan lose out in the struggle for control of the railroads, Nakajima took the alternative of negotiating separately for the needs of the Japanese forces. The Amur and Trans-Baikal railways were so disrupted that no arrangements could be made. However, on the Ussuri line Nakajima was able to secure for the use of Japanese troops three trains of thirty cars each per day.[9]

Acceleration of Economic Planning

While the army was completing its work on the military phase of the expedition, the Foreign Ministry busied itself with the economic aspects. News from America showed that there was no time to lose. On July 16, Consul General Yada Chōnosuke cabled from

[4] *Ibid.*, I, 72–74.
[5] *Ibid.;* MacMurray to Lansing, July 20, 1918, *USFR, 1918, Russia,* II, 298; and MacMurray to Lansing, July 20, 1918, *ibid.*, II, 299.
[6] MacMurray to Lansing, August 8, 1918, *ibid.*, II, 334–35.
[7] Japan, Sambō Hombu, *Shiberia Shuppei-shi,* IV, 853–68, 970–72.
[8] *Ibid.*, IV, 683–704.
[9] *Ibid.*, IV, 704.

New York a newspaper report that President Wilson was considering sending a group of businessmen to Russia, headed by Daniel Willard and Frank A. Vanderlip, president of the National City Bank, and creating a single company with capital of from fifty to one hundred million dollars, to carry on America's economic program in Russia.[10] The next day this story received general confirmation in an aide-memoire, which Secretary Lansing distributed to the Allied ambassadors in Washington, explaining the action it was proposed to take in Siberia.[11] The last paragraph contained the following announcement:

It is the hope and purpose of the government of the United States to take advantage of the earliest opportunity to send to Siberia a commission of merchants, agricultural experts, labor advisers, Red Cross representatives, and agents of the Young Men's Christian Association accustomed to organizing the best methods of spreading useful information and rendering educational help of a modest sort, in order in some systematic manner to relieve the immediate economic necessities of the people there in every way for which opportunity may open.

To many in the Japanese Foreign Ministry, this was a virtual declaration of the economic war they had feared. On July 23, Marquis Kimura submitted a revision of Arita's recommendations of June 6.[12] On the morning of July 26, Foreign Minister Gotō called together an important group of interested officials to discuss the question at his official residence. Those present included, from the Finance Ministry, Baron Megata Tanetaro (an elderly retired financier), Minobe Shunkichi (president of the Bank of Korea), and Matsumoto Osamu (chief of the National Treasury section); from the Ministry of Agriculture and Commerce, Baron Itō Bunkichi (an official in its temporary industrial research bureau who had recently returned from a special economic mission to the United States); and from the Foreign Ministry, Obata Yukichi

[10] Gotō to Kikuchi (at Vladivostok) and Satō (at Harbin), July 25, 1918, JGK, RKI, SB, pp. 165–67.
[11] Aide-Memoire, from the U.S. secretary of state to the Allied ambassadors, July 17, 1918, USFR, 1918, Russia, II, 287–90.
[12] Japan, Gaimushō Kiroku, "Shiberia Keizai Enjo Kankei Zakken, I'inkai no Seiritsu ni kansuru Ken" (hereafter, JGK, SKE, IS).

(chief of the Political Affairs Bureau), Nakamura Takashi (chief of the Commercial Affairs Bureau), and the four key planners—Matsuoka Yōsuke, Marquis Kimura Ei'ichi, Hirota Kōki,[13] and Arita Hachiro.

At this meeting Matsuoka introduced the subject by summarizing various consular and military reports on economic conditions in the Amur basin and distributed copies of a proposal that he had drawn up along the general lines of the previous Arita and Kimura drafts. Matsuoka recommended that a Russian trading syndicate of private industrialists be organized to extend relief and acquire economic concessions in Siberia and northern Manchuria. The government, of course, would select the personnel of the syndicate, help it to raise money, itself invest from twenty to thirty million yen, facilitate its relations with the army, and supervise and protect its activities. This could best be done through a Siberian relief commission within the Foreign Ministry, chaired by a Foreign Ministry official, with representatives from various other ministries, the railroad board, banks, and the syndicate. The commission would be assisted locally, of course, by the consulates, but, in addition, it would send out its own economic committees to important cities and attach its own liaison committees to units of the expeditionary force in these areas.

Although Obata and Nakamura thought the government had no business seeking economic concessions—these ought to be left to private concerns—the others present agreed that government support and supervision were necessary to avoid rousing the hostility of the powers by the competitive activities of private enterprise. Baron Itō had in fact come prepared with a proposal of his own to similar effect. On the basis of this understanding, Matsumoto, Itō, and Kimura were asked to draft a plan of organization to be considered by the group on July 29.

Marquis Kimura seems to have assumed the drafting responsi-

[13] The person listed in the minutes of the meeting (*JGK, SKE, IS*) is Hirota Morinobu, one of the secretaries of the foreign minister; but Okamoto Suemasa, author of the Foreign Ministry's official history of the Siberian expedition, believes this should be Hirota Kōki, who became very active in the work of the temporary Siberian economic assistance committee.

bility. Following the lines of Matsuoka's proposal, he brought in a "draft cabinet proposal," a "draft ordinance" setting up a temporary Siberian economic assistance committee under the Foreign Ministry, and a "draft policy of economic assistance to Siberia" outlining the committee's proposed activities. Kimura pointed out that while the committee was a deliberative body in form, it would in fact exercise supervisory authority as well. Suspecting that the Foreign Ministry might use the committee to assume a dominant position in the civilian bureaucracy, the representatives of finance, agriculture, and commerce at first protested that the committee should limit itself to deliberation, leaving the execution of policies to the established ministries. However, in the end they seem to have capitulated. Two other points were left unstated in the drafts: the relationship of the program to any program the United States might undertake, a problem on which the group could not agree; and the inclusion of northern Manchuria in the concept of "Siberia," on which they did agree, although they did not say so openly.

Anxious Waiting

While Gotō proceeded with the formulation of economic plans, he was heartened by news from London, Paris, and Rome. On July 25, in accordance with the foreign minister's instructions, Ambassador Chinda called on Under Secretary Lord Robert Cecil to explain the American proposal, together with the Japanese reply and the proposed declaration.[14] The following day, Ambassador Matsui called on Foreign Minister Pichon in Paris; and Ambassador Ijūin called on Foreign Minister Baron Sonnino in Rome. In each case the reply was the same: wholehearted support for Japan's position.

The American reaction was the crucial one. As the days dragged by, the Japanese government waited more and more impatiently, more and more fearfully. Ambassador Ishii, of course, was con-

[14] Japan, Gaimushō, *Shiberia Shuppei Mondai, Dai Ippen, Shiberia Shuppei ni itaru Kōshō Keika,* I (1922), 57–59.

ducting the negotiations in Washington, but Foreign Minister Gotō thought it might be well also to confer with Ambassador Morris in Tokyo. After all, Morris had been one of Wilson's disciples at Princeton and perhaps the President could be influenced indirectly through him. Late in the evening of July 22 and again on the afternoon of July 26, Gotō paid confidential visits to the United States embassy.[15] He did his best to persuade Morris of the reasonableness of the reservations Japan had made in its reply, but Morris was not to be moved. Instead, he took the opportunity to warn Gotō that the United States had heard rumors that, contrary to American policy, the Japanese government was supporting Horvat and that it intended to occupy northern Manchuria and the Chinese Eastern Railway. Gotō readily admitted Japan's interest in Horvat, but declared that it would discontinue such aid and cooperate wholeheartedly with America's policy of treating all Russian factions with impartiality. As for the second question, Gotō admitted also that a second division was being readied for dispatch to Harbin and tried hard to convince Morris of the need for such action; he succeeded only in eliciting the warning that any Japanese occupation of northern Manchuria or of the Chinese Eastern Railway would defeat the purposes of the joint expedition.[16]

The warning served only to heighten the fears of the Japanese government. What if the United States should insist on the limits set forth in its original proposal? What if it should refuse to participate in the expedition unless Japan agreed to station a single division at Vladivostok? The army was not disposed to brook any further interference in its plans, and the cabinet was highly indignant over the overruling of its decisions by the advisory council.[17] As the pressure mounted, Premier Terauchi became more and more convinced that, whatever the American response, Japan

[15] Morris to Lansing, July 23, 1918, *USFR, 1918, Russia,* II, 300–301; Tsurumi Yūsuke, *Gotō Shimpei* (Tokyo: Gotō Shimpei Denki Hensankai), III (1938), 925–27. Tsurumi acted as Gotō's interpreter and aide on these occasions.

[16] See instructions to Morris in Polk to Morris, July 19, 1918, *USFR, 1918, Russia,* II, 297–98.

[17] Hara, *Hara Kei Nikki,* VII, 457.

would have to carry out the decisions already made.[18] But of course there was always Hara and the threat that, if the government ignored him, he might join forces with Katō Komei and bring down the cabinet. Would he agree to act in opposition to American policy? Chief Cabinet Secretary Kodama and Baron Den talked again and again with Hara's Secretary General Yokota, but Hara was determined to hold to his position. He gave clear warning that he would agree to no action which did not have the approval of America.[19] And Itō Miyoji was prepared to join him.

American Rejection of the "Counterproposal"

At 9:40 on the evening of July 27, the long-awaited word from Ambassador Ishii finally arrived at the Foreign Ministry in Tokyo.[20] The ambassador had called on Acting Secretary of State Polk on July 24 to deliver the Japanese reply and to leave a copy of the proposed declaration. At the same time he had emphasized that the 7,000 men requested of Japan by the United States would be completely inadequate for the task; it would require a full peacetime division—about 12,000 men—and possibly more later. The acting secretary had then communicated with President Wilson.

On the following day Polk explained to the ambassador that, as a result of a conference with the secretary of war and President Wilson, he was authorized to state frankly that, "although the Japanese government's reply speaks of agreeing with our proposal," it did not in fact do so. It talked of sending more than the specified number of men at the outset and additional troops later as the situation might require. This was nothing more nor less than a "counterproposal." The American government was ready to acknowledge "the right" of the Japanese army to command the ex-

[18] Ibid., VII, 456.

[19] Ibid., VII, 459–60, reporting a talk between Hara and Itō Miyoji on July 27, 1918.

[20] Japanese text, from which the excerpts were translated, in Japan, Gaimushō, Shiberia Shuppei Mondai, I, 59–62; Japan, Sambō Hombu, Shiberia Shuppei-shi, I, 60–63; and summary in Japan, Kaigun Gunreibu, Taishō Yon-nen naishi Kyū-nen Kaigun Senshi, I (1924), 193–94. Summary account in English of the Ishii-Polk conversations in Polk to President Wilson, July 24, 1918, USFR, 1918, Russia, II, 301–2; and Polk to Morris, July 27, 1918, ibid., II, 306–7.

pedition and for the sake of "harmony" would not object to the "10,000 to 12,000 men" mentioned. But the number must be agreed upon beforehand, and the question of sending more troops later was a "separate question" that could be discussed when "the necessity arises." The American government was in no position to send a "large number of troops." In fact, a "large number" would so excite the "fears of the Russian people" about "Allied intervention" as to defeat the purposes of the expedition. In conclusion, unless the Japanese government assented to these points, "America would be forced to withdraw from this venture and assume a disinterested position."

At 3 p.m. on July 28, a second wire arrived from Ishii, reporting three specific changes requested by the United States in the proposed Japanese declaration. The phrase, "in this expedition" should be added to the phrase "in harmony with the Allies" in the next to the last sentence in the first paragraph, so that the Allies would know that the declaration did not refer to the intervention they had been proposing. The phrase which followed, "having regard at the same time to the special position of Japan," should be eliminated lest it arouse the fears of the Russian people. And the last half of the next sentence—"and, if called for by the further exigencies of the situation, another detachment will eventually be ordered to operate and to maintain order along the Siberian railway"—should be deleted in order to indicate that operations would be limited to the Vladivostok area.

DECLARATION AS DRAWN UP BY JAPAN	AS REVISED BY AMERICA
The Japanese Government, being anxious to fall in with the desires of the American Government and also to act in harmony with the Allies *and having regard at the same time to the special position of Japan,* have decided to proceed at once to dispatch suitable forces for the proposed mission. A certain number of these troops will be sent forthwith to Vladivostok *and, if called for by the further exigencies of the situation, another detachment will eventually be ordered to operate and to maintain order along the Siberian Railway.*	The Japanese Government being anxious to fall in with the desires of the American Government and also to act in harmony with the Allies *in this expedition,* have decided to proceed at once to dispatch suitable forces for the proposed mission. A certain number of these troops will be sent forthwith to Vladivostok.

Premier Terauchi greeted the news with bitterness. It seemed clear to him that the United States sought to bind Japan "hand and foot." If Japan were to agree, it would be "unable to move a single step beyond Vladivostok." [21] This would completely defeat Japan's purposes. His cabinet colleagues were equally resentful. After talking with them, the premier was strongly inclined to send troops as the government had already determined, refusing to make the revisions in the declaration or to give the private assurances which Washington had requested.[22]

For Baron Gotō, the worst of his fears had been realized. As his friend and biographer puts it, his "heart must have been cold with grief." [23] He had been appointed foreign minister largely in the belief that he could secure the understanding of America where his predecessor had failed. If, now that the government had taken a fundamental decision, he too failed to win America's approval, he knew that he too would be forced to accept the responsibility. If only there were some way for Japan to appease America without at the same time abandoning its plans! Once again Viscount Itō found a way out.

"Apparent" and "Hidden" Meanings

On July 29, after talking with Terauchi, Gotō hurried over to Itō's home.[24] He found, to his great relief that Itō was not at all disposed to believe that a break with America threatened or even that new negotiations would have to be undertaken. He still maintained there were no basic differences of view between Japan and America. As he told the advisory council three days later,[25] it was important not to be misled by the "apparent" meaning of the American reply; if one examined the "hidden" meaning carefully, it was clear that America had no objection "in principle" to the

[21] Conversation between Terauchi and Itō Miyoji, July 30, 1918, in Itō Miyoji, "Sui'usō Nikki," pp. 1371–72.
[22] Conversation on July 30 between Terauchi and the Seiyūkai director Noda Utarō, who relayed it to Hara. Hara, *Hara Kei Nikki*, VII, 465.
[23] Tsurumi, *Gotō Shimpei*, III, 929.
[24] Itō, "Sui'usō Nikki," pp. 1370–74.
[25] *Ibid.*, pp. 1389–1442.

kind of expedition Japan had in mind. That was clear from the concession of supreme command to Japan. Moreover, the reasonableness of Japan's doubling the number of troops was recognized, and although America feared the effect on the Russian people of agreeing then to the dispatch of reinforcements, it had no objection to their being sent as a matter of "principle" and would be ready later to discuss the need for them.

Why, then, did the United States government insist that the Japanese government should agree in advance to limitations on the number of troops and on the area in which they were to operate? Simply because America still feared that Japan intended to send the large expedition it had been discussing with the Allies in the spring. Ambassador Ishii had failed to convince Washington that this was not Japan's intention. Itō was sure that, if Ishii were properly instructed, he would be able to calm American fears and to persuade Washington confidentially to give up the limitations it sought to impose. Once a private understanding had been reached, Itō saw no reason why Japan should not adopt Polk's suggestion for changes in the public declaration.

As Itō explained, America had no real objection to the kind of action proposed by Japan in the Trans-Baikal Territory or "Siberia," obviously having decided that it was necessary. On the other hand, the United States had officially committed itself many times against any intervention and would "lose face" if it publicly reversed itself. Confronted by this dilemma, the United States government appeared ready to accept intervention privately, but publicly, as a matter of "formality," felt it necessary to insist its position was unchanged. There was no reason why Japan should not welcome the opportunity to help its friend "save face" by accepting the revised declaration and then proceeding to send the troops as planned.

This was precisely the kind of solution the foreign minister had been seeking. He immediately sped to Odawara to discuss it with Prince Yamagata. As on his visit of eleven days earlier to discuss the Itō redraft of the declaration, Gotō found the prince anxious to restrain the cabinet from taking any position that would either delay the expedition or antagonize America. Itō's recommendations offered the best solution.[26] The foreign minister returned to Tokyo, "vivacious and in excellent spirits." [27]

A meeting of the cabinet was scheduled for July 31, to be followed by a meeting of the advisory council on August 1. In the hope of persuading the premier that the Washington revisions could be accepted without harm, Itō talked with Terauchi on July 30 and even showed him a draft of a confidential understanding about areas and numbers, which he thought Ishii could and should explain to the American government.[28] But, Terauchi refused to commit himself. Determined if necessary to carry his recommendations to the advisory council, Itō then called Hara Kei on the telephone and assured him of his intention to join Hara in insisting that the changes in the declaration must be made before any troops were sent. Itō knew that Foreign Minister Gotō was to call on Hara later that evening, and he urged Hara to take the opportunity to strengthen Gotō's resolution to take the same stand in the cabinet. When Gotō did call a short time later, Hara had no need to press the case, for the foreign minister was already sufficiently resolved and, moreover, confident that, under pressure from Yamagata, Terauchi would "quiet down" and the cabinet would follow suit.[29]

But Gotō's assurance proved too sanguine. When the cabinet met on July 31, it broke into revolt. The extremists argued hotly that the cabinet had already conceded too much. It would "lose face" if it conceded any more;[30] "the empire should adhere to its former declaration." Gotō repeated that a private understanding with the United States was all that was needed, and Terauchi finally sent the chief cabinet secretary to Itō for a copy of the reservations he had proposed to Ishii. Before the secretary returned, the meeting dissolved in uproar, leaving Terauchi and Gotō to

---

[26] As Gotō told Hara, July 30, 1918, Hara, *Hara Kei Nikki*, VII, 463.
[27] Tsurumi, *Gotō Shimpei*, III, 928.
[28] Itō, "Sui'usō Nikki," pp. 1371–72.
[29] Hara, *Hara Kei Nikki*, VII, 463.
[30] Account of the meeting given to Viscount Itō by Chief Cabinet Secretary Kodama that morning. Itō, "Sui'usō Nikki," pp. 1374–77.

work out a statement that the cabinet could accept at its emergency session the next morning before the advisory council met.

Whether Terauchi took a strong position with Gotō that afternoon and evening or whether the cabinet extremists, who may have included War Minister Ōshima and Communications Minister Baron Den, persuaded Terauchi the next morning,[31] the cabinet finally decided to reject the Itō-Gotō proposal and to insist that the declaration would have to provide for sending Japanese troops to other parts of the Amur basin in addition to Vladivostok. It was also agreed to instruct Ishii to inform the American government that Japan was accepting the American invitation and was immediately sending troops on the understanding that the numbers and area would have to be determined by necessity, as previously explained.

The Council Decision

When the premier opened the advisory council meeting at three that afternoon, he had Gotō explain the government's attitude and hand out copies of the draft reply Ishii was to present to the American government:[32]

DRAFT REPLY, PROPOSED BY THE JAPANESE CABINET,
TO THE AMERICAN REPLY OF JULY 25, 1918

1. The Imperial government deeply appreciates the fact that in replying to the Imperial government's reply to the American proposal to send troops, the United States government expressed its views frankly.

2. As for the question raised by the United States government about the number and disposition of the troops required, we do not believe that there is any difference in the view of the United States and Japa-

---

[31] Gotō told Hara on August 2 that his presence had been required at court, so that he was unable to be present to defend his position at the emergency cabinet meeting. Hara, *Hara Kei Nikki*, VII, 468.

[32] *JGK, RKI, SK, CKH,* confirmed by comparison with the final reply sent to Ishii on August 1, given in Japan, Gaimushō, *Shiberia Shuppei Mondai*, I, 63, and Japan, Sambō Hombu, *Shiberia Shuppei-shi*, I, 65–66, with the changes indicated in Itō, "Sui'usō Nikki," pp. 1382–84.

nese governments in regard to the basic objective; for we do not hesitate to say from the beginning the Imperial government does not plan to send excessively large forces inconsistent with the objective in view.

3. The Imperial government, believing that it is extremely important to maintain perfect harmony between the United States and Japan in view of the general relations between them, is immediately sending forces to Vladivostok and believes it urgent to assist in the rescue of the Czechoslovak forces; and consequently, in reply to the United States government's reply just received, it is happy to express its acceptance on the basis of the following understanding:

1) If necessary in order to aid the Czechoslovak forces, the Imperial government will send troops to places other than Vladivostok.

2) Depending on how the situation develops, it may be necessary to send reinforcements.

Gotō then went on to say that, in accordance with the "understanding" expressed in the draft reply, his government could not fully accept all the deletions America had suggested and in particular a provision for operations in areas other than Vladivostok must be included. The phrase "in this expedition" might be inserted and reference to Japan's "special position" might be eliminated, but the only change in the crucial last part of the last sentence in that paragraph which could be accepted was as follows:[33]

ORIGINAL JAPANESE DRAFT DECLARATION	REVISION REQUESTED BY THE UNITED STATES GOVERNMENT
A certain number of these troops will be sent forthwith to Vladivostok and, if called for by the further exigencies of the situation, another detachment will eventually be ordered to operate and to maintain order along the Siberian railway.	A certain number of these troops will be sent forthwith to Vladivostok.

REVISION ACCEPTABLE TO THE
JAPANESE CABINET

We are equipping troops forthwith and will send them first to Vladivostok; later as the situation requires, they will gradually be moved into other areas.

The government members braced themselves for the inevitable assault. Viscount Itō immediately took the floor and launched upon

[33] From Gotō's speech in the Advisory Council on Foreign Relations, August 1, 1918, as reported in Itō, "Sui'usō Nikki," p. 1386.

a lengthy exposition of his views on the "hidden meaning" of the American reply and on the ease with which American approval of the Japanese plans could be obtained if Ishii made these plans sufficiently clear. He urged the council, consequently, to approve the government's draft reply, which conformed so well to the position he had been recommending.

On the other hand, Itō vigorously attacked the government's refusal to accept the proposed American changes, in the declaration. True, these changes seemed to limit Japan's actions to Vladivostok, but this was simply a matter of "formality" motivated by the American desire to "save face" publicly in a matter on which its views had altered privately. The revisions would not affect Japan's action; they were vital to the public position of the American government. He was convinced that the United States would insist on them to the end. And what if the Japanese government resisted to the end? Did it intend to "act independently"? "We are not," Itō warned the government, "so resolved."

Hara then rose to add his support in favor of accepting the change in wording.[34] And he went even further in his attack on the cabinet to argue that the draft reply should also be revised. If the government meant to accept the American proposal, as it was rightly—and specifically—pledged to do at one point in the reply, then it should do so without reservations. The reference to any confidential "understanding" might well be deleted.

Makino and Inukai seemed to agree with Hara, but Itō rose to insist on retaining these passages in the declaration. He agreed that they were perhaps awkwardly stated, but he felt that the substance should be included, so that Ishii would not again fail to secure American acquiescence before the troops were sent. After suggesting corrections in grammar in the second paragraph of the proposed reply,[35] Itō offered the following revision of the last part of paragraph three:

[34] Hara, *Hara Kei Nikki*, VII, 466–67; and Itō, "Sui'usō Nikki," pp. 1443–44.
[35] In the last clause, following the semicolon, Itō recommended that the "for" be changed to "and," and that the phrase "does not plan" be changed to "has not planned." Itō, "Sui'usō Nikki," pp. 1382–84.

ORIGINAL DRAFT REPLY	REVISION BY VISCOUNT ITŌ
and consequently, in reply to the United States government's reply just received, it is happy to express its acceptance on the basis of the following understanding:	and consequently, in reply to the United States government's reply just received, it anticipates that in order to support the Czechoslovak forces, it will be necessary to advance beyond Vladivostok and to increase this assistance
1. If necessary in order to aid the Czechoslovak forces, the Imperial government will send troops to places other than Vladivostok.	in response to circumstances as they develop. It gladly accepts [the United States government's proposal] and expresses its intentions to respect the
2. Depending on how the situation develops, it may be necessary to send reinforcements.	United States government's wishes in revising the draft declaration.

This wording seemed less objectionable to Hara and he gave his assent. The united stand of Itō and Hara gradually won over most of the council members. Somewhat reluctantly the premier accepted their recommendations, whereupon the council agreed to forward the revised reply to Ishii, to issue the revised declaration, and to order up the troops at once. In accordance with these decisions, the foreign minister immediately sent off the reply to Ambassador Ishii in Washington. The following morning, Terauchi secured the formal approval of his hostile cabinet.[36] The Imperial sanction was then secured and mobilization orders were approved at 1:45 P.M.[37]

Then, lest Ambassador Ishii should not understand exactly what Tokyo's reply really meant, Foreign Minister Gotō sent him more detailed information about the government's plans, as follows:

1. The object of the present expedition being solely to support the Czech forces, the Imperial government does not hesitate to say that it has no intention of using this as an excuse to send a large number of troops and of taking action beyond this objective.

2. After sending troops with the announced objective of supporting the Czechoslovak forces, we must expect to achieve the objective without fail. If we are to limit the sphere of action of our troops to the Vladivostok area and merely look on at the dangers to the Czechoslovak forces in other areas, the expedition would, we believe, end almost meaninglessly.

3. In particular, the extreme insecurity of the position of the Czech-

---

[36] Ibid., pp. 1450–53; and Japan, Sambō Hombu, Shiberia Shuppei-shi, I, 66.
[37] Extract from Uehara's diary of August 2, 1918, in Araki, Gensui Uehara, II, 145.

oslovak forces at the present time, faced with German and Austrian prisoners of war and Bolshevik troops in the Russian Far East, being clear from various reports, it is reported that the situation of the Czechoslovak forces moving out from Vladivostok will soon be serious. If the empire, because it had not yet conferred with the United States, refrained from moving up its Vladivostok garrison, so that the opportunity were finally lost, in view of the stated objectives, the empire and the Allies would suffer an unbearable loss of prestige. This is the reason why the empire anticipates in its above-mentioned reply to America that in time of emergency it may be necessary to move its forces beyond Vladivostok or to increase their strength, without waiting every time to confer with the United States; but, of course, in every case, we shall endeavor as soon as possible to inform the United States government of the circumstances and to convince it that the action is necessary and reasonable.

4. With the understanding that this reply completes the negotiations on this matter, the Imperial government will immediately dispatch troops to Vladivostok.[38]

And, lest the military authorities misinterpret what the government meant, Premier Terauchi drafted a note to War Minister Ōshima, which was passed on to Chief of Staff Uehara.[39] Terauchi explained that Japan had agreed to send no more than one division, for the present, to Vladivostok. It had also privately reserved the right to send another to Siberia as events determined. Before doing so, the army should consult with him.

At 6 P.M. on August 2, 1918, the declaration announcing the Japanese government's decision to send an expedition to Siberia was promulgated in a special edition of the *Official Gazette*.

The Meaning of the Decision

At the time the expedition was launched, it appeared that the liberal faction within the government, led by the young genro Marquis Saionji, the Seiyūkai president Hara Kei, and the Peers member Baron Makino had with the support of America, won a signal victory. For more than six months the interventionist leaders—Prince

[38] Gotō to Ishii, August 2, 1918, Japan, Gaimushō, *Shiberia Shuppei Mondai*, I, 63–64.

[39] Japan, Sambō Hombu, *Shiberia Shuppei-shi*, I, 66.

Yamagata, Army Chief of Staff Uehara, Army Vice Chief of Staff
Tanaka, Premier Terauchi, War Minister Ōshima, and Foreign
Minister Gotō—had worked strenuously to prepare the way for a
large expedition to the Amur basin to bolster a pro-Japanese government in the Russian territories, gain control of the Chinese Eastern
Railway and the Siberian railways east of Irkutsk, and harness the
region to the Japanese economy. At last it appeared that the pro-
interventionist forces had shelved these far-reaching plans and had
agreed to accept a very limited expedition, based on the American
conception and devoted solely to rescuing the Czechoslovak forces.

In the official declaration promulgated on August 2, the Japanese
government explained publicly that it was sending "suitable forces"
to Vladivostok in order to "relieve pressure" being exerted by the
German and Austrian prisoners of war on the Czechoslovaks passing through Siberia and that its purpose in so doing was solely "to
fall in with the desires of the American government and also to
act in harmony with the Allies." In its negotiations with the American government Japan had refused to limit beforehand either the
number of troops or the area of operations. However, it had insisted
on these reservations on the sole grounds that the plight of the
Czechoslovaks might require more extended support than the
American government envisaged. To reassure the United States,
it had indicated that no more than 10,000 to 12,000 men would
be sent to Vladivostok at first and had promised that if the "need"
arose for more men or for a movement westward, the Japanese
government, in so far as time permitted, would consult with the
United States and Allied governments before taking the appropriate action.[40] Within the Advisory Council on Foreign Relations, it
was understood that the government was already convinced of the
"need" and hoped soon to send a second division into the Trans-
Baikal Territory to "protect" the Siberian railway, but that it would
not do so until after the initial troops had been sent to Vladivostok
and after it had conferred again with the Advisory Council.

[40] Polk to President Wilson, August 3, 1918, reporting conversation between
Polk and Ambassador Ishii that day. *USFR, 1918, Russia,* II, 325–26.

The victory of American policy and the Japanese liberals was more apparent than real. As the Japanese adage puts it, "proof is better than argument." Once the expedition was begun, the pledges made by the Terauchi government were largely ignored. Without prior consultation with either the United States government or the advisory council, by mid-October the army had sent more than three and a half divisions into the Amur basin, and it then proceeded to secure the railway network by a pincers movement between Vladivostok and Khabarovsk in the east and Manchouli and Chita in the west.[41] A few months later it increased its forces to between four and five divisions, and in 1920 it expanded its field of operations to include the island of Sakhalin. When the American and Allied forces evacuated Siberia in that year, the Japanese army elected to remain until 1922 in the Amur basin and until 1925 on the island of Sakhalin. Throughout this period, the army sought energetically to advance the interests of its White Russian protégés, to secure control of the Siberian railways for itself, and, especially through the Siberian economic assistance committee, to integrate the economy of the region with that of Japan.

These activities conformed so closely to the original plans of the government interventionists that one is driven to conclude that the concessions made in July and August, 1918, in the public declaration, in the notes to America, and in the discussions of the Advisory Council on Foreign Relations, represented a bargain in words rather than a meeting of minds. In fact, the interventionists had won.

Although the agreement was extremely superficial, the fact that it was striven for at all indicates that an important stage had been reached in the political development of Japan. By 1918 power was multiple. Under the Meiji constitution, the emperor exercised his sovereign powers through a variety of individuals and bodies, such as the imperial household, the privy council, the cabinet, the diet, the civilian ministries, and the armed forces. Since the emperor

[41] For a summary of army operations, see Japan, Sambō Hombu, *Shiberia Shuppei-shi*, I, 111–35.

did not usually participate actively in policy making and since supreme authority was not delegated to any other single official or organ, a struggle for control had early developed among various bureaucratic cliques. By 1918 the Chōshū clique under Prince Yamagata was clearly the single most powerful directing and co-ordinating force in the government; but, as the events of the first half of 1918 show, its power was in decline. New centers of control had developed. In the diet, political party leaders had grown strong. In the bureaucracy, clan cliques persisted, but in addition new bureaucratic leaders were beginning to show a spirit of independ-ence. As the clan cliques were declining in influence, the newer forces were struggling to take over. The long argument within the Japanese government over the Siberian expedition represents one of the critical points in that struggle: the last important effort by the Chōshū clique to retain control.

The fact that only a verbal agreement could be achieved shows how deeply divided these new contenders were. They were not, however, equally strong or equally determined. The capitulation of the noninterventionists shows once more how weak were many of the liberal opponents of the Chōshū clique. Saionji, Hara, and Makino did not pretend to represent the people, but they did repre-sent the growing civilian forces opposed to a continuation of bureau-cratic, clan rule. Yet, whether from clique ties, bureaucratic inter-ests, considerations of political alliance, or other unknown pres-sures, they gave way on the issue of the Siberian expedition when they must have known that only the military extremists could benefit.

The long argument over the Siberian expedition also represents an important stage in the long struggle within the Japanese govern-ment over one of the most basic questions of its foreign policy: whether to give priority to relations with the West or to interests on the Asian continent. When the Japanese emerged into the modern world in the middle of the nineteenth century, they were deter-mined to become a wealthy and powerful independent nation. Unfortunately they were endowed with little arable land and few industrial minerals with which to realize their ambition. From the beginning they were dependent on foreign sources of raw materials and the markets necessary for modernization; they were also partly dependent for military protection. Broadly speaking, the Japanese had two alternatives: a strong alliance with the West, from which would flow goods, services, ideas, and military support, or a sphere of their own on the Asian continent by means of which they might become independent of the West. Few statesmen were ever prepared to pursue one policy to the total exclusion of the other. Even the proponents of the great east Asian war felt it necessary first to secure an alliance with Germany and an understanding with Russia. On the other hand, there were always extremists; and for the moderates there was always the question of degree.

In the case of the Siberian expedition, the anti-interventionists were clearly champions of a "West first" policy. Hara and Makino made it very clear that, except in case of an attack on Japan itself they would not support an expedition which did not have America's approval. No doubt, their attitude was the same toward the European Allies, but there was never any question about their position. It is clear that, in the view of this liberal faction in the coalition, the Japanese government undertook the expedition to do precisely what the declaration said: "to fall in with the desires of the American government and also to act in harmony with the Allies."

There was, of course, another reason given in the declaration: the desire to safeguard "the special position of Japan." Although the exact meaning of this phrase was not spelled out, the long discussions within the government reveal that to the interventionists this phrase represented the real reason for Japan's participation in the expedition.

The interventionists were less inclined to look to the West for help; they were more inclined to solidify Japan's position in Asia. Before the Russian Revolution, the Chōshū clique and others had come to the conclusion that Japan could overcome its military and economic weaknesses only by securing an incontestable position in China. When the October Revolution appeared to reduce the Amur basin to a state of dissolution similar to that of China, they saw the new situation as a possible threat to their Chinese policy; and they concluded quite naturally that policies similar to those they were applying in China would work equally well in the basin of the Amur.

The overthrow of the Imperial regime by moderate socialists and then of the moderate socialist regime by small bands of Bolsheviks and leftist Social Revolutionaries seemed to the interventionists to threaten to turn the Amur basin over to either a hostile Bolshevik, a hostile German, or a competitive Allied power that would destroy the stability of Russo-Japanese relations in northeast Asia, eliminate Japanese trade and investments in the region, interfere with Japan's plans in China, and weaken the security of the home islands themselves. To overcome these threats and at the same time advance Japan's continental position, the interventionists early resolved that the best policy would be to establish Japan's political and economic hegemony in the Amur region by sending an expedition in support of a pro-Japanese regime.

There were some "Asia first" extremists, like Motono and Uehara, who would have disregarded all opposition to achieve their objectives; but, the controlling Chōshū clique were more moderate men. They believed strongly in their Asian objectives, they wanted to secure Japanese control of the Amur basin, but they recognized that success required the cooperation of Hara and Makino at home and the support of the Allies and particularly America abroad. For six months these reservations restrained action and indeed might have forestalled it altogether had not the American invitation arrived to break the deadlock. The American invitation enabled the "interventionists" and the "noninterventionists," for quite different reasons, to agree on an expedition.

Although essential for launching the expedition, this superficial agreement rapidly dissolved thereafter. The Chōshū clique lost control. Hara took over the cabinet; the pro-Asian military extremists, led by Uehara, took over the expedition. Each pursued its own policy, the cabinet through diplomacy with the West, the army through war in Siberia. In this first round in the struggle to control the government—and eventually all Asia—the military extremists were finally brought to defeat in 1922, but the issue was not fully resolved until the greater cataclysm of the Second World War.

CHRONOLOGY

1916

October 9 λ   Terauchi is appointed premier.

1917

April 20	Government-supported parties win in special general election for the diet.
June 5	Advisory Council on Foreign Relations is established.
July 25–26	At Inter-Allied Conference in Paris, France suggests Japanese expedition to Russian front.
Sometime in October	Japanese army rejects "European expedition."
November 1	British open talks with United States on possibility of Japanese or American expedition to Russia.
November 7	Bolsheviks seize power in Petrograd.
November 12	Advisory Council on Foreign Relations rejects expedition to European Russia.
November 14–16	Tanaka discusses with Chinese the possibility of joint Sino-Japanese defense agreement.
Sometime in November	Japanese navy proposes sending fleet unit to Vladivostok, but is dissuaded by Britain.
	Japanese army prepares a plan for sending troops to the Russian Far East to protect foreign residents.
November 29–December 3	Inter-Allied Conference on the Russian problem in Paris rejects French proposal for U.S.-Japanese expedition to Siberia.
December 10	Balfour's proposal for U.S. expedition to Vladivostok is rejected by Chinda.
	Nishihara joins Andreev in movement for an independent, anti-soviet Siberia.

1917 (*Continued*)

December 12   Bolsheviks gain control of the Harbin soviet.
December 17   Advisory Council on Foreign Relations reserves judgment on expedition question.
December 18   Semenov establishes base at Manchouli.
December 26   Chinese troops, at request of Allies, restore Horvat to power in Harbin.
               British urge sending joint Allied troops to Vladivostok.
December 27   Advisory Council on Foreign Relations splits into "interventionist" and "anti-interventionist" factions.

1918

January 1   Cecil reveals to Chinda that Britain has ordered a warship to Vladivostok.
Early January Japanese army sends Nakajima and Sakabe to Russian Far East.
               Semenov secures Chinese Eastern Railway zone from Hailar to the border.
January 3   Terauchi and Katō decide to send warships immediately to Vladivostok.
January 8   France proposes to United States a joint Allied expedition to Irkutsk.
January 12   Japanese warship *Iwami* arrives at Vladivostok.
January 14   British warship *HMS Suffolk* arrives at Vladivostok.
Middle of   Semenov begins offensive toward Chita, but soon
January   withdraws.
January 18   Japanese warship *Asahi* arrives at Vladivostok.
About   Ussuri Cossack army elects Ivan Kalmykov as
January 22   ataman and accepts Japanese and British liaison officers.
January 28   Britain proposes to United States that Japan be invited to intervene in Siberia on behalf of Allies.
January 30   Amur Cossack army accepts Japanese liaison officer.
Sometime in   Japanese army expands expeditionary plans.
January

1918 (*Continued*)

Early in February	Far Eastern Committee for the Defense of the Fatherland and the Constituent Assembly is organized in Harbin.
February 5	✘ Motono begins to exchange views with Allies about expedition to Siberia.
February 7	United States rejects British proposal to invite Japanese intervention in Siberia.
February 12	France approves Motono's ideas about expedition.
February 19	France presses United States to accept Japan as Allied mandatory in Siberia.
February 21	Nakajima urges Horvat to form a government. Chinese cabinet agrees to accept Japanese proposal to negotiate military agreement.
By February 25	Japanese government agrees to supply Semenovists and Kalmykov detachment through Far Eastern Committee in Harbin.
February 25	Tuan Ch'i-jui is appointed commissioner of the war participation board in Peking; Nishihara is requested to go to Peking.
February 28	Joint Siberia Planning Committee, comprising representatives of the Japanese Army General Staff and War Ministry is set up secretly under Tanaka. Araki is sent to the continent to assist Nakajima.
Sometime in February	Japanese army prepares revised plan to send troops to Trans-Baikal territory.
March 1	USS *Brooklyn* arrives at Vladivostok. Horvat, Kudashev, and Putilov in Peking announce support for Semenov's movement and the Far Eastern Committee in Harbin.
March 2	China agrees to negotiate defense agreements with Japan.
March 5	Red Guard forces Semenov across Manchurian border. United States rejects Motono's ideas for expedition.
March 6	Britain offers to support Japanese expedition to Cheliabinsk.
March 7	Japanese commander in Vladivostok is given discretionary powers.
About March 8	British and French agree to support Semenov.

1918 (*Continued*)

March 11   Chinese accept soviet demand to quarantine
                Semenov's forces until April 5.
March 9   Advisory Council on Foreign Relations considers
                report on Motono's negotiations.
                Britain announces support for Kalmykov and asks
                Japan's attitude.
                Japanese navy orders reinforcements to Eikō
                Wan.
March 15   Yamagata writes to Terauchi, Motono, and Gotō,
                opposing expedition without American support.
March 17   Allied Supreme War Council asks United States
                to accept Japan as Allied mandatory in Siberia.
                Advisory Council on Foreign Relations adopts
                reply to U.S. note of March 5, reassuring United
                States that Japan would send no expedition with-
                out American agreement.
March 18   Japanese cabinet adopts reply to British note re-
                ceived March 11.
March 23   Tuan Ch'i-jui resumes premiership in Peking.
March 25   Japan and China formally agree to begin negotia-
                tion of joint defense agreements.
March 26   Soviet government permits Czechoslovaks to leave
                Russia via Trans-Siberian Railroad.
March 27   Britain announces decision to supply seed corn
                to Ussuri Cossacks and asks Japan's attitude.
                Stevens and Horvat conclude agreement concern-
                ing American technical help for Chinese Eastern
                Railway.
Sometime in   Japanese army's Joint Siberia Planning Commit-
  March   tee revises plan for sending troops to Russian Far
                East.
April 2   Japan tells Britain it doubts wisdom of supplying
                Kalmykov.
                Motono pleads with Terauchi for expedition de-
                cision.
April 4   Three Japanese clerks are murdered in Vladi-
                vostok.
April 5   Japanese land at Vladivostok, followed by British.
                Japanese navy orders limits on operations.
April 10   Genro reject Motono's plea for expedition de-
                cision.
April 16   Britain tells Japan it will not supply Kalmykov.

1918 (*Continued*)

April 21	Japanese war minister secretly recommends "positive aid" for Horvat.
About April 21	Semenov begins offensive in Trans-Baikal Territory.
April 23	Motono is forced to resign as foreign minister and is replaced by Gotō.
April 25	Advance Czechoslovak echelons reach Vladivostok; soviet takes over the city.
Early May	Semenov proclaims Temporary Government of Trans-Baikal Territory.
May 3	Tanaka threatens to withdraw Japanese support if Tuan government delays military agreement.
May 6	Ishii informs Lansing that Japanese government is not averse to a joint expedition if under Japanese command.
May 9	Semenov stops advance at Aga station.
May 14	Chinese and Japanese delegations agree on draft of joint military agreement.
	Japanese cabinet accepts army recommendation to send military instructors, money, munitions, and railway technicians to secure control of Chinese Eastern Railway.
Mid-May	Kolchak-Semenov conference at Manchouli ends in break between the two men.
May 16	Sino-Japanese military agreement is signed in Peking.
May 19	Sino-Japanese naval agreement is signed in Peking.
May 21	Mutō wins Semenov's agreement not to admit American engineers to Trans-Baikal Railway.
May 25	Trotskii orders Czechoslovaks disarmed along Penza-Omsk line; Czechoslovaks and anti-Bolshevik Russians begin seizing cities along Trans-Siberian Railroad.
May 27	Semenov's detachment is forced to retreat.
May 30	British reveal declining interest in Semenov.
Late May	Horvat breaks with Kolchak, who leaves Harbin.
June 7	Allied Supreme War Council asks if Japan would accept invitation for joint expedition.
	First proposal for Japanese economic mission to Siberia is drawn up in the Foreign Ministry.

1918 (*Continued*)

June 13	Mutō begins to organize volunteer Japanese force in Manchuria to aid Semenov.
June 17–20	Advisory Council on Foreign Relations agrees to defer decision on Allied request of June 7 until United States is in agreement.
June 18	Under pressure from Saitō, Premier Tuan orders Chinese border guards to give Semenov's detachment refuge in China.
June 20	French instruct Czechoslovaks to hold their positions along the Trans-Siberian Railroad.
June 21	Advisory Council's decision of June 20 is communicated to the Allies and America.
June 28	Czechoslovak commander informs Allied consuls at Vladivostok of plans for coup; Japanese and British commanders pledge support.
June 29	Czechoslovaks seize Vladivostok.
July 2	Czechoslovaks at Vladivostok move northward; British and American naval commanders pledge support.
July 3	Allied Supreme War Council requests United States to join in Inter-Allied expedition to Siberia.
July 4	Japanese cabinet decides to aid the Czechoslovaks.
July 5	United States decides to invite Japan to join in expedition to rescue the Czechoslovaks.
July 6	An Allied protectorate is proclaimed over Vladivostok.
	Horvat declares Chinese Eastern Railway closed to Czechoslovaks.
July 8	United States invites Japan to participate in joint expedition.
July 9	Horvat proclaims an all-Russian government at Grodekovo.
July 10	Britain orders troops to Vladivostok; France follows suit.
	Japanese interventionists decide to exploit the American proposal.
July 12	Japanese warships bring ordnance and instructors to the Czechoslovaks.
	Japanese cabinet approves interventionists' plans.

1918 (*Continued*)

July 15   Horvat and the Czechoslovaks are brought into
                   agreement.
                   Genro decide to leave decision on interventionists'
                   plans to Advisory Council on Foreign Relations.
                   Emergency Japanese cabinet meeting in after-
                   noon.
                   Seiyūkai party directors support Hara's decision
                   to resign from the advisory council rather than
                   approve interventionists' plans.
July 16   Advisory Council on Foreign Relations meets;
                   "interventionists" clash with "anti-intervention-
                   ists" over reply to United States.
                   Mobilization of Japan's Twelfth Division is or-
                   dered; Japanese army readies plan for "inde-
                   pendent" expedition to Trans-Baikal territory.
July 17   United States issues aide-memoire to Allied am-
                   bassadors, explaining proposed action in Siberia.
                   Advisory Council on Foreign Relations meets to
                   consider Ito's revision of proposed reply to United
                   States. After further revisions, reply as approved
                   is in ostensible general agreement with U.S.
                   proposal. Revision of proposed public declaration
                   is required to make it accord with approved reply.
July 18   Advisory Council on Foreign Relations approves
                   Itō's revision of declaration; Imperial sanction is
                   given to declaration as revised.
July 19   Japanese declaration is communicated to U.S.
                   government.
July 20   Japanese military plans are revised and Japan
                   notifies China of need to bring the joint military
                   and naval agreements into effect.
July 24–25   Ishii-Polk conversations in Washington.
July 25   Britain supports Japan's stand.
July 26   France and Italy support Japan's stand.
                   Meeting at Japanese Foreign Ministry of officials
                   from Foreign Ministry, Finance Ministry, and
                   Agriculture and Commerce Ministry, to discuss
                   plans for economic activity in Siberia.
July 27   U.S. reply, rejecting Japanese government's
                   stand, arrives in Tokyo.

1918 (*Continued*)

July 28	Tokyo receives U.S. request for revisions in Japan's declaration to restrict expedition to Vladivostok only.
July 29	Plans for Japanese temporary Siberian economic assistance committee under Foreign Ministry are completed.
July 31	Japanese cabinet meeting breaks up in mood to reject revisions of declaration requested by United States.
August 1	Japanese cabinet insists on unrestricted number of troops and area of operations of expedition. Japanese Advisory Council on Foreign Relations rejects cabinet decision and adopts Itō's proposal to revise declaration as requested by United States, with private explanation to United States that Japan would go beyond it.
August 2	Japanese cabinet accepts advisory council's decision. Imperial sanction is given. The declaration is issued.

LIST OF APPENDIXES

A. Memorandum of the Ideas Developed at the Inter-Allied Conference in Paris on December 3, 1917
B. Plan to Send Troops to the Russian Far East to Protect Foreign Residents, November, 1917
C. Plan to Reinforce the Maritime Territory, Late January, 1918
D. Summary of the Plan to Send Troops to the Trans-Baikal Territory Area, February, 1918
E. Agenda Preparatory to a Japanese Expedition
F. Plan for Sending an Emergency Detachment to Vladivostok, March, 1918
G. Plan for Sending Troops to the Russian Far East, March, 1918
H. Summary Table of Organization of the Maritime Territory Expeditionary Force, Reviewed July 12, 1918
I. Summary Table of Aid Given by Allied Countries to the Committee for the Defense of the Fatherland and the Constituent Assembly and to the Ussuri Cossacks, to April 30, 1918
J. Ordnance Supplied to Russian and Czechoslovak Forces by Japan Prior to August 2, 1918
K. Draft of an Agreement for Military Transportation and Military Communication on the Russian Railroads, March, 1918
L. Proclamation of the Temporary Government of the Trans-Baikal Territory, May, 1918
M. Agreement between the Commander of the Trans-Baikal Front and the Command of the Chinese Troops, July 30, 1918
N. Sino-Japanese Joint Defensive Military Agreement, May 16, 1918
O. Sino-Japanese Joint Defensive Naval Agreement, May 19, 1918

APPENDIX A

MEMORANDUM OF THE IDEAS DEVELOPED AT THE INTER-ALLIED CONFERENCE IN PARIS ON DECEMBER 3, 1917[1]

Secret   Le 4 Décembre 1917

MEMORANDUM

au sujet des mesures à prendre à l'égard de la Russie

La Russie est dans un état d'anarchie et de désordre qui met en péril sa puissance militaire, politique, et ses richesses économiques.

I

Les conséquences de cette situation sont:

a) *Communications rompues de l'Occident avec la Russie et avec la Roumanie*

En effet, les communications de l'Occident avec la Russie par Arkhangelsk, par Port-Mourman et par la Suède, sont fermées par la saison ou interceptées par l'émeute.

Cette situation accélère la désagrégation de l'armée russe, et menace l'existence même de l'armée roumaine encore vigoureuse.

b) *Cessation prochaine de la résistance sur le front russe*

Quel que soit le sort réservé aux négociations d'armistice actuellement en cours,* la résistance russe est sur le point de prendre fin:

le peuple russe, gangréné par la propagande germano-maximaliste, semble vouloir la paix; les éléments, désireux de poursuivre la lutte sont entraînés dans le désarroi général et réduits à l'impuissance.

* Depuis le 2 Décembre, midi.

[1] Transmitted to Japanese Ambassador Matsui by Marshal Foch the following day. *JGK, RKI, SK, HMSK* (in French).

l'armée se dissocie. La désagrégation est déjà commencée sur les fronts Nord; son développement vers les fronts Sud est inévitable.

c) *Large extension de la conquete allemande*

Sans parler des résultats militaires, de la disparition de la force organisée devant lui, l'ennemi va pouvoir mettre la main sur les centres de résistance du front russe.

Mais en outre, il va, sans difficultés, pouvoir s'emparer des foyers de productions militaires et economiques (armement et produits manufacturés), ainsi que des richesses naturelles du pays, pour en faire son bien, et les exploiter à l'avenir.

C'est ainsi qu'il va lui être possible de gagner d'abord Petrograd, oú est concentrée la majeure partie des usines de guerre; puis de s'emparer des centres industriels de la région de Moscou, d'atteindre sans doute le riche bassin du Donetz (charbon, industries, céréales) et d'aller peut-être même jusqu'à Vladivostock* débouché sur le Pacifique, et tête du chemin de fer qui relie l'Europe à cette mer.

À la faveur de cette extension, il disposera des ressources qui lui manquent, rompant ainsi pratiquement le blocus des Alliés, et s'assurant de larges moyens d'existence dans le présent. Il aura, en outre, constitué un vaste domaine économique et dressé une carte de guerre impressionnante, avantages incontestables comme éléments de discussion, lors du règlement de la paix. Pour l'avenir, il aura enfin organisé une base de départ favorable à son effort industriel et commercial, mettant en péril le développement économiques des pays d'Êxtreme-Orient, notamment États-Unis, Japon, et rompant l'équilibre de l'Orient Asiatique.

Ces résultats considérables, il peut les obtenir sans sacrifices de forces importantes. Il peut en effet maintenir à la fois le gros de ses troupes en Occident et, grâce à l'état de décomposition de la Russie, conquérir la Russie, même la Sibérie, menacer la Corée, paraître sur le Pacifique, et réaliser la prise de possession du vaste domaine envisagé ci-dessus (Russie, Sibérie), par des détachements relativement faibles, occupant des points habilement choisis, si par des dispositions particulières et rapides, l'Entente ne s'oppose pas à ses progrès.

II

Il sera tout autrement si, par ces dispositions, l'Entente vise:

1. *au point de vue militaire:*
   d'abord a soutenir et renforcer tous les éléments de résistance qui éxistent encore sur le front oriental, en Russie et en Roumanie.

* Les dépêches du 2 Décembre signalent la prise de possession de cette ville par les maximalistes.

2. *au point de vue économique:*
à empêcher la conquête par les Allemands de la Russie désorganisée.

En ce qui concerne le *point de vue militaire,* la situation générale des forces alliées est moins défavorable sur les fronts Sud-Ouest et roumain que dans la partie septentrionale du théâtre d'opérations.

L'armée roumaine, forte de 15 divisions, d'une valeur éprouvée, constitue un noyau de forces solide qui permettra, s'il continue à être ravitaillé, de réaliser le groupement de tous les éléments du Sud de la Russie capables de prolonger la lutte (éléments ukraines-cosaques-peuplades du Caucase-elements tchéco-slovaques organisés).

Les Chefs des Missions française et anglaise de ce pays ont été invités à diriger leur activité dans ce sens.

Mais, pour que les noyaux de résistance ainsi constitués puissent vivre, recevoir les armes et les munitions nécessaires, pour qu'ils puissent ensuite être développés, il faut d'abord maintenir avec eux la seule communication encore possible: le *Transsibérien,* puis renforcer au besoin les éléments russo-roumains par de nouveaux contingents, préparer même une intervention militaire par l'envoi de troupes à leur appui.

Au point de vue économique, pour limiter l'extension allemande en Russie et en Asie, c'est encore l'organisation des éléments de résistance envisagés ci-dessus qui constitue le moyen le plus efficace, mais à la condition, toujours, que ces éléments soient ravitaillés par le Transsibérien.

La première mesure à adopter consiste donc à prendre possession de la voie ferrée du Transsibérien, à Vladivostock d'abord, puis à Kharbin, et de là jusqu'à Moscou, au moyen de détachments qui étendraient progressivement leur action le long de la ligne.

Dans ces conditions, et même si nous ne parvenions pas ainsi à soutenir la résistance roumaine, l'occupation réalisée par des détachements de l'Entente du Transsibérien en rendrait l'emploi difficile aux Empires Centraux et interdirait par là une expansion facile des Allemands en Orient.

Le Japon et l'Amérique sont, par leur situation géographique et l'état de leurs moyens militaires, les seules puissances de l'Entente en état de réaliser cette occupation.

L'opération ne doit pas être un acte d'hostilité vis-à-vis de la Russie, mais elle demande à être présentée comme un appui sous forme de ravitaillement en vivres et autres matières. Elle serait donnée comme une mesure de sûreté réalisée par des détachements de police pour assurer la garde des approvisionnements existant à Vladivostock et les faire arriver à Moscou.

Le chemin de fer Transsibérien étant militairement tenu, des trans-
ports de troupes, destinées à venir renforcer les centres de résistance
constituée dans la Russie méridionale, pourraient être envisagés ulté-
rieurement.

En résumé, il conviendrait:

1) De prendre possession immédiatement du Transsibérien par Vladivostock et Kharbin.
2) D'assurer par cette voie le ravitaillement en matériel de guerre des
   groupes de résistance formés en Russie méridionale.
3) De préparer au besoin des secours militaires ultérieurs à ces combat-
   tants.
4) D'arrêter, en tous cas, la pénétration de l'élément germain, qui, à
   travers la Russie et la Sibérie, menace, si on s'y oppose sans retard, la
   Corée et le Pacifique.

Une fois de plus, les États-Unis et le Japon sont, par leur situation
géographique et l'état de leur moyens militaires, les seules puissances de
l'Entente qui puissent réaliser ce programme, aussi indispensable à
leurs intérèts propres qu'aux intérèts généraux de la Coalition.

Telles sont les idées qui ont été développées à la Conference du 3
Décembre 1917, à laquelle prenaient part les représentants de l'Angle-
terre, de l'Italie, des États-Unis, du Japon et auxquelles s'est arrêtée la
Conference.

(signé) F. FOCH

PLAN TO SEND TROOPS TO THE RUSSIAN FAR EAST TO
PROTECT FOREIGN RESIDENTS, NOVEMBER, 1917[1]

I. Object of sending troops:

To protect Japanese nationals living in strategic places in North
Manchuria and the Maritime Territory; and to make preparations
for military operations which may be undertaken later.

II. Basis of decision on the number of troops:

The number of troops to be determined on the basis of the number of residents there, the strength of Russian forces in these areas,
the convenience for military operations which may be undertaken
later, and the desirability of occupying a commanding position in
case the Allies jointly send troops.

III. Chain of command:

The Kwantung Government General and the Maritime Territory
Temporary Detachment Headquarters will be assigned the duty of
protecting foreign residents. In addition to the forces under the
Kwantung Government General's command, necessary reinforce
ments will be sent from Japan and Korea. Forces organized in
Japan will be assigned to the Maritime Territory Temporary Detachment Headquarters. The areas of responsibility of the Kwantung Government General and the Maritime Territory Temporary
Detachment Headquarters are generally to be delimited by the Mu-
tan-kiang Station on the Chinese Eastern Railway, east of Harbin.
The Kwantung Government General will be responsible for protecting residents in Northwest Manchuria and the Maritime Territory Temporary Detachment Headquarters will be responsible for
protecting residents in Northeast Manchuria and the Maritime Territory.

[1] Drawn up by the Japanese Army General Staff Headquarters, November,
1917. Japan, Sambō Hombu, *Shiberia Shuppei-shi*, I, Appendix, 29–33.

IV. Summary of the strength and organization of troops to be used to protect residents:

A. Forces to be attached to the Kwantung Government General

1. North Manchuria Temporary Detachment
2. North Manchuria Temporary Detachment Headquarters (with a major general or lieutenant general as commander plus necessary staff)
3. Temporary Detached 1st Infantry Regiment Headquarters (a colonel or lieutenant colonel as commander plus staff to direct 3 infantry battalions) 3 infantry battalions (each battalion to be made up of 3 companies and a machine gun unit; each company, about 120 guns)
   To be organized from forces in Manchuria (roughly 1 battalion and 1 infantry regiment)
4. Temporary Detached 2d Infantry Regiment Headquarters (a colonel or lieutenant colonel as commander plus staff to direct 2 infantry battalions) 2 infantry battalions (battalions to be organized the same as above)
   To be organized by the 40th Infantry Brigade in Korea
5. Temporary Detached 1st Cavalry Company
6. Temporary Detached 1st Field Artillery Battalion (consisting of 2 companies, each company having 4 artillery pieces)
7. Temporary Detached 1st Engineering Company
   To be organized from forces in Manchuria
8. Temporary Detached 1st Radio Unit (to establish 2 radio stations)
9. Temporary Detached 1st Field Signal Company
10. Temporary Detached 1st Railway Company
    To be organized in Japan

B. Maritime Territory Temporary Detachment

1. Maritime Territory Temporary Detachment Headquarters (with a major general or lieutenant general as commander with necessary staff)
   To be organized in Japan
2. Temporary Detached 3d Infantry Regiment (same organization as the 1st Regiment)
   To be organized from some division in Japan (generally 1 battalion per infantry regiment)
3. Temporary Detached 4th Infantry Regiment (same organization as the 1st Regiment)
4. Temporary Detached 2d Cavalry Company

5. Temporary Detached 2d Field Artillery Battalion (consisting of 2 companies, each company having 4 artillery pieces)
6. Temporary Detached 2d Engineering Company
   To be organized from some regiment in Japan
7. Temporary Detached 2d Radio Unit (to establish 3 radio stations)
8. Temporary Detached 2d Field Signal Company
9. Temporary Detached 2d Railway Company
   To be organized in Japan

Note: The strength of forces to be organized from those stationed in Manchuria is indicated at the minimum. The Kwantung Government General may use other forces under its command if conditions warrant.

V. Movement of forces responsible for the protection of foreign residents:

A. The main strength of the Maritime Territory Temporary Detachment will be in Vladivostok, with elements in Khabarovsk and other strategic places. Besides protecting the residents within the area of their responsibility, they will guard the railways and telegraph facilities.

B. The main strength of the North Manchuria Temporary Detachment will be in Harbin, with elements in Tsitsihar and other strategic places. Besides protecting the residents within the area of their responsibility, they will guard the railways and telegraph facilities.

C. If necessary to prevent dissipation of strength while trying to protect foreign residents, foreign residents will be appropriately assembled.

VI. The war minister is responsible for transportation and supply, but in carrying out these responsibilities, he is to consult the chief of the army general staff.

PLAN TO REINFORCE THE MARITIME TERRITORY, LATE
JANUARY, 1918 [1]

I. Object of reinforcements:

   A. Principally to suppress the Bolshevik uprising and hostile activity in the vicinity of the Southern Ussuri and along the
railroad in the Maritime Territory, so as to accomplish the
objective of protecting foreign residents.

   B. To pacify the area and to protect those citizens of the Territory
who have moderate ideas; in short, to assist their independence.

   C. To protect the railroads and other systems of communication
and transportation.

II. Strength and organization:

   D. To send as reinforcement a force built around one division,
wartime organization, and join it to the Maritime Territory
Temporary Detachment (changing part of its organization)
to form the Maritime Territory Expeditionary Force, organized
according to the appended table.

   When the Force Headquarters lands in the Maritime Territory,
the Maritime Territory Temporary Detachment will be attached
to it.

III. Summary of movement:

   E. The Maritime Territory Expeditionary Force will locate its
main strength in Vladivostok and Nikolsk-Ussuriisk, and an
element in Kharbarovsk; then, moving into areas where necessary, it will suppress Bolshevik and other uprisings or hostile
activities.

   In addition, in order to pacify the area and protect the communication and transportation system, it will dispose defense
units along the railroad and at other strategic places in the
Territory.

[1] Adopted by the Japanese Army General Staff Headquarters at the end of
January 1918, this is a revision of the Headquarters' Plan of November, 1917.
Japan, Sambō Hombu, *Shiberia Shuppei-shi,* I, Appendix, 35–36.

It will dispatch a force to either the Maritime or Amur Territories depending on conditions.

F. It will secretly make the necessary preparations for operations against Russia, which may be expected to develop in the future; and, depending on circumstances, will confiscate railroad rolling stock.

IV. Transportation:

G. Reinforcements, after having been mobilized or organized, will be transported by rail to the point of embarkation, thence by ship to the harbor of Vladivostok. These details will be decided on separately.

V. Supply:

H. The main supply system will be set up in Vladivostok; and supplies to Nokol'sk-Ussuriisk and Kharbarovsk areas will be mainly by auxiliary overland lines of communications, depending primarily on the railroad.

APPENDED TABLE 1

ORGANIZATION OF THE MARITIME TERRITORY EXPEDITIONARY FORCE

Forces	No.	Summary
Force headquarters	1	With the staff to control the various forces below
Permanent division	1	Use 3d Division
Maritime Territory Temporary Detachment	1	To reduce headquarters organization, exclude field signal company and railway company
"Otsu" cavalry regiment	1	Use 3d Cavalry Regiment
Field signal unit		For one of the two companies, use
Headquarters	1	Temporary Detached 2d Field
Companies	2	Signal Co.
Radio unit	1	Use Temporary Detached 2d Radio Unit
Air unit	1	Use air squad attached to Maritime Territory Detachment Headquarters
Bridging columns	3	
Force line-of-communications department	1	

Note (in the original): Unless specifically designated otherwise, all forces are wartime organization.

SUMMARY OF THE PLAN TO SEND TROOPS TO THE
TRANS-BAIKAL TERRITORY AREA, FEBRUARY, 1918 [1]

I. Policy:
   To aid Cossack troops in the vicinity of Chita, to sweep aside the
   Bolsheviks in Trans-Baikal Territory, and to protect the residents
   of the Territory who have moderate ideas; in short, to assist (the
   Territory's) independence.

II. Basis for decision as to strength:
   The Trans-Baikal Territory Expeditionary Force will consist of
   sufficient troops to destroy the Bolshevik troops and the German
   and Austrian prisoners-of-war who are in the Territory; the Kwantung Government General will have under its command the strength
   required to guard securely the Chinese Eastern Railway.

III. Summary of strength and organization:
   A. Trans-Baikal Territory Expeditionary Force
      Force Headquarters
      2 permanent divisions (wartime organization)
      7th Division (emergency preparation)
      40th Infantry Brigade (emergency preparation)
      1 "Kō" cavalry brigade (wartime organization)
      3 "Otsu" cavalry regiments (2: wartime organization; 1: being
         the 7th Cavalry Regiment, emergency preparation)
      Field signal unit (headquarters plus 3 companies)
      Radio unit (headquarters and 3 platoons)
      1 air battalion (headquarters and 3 companies, 18 planes)
      Railway unit: some
      Necessary line-of-communications troops
      But, a part of the above is to be attached to the Kwantung

[1] Adopted by the Japanese Army General Staff Headquarters, February, 1918.
Japan, Sambō Hombu, *Shiberia Shuppei-shi*, I, Appendix, 37–39.

Government General in order to guard the Chinese Eastern Railway as the force advances.

B. Forces under the Kwantung Government General:

Forces properly assigned (7th Division and 7th Cavalry Regiment)

Forces provided for above

Railway unit and some other line-of-communications forces

IV. Summary of movement:

With the forces properly assigned and those sent from Korea and Japan, the Kwantung Government General will advance immediately into the Trans-Baikal Territory and will undertake to execute the policy. After the Trans-Baikal Territory Expeditionary Force Headquarters assumes its duties, the Kwantung Government General will be responsible chiefly for guarding the Chinese Eastern Railway and for line-of-communications duty east of (and including) Manchouli.

When the Trans-Baikal Territory Expeditionary Force Headquarters arrives in the Trans-Baikal Territory, it will be responsible for carrying out the policy by directing the various troops and staffs west of Manchouli (and excluding it).

APPENDIX E

AGENDA PREPARATORY TO A JAPANESE EXPEDITION [1]

I. Decision as to the strength to be used and preparations of matériel needed by them:

First, one division should be sent to the Maritime Territory area and 2 divisions to the Trans-Baikal Territory area; these to be supported by the 7th Division in Manchuria and the 40th Infantry Brigade in Korea.

Second, send roughly the same strength to both areas; and equip about 3 divisions to conduct operations with Chinese forces from the Mongolian area to the Trans-Baikal Territory or to reinforce any area where they may be needed temporarily. Have the matériel needed for operations prepared for 10 divisions (total above strength).

II. Negotiate a joint Sino-Japanese military agreement:

In order to have the Chinese troops cooperate with us in the expedition now planned and in operations against Russia and Germany which may develop in the future, and since it will be necessary to have close mutual assistance in supplying munitions, propose the conclusion of a Sino-Japanese military agreement. After negotiations by committees of both countries, an agreement was signed on May 16.

III. Handling of preparatory arrangements in Vladivostok and Harbin:

Enlarge the already established intelligence network; and in order to have various preparations made for the expedition, after March send necessary personnel to Vladivostok and Harbin. In Vladivostok, have these directed by Major General Nakajima Masatake; and in Harbin, by Major General Mutō Nobuyoshi.

[1] Drawn up by the Joint Committee of the War Department and the Army General Staff Headquarters (the Siberia Planning Committee), which was organized on February 28, 1918, under the chairmanship of the vice chief of the army general staff, Lieutenant General Tanaka Gi'ichi; and action taken on it. Japan, Sambō Hombu, *Shiberia Shuppei-shi*, I, 36–38.

IV. Aid to Semenov detachment:

Supply weapons and other matériel to Semenov. Attach some officers and men to him in order to direct the actions of the detachment and to give instruction in the use of the weapons.

V. Change in the annual mobilization plan:

Since the Army Mobilization Plan of 1918 was drawn up for operations using either all of Japan's forces or a large corps, it is inadequate for sending part of those forces in an expeditionary force. Moreover, the period of mobilization stretches across both years. Therefore, the new plan should be abolished and a request made that the plan for 1917 be imitated.

March 9, 1918. Emergency instructions for Army Mobilization Plan of 1918 were issued.

VI. Preparations for sending troops to Vladivostok in emergency:

Since the personnel of the naval landing unit of the Japanese warship sent to Vladivostok is no more than about 500 men, in order to assist them as soon as needed and to help them hold their position, Army General Staff Headquarters should draw up a plan for sending there (Vladivostok) in March the main strength (about 800 men) of the 74th Infantry Regiment at Hamhŭng; to transport them, the navy repair ship *Kantō Maru* should be used.

April 4 incident.

April 5, dawn-landing.

VII. Preparations for revising organization and equipment:

In order to keep up with advances in military technique, in view of the future opportunities of the national forces, a "proposal for revising organization and equipment" was drawn up; and on the basis of this, the forces began to be systematically equipped with new weapons in order to be ready for an expedition.

PLAN FOR SENDING AN EMERGENCY DETACHMENT TO
VLADIVOSTOK, MARCH, 1918 [1]

I. Objective:
    A. To have army troops support the naval landing units of the
    Imperial Fleet at Vladivostok, in advance of the Imperial
    Army expedition to the Russian Far East; and to work together
    with them to prepare the way for a later army expedition.
II. Strength and organization:
    B. There should be sent for the above purpose the 74th Infantry
    Regiment (lacking one battalion, but including a machine-gun
    unit) stationed at Hamhŭng [Kankō].[2]
    C. The above force will be placed on "emergency preparation,"
    with no field train or combat train attached, but carrying with
    it combat train articles and metal boxes, baggage and cooking
    utensils.
    D. In addition to what he wears and in addition to the combat
    train load, each man will carry 200 shells for each rifle and
    15,000 rounds for each machine gun.
    E. Depending on circumstances, 1 battalion (including a ma-
    chine-gun unit) and, if necessary, some artillery and engineer-
    ing troops of the 73d Infantry Regiment stationed at Nanam
    [Ranan] will be sent as reinforcements.
III. Transportation:
    F. The 74th Infantry Regiment (lacking 1 battalion, but includ-
    ing a machine-gun unit) will embark at Sohojin [Seikoshin]
    on the navy transport *Kantō Maru* and will be sent to Vladivos-
    tok.

[1] Drawn up in March, 1918, by the Siberia Planning Committee. Japan,
Sambō Hombu, *Shiberia Shuppei-shi*, I, Appendix, 69–71.
[2] Korean place names are given in transliteration from the Korean, followed,
for ease in identification, by a bracketed transliteration from the Japanese.

G. The transportation of reinforcements from Nanam [Ranan] will be determined when the time comes.

IV. Chain of command:

H. At the time of embarkation of the force to be sent as an emergency detachment to Vladivostok, it will come under the command of the Imperial Fleet Commander at Vladivostok.

V. Summary of operations:

I. The force to be sent as an emergency detachment to Vladivostok will debark at Vladivostok and seek to achieve its objective as directed by the Imperial Fleet Commander at Vladivostok.

J. After the arrival of the forces of the First Force,[3] depending on circumstances, a part will return to their original station, but the major part will be assigned to occupy the Ussuri district.

VI. Supply:

K. The 74th Infantry Regiment (lacking 1 battalion, but including a machine-gun unit) will carry with it a 10-day reserve of food and fodder.

L. Reserve food and fodder for about 30 days will be transported for the above unit by a naval transport ship from Ch'ŏngjin [Seishin] to Vladivostok.

M. The Commander of the Korean Army will be responsible for supply.

[3] The "First Force" referred to in the Plan of March, 1918, Appendix G.

APPENDIX G

PLAN FOR SENDING TROOPS TO THE RUSSIAN FAR
EAST, MARCH, 1918[1]

I. Policy of sending troops:
   A. The Imperial Army is to maintain peace in the Far East by occupying various strategic points in Russian territory east of Lake Baikal and along the Chinese Eastern Railway, and by assisting the Russian moderates; and to make necessary preparations for operations against Russia and Germany, which may develop in the future. To do this, one force shall be sent to the Maritime Territory and a second to the Trans-Baikal Territory; and they shall take special defensive measures outside the area of their operations.

   When the above operations are carried out, we shall have the Chinese forces cooperate with us.

II. Summary of operations:
   B. Maritime Territory area.

   The First Force will occupy Vladivostok, Nikol'sk-Ussuriisk and Khabarovsk; then, by extending its zone of occupation along the Amur Railroad line and the Amur river bank, it will suppress the Russian Bolsheviks and prevent the German invasion plan from being carried out.

   C. Trans-Baikal area.
      1. The Kwantung Governor General will use the 7th Division, the 40th Infantry Brigade and other forces to advance immediately by the Chinese Eastern Railway into the Trans-Baikal Territory. The Second Force will be used to secure the area.

[1] Adopted by the Japanese Army General Staff Headquarters, March, 1918. A "Summary of Appendix," adopted in the last ten days of June, 1918, and accompanying tables follow. Japan, Sambō Hombu, *Shiberia Shuppei-shi,* I, Appendix, 39–48.

2. The Second Force will immediately advance to the vicinity of Chita; and thereafter, by extending its zone of occupation to the vicinity of Lake Baikal, it will suppress the Russian Bolsheviks and thwart the German plans to invade the Far East.

3. After the Second Force Commander arrives in the Trans-Baikal Territory, the Kwantung Government General will use the 40th Infantry Brigade and the other forces to carry out the duty of guarding the railroad in the Kwantung Government General guard district and for line-of-communications duty there for the Second Force.

4. Depending on circumstances, a force shall be sent to the central Mongolian area and, in cooperation with Chinese troops, shall advance from that area toward the Trans-Baikal Territory.

III. Measures to be taken in case of necessity after it is decided that troops must be sent:

D. The 7th Division and the 40th Infantry Brigade will make emergency preparations and take the necessary action.

E. Transportation and communication arrangements will be made.

F. Ammunition and other supplies will be prepared; and other vital matériel will be assembled at necessary points.

IV. Operational zones and guard districts:

G. The boundary between the First Force's operational zone and the Kwantung Government General's guard district will be Mu-tan-kiang (included in the Kwantung Government General's guard district). The boundary between the Second Force's operational zone and the Kwantung Government General's guard district will be the Russo-Chinese border.

V. Classification of strength and equipment:

H. For operations, the classification of strength will be as in appended Tables 1 and 2.

I. The above forces will be equipped by the Army Mobilization Plan for 1917; and what that plan does not provide for will be done under temporary organization.

J. If conditions require that the command of the First and Second Forces be unified, a supreme command organization will be sent.

K. As the situation develops, reinforcements will be sent to the extent that transportation facilities permit.

VI. Transportation:

L. For forces sent from Japan, after their mobilization or organization has been completed, they will be transported by railroad to embarkation points.

Embarkation points are scheduled as follows: Yokohama, Osaka, Ujina, Moji.

M. The First Force will be transported to Vladivostok or a harbor nearby and, after disembarking, will use for its operations mainly the Ussuri and the Amur railroads.

N. The Second Force will be transported to either Masan [Masan] or Pusan [Fusan] and Talien [Dairen] and, after disembarking, will proceed to Changchun via the Korean and South Manchurian railways; and thereafter, it will use for its operations the Chinese Eastern and the Amur railways.

VII. Defense beyond the zones of operations:

O. Kwantung Governor General and Commander of the Korean Army have their regular responsibility for defense in areas under their jurisdiction.

Additional defense will be carried out as needed.

P. The rear guard units assigned to the Kwantung Governor General, after debarking at Masan [Masan], Pusan [Fusan], or Talien [Dairen], will be attached to his command.

VIII. Line-of-communications duty:

Q. Essential matériel for the First Force will be mainly accumulated at Vladivostok and Khabarovsk, and for the Second Force and the forces under the command of the Kwantung Governor General, at Manchouli and Harbin. They will be transported mainly by rail and water; later, if necessary, an overland line-of-communications will be set up.

IX. Reports about the sea:

R. Vital information about the sea will be exchanged with the navy as provided by the Japanese Imperial Plan for operations against Russia for the year 1918. Details will be worked out according to circumstances.

SUMMARY OF APPENDIX[2]

I. Although the expeditionary forces number only about one half the strength of the German and Austrian prisoners of war and Russian Bolshevik forces now in the Russian Far East, it is believed that, because of the superior quality of our troops, operational superiority can be anticipated. However, our strength is to be increased, par-

[2] Approved by the Japanese Army General Staff Headquarters, in the last ten days of June and transmitted to the minister of war.

ticularly because of the large size of the area of operations in the Maritime Territory. Our comparative strength is as follows:

Maritime Territory area:
    German and Austrian prisoners of war in the Maritime Territory and along the Amur Railroad, about 5,000.
    Bolshevik forces in that area, about 9,000. Total, 14,000.
    Combatant strength of our expeditionary force, 19,000.
Trans-Baikal Territory area:
    German and Austrian prisoners of war in Trans-Baikal Territory and the Irkutsk district, about 93,000.
    Bolshevik forces in that area, about 10,000.
    Combatant strength of our expeditionary force, about 51,000.
    In addition, Chinese troops which can be scheduled for joint operations in this area, about 10,000.

II. Timetable of operations for the Maritime Territory Expeditionary Force is generally as follows:

Debarkation at Vladivostok, about 24 days after the 10th day following the issuance of the mobilization order.
    Depending on circumstances, before the Force debarks, a part of the Force in Korea will be dispatched; and, in cooperation with the naval landing units, it will secure the occupation of Vladivostok.
Arrival at Khabarovsk of the leading element of the Force (about 190 *ri* [463.5 miles] overland from Vladivostok):
    a. If the Ussuri Railroad can be used completely, about 5 days after debarking at Vladivostok.
    b. If the Ussuri Railroad cannot be used, about 2 months after debarking at Vladivostok.
Arrival at Blagoveshchensk of the leading element of the Force (about 190 *ri* [463.5 miles] overland from Khabarovsk):
    If it goes both by foot and by water, about 1 month after leaving Khabarovsk.
Since the Ussuri is almost completely in the hands of the Bolsheviks at present, the Maritime Territory Expeditionary Force will have to advance northward entirely on foot.
This disadvantageous situation will prolong the duration of the expedition; and the power of the enemy will increase. Furthermore, the freezing of the Amur river in winter will make it impossible to use.

III. Timetable of operations for the Trans-Baikal Territory Expeditionary Force is generally as follows:

Arrival at Manchouli of forces under the Kwantung Governor

General, about 15 days following the 8th day after the mobilization order is issued.

Arrival of the leading element of the Force at Manchouli, about 24 days after the mobilization order has been issued.

Completion of the concentration of the Force in the vicinity of Chita (about 140 *ri* [341.6 miles] overland from Manchouli):

Repairing the railroad in the Trans-Baikal Territory as it advances, at most about 4 months after mobilization orders have been issued; but, if conditions are good, it might be shortened to about 3 months.

Arrival of the main strength of the Force at Verkhneudinsk (about 130 *ri* [317.2 miles] overland from Chita):

Going by foot, about 2 months after leaving Chita.

If Pusan [Fusan] were used as the debarkation point for the main strength of the force, it would shorten the time of maritime transportation; and if proper connections were made with railroad transportation, the general transportation time could be shortened.

According to a recent investigation, the Chinese Eastern Railway could, at the very beginning of the expedition, provide about 3 trains a day; after about a month, with the situation improved by an increase in the rolling stock, it could provide about 5 trains a day. If the transportation had to be carried out, using only 3 trains throughout, the concentration of the force would be delayed by about 2 months.

IV. Expenses required for the above forces:

First year of the expedition (from 1st to 12th month of the expedition), about 300,010,000 yen; and after that, about 295,000,000 yen. The basis for this calculation is the cost per man or horse for the 1st month of the expedition, 185 yen; and the cost for each month thereafter, 106 yen.

V. The action taken by Russia and Germany, particularly Germany, in opposing our expedition will have a direct connection with the military situation in Europe. Although this cannot be foreseen immediately, evidences of bold German military management in the areas up to now indicate that Germany is inciting Russia and becoming its vanguard, and that it plans future revenge by sending large forces to the Far East. It is vital for the empire to be resolved early.

In that case, if we compare their and our advantages in transporting and concentrating forces in Eastern Siberia, it is clear that, if we were to advance to the Irkutsk district or west of it, we should always have the disadvantage of facing many with few; and, in addition, as a consequence of advancing west, the supply of the forces being difficult, we could not anticipate carrying out rapid and bold operations.

In contrast to this, if we select a point of concentration in central Trans-Baikal Territory, we should, for about the first half year, have considerable superiority over the enemy; and thereafter, even if the enemy developed superior strength, we would have the advantage of being able to destroy him repeatedly as he advanced past the great obstacle of Lake Baikal; therefore, this policy is believed to be best for the Imperial Forces. Even if several years from now, as a result of changes in the European military situation, Germany were to come against us with a large force, it should be not at all difficult, considering the comparative advantages of transportation, to make use of the Trans-Baikal terrain and, with Japanese and Chinese forces operating jointly, to destroy the enemy forces.

APPENDED TABLE 1

CLASSIFICATION TABLE OF STRENGTH OF EXPEDITION TO THE RUSSIAN FAR EAST, AS REVISED JUNE 7, 1918[a]

Forces	1st Force, Maritime			2d Force, Trans-Baikal			Forces under Kwantung Government General			Totals		
	I	II	Total	I	II	Total	I	II	Total	I	II	Total
Force headquarters	1		1	1		1				2		2
Permanent divisions	1 (Div. 12)	1 (Div. 5)	2	3 (Divs. 3, 7, 14)	2 (Divs. 1, 4)	5				4	3	7
Infantry brigades							1 (Brig. 40e)		1e	1e		1e
"Kō" cavalry brigades	1 (Brig. 1)		1	1 (Brig. 4)	2	3				2	2	4
"Otsu" cavalry regiments	1	1	2	3	2	5				4	3	7
Mountain artillery regiments and supply units	1 (Regt. 3)		1	1 (Regt. 1)		1				2		2
Medium artillery Brigades					1	1					1	1
Regiments and supply units	1		1	1 bn. t		1 bn. t				1 bn. t	1	1 regt. + 1 bn. t
Independent construction battalions	1 (Bn. 5)		1	1 (Bn. 1)	1	2				2	1	3

Unit	I	II			I	II		
Rear-guard								
Infantry battalions	1	2	4	8	8	4	12	12
Cavalry companies			2			2	2	2
Field artillery companies			4			4	4	4
Engineering companies			2			2	2	2
Field signal unit								
Headquarters	1		1		2		2	
Companies	1	3	4	8	5	6	11	
Field searchlight units			1	1		1	1	
Radio units	1t	1t	1t	2t		4	2t	
Air units	1t	1t	1t	2t		4	2t	
Bridging columns	1	2	3	4	6	5	4	9

Note (in the original): In the columns marked "I" (First Echelon) are indicated the forces to be mobilized or organized first and transported. In the columns marked "II" (Second Echelon and after) are the forces which will be equipped and sent later as they are needed. The order of battle will consist at first of the forces of the First Echelon column; after that, the order will be changed as these are reinforced.

In this table, t indicates forces under temporary organization, while e indicates forces under emergency preparation. However, the 7th Division and the 7th Cavalry Regiment will be under emergency preparation in the First Echelon and mobilized in the Second Echelon. For forces (except permanent divisions) which are to be equipped in the Second Echelon and later, the exact unit numbers will be designated later.

a Appended to the Plan of March, 1918, as revised on June 7, 1918, principally by the addition of 1 medium artillery battalion and 2 bridging columns to the Second Force.

APPENDED TABLE 2

CLASSIFICATION TABLE OF STRENGTH OF EXPEDITION TO THE RUSSIAN FAR EAST, AS REVISED JUNE 7, 1918

Line-of-Communications Forces	1st Force, Maritime			2d Force, Trans-Baikal			Forces under Kwantung Government General			Totals		
	I	II	Total	I	II	Total	I	II	Total	I	II	Total
Army staffs	1		1	1		1				2		2
Headquarters	4		4	4	8	12	4		4	12	8	20
Field signal unit												
Headquarters	1		1	1		1				2		2
Companies	1		1	1	3	4	1		1	3	3	6
Supply												
Field artillery depots	1		1	1		1				2		2
Field engineering depots	1		1	1		1				2		2
Reserve horse depots	1		1	1		1				2		2
Transportation columns	2	2	4	4	6	10				6	8	14
Transportation inspection units	4	4	8	8	12	20				12	16	28
Clothing replacement departments	1		1	1		1				2		2
Reserve field hospital												
Headquarters	1		1	1		1				2		2
Squads	1	1	2	2	3	5				3	4	7
Field medical supply depots	1		1	1		1				2		2
Casualty clearing department												
Headquarters	1		1	1		1				2		2
Squads	1	1	2	2	3	5				3	4	7
Hospitals	2		2	3		3	1		1	6		6

Veterinary hospitals	1	1	1		2		2
Independent engineering battalions	1	1	2		3		3
Rear-guard engineering companies		2	2		2		2
Special Forces							
Railroad brigade headquarters		1	1		1		1
Railroad regiments	1 (−1 bn.)	1 (+1 bn.)	1 (+1 bn.)		2		2
Railroad brigade warehouses	1 sec.	1 (−1 sec.)	1 (−1 sec.)		1		1
Railroad handcar units	2	3	3	5	5	5	5
Motor transport units	1t	1t	1t		1t		1t
Transport service units							
Land	18	26	51	25	50	25	75
Water	2	1	2	1	3	1	4
Construction	1	1	2	1	2	1	3

CLASSIFICATION TABLE OF STRENGTH OF EXPEDITION TO THE RUSSIAN FAR EAST, AS REVISED JUNE 7, 1918

Special Forces	1st Force, Maritime			2d Force, Trans-Baikal			Forces under Kwantung Government General			Totals		
	I	II	Total	I	II	Total	I	II	Total	I	II	Total
Field fortification departments	1		1	1		1				2		2
Field construction departments	1		1	1		1				2		2
Field collecting departments				1t		1t				1t		1t
Rations and forage departments				2		2				2		2
Horse purchasing departments				1		1				1		1
Temporary map departments	1t		1t	1t		1t				2t		2t
Field medical departments "Kō" "Otsu"					1	1					1	1
Main storage depots Field artillery							1		1	1		1
Field engineering							1		1	1		1
Field commissary							1		1	1		1

Note (in the original): See Note, Appended Table 1.

APPENDIX H

SUMMARY TABLE OF ORGANIZATION OF THE MARITIME TERRITORY EXPEDITIONARY FORCE, REVIEWED JULY 12, 1918

Forces	No. of Units	No. of Men	No. of Horses	Summary of Organization
12th Division, Division Headquarters	1	280	40	With wartime organization, independent div. hq. as standard, attach to it a communications officer.
Infantry				
12th and 35th Brigade Headquarters	2	20 (10 each)	10 (5 each)	Generally peacetime.
14th, 24th, 47th, and 72d Regiments	4	6100 (1525 each)	400 (100 each)	Each regt.: hq. (with signal dept.), 3 bns., 1 special artillery unit (2 cannon). Each bn.: hq., 4 cos., 1 machine gun unit (4 machine guns). Regt. & bn. hq. have small trains; co., 2 platoons of about 100 persons.
12th Cavalry Regiment	1	290	260	Regt. has hq. (with signal dept. squad), 2 cos.; each co. about 120 mounted men.
12th Field Artillery Regiment	1	380	290	Regt. has hq., 2 bns. Each bn. has hq., 2 cos. Each co. has 4 cannon, 2 caissons. Regt. and bn. hq. have signal squads. Total shells carried by regt., 1376 (86 per cannon).
Medical Artillery Battalion	1	390	310	Bn. has hq., 2 cos. Each co. has 4, 1905-type, 15-cm howitzers; 18 caissons. Total shells carried by bn., 576 (72 per howitzer).

SUMMARY TABLE OF ORGANIZATION OF THE MARITIME
TERRITORY EXPEDITIONARY FORCE,
REVIEWED JULY 12, 1918 (*Continued*)

Forces	No. of Units	No. of Men	No. of Horses	Summary of Organization
12th Engineering Battalion	1	380	50	Bn. has hq., 2 cos., small train, and personnel for div. telephone unit. Each co., about 180 men.
1st Field Signal Unit	1	230	50	Corresponds to about ⅔ field signal co., wartime organization, but carry equipment of 1 co.
1st Radio Unit	1	250	80	Able to set up 3 radio stations.
1st Air Unit	1	170	60	9 airplanes (including 3 reserve), pilots.
1st Casualty Collecting Squad	1	110	1	With capacity equal to wartime organization, field reserve hospital.
1st Railway Unit	1	280	10	Has hq., 2 cos. Ability of 1 co., wartime organization, for normal operation and repair of railroad.
1st Temporary Mapping Department	1	110	2	Has hq., 1 location squad, 4 topographic squads.
1st Fuel Gathering Depot	1	20	0	Same as wartime organization.

Note (in the original): Total number of men, about 8,910; horses, about 1,560.

Source: Japan, Sambō Hombu, *Shiberia Shuppei-shi*, Vol. I, Appendix II.

SUMMARY TABLE OF AID GIVEN BY ALLIED COUNTRIES
TO THE COMMITTEE FOR THE DEFENSE OF THE FATHER-
LAND AND THE CONSTITUENT ASSEMBLY AND TO THE
USSURI COSSACKS, TO APRIL 30, 1918

| | Source | | | To Ussuri Cossacks |
Type of Aid	Japan	Britain	France	by Japan
Weapons and munitions				
Heavy guns	2			
Field guns	16	2		
Mountain guns	4		4	
Infantry rifles	2500			
Carbines	3000			
Pistols	1100			
Machine guns	50		2	
Personnel				
Ordnance instructors	31	unknown	5	
Money	about 100,000 rubles	about £10,000 (500,000 rubles) monthly		about 100,000 rubles

Note (in the original): At their greatest number, Japanese ordnance instructors totaled 50 men.

In addition to the above, Japan supplied considerable communications equipment and first-aid packets to the Committee for the Defense of the Fatherland and the Constituent Assembly.

About 80 men in the United States' Russian Railway Service Corps were assigned to give technical instruction on the Chinese Eastern Railway.

Source: Japan, Sambō Hombu, Shiberia Shuppei-shi, III, 1070, facing.

ORDNANCE SUPPLIED TO RUSSIAN AND CZECHOSLO-
VAK FORCES BY JAPAN PRIOR TO AUGUST 2, 1918[1]

TO THE SEMENOV DETACHMENT*

Bayonets: *on March 4,†* 5,000; *on May 27,* 2,000.

Infantry rifles (1897): *on March 4,* 2,000 rifles, 400 spare parts.

Infantry rifles (1905): *on May 27,* 1,000 rifles, 100 spare parts.

Carbines (1905): *on March 4,* 3,000 carbines, 300 spare parts; *on May 27,* 1,000 carbines, 100 spare parts.

Rifle clips (1905): *on March 4,* 7,500,000 cartons; *on May 27,* 1,000,000 cartons.

Pistols: *on March 4,* 200 pistols, 20,000 cartridges.

Machine guns (1905): *on March 4,* 50 guns, 50 extra barrels, 2,000,000 cartons of cartridge belts, 8 "Kō" tool boxes, 544 "Kō" ammo boxes, 52 horse harness packs for guns, 10 horse harness packs for tool boxes, 138 horse harness packs for ammo boxes; *on May 27,* 10 extra barrels, 100,000 cartons of cartridge belts; *on June 15,* 70 firing pins.

For rapid-firing field-gun (1898): *on March 4,* 8 gun carriages, 8 ammo carriages for shrapnel, 8 ammo carriages for shells, 400 train ammo boxes for shrapnel, 1,800 train ammo boxes for shells, 10,000 cartridge cases of shells, 5,000 cartridge cases of shrapnel; *on March 13,* 600 train ammo boxes for shrapnel; *on May 27,* 4,000 cartridge cases of shells.

Horse harnesses: *on March 4,* 62 artillery draft harnesses for front (mid.), 30 artillery draft harnesses for rear, 30 riding saddles; *on March 29,* 16 artillery draft harnesses for front (mid.), 8 artillery draft harnesses for rear; *on May 27,* 14 artillery draft harnesses for front

---

* Included in the weapons sent to the Semenov Detachment on March 4, 1918, were 1,000 infantry rifles, 1,000 carbines, and 20 machine guns, carried by Japanese officers detailed to it at Harbin.

† All dates are in the year 1918.

[1] Extracts from Tables 16 and 17 in Japan, Sambō Hombu, *Shiberia Shuppeishi,* Vol. I, Appendix.

(mid.), 6 artillery draft harnesses for rear; *on July 9,* 16 artillery draft harnesses for front (mid.), 8 artillery draft harnesses for rear.

For rapid-firing mountain gun (1898): *on March 9,* 4 gun carriages, 4 ammo boxes for shrapnel, 4 ammo boxes for shells, 2 #1 tool boxes, 2 #2 tool boxes, 1 spare part, 16 horse harnesses for pulling guns, 2 horse harnesses for pulling ammo boxes, 4,000 cases of shells, 4,000 cases of shrapnel; *on March 13,* 572 train ammo boxes for shrapnel, 233 train ammo boxes for shells.

For 3-inch field gun (old Russian type): *on March 29,* 8 gun carriages, 6,700 cases of shrapnel; *on May 27,* 4,000 cases of shrapnel; *on July 9,* 8 gun carriages, 5,000 cases of shrapnel.

For 12-cm howitzer (1905): *on May 27,* 2 gun carriages, 4 ammo carriages, 1,000 cases of armor-piercing shells.

For 15-cm howitzer (1905): *on March 4,* 2 gun carriages, 4 ammo carriages, 1,000 cases of armor-piercing shells; *on May 27,* 250 cases of armor-piercing shells, 220 cases of shrapnel.

Rifle grenade launchers: *on March 4,* 10 rifles, 1,000 shells, 2,000 illuminating shells.

Hand grenades: *on March 4,* 10,000 grenades.

Portable tool kits: *on March 13,* 1 blacksmith, 2 gunsmith, 1 harness-making.

Signal instruments: *on March 29,* 1.

Cold-proof overcoats: *in June–July,* 3,000.

Messkits: *in June–July,* 500.

TO THE KALMYKOV DETACHMENT
(all on March 13)

Bayonets: 500.

Infantry rifles (1905): 500 rifles, 50 spare parts.

Rifle clips (1905): 750,000 cartons.

TO THE CZECHOSLOVAK FORCES
(all on July 4)

Rifle clips (1905): 280,000 cartons.

Machine guns (1905): 20 guns, 200,000 cartons of cartridge belts, 3 "Kō" tool boxes, 20 "Kō" ammo boxes, 22 horse harness packs for guns, 3 horse harness packs for tool boxes.

For rapid-firing mountain gun (1898): 6 gun carriages, 6 ammo boxes for shrapnel, 6 ammo boxes for shells, 3 #1 tool boxes, 3 #2 tool boxes, 1 spare part, 24 horse harnesses for pulling guns, 15 horse harnesses for pulling ammo boxes, 500 cases of shells, 500 cases of shrapnel.

Portable tool kits: 1 blacksmith, 1 gunsmith.

DRAFT OF AN AGREEMENT FOR MILITARY TRANSPOR-
TATION AND MILITARY COMMUNICATION ON THE RUS-
SIAN RAILROADS, MARCH, 1918[1]

The Japanese Imperial military representative and the Russian railroad representative, on ———, at Harbin, agree to the following arrangements for the military transportation and military communications of Japanese forces on the Chinese Eastern, Ussuri, Amur and Trans-Baikal railroads:

Article I. In the eventuality of a movement of Japanese Imperial forces from North Manchuria and the Maritime Territory into eastern Siberia, the Russian railroads in this zone of operations will be responsible for the transport of the men, horses and munitions of the Japanese Imperial forces, and will supply telegraph lines for other than railroad use to be used exclusively by Japanese forces.

Article II. At the very beginning of the movement of the Japanese Imperial forces, the minimum strength for military transportation which the Chinese Eastern and Ussuri railroads are responsible for is as follows:

Transport Zone	No. of Trains	No. of Cars Attached
Changchun–Harbin	4–5	40–45
Harbin–Manchouli	4–5	40–45
Vladivostok–Khabarovsk	3–4	40–45
Vladivostok–Harbin	2	35–45

Article III. The military transportation strength between Changchun and Harbin, and between Harbin and Manchouli will gradually be increased to 8 to 10 trains and even more, should special necessity arise.

[1] Given to Major-General Mutō Nobuyoshi by the Japanese central military authorities in March, 1918, for negotiation with General Horvat. Japan, Sambō Hombu, *Shiberia Shuppei-shi,* IV, Appendix IV, 35–38.

However, when military transportation declines, there is no objection to restoring some of the above-mentioned trains to service.

Article IV. The standard for the Amur and Trans-Baikal railroads will be to take over the military transport facilities of the Ussuri and Chinese Eastern railways respectively.

Article V. The minimum number of the railroads' local telegraph lines suitable for long-distance communications, which are offered for the exclusive use of the Japanese forces, will at the very beginning of the movement of the Japanese Imperial forces, be as in Article II; thereafter, as in Article III.

Article VI. After the military transportation has been completed as provided in Article I, the Japanese Imperial forces will assist the Russian railroads in the following ways:

1) By sending railroad technical experts and mechanics to the railroad shops;
2) By transferring as much soft coal as possible;
3) If necessary, in order to increase the transportation strength, by having the Japanese Imperial forces accept responsibility for their own transportation between Changchun and Harbin, and in other districts.

Article VII. The Japanese Imperial forces will do the following in order to insure military communications:

1) Send communications personnel to necessary signal stations and railroad stations;
2) Be responsible for the maintenance of the lines for their exclusive use;
3) In order to carry out "1" and "2" above, be responsible for the necessary tools and repair materials.

Article VIII. In order to complete the liaison of the military transportation and military communications on the Chinese Eastern, Ussuri, Amur and Zabaikal railroads, the Japanese Imperial forces will detail commissioned officers or railroad and communications workers under the direction of the representative of the Japanese Imperial forces to each railroad administrative department, transport office, important railroad station and communications administrative department.

Article IX. The expenses of military transportation of the Japanese Imperial forces on the Chinese Eastern, Ussuri, Amur and Zabaikal railroads will be paid to the Russian railroad representative by the representative of the Japanese Imperial forces, according to the standard fare set for military transportation on these railroads; and compensation for the exclusive use of telegraph lines, on the basis of a percentage of the current receipts of these lines.

Article X. Matters of detail necessary in order to execute this agreement will be determined separately by the proper authorities, under the direction of the representative of the Japanese Imperial forces and the representative of the Russian railroads.

Article XI. This agreement will be effective from the day it is signed by the Japanese Imperial forces representative and the Russian railroad representative. It will be void upon the withdrawal of the Japanese Imperial forces from the Russian Far East and the district along the Chinese Eastern Railway.

APPENDIX L

PROCLAMATION OF THE TEMPORARY GOVERNMENT OF
THE TRANS-BAIKAL TERRITORY, MAY, 1918[1]

In view of the importance of the responsibilities it is undertaking, the
Temporary Government of the Trans-Baikal Territory feels it essential
at the outset to announce to the general public its policies and procedures in the present situation. First of all, we must express our gratitude to the Allied powers for having several times declared their respect
for the territorial integrity of Siberia. Moreover, we are confident in
anticipating close relations with the Allied powers in the difficult path
that lies ahead for our government. The Territorial Government, wield-
ing all military power, will be the sole organ to lead the Siberian people forward toward the securing of democratic rights, the development
of the economy and the establishment of Siberian self-government, on
the basis of equality, justice, and equity. We shall establish the indispensable conditions for calling quickly a Siberian legislative assembly,
which will be the proper organ of authority of a self-governing Siberia.
A Siberian government will be set up by the Siberian assembly.

The government will gradually restore the organs of republican self-
government which existed before the invasion of Bolshevik authority;
and we are confident that these organs will not interfere with the objectives or obstruct the attainment of these objectives, as announced by
the detachment.

In view of the extreme importance placed by all civilized countries
on the establishment of a system of justice to protect the people's rights,
lives and property, the government intends to restore by degrees the
laws relating to justice established during the period of the Russian
provisional government. When it becomes necessary to revise them, they

[1] Issued by Gregorii Semenov, May, 1918. From the Japanese, as contained in
Mutō (at Changchun) to Vice Chief Tanaka, May 21, 1918, in *JGK, RKI, HK,*
Vol. II.

will be referred to the Siberian legislative assembly or to the body which has authority to revise them according to the laws of the Russian provisional government.

The government will also take particular care to select suitable persons to restore the banking facilities which have been disrupted and to readjust agriculture, which has been desolated.

APPENDIX M

AGREEMENT BETWEEN THE COMMANDER OF THE TRANS-BAIKAL FRONT AND THE COMMAND OF THE CHINESE TROOPS, JULY 30, 1918[1]

We the undersigned, on the one hand, the Chief of Staff of the Commander in Chief of the Chinese troops temporarily guarding the Chinese Eastern Railway Zone in the Province of Heilungkiang, and on the other hand, the Commander of the Trans-Baikal Front, in order to maintain peace between the Chinese Republic and the Russian Republic of Soviets, agree to the following:

1. For 5 weeks, we shall endeavor to take all measures for the disarmament of Semenov (the Special Manchurian Detachment).

During this time, we guarantee not to permit Semenov and the Special Manchurian Detachment to cross the Russo-Chinese border. We shall inform each other about the outcome of this at appropriate times.

2. In no instance do the Soviet troops of the Trans-Baikal Front have the right to cross the Russo-Chinese border, nor likewise do the troops of the Chinese Republic have the right to cross the Russo-Chinese border.

3. The Soviet troops of the Trans-Baikal Front will dispose their main forces in Dauriia station on the Chita side.

4. For the convenience of the troops, in view of the existence of water at Railroad Siding 86, advance posts of Chinese and Soviet troops, their numbers not to exceed 60 men each, will be stationed there.

[1] Vsesoiuznaia Kommunisticheskaia Partiia, *Sergei Lazo,* comp. G. Reikhberg, A. Romanov, and P. Krol', p. 83. Russian text, no source given.

5. All of the above conditions enter into force from the day when this instrument is signed by both sides.

> Chief of Staff of the Commander in Chief of the Chinese troops temporarily guarding the Chinese Eastern Railway Zone in the Province of Heilungkiang   (*Signature*)[2]

> Senior adjutant of the Staff of the Commander in Chief of the Chinese troops   (*Signature*)

> Commander of the Trans-Baikal Front, S. Lazo
> Chief of Staff of the Trans-Baikal Front, Russkis
> July 30, 1918, Matsievskaia Station

[2] Chinese signatures are not given.

SINO-JAPANESE JOINT DEFENSIVE MILITARY AGREE-MENT, MAY 16, 1918 [1]

1. China and Japan, realizing the fact that the gradual extension of enemy influence towards the east may jeopardize the peace of the two countries, consider it their mutual duty, as participants in the war, to take concerted action against the common enemy.

2. As regards military cooperation, each country shall pay due respect to the prestige and interests of the other country, and both parties shall be considered to be on an equal footing.

3. When the time comes to take action in accordance with this agreement, the two countries shall instruct their military and civil officials and people to adopt a friendly attitude towards those of the other country in the military areas. The Chinese officials shall do their best to aid the Japanese troops in the said areas so that no obstacles shall arise to impede their movements, and the Japanese troops shall respect the sovereignty of China, and shall not be allowed to act in a manner contrary to the local customs and cause inconvenience to the people.

4. The Japanese troops in Chinese territory shall be withdrawn as soon as military operations cease.

5. Whenever troops have to be dispatched outside Chinese territory, the two countries shall dispatch them jointly whenever necessary.

6. The military areas and other matters relating to the military operations shall be decided by the military authorities of the two countries whenever necessary, in accordance with the military strength of each country.

[1] Signed on May 16, 1918, by representatives of the military authorities of China and Japan. From the English language text as officially given out by the Foreign Ministry in Peking, enclosed in Reinsch to Lansing, June 6, 1918, *USFR, 1918,* pp. 224–25; compared with the Chinese language text in Chinese Ministry of Foreign Affairs, *Chung-Jih Tiao Yueh Hui-tsuan,* pp. 469–71, and with the Japanese Language text in Gaimushō, *Taishō 7 nen Hen-roku Jōyaku Isan,* pp. 413–17.

7. In order to facilitate matters, in the course of the military cooperation the military authorities of the two countries shall observe the arrangements:

a) In regard to the making of all arrangements for carrying on military operations, both countries shall appoint deputies who shall arrange all matters regarding cooperation.

b) In order to secure rapid transportation by land or water and rapid communication, both sides shall cooperate to this end.

c) When occasion arises the two commanders in chief shall arrange all necessary military constructions such as military railways, telegraph and telephone lines. These shall all be removed at the conclusion of the military operations.

d) Regarding the necessary military supplies and materials required for taking concerted action against the enemy, the two countries shall supply each other to such an extent as not to affect the supplying of ordinary demands.

e) The two countries shall assist each other in carrying out sanitary measures for the troops in the military areas.

f) With regard to the question of military experts for direct military operations, should the necessity arise for mutual assistance, if one country requests the assistance of such experts, the other shall supply it.

g) In the areas in which military operations are taking place, intelligence agencies may be established, and the two countries shall exchange important military maps and military reports. The intelligence agencies of the two countries shall exchange information and render mutual assistance.

h) All secret passwords shall be agreed upon mutually.

The question as to which of the above arrangements shall be considered first, and which shall be first entered upon shall be mutually arranged in a separate agreement, before the actual commencement of hostilities.[2]

8. When military transportation necessitates the use of the Chinese Eastern Railway, the provisions in the original treaty regarding the management and protection of the said railway shall be respected. The method of transportation shall be decided upon at the time.

9. Regarding the enforcement of the details in this agreement, it shall be decided upon by delegates appointed by the military authorities of the two countries.

10. This agreement and the supplementary articles therein shall

[2] The first Supplementary Agreement was not signed until September 6, 1918.

not be published by the two Governments, but shall be considered as military secrets.

11. This agreement shall be signed and sealed by the military delegates of the two countries and recognized by the two Governments before it becomes operative. The time for commencing actual military operations shall be decided by the highest military organs of the two countries. This agreement and all the details arising from this agreement shall become null and void as soon as the military operations of China and Japan against the enemy countries of Germany and Austria come to an end.

12. Two copies of this agreement shall be written in the Chinese language, and two corresponding copies in the Japanese language, and each party shall keep one copy of the agreement in each language.

SINO-JAPANESE JOINT DEFENSIVE NAVAL AGREEMENT,
MAY 19, 1918 [1]

1. Same as Article 1 of military agreement.
2. Same as Article 2 of military agreement.
3. When the time comes to take action in accordance with this agreement, the two countries shall instruct their naval officers and all officials and people to adopt a friendly attitude toward those of the other country in the military areas, and mutually assist each other with a view to overcoming the enemy.
4. A separate agreement shall be drawn up regarding the field of activity and the duties of the participants when the time comes for taking action against the enemy.
5. When the time comes for action, the naval authorities of China and Japan shall cooperate with a view to taking efficient measures as follows:

a) Same as Article 7(*a*) of the military agreement.
b) Same as Article 7(*b*) of the military agreement.
c) In all matters relating to shipbuilding and repairs and naval equipment and supplies, both countries shall mutually assist each according to its power. This also applies to necessary military articles.
d) Same as Article 7(*f*) of military agreement.
e) Same as Article 7(*g*) of military agreement. Substitute "naval" for "military" wherever used.
f) Same as Article 7(*g*) of military agreement.

6. Same as Article 9 of military agreement, except that "naval" should be substituted for "military" wherever used.

[1] Signed on May 19, 1918, by representatives of the naval authorities of China and Japan, together with Explanatory Note. Reinsch to Lansing, June 6, 1918, *USFR, 1918,* pp. 225–26; compared with Chinese and Japanese language texts in same sources as for Military Agreement.

7. Same as Article 10, with "naval" substituted for "military."
8. Same as Article 11, with "naval" substituted for "military."
9. Same as Article 12.

EXPLANATORY NOTE, REGARDING THE "SINO-JAPANESE JOINT DEFENSIVE NAVAL AGREEMENT"

I

The navies of the two countries of China and Japan, looking toward the accomplishment of their mutual efforts in the war, in order mutually to carry out their purposes as outlined in Article I, are agreed to render each other mutual assistance in the hope that these military efforts may be fully accomplished.

II

Article 5 of the agreement is explained as follows:

The term "deputies" as used in clause (*a*) of Article 5 of the naval agreement is defined as naval attachés of each Legation, and naval officers stationed in other places, and others to be mutually appointed in case of necessity.

In clause (*c*) of Article 5, the term "necessary supplies" shall be defined as "metallic articles." "Necessary military articles" shall be defined as "combustibles, provisions, ammunition, such as are required in military operations." They shall be supplied by each country according to its power.

With reference to clause (*e*) of Article 5, charts are to be supplied upon the request of either country.

In a place within which military operations are taking place, should it be found necessary by both sides to make surveys and soundings of any bays, such surveys and soundings shall be done by the naval authorities of the country in which the bays are situated.

BIBLIOGRAPHY

ABBREVIATIONS

CRMFADD	Chinese Republic, Ministry of Foreign Affairs, *Diplomatic Documents*.
JGK	Japan, Gaimushō Kiroku. Indicates a file of official manuscript materials in the archives of the Japanese Ministry of Foreign Affairs. Letters following these designate the title of the specific file, translations of which will be found in the Bibliography.
JGK, KZ	Japan, Gaimushō Kiroku, Kengen Zassan.
JGK, RKI, CGMU	Japan, Gaimushō Kiroku, Rokoku Kakumei Ikken: Chiekku Gundan "Minzoku Undō."
JGK, RKI, HK	Japan, Gaimushō Kiroku, Rokoku Kakumei Ikken: Han-Kagekiha Kankei.
JGK, RKI, SB	Japan, Gaimushō Kiroku, Rokoku Kakumei Ikken: Shiberia ni tai suru Beikoku no Riken Kito sono ta Taido Zakken.
JGK, RKI, SC	Japan, Gaimushō Kiroku, Rokoku Kakumei Ikken: Sankō Chōsho.
JGK, RKI, SK, CKH	Japan, Gaimushō Kiroku, Rokoku Kakumei Ikken: Shuppei Kankei: Chiekku Kyūen Hahei.
JGK, RKI, SK, EBFK	Japan, Gaimushō Kiroku, Rokoku Kakumei Ikken: Shuppei Kankei: Ei-Bei-Futsu no Kōshō.
JGK, RKI, SK, HMSK	Japan, Gaimushō Kiroku, Rokoku Kakumei Ikken: Shuppei Kankei: Hon Mondai Shinchoku Keika.
JGK, RKI, SK, SSK	Japan, Gaimushō Kiroku, Rokoku Kakumei Ikken: Shuppei Kankei: Shiberia Shuppei Kōshō.
JGK, RKI, TT	Japan, Gaimushō Kiroku, Rokoku Kakumei Ikken: Teikoku no Taidō.
JGK, SKE, IS	Japan, Gaimushō Kiroku, Shiberia Keizai Enjo Kankei Zakken: I'nkai no Seiritsu ni kansuru Ken.
JGK, SKZ	Japan, Gaimushō Kiroku, Sho-shūshi Kankei Zakken: Gaikō Shiryō-shū Kankei.
JKK	Japan, Kaigunshō Kiroku. Indicates a file of official manuscript materials found in the archives of the former Japanese Navy Ministry. Letters following these designate the title of the specific file, translations of which will be found in the Bibliography.
JKK, GTBO	Japan, Kaigunshō Kiroku, Gaikoku Taishikan-tsuki Bukan Ōfuku-sho: Kaigunshō Fukkan.

JRK   Japan, Rikugunshō Kiroku. Indicates a file of official
                          manuscript materials found in the archives of the
                          former Japanese Army Ministry. Letters following
                          these designate the title of the specific file, transla-
                          tions of which will be found in the Bibliography.
JRK, MDN   Japan, Rikugunshō Kiroku, Mitsu Dai Nikki.
JRK, OJDN   Japan, Rikugunshō Kiroku, Ō Ju Dai Nikki.
USFR   United States, Department of State, *Papers Relating
                          to the Foreign Relations of the United States.*

MANUSCRIPT MATERIALS

Official

JAPAN. Gaimushō (Foreign Ministry)

Most of the voluminous files of the Foreign Ministry relating to the Siberian
expedition have been preserved in the ministry's archives in Tokyo. Not all titles
of relevant files are listed below because many of the files contain duplications of
important instructions, reports, and other items. Those which are listed proved
most useful in this project. They can be located by the MT numbers in the
Meiji-Taishō section (materials 1868–1925) of the Gaimushō Genson Kiroku
Mokuroku (Index of the Extant Archives of the Foreign Ministry), compiled in
1947 by the ministry's archives and documents section. It should be noted that
some, but not all, of the cited material is available on microfilm in the Library
of Congress, Washington, D.C. The microfilm numbers do not correspond with
those of the ministry files.

Kengen Zassan (Miscellaneous Collection of Memorials), Vol. II. File
Number MT 1.1.1.46 (2). A collection of recommendations relat-
ing to China and Russia policy, 1917–20.
Rokoku Kakumei Ikken (Russian Revolution): Chiekku Gundan "Minzoku Undō": Rengōkoku-gawa no Enjo (Czech Corps National
Movement: Allied Assistance), Vol. I. File number MT 1.6.3.24–40.
April, 1918, to August, 1918.
——Han-kagekiha Kankei (Materials relating to Anti-Bolshevik Activities), Vols. I–III. File number MT 1.6.3.24.29. Telegrams exchanged between the Army General Staff Headquarters and the
Foreign Ministry at home and military officers and diplomatic officials in China, north Manchuria and Siberia, relating to the activities of anti-Bolshevik factions, especially in the Amur basin. These
files, which are part of a large series, cover the period from January
to August, 1918.
——Sankō Chōsho (Research Reports for Reference), Vols. I–II. File
number MT 1.6.3.24–3. Confidential studies, made by the Foreign
Ministry, of changes in Russia. Some Foreign Ministry telegrams are
included. April, 1917, to June, 1918.

———Shiberia ni tai suru Beikoku no Riken Kito sono ta Taido Zakken (Miscellaneous Materials Relating to American Projects for Acquiring Rights in Siberia and to Other American Attitudes). File number MT 1.6.3.24.5. Rumors and reports of American concession hunting and railroad activities in Siberia, June, 1917, to July, 1921.

———Shuppei Kankei: Chiekku Kyūen Hahei (Materials Relating to the Expedition: The sending of Troops to Rescue the Czechs). File number MT 1.6.3.24.15–13. July, 1918, to March, 1920.

———Shuppei Kankei: Ei-Bei-Futsu no Kōshō (Materials Relating to the Expedition: Negotiations with England, America, and France), Vols. I–II. File number MT 1.6.3.24.15.4. Diplomatic instructions and reports, February, 1918, to January, 1919.

———Shuppei Kankei: Hon Mondai Shinchoku Keika (Materials Relating to the Expedition: The Development of This Question). File number MT 1.6.3.25.15.1. December, 1917, to March, 1918.

———Shuppei Kankei: Shiberia Shuppei Kōshō (Materials Relating to the Expedition: Negotiations for the Siberian Expedition). File number MT 1.6.3.24.15.2. Relevant diplomatic telegrams, February to March, 1918, plus a summary of the key negotiations, prepared for current use, which seems to have formed the basis for the confidential history, compiled later by Okamoto Hidemasa (listed below).

———Teikoku no Taido (Japan's Attitude), Vols. I–IV. File number MT 1.6.3.24.12. Valuable collection of recommendations and decisions of high government officials and organs, December, 1917, to June, 1924.

Shiberia Keizai Enjo Kankei Zakken: I'inkai no Seiritsu ni kansuru Ken (Miscellaneous Matters Relating to Siberian Economic Assistance: Matters concerning the Establishment of the Committee). File number MT 3.41.4.23. June 7 to September 17, 1918.

Sho-Shūshi Kankei Zakken: Gaikō Shiryō-shū Kankei, (Various Matters Relating to Past Events: Related to the Collection of Diplomatic Source Materials), Vol. III. File number N 2.1.0.4–1. Useful collection of the statements of important officials, concerning certain phases of Japan's foreign relations of which they had some personal knowledge, recorded mostly in 1939 by the Ministry of Foreign Affairs.

JAPAN. Kaigunshō (Navy Ministry)

Most of the extant Navy Ministry archives (now held in RG 242, War Records Division, National Archives, Washington, D.C.) relating to the Siberian expedition concern operations after the expedition was begun. Fortunately, copies of many useful Navy Ministry materials were included in the Foreign Ministry files listed above. File numbers are those assigned by the National Archives.

Gaikoku Taishikan-tsuki Bukan Ōfuku-sho: Kaigunshō Fukkan (Correspondence with Attachés of Foreign Legations: Navy Ministry Adjutant), November, 1917–December, 1918. File number NA 8821. Originals of incoming correspondence from the British embassy, Tokyo, to the Navy Ministry and copies of the Navy Ministry replies, chronologically arranged. One of series, 1906–1936.

JAPAN. Rikugunshō (War Ministry)

Like the Navy Ministry's archives, these too are now held in RG 242, War Records Division, National Archives, Washington, D.C., and those surviving, which concern the Siberian expedition, relate chiefly to operations after the expedition was begun. The Foreign Ministry files contain many important War Ministry items not located here. File numbers are those assigned by the National Archives.

Mitsu Dai Nikki (Great Daily Record of Messages Received, Confidential), 1917–18. File numbers NA 14628–14631, 14632–14635. Handwritten copies of confidential correspondence, reports, etc., received, arranged chronologically, under subject heads, and indexed in tied volumes. Part of a voluminous series, extant for 1873–1940.

Ō Ju Dai Nikki (Great Daily Record of European War Messages Received, Unrestricted) January–July, 1918. File numbers NA 14399–14405. Copies of unrestricted correspondence and reports received, relating to Japanese military operations in the First World War, including some relating to possible operations in Siberia. Part of series, 1914–1926.

UNITED STATES. Department of State

No attempt was made to survey exhaustively the archives of the Department of State in the National Archives, Washington, D.C., inasmuch as those relating to the Siberian expedition were used especially by Bock, Tompkins, and Williams in their works listed below, and the formation of American policy, except in so far as it affected Japanese policy, is beyond the scope of this work. A few items in the record groups proved useful.

Record Group 59. General Records of the Department of State, especially correspondence filed under 861.00, entitled "Political Conditions in Russia."

Record Group 84. Records of the Foreign Service Posts of the United States. Most of the post records of consulates in Siberia and north Manchuria for the period of 1917–18 were not recovered. Fortunately, a portion of the archives of the American consulate at Vladivostok for these years was evacuated to Japan and later sent to Washington.

Unofficial

Aoki, Arata. Uchida Kōsai Denki Genkō (Draft Biography of Uchida Kōsai). Based on Uchida's personal diary and on Foreign Ministry archival materials, by Aoki, who served as second secretary to the Japanese embassy in Russia during the latter part of Uchida's ambassadorship there, and as private secretary to the foreign minister, when Uchida assumed that post in 1918 in the Hara cabinet. Part nine covers the period of his ambassadorship to Russia, December, 1916–July, 1918.

Itō, Miyoji. Sui'usō Nikki: Gaikō Chōsakai Kaigi Hikki (Green Rain Villa Diary: Notes of the Meetings of the Advisory Council on Foreign Relations). A handwritten copy of Itō's "Diary," recording private conversations and speeches made in the council in the spring and early summer of 1918, relating to the Siberian expedition, copied from the Itō family archives by the former parliamentary vice minister of foreign affairs, Matsumoto Tadao, and now in the Matsumoto collection of the Foreign Ministry's archives under the file number MT 1.1.1.10. An invaluable source. That part of the diary which Matsumoto had, concerning the establishment of the council, subtitled "Taishō Roku-nen Roku-gatsu yori: Rinji Gaikō Chōsakai Kansei no Bu," unfortunately was destroyed by fire in February, 1942; but the concluding part in seven folders, relating to the twenty-six meetings of the council from October 22, 1918, to December 22, 1919, subtitled "Hara Naikaku Seiritsu go," has been recovered by the Foreign Ministry and is filed under the number above.

PRINTED MATERIALS

Official

CHINA. Wai-Chiao-Pu (Ministry of Foreign Affairs)

Wai-chiao Wen-tu: Chung-Jih Chün-shin Hsieh-ting An (Diplomatic Documents: Sino-Japanese Military Agreements for Common Defense). Peking, 1921.

JAPAN. Gaimushō (Foreign Ministry)

Gaimushō Kōhyō-shū (Collection of Public Announcements of the Foreign Ministry) Tokyo, 1919– .

Gaimushō Nenkan (Yearbook of the Ministry of Foreign Affairs). Annual.

Gaimushō Shokuin-roku (Personnel Roster of the Ministry of Foreign Affairs). Annual.
Nichi-Ro Kōshō-shi (History of Negotiations between Japan and Russia), Vols. I–II. February, 1944. Written by Tanaka Bun'ichiro and issued as a classified publication.
Rokoku ni okeru "Chiekko Surovakkii" Guntai (Czechoslovak Forces in Russia). June 27, 1918.
Shiberia Shuppei Mondai (The Siberian Expedition Question): Dai Ippen: Shiberia Shuppei ni itaru Kōshō Keika (Vol. I: The Course of the Negotiations Leading Up to the Siberian Expedition); Dai Nihen: Rengōkoku Kyōdō Shuppei Igo Beikoku Teppei ni itaru Made no Keika (Vol. II: From the Beginning of the Inter-Allied Expedition to the Withdrawal of American Troops). November, 1922. A formerly classified account written by Okamoto Hidemasa.
Teikoku Gikai ni okeru Gaimu Daijin Enzetsu-shū (Collection of the Speeches by the Minister of Foreign Affairs in the Imperial Diet). May, 1934.

JAPAN. Kaigun Gunreibu (Navy General Staff)
Taishō Yon-nen naishi Kyū-nen Kaigun Senshi (Naval War History, 1915–1920). Vols. I–IV. 1924.

JAPAN. Sambō Hombu (Army General Staff Headquarters)
Taishō Shichi-nen naishi Jūichi-nen Shiberia Shuppei-shi (History of the Siberian Expedition, 1918–1922). Vols. I–VII. 1924.

UNITED STATES. Department of State
Papers Relating to the Foreign Relations of the United States, 1917, Supplement 2, The World War. Washington: GPO, 1932.
——1918, Russia, Vols. I–III. Washington: GPO, 1931–32.
——The Lansing Papers, 1914–1920, Vols. I–II. Washington: GPO, 1940.

USSR. Tsentral'nyi Arkhiv RSFSR, Arkhiv Oktiabr'skoi Revoliutsii (Central Archives, RSFSR, Archives of the October Revolution). Iaponskaia Interventsiia 1918–1922 gg. v Dokumentakh (Japanese Intervention, 1918–22, in Documents). Ed. I. Mints. Moscow, 1934.
Vsesoiuznaia Kommunisticheskaia Partiia (bol'shevikov), Chita Okruzhnyi Komitet (All-Union Communist Party [Bolshevik], Chita Regional Committee). Partizany (Partisans). Chita, 1929.
Vsesoiuznaia Kommunisticheskaia Partiia, Tsentral'nyi Ispolnitel'nyi Komitet, Sekretariat Glavnoi Redaktsii Istorii Grazhdanskoi Voiny v SSSR (All-Union Communist Party, Central Executive Committee,

Secretariat of the Editor-in-Chief of the History of the Civil War in the USSR). Sergei Lazo, Vospominaniia i Dokumenty (Memoirs and Documents). Comp. G. Reikhberg, A. Romanov, and P. Krol'. Moscow: Gosizdat, 1938.

Unofficial

Unfortunately, very few able accounts of the Siberian expedition by serious Japanese scholars are available to the public, largely because the official archival materials were classified and private archives are difficult of access and because until 1945 scholars were discouraged from writing critically of government activities, particularly those involving the military. The one notable exception is the excellent recent work by Hosoya Chihiro, entitled *Shiberia Shuppei ni Shiteki Kenkyū* (Historical Study of the Siberian Expedition) (Tokyo: Yūhikaku, 1955). Published too late to be of use in this study, it makes thorough use of the archives of the Foreign Ministry and of published Western and Russian materials to analyze the origins of Western as well as Japanese policies.

Japanese biographies present different problems. Often they are compiled by specially organized societies which stress primarily the reminiscences of friends concerning the personality rather than the policies of the subject. A few, however, quote extensively from private and governmental archives.

Alekseev, S. A., comp. Nachalo Grazhdanskoi Voiny (Beginning of the Civil War). Volume III in the series Revoliutsiia i Grazhdanskaia Voina v Opisaniiakh Belogvardeitsey (Revolution and Civil War in the Memoirs of the White Guards). Moscow: Gosizdat, 1926.

Araki Sadao, comp. Gensui Uehara Yūsaku Den (Biography of Field Marshal Uehara Yūsaku). Vols. I–II. Tokyo: Gensui Uehara Yūsaku Denki Hankō-kai, 1937.

Bokudō Sensei Denki Kankō-kai, comp. Inukai Bokudō Den (Biography of Inukai Bokudō). Vols. I–III. Tokyo: comp., 1938.

Borodavkin, V. "Vospominaniia Komandira" (Memoirs of a Commander), in Vsesoiuznaia Kommunsticheskaia Partiia, Sergei Lazo, pp. 43–47.

Budberg, Baron Aleksei. "Dnevnik" (Diary), Arkhiv Russkoi Revoliutsii (Archives of the Russian Revolution), VII (1923), 197–312.

Butsevich, Aleksandr. "Pervye Dni Chekho-slovakov v Cheliabinskom Raione" (First Days of the Czechoslovaks in the Cheliabinsk Area), Proletarskaia Revoliutsiia (Proletarian Revolution), No. 5 (1922), pp. 262–74.

Chang Chung-fu. Chung-Hua-Min-Kuo Wai-chiao Shih (Diplomatic History of the Chinese Republic). Vol. I. Peking: Cheng Chung Shu-chü, 1943.

Chuchin, F. "Imperialisticheskaia Interventsiia na Dal'nem Vostoke i v Sibiri (1917–1919 gg.)" (Imperialistic Intervention in the Far East and in Siberia, 1917–1919), Proletarskaia Revolutsiia (Proletarian Revolution), No. 106 (November, 1930), pp. 21–51.

Den Kenjiro Denki Hensankai, comp. Den Kenjiro Denki (Biography of Den Kenjiro). Tokyo: comp., 1932.

Dmitriev. "Oktiabr'skaia Revoliutsiia v Sibiri" (October Revolution in Siberia), *Severnaia Aziia* (Northern Asia), III, Nos. 5–6 (1927), 5–21.

Fischer, Louis. The Soviets in World Affairs. Vols. I–II. London: Cape & Smith, 1930.

Frid, D. "Cheshskie Voennoplennye, Bor'be s Chekhoslovatskim Miatezhom" (Czech Prisoners-of-War, the Struggle with the Czechoslovak Insurrection), *Proletarskaia Revoliutsiia* (Proletarian Revolution), No. 76 (May, 1928), pp. 158–65.

Fukunami Sadao and Navy Captain Ishihara Kitao. Katō Kanji Taishō Den (Biography of Admiral Katō Kanji). Tokyo: Katō Kanji Taishō Denki Hensan-kai, 1941.

Germanov, I. (M. Frumkin). "K Istorii Chekho-Slovatskogo Nastupheniia i Sverzheniia Sovetskoi Vlasti v Sibiri" (Toward a History of the Czechoslovak Uprising and the Overthrow of the Soviet Power in Siberia), *Proletarskaia Revoliutsiia* (Proletarian Revolution), No. 4 (1922), pp. 16–23.

Hara Kei. Hara Kei Nikki (Diary of Hara Kei). Ed. Hara Kei'ichiro. Vols. I–IX. Tokyo: Kengensha, 1950–52.

House, Edward Mandell. Intimate Papers of Colonel House. Ed. Charles Seymour. Vols. I–IV. Boston: Houghton Mifflin, 1926–28.

Itō Masanori. Kokubō Shi (History of National Defense). Vol. IV in the series Kendai Nihon Bummei-shi (History of the Civilization of Modern Japan). Tokyo: Tōyō Keizai Shimpō-sha Shuppan-bu, 1941.

Itō Masanori, ed. Katō Kōmei. Vols. I–II. Tokyo: Katō Haku Denki Hensan Iin-kai, 1929.

Ivanov, M. "Oktiabr' v Sibiri: 1917 god v Kharbine" (October in Siberia: 1917 in Harbin), *Proletarskaia Revoliutsiia* (Proletarian Revolution), No. 10 (October, 1922), pp. 375–88.

Katakura Tōjiro. Fushi Terauchi Gensui (The Field Marshals Terauchi, Father and Son). Tokyo: Ajia Seinen-sha, 1944.

Kawatani Shitao. Tanaka Gi'ichi Den (Biography of Tanaka Gi'ichi). Tokyo: Tanaka Gi'ichi Den Sanjo, 1929.

Khabas, R. "K Istorii Bor'by s Chekhoslovatskim Miatezhom" (Toward a History of the Struggle with the Czechoslovak Insurrection), *Proletarskaia Revoliutsiia* (Proletarian Revolution), No. 76 (May, 1928), pp. 56–65.

Khaptaev, P. T. Buriat-Mongoliia v Period Oktiabr'skoi Revoliutsii (Buriat-Mongolia in the Period of the October Socialist Revolution). Ogiz, Irkutskoe Oblastnoe Izdatel'stvo, 1947.

"Khronika Sobytii na Tikhom Okeane 1914–1918 gg" (Chronology of Events in the Pacific Ocean Area, 1914–1918), *Tikhii Okean* (Pacific Ocean), III, No. 9 (July-September, 1936), 219–67.

Klark-Ansonova, A. "Drug" (Friend), in Vsesoiuznaia Kommunisticheskaia Partiia, Sergei Lazo, p. 47.

Kuribara Hirota. Hakushaku Itō Miyoji (Count Itō Miyoji). Vols. I–II. Tokyo: Shinteikai, 1938.

Kuroda Koshiro, ed. Gensui Terauchi Hakushaku Den (Biography of Field Marshal Count Terauchi). Tokyo: Gensui Terauchi Hakushaku Denki Hensansho, 1920.

Lazo, O. "Komanduiushchii Frontom" (Commander at the Front), in Vsesoiuznaia Kommunisticheskaia Partiia, Sergei Lazo, pp. 56–58.

Liu Yen. Ou-chan Ch'i-chien Chung-Jih Chiao-she Shih (A History of Sino-Japanese Negotiations during the European War). Shanghai: author, 1921.

Maksakov, V. V., and A. Turunov, eds. Khronika Grazhdanskoi Voiny v Sibiri (1917–1918) (Chronology of the Civil War in Siberia). Moscow: Gosizdat, 1926.

Matsushita Yoshio. Kindai Nihon Gunji-shi (History of Japan's Military Affairs in Modern Times). Tokyo: Kigen-sha, 1941.

Matveev, N. M. "Bor'ba za Sovety v Zabaikal'e" (Struggle for the Soviet in Trans-Baikal), in Vsesoiuznaia Kommunisticheskaia Partiia, Sergei Lazo, pp. 22–42.

Nabokov, K. D. Ispytaniia Diplomata. Stockholm, Severnye Ogni, 1921. Available in an English translation *The Ordeal of a Diplomat*. London: Duckworth & Co., 1921.

Nishihara Kamezō. Yume no Shichi-jū-yo-nen: Nishihara Kamezō Jiden (More Than 70 Dream-like Years: The Autobiography of Nishihara Kamezō). Comp. Murajima Nagisa. Kumobara Mura, 1949.

"Oktiabr' v Sibiri, I: Blagoveshchensk" (October in Siberia, I: Blagoveshchensk), the recorded words of "Comrade" Bodesko, *Proletarskaia Revoliutsiia* (Proletarian Revolution), No. 10 (October, 1922), pp. 362–65.

"Oktiabr' v Sibiri, II: Khabarovsk" (October in Siberia, II: Khabarovsk), the recorded words of "Comrade" Gavrilov, *Proletarskaia Revoliutsiia* (Proletarian Revolution), No. 10 (October, 1922), pp. 365–68.

"Oktiabr' v Sibiri, III: Vladivostok" (October in Siberia, III: Vladivostok), the recorded words of "Comrade" Kushnarev, *Proletarskaia Revoliutsiia* (Proletarian Revolution), No. 10 (October, 1922), pp. 370–5.

Ōtsu Jun'ichiro. Dai Nihon Kensei-shi (Constitutional History of Greater Japan). Vols. I–X. Tokyo: Hōbunkan, 1927.

Palmer, Frederick. Bliss, Peacemaker: The Life and the Letters of General Tasker Howard Bliss. New York: Dodd, Mead, 1934.

Parfenov, P. S. Uroki Proshlogo: Grazhdanskaia Voina v Sibiri 1918, 1919, 1920 gg. (Lessons of the Past: Civil War in Siberia, 1918, 1919, 1920). Harbin, 1921. Reissued with only minor changes, under the title *Grazhdanskaia Voina v Sibiri 1918–1920* (Civil War in Siberia, 1918–1920) (Moscow: Gosizdat, 1924), by the Komissiia po Istorii Oktiabr'skei Revoliutsii of the VKP(b) (Commission for the History of the October Revolution of the All-Union Communist Party [Bolshevik]).

Parfenov, V. The Intervention in Siberia in 1918–1922. New York: The Workers Library Publishers, 1941.

Pomerantseva, A. "V Krasnoiarske" (In Krasnoiarsk), in Vsesoiuznaia Kommunisticheskaia Partiia, Sergei Lazo, pp. 11–12.

Popov, K. A., ed. Dopros Kolchaka (The Examination of Kolchak). Leningrad: Gosizdat., 1925.

Pozdeev, P. "Sovetizatsiia Zabaikal'ia v Usloviiakh Interventsii 1918 g." (The Sovietization of Zabaikalia under the Conditions of Intervention, 1918), *Proletarskaia Revoliutsiia* (Proletarian Revolution), No. 34 (November, 1924), pp. 185–95.

Reikhberg, Georgii Evgen'evich. "Bol'sheviki Dal'nego Vostoka v Bor'be s Iaponskoi Interventsiei (1918–1922 gg.) (Bolsheviks of the Far East in the Struggle with the Japanese Intervention [1918–1922], *Proletarskaia Revoliutsiia* (Proletarian Revolution), No. 3 (1939), pp. 77–114.

——Iaponskaia Interventsiia na Dal'nem Vostoke, 1918–1922 gg. Kratkii ocherk (Japanese Intervention in the Far East, 1918–1922: Short Course). Moscow: Gosuradstvennoe Sotsial'no-Ekonomicheskoe Izdatel'stvo, 1935.

Sakatani Yoshiro, comp. Segai Inoue Kō Den (Biography of the Extraordinary Marquis Inoue). Vols. I–V. Tokyo, 1930.

Semenov, Grigorii Mikhailovich. O Sebe (About Myself). Harbin: Zaria, 1938.

Shōda Kazue. Kiku Bun Ne (The Spreading Roots of the Chrysanthemum). Privately published, 1918.

Shumiatskii, Boris. "Organizatsii S.-D. Bol'shevikov Sibiri v 1917 g." (Organization of the S-D Bolsheviks of Siberia in 1917). Introductory article in *Khronika Grazhdanskoi Voiny v Sibiri* (1917–1918), ed. Maksakov and Turunov, pp. 3–27.

Shumiatskii, Ia. "Ot Fevralia k Oktiabriu v Irkutske" (From February to October in Irkutske), *Katorga i Ssylka* (Forced Labor and Exile), LXXXVII (1932), 56–78.

Sibirskii Kraevoi Sovet Professional'nykh Soiuzov (Siberian Regional Soviet of Trade Unions). Profsoiuzy Sibiri v Bor'be za Vlast' Sovetov, 1917–1919 gg. (Trade Unions in the Struggle for Power of the Soviets, 1917–1919). Comp. V. Shemelev, ed. V. Vegman. Novosibirsk, 1928.

Smirnov, M. I. "Admiral Kolchak," *The Slavonic and East European Review*, XI, No. 32 (January, 1933), 373–87.

Sokolov, V. N. "Oktiabr za Baikalom (Ianvar-Fevral 1918 g.)" (October in Trans-Baikal [January-February, 1918]), *Proletarskaia Revoliutsiia* (Proletarian Revolution), No. 10 (October, 1922), pp. 389–91.

Sviderskii-Politovskii, T. "V Gostiakh u Chekhov" (A Guest of the Czechs), *Katorga i Ssylka*, CVIII (1933), 20–35.

Teodorovich, I. A., ed. Piatnadtsat' Let Oktiabria: Sbornik Statei iz Zhurnala *Katorga i Ssylka*, No. 11–12 za 1932 god. (Fifteenth Anniversary of October: Collection of Articles from the Magazine *Forced Labor and Exile*, Nos. 11 and 12, 1932). Moscow: Izdatel'stvo Vsesoiuznego Obshchestva Politicheskikh Katorzhan i Ssyl'noposelentsev, 1932.

Tokutomi I'ichiro, comp. Kōshaku Matsukata Masayoshi Den (Biography of Prince Matsukata Masayoshi). Vols. I–II. Tokyo: Kōshaku Matsukata Masayoshi Denki Hensan-kai, 1935.

——Kōshaku Yamagata Aritomo Den (Biography of Prince Yamagata Aritomo). Vols. I–III. Tokyo: Yamagata Aritomo Kō Kinen Jigyōkai, 1933.

Tsurumi Yusukc. Gotō Shimpei. Vols. I–IV. Tokyo: Gotō Shimpei Denki Hensan-Kai, 1938.

Velt'man, V. "Fevral'skaia Revoliutsiia v Sibiri" (February Days in Siberia), *Proletarskaia Revolutsiia* (Proletarian Revolution), No. 38 (March, 1925), pp. 167–200.

Vilenskii-Sibiriakov, V. "Bor'ba za Sovetskii Sibir'" (Struggle for a Soviet Siberia), *Severnaia Aziia* (Northern Asia), 1926, pp. 47–66.

——Chernaia Godina Sibirskoi Reaktsii: Interventsiia v Sibiri (Evil Times of the Siberian Reaction: Intervention in Siberia). Moscow: V.Ts.I.K. Sovetov R.S.K.i. K Deputatov, 1919.

Wang Yun-sheng. Liu Shih Nien Lai Chung Kuo Yu Jih Pen (Sixty Years of Sino-Japanese Relations). Vols. I–VIII. Tientsin: Ta Kung Pao, 1932–34.

White, John Albert. The Siberian Intervention. Princeton: Princeton University Press, 1950.

Zaidan Hōjin Kaigun Yūshū-kai, comp. Kinsei Teikoku Kaigun Shiyō (Short History of the Imperial Navy in Modern Times). Tokyo: comp., 1938.

INDEX

Abo, Rear Admiral, 62
Achinsk, 35
Adrianovka, 77, 85
Advisory Council on Foreign Relations, *see under* Japan
Agarev, mayor of Vladivostok, 169
Aga Station, 194
Aksha, 185
Alekshin, agent for Japan, 80
Alexandrov, member of the Far Eastern Committee, 84
Alexandrovich, Michael, 257*n*
Allied Supreme War Council: urges United States to approve Japanese expedition, 134–35, 262; urges Japan to send expedition, 223, 225–32
Allies, 3–4; Japan's negotiations with, 28–35, 122–35, 213–32, 296–307; importance of Vladivostok to, 38–40; action at Harbin against Bolsheviks, 40–48; Motono's desire to conciliate, 56; negotiations with anti-Bolsheviks, 87–109, 168, 180, 353; pressure on United States, 133–35; attitude toward landing of Japanese marines at Vladivostok, 147; and Soviet government, 221–23; and support of Czechoslovaks, 239–53; *see also* France, Great Britain, Italy, Japan
All-Russian Constituent Assembly, 71–72
All-Siberian Cooperative Congress (Jan., 1918), 73
American Advisory Commission of Railway Experts, 123–24, 177
Amur basin, 4, 5 (*map*): Japan's interests in, 37, 40–41; China's and Russia's interests in, 40–41; Motono's plan for military expedition into, 55; Japanese intelligence officers in, 69; revolutionary conditions in, 69–72; Japanese army in, 309

Amur Cossacks, 69–71, 77–82, 109, 254–55; *see also* Gamov
Amur Railway, 176, 356–58
Amur Territory, Horvat's concessions to Japan in, 179–80; *see also* Chita; Soviet governments in Amur Basin
Andreev, Russian agent, 49, 79
Anfu clique, 114, 115
Ansho Jun'ichi, 209
Anti-Bolshevik organizations in Siberia, 4, 106; in southern Russia, 34; Siberian regionalists conference at Tomsk, 72–73; Far Eastern Committee, 84–85; in Trans-Baikal Territory, 85–87; activities in Amur basin, 87–109; Nakajima's evaluation of, 107–8; provisional duma at Tomsk, 108; and China, 110–11, 189–90; use of, against German expansion into Siberia, 125; attitude of British and French toward, 127; west Siberian army at Omsk, 237; Union for the Regeneration of Russia, 239–40; aid supplied by Allies to, 353; ordnance supplied to, by Japan, 354–55; *see also* Andreev; Czechoslovaks; Derber; Gamov; Horvat; Kaledin; Kalmykov; Kolchak; Semenov
Aoki Nobuzumi, 53
Aoshima (ship), 252
Araki Sadao, 97; Nakajima's conference with, 106; and Semenov, 209–10; and Horvat, 255; and Pflug, 258
Aralov, N., 235
Arima Ryokitsu, 104, 151
Arita Hachiro, 217, 295
Arkus, member of Harbin Soviet, 46
Army, Japanese, *see under* Japan
Army General Staff Headquarters, *see* Japan; Army
Asahi (ship), 3, 62, 63
Asakage (ship), 3, 253

Austria-Hungary, 3, 162, 165; effect of Russian Revolution on, 28, 32; see also Prisoners of war in Siberia

Balakshin, A. A., 240n
Balfour, Arthur James, 29; attitude toward Foch plan, 33; attitude toward Bolsheviks at Vladivostok, 39–40; and Chinda, 222–26, 230–31
Baliasin, Bolshevik leader in Trans-Baikal Territory, 81, 81n
Bank of Korea, 14, 18
Bargut Mongols, 44
Barnaul, 35
Beneš, Edvard, 234, 239
Berezovskii, commandant of Dauriia stockade, 45
Bion de la Pomarède, French military attaché in China, 91
Black Ocean Society (or Gen'yōsha), 48
Blagoveshchensk, 35, 75, 80, 108, 343
Bolsheviks: seizure of power in central Siberian cities, 35; tactics in seizing power, 38, 73–74; in Vladivostok, 38, 51, 105, 156–60; in Harbin 41–42, 45–48, 51; attitude of Japanese army toward, in Maritime Territory, 51; limited appeal of, in Amur basin, 71–72; support in election to Russian Constituent Assembly, 71; coalition with left-wing Social Revolutionaries, 73–75; in Khabarovsk, 74; in Blagoveshchensk, 75, 108; in Irkutsk, 75; in Chita, 80–82; authority in Amur basin, 108–9; attitude toward Vladivostok landings, 148; attitude of Japanese navy toward, in Vladivostok, 159–60; activity among Czechoslovaks, 234–35; see also entries beginning Soviet
Borodavkin, V., 196
Borzia, 193, 197
Brest-Litovsk, Treaty of, 157, 191
Brooklyn (ship), 3, 65, 143
Brusilov, A. A., 44
Budberg, Aleksei, 255n
Buriat Mongols, 43–44, 70, 208
Butin, I. A., 185

Cabinet, Japanese, see under Japan
Caldwell, John K., 263

Caucasian peoples, 32
Cecil, Lord Robert, 60; and Chinda, 128, 222, 231, 243, 296
Central Executive Committee: Far Eastern Regional, at Khabarovsk, 74, 160; Siberian ('Tsentrosibir'), at Irkutsk, 109, 149, 184; of Trans-Baikal Territory, at Chita, 184; see also Soviet governments in Amur basin
Čerensky, and charges of Allied complicity in the Czechoslovak uprising, 238
Chang Tsung-hsiang, 114, 116–17, 119–21, 188
Chechikov, Russian businessman, 176
Cheliabinsk, 93, 235–36, 240–41; as objective of Japanese expedition desired by Britain and France, 128–29, 132–33, 227–28, 229–32
Ch'en Ch'i-mei, 13
Chin, General, 188
China: ship to Vladivostok, 3–4; and Horvat, 45–48, 110–11, 189–91; troops to Harbin, 45–48, 83; and Semenov, 110–12, 180–81, 183–84, 199, 207–12; troops to Chinese Eastern Railway Zone, 110–11; troops to Outer Mongolia and Sinkiang, 110; negotiations with soviet forces on Manchurian border, 111–13, 180, 183–84, 207–8, 361–62; see also Chinese Eastern Railway; Chinese Eastern Railway Zone; and specific persons and places
——relations with Japan: "twenty-one demands," 12–13, 164; Japanese support for local revolts against Yuan Shih-k'ai, 13–14; economic coalition plans and "Nishihara loans," 14–15, 15n, 27, 53, 114–15, 120–21, 188–89; Japanese support for Tuan Ch'i-jui, 14–15, 27, 113, 115, 120; negotiations for Joint Defensive Military and Naval Agreements, 14–15, 52–53, 113–21, 161–65, 188–89, 292–93, 363–67; Terauchi government's coalition policy, 14–15, 18; effect of Russian Revolution on, 37, 317; negotiations concerning Semenov, 209–12; negotiations concerning Siberian expedition, 292–93
China League (Tai-Shi Rengōkai), 13

Chinda Sutemi: negotiations with Allies, 33, 88; attitude toward Bolsheviks at Vladivostok, 39–40; and Lord Robert Cecil, 61, 128, 222, 243, 296; considered as successor to Motono, 213; and Balfour, 222-26, 230–31

Chinese Eastern Railway, 29; Chinese troops and, 85; Horvat and, 100, 189–91, 268; Japan's desire to control, 106, 176–80, 203, 292, 297, 344; U. S. agreement with, 123–24, 177; China's fear that Japan might take over, 165; administration chain of command (late April, 1918), 175; board of directors reorganized as shadow Russian government, 189–91

Chinese Eastern Railway Zone, 41, 45–46; Japan's plans for sending troops to, 103, 340–45

Chin Yün-p'eng, 53

Chita, 35; activities of Bolsheviks in, 75–82; Semenov's offensive against, 85; Japan's plans for sending troops to, 103, 340–45

Chōshū clan clique, 8–27, *passim*; influence in Terauchi's cabinet, 18; views on foreign policy, 23–27; representatives on Advisory Council on Foreign Relations, 26; attitude toward European Russia expedition, 31–32; and Siberian expedition, 48–49, 50; attitude toward Motono's negotiations, 137; concern over America's opposition to intervention, 141–42; and Goto, 218–19; reaction to American proposal for Siberian expedition, 264–74; power of, 310; loss of control, 312

Chronology, 315–22

Chu T'ung-feng, 53

Clan cliques, Japanese, 8–27, 310; Hizen, 8–10; Satsuma, 8–10, 20, 26, 155; Tosa, 8–10; *see also* Chōshū clan clique

Clemenceau, Georges, 34

Cliques, Japanese, *see* Clan cliques; Shidehara clique; "Teidai"; Zaibatsu

Congress of Soviets: Third Far Eastern Regional, at Khabarovsk, 74; Third East Siberian, at Irkutsk, 75; Second All-Siberian, at Irkutsk, 109, 184; *see also* Soviet governments in Amur basin

Constituent Assembly, All-Russian, 71–72

Cooperative Congress, All-Siberian, 73

Corbeil, Colonel, 240

Cossacks, 32; and Bolsheviks, 76–82; Nakajima and, 77–82; Japan's dependence on, 109; *see also* Amur Cossacks; Trans-Baikal Cossacks; Ussuri Cossacks

Council of People's Commissars (Sovnarkom): Far Eastern Regional, at Khabarovsk, 74; Siberian, at Irkutsk, 109, *see also* Soviet governments in Amur basin

Crabbe, secretary at the Russian legation in Peking, 175

Czechoslovaks in Siberia, 3–4, 32; uprising of, 233–42; and Allied support of, 239–53, 260–90; and Japan, 243–47, 306–8, 355; Nikol'sk falls to, 252; movement against Amur basin, 258; and Semenov, 258–59; differences between Horvat and, 268–69; for relations with individual countries, *see under* specific countries

Dauriia, 45, 111–12, 193

Declaration of London, *see* London, Declaration of

Den Kenjiro, 16, 18, 137, 298

Denny, Captain, 87

Derber, Peter, 167–72, 249–50, 256

Diet, Japanese, *see under* Japan

Dietrichs, M. K., 236, 245; requests aid of Japan, 246, 250; in Vladivostok, 247; and Horvat, 269

Domanevskii, Lieutenant General, 83, 94

Dōshikai (political party), 16

Dragovich, Lieutenant Colonel, 181

Dunlop, Major, 79, 95, 96

Economic assistance to Siberia: planned by Japan, 217–18, 293–96; planned by United States, 294

Economic concessions: reported sought by Japan from Horvat, 106–7, 176–80; reported sought by United States in Russian Far East, 122–25, 177–78, 215–16, 293–94

Eikō Wan, 151

Elder statesmen, *see* Genro

Emerson, George H., 124
Expansionist societies, 48, 102
Expeditions: Amur basin, as limit of Japanese activity, 128, 220, 222, 227–28, 230; European Russia, discussed, 29–36, 325–28; Irkutsk, proposed by France, 89–91; Vladivostok, see Vladivostok; West Siberia, desired by Allies, 127–29, 132–33, 219–32
Ezerski, Count, 87

Far Eastern Committee for the Defense of the Fatherland and the Constituent Assembly, 84–85, 94, 101, 106, 109, 174, 353
First World War: and Russian Revolution, 28; Vladivostok in, 38
Foch, Ferdinand, proposal for Japanese expedition to European Russia, 32–33, 89, 128, 325–28
Foreign Ministry, Japanese, see under Japan
France: threat of Russian Revolution to, 28, 31–32; and Soviet authorities in Moscow, 34, 157, 186, 221; supports Semenov and the Far Eastern Committee, 91, 99–100, 185–86, 353; and Czechoslovak Corps, 233, 235, 238–53; see also Allies
——relations with Great Britain, 31–35, 89, 127–29, 185–86; see also under Allied Supreme War Council; Allies
——relations with Japan: early French interest in Japanese expedition, 29; Foch plan for joint intervention, 31–35; French proposal of Irkutsk expedition, 89–91; concerning Semenov, 99–100; French support of Motono proposal, 126–29; see also Allied Supreme War Council; Allies
——relations with United States, see under United States
Fujita Hisanori, 62n
Fushimi Sadayoshi, 63

Gaida, Staff Captain, 237, 240
Gamov, Ataman, 80, 255, 255n
Genro (elder statesmen), 8–10, 19,

155, 156n, 269–74; see also Matsukata Masayoshi; Ōkuma Shigenobu; Saionji Kimmochi; Yamagata Aritomo
Gen'yōsha (or Black Ocean Society), 48
Germany: colonies in Asia, Japan's claims to, 15; advantages from Russian Revolution to, feared by Allies, 28, 32; Japan's refusal to join Soviet authorities in peace negotiations with, 33–34; Japan's fear of, in Far East, 94, 114–15, 118, 125, 131–33, 139–40, 182, 202, 214, 222–23, 225, 246; Allies' fear of Japanese coalition with, 129; Russia's peace with, at Brest-Litovsk, 157; in Sino-Japanese defense agreements, 162, 165; see also Prisoners of war in Siberia
Glukharev, B., 257
Gotō Shimpei: and Japan's Chinese policy, 15n, 16; appointed home minister, 18; and election of diet, 22, 23; and Japan's foreign policy, 24; member of Advisory Council on Foreign Relations, 26; and Motono's policy, 137; successor to Motono as foreign minister, 156; attitude toward United States, 213–21, 264–67; policy of "aggressive defense," 213–19; attitude toward Siberian expedition, 269–83; and meeting of Advisory Council (July 16), 274–83; revision of draft agreement, 283–85; and draft declaration, 287; and Morris, 297; reaction to American reply to declaration, 300
Graves, William S., cited, 6
Great Britain: ships at Vladivostok, 3–4, 60–67, 143–46; effect of Bolshevik Revolution on, 28; rejection of Foch plan, 33–34; policy of supporting anti-German regimes in Russia, 34–35, 127, 186, 223; and Soviet authorities in Moscow, 34, 157–58, 186, 221; and Kalmykov, 79–80, 95–97, 166–67; and Semenov, 87–88, 92–95, 99–100, 185–86; landing of marines at Vladivostok, 147; and Derber, 168, 249; and Kolchak, 191–92, 198, 204–205,

207; and Czechoslovak uprising, 242–53; see also Allies

——relations with France, 31–35, 89, 127–29, 185–86; see also under Allied Supreme War Council; Allies

——relations with Japan: early British interest in Japanese expedition to European Russia, 29; concerning expedition to Siberia, 31–35, 122–26, 131–33, 140–42, 221–25; concerning the sending of ships to Vladivostok, 39–40; concerning Semenov, 88, 99–100, 186, 222–23, 225, 231; concerning Kalmykov 95–97, 166–67; concerning Japanese landings at Vladivostok, 147, 157–58; concerning Kolchak, 172, 204–6; concerning possibility of Soviet invitation to intervene, 221–23; see also Allied Supreme War Council; Allies; Balfour; Cecil; Greene

——relations with United States, see under United States

Greene, Sir Connyngham, 39, 97, 132, 133

Grishin-Almazov, Colonel, 237

Grodekovo, 166, 256, 268

Gubel'man, Bolshevik political commissar of forces on the Trans-Baikal front, 196

Gunji kyodo i'in-kai, see Japan: Siberia Planning Committee

Hai Jung (ship), 3

Hailar, 109

Halainor, falls to Semenov, 193

Hara Kei: head of Seiyūkai, 19, 24, 273–74; member of Advisory Council on Foreign Relations, 25, 26; noninterventionist views, 58, 137, 155, 224, 228–29, 269–74, 278–79, 282–85, 298; on American proposal, 305–6, 307; becomes premier, 312

Harbin: Bolshevik activity in, 35–36; Allied action against Bolsheviks at, 40–48; conditions in 1918, 83; Semenov in, 92–95, 105–6; Americans in, 124; Horvat and Kolchak at, 204–7; Japanese troops to be sent to, 331, 336, 342

Hayashi Gonsuki, 120, 177, 188, 253, 268

Heilungkiang Province, 110, 208

Hioki Masu, 14

Hirata Tōsuke, Chōshū leader in House of Peers, 10, 14, 21; and Japan's foreign policy, 24; member of Advisory Council on Foreign Relations, 26, 59; attitude toward Siberian expedition, 138–39, 154, 228, 269, 279

Hirota Kōki, 217, 295

Hirota Morinobu, 295n

Hizen (ship), 105, 151, 153

Hizen clan clique, 8–10

Horvat, Dmitrii Leonidovich, 41–42, 45–47, 83, 109; and Semenov, 100–101, 198; Nakajima and, 106–8; Allies' support of, 169; attitude toward, in Vladivostok, 169–70; relations with Japan, 171–80, 201–3, 231–32, 297; conference in Peking, 189–91; and Kolchak, 206; proclamation of a government by, 253–58; differences between Czechoslovaks and, 268–69

House, E. M., 33, 34

Ijūin Hikokichi, 296

Iman, 79, 95–97, 166

I-mien-p'o, 254

Imperial Reserve Association, 102

Inagaki, General, 29

Independents, in Japanese politics, 20–23

Inostrantsev, General, 240

Intelligence organization, Japanese, reconnaissance in Siberia, 60–82

Inter-Allied Conference at Paris (Nov. 29–Dec. 3, 1917), 29, 31–35, 325–28

Inter-Allied expedition: proposed by Foch, 29–35; to Vladivostok, urged by Britain, 60–61; Allied hopes for Soviet invitation for, 157–59, 221–22, 226; idea of, accepted by Gotō, 218–19; discussed by Japan and United States, 219–21; Japan's participation in, requested by Allied Supreme War Council (q.v.), 225–26; discussed by Advisory Council on

Inter-Allied expedition (*Cont.*)
Foreign Relations, 227–29; proposed by United States, 260–64; effect of Czechoslovak uprising on, 242–45; and Japan-United States negotiations, 296–307; *see also* Allies; Japan

Interventionists: versus noninterventionists, 56–59, 141, 232; and American proposal, 265, 266–67, 269–74, 307–8; attitude toward the West, 311–12; *see also* Gotō Shimpei; Ōshima Ken'ichi; Tanaka Gi'ichi; Terauchi Masatake; Uehara Yūsaku

Inukai Tsuyoshi: leader of the Kokumintō party, 21, 22, 24; member of Advisory Council on Foreign Relations, 25, 26; attitude toward Siberian expedition, 228, 269, 276–77, 280–81; on American proposal, 305–6

Irkutsk, 35, 70; falls to Bolsheviks, 75; Third Congress of East Siberian Soviets at, 75; France proposes expedition to, 89–91; Second All-Siberian Congress of Soviets at, 109, 184; Siberian Council of People's Commissars at, 109; as westernmost limit of Japanese military action, 128, 220, 222, 227–28, 230; Central Executive Committee of Siberian Soviets, 149; falls to Czechoslovaks, 258

Ishii Kikujiro: as foreign minister of Japan, 12; as ambassador in United States, 219–21

Ishimitsu Makiyo, 80

Ishinkai (political party), 23, 26

Italy, 34, 134, 296

Itō Bunkichi, 294

Itō Hirobumi, 24, 155

Itō Miyoji, 24–25; member of Advisory Council on Foreign Relations, 26; supports Motono's plan, 57–58, 137, 139; declines to be foreign minister, 213; drafts reply to Allied proposal for Inter-Allied expedition, 224, 229; urges acceptance of American proposal with "understandings," 266, 269, 276*n*, 281–85; helps Gotō redraft declaration, 288–90; brings Japanese government to decision on expedition despite U.S. objections, 299–307

Iwami (ship), 3, 62, 63

Iwasaki Yataro, 20

Japan: archives as source material, 6–7; government of, 7; clan cliques and political parties in, 8–27; secret treaty with Russia (*1916*), 12, 36; foreign policy and the Chōshū clique, 23–27; initial attitude toward October Revolution, 28–35; interests in Asiatic Russia, 36–37; problems raised by Russian Revolution, 36–38; Motono's plans for Siberian expedition, 53–56; initial opposition and support of Siberian expedition, 56–59; activity in Vladivostok, 65–67; and Semenov, 92–95, 97–100, 105–6; and Horvat, 106–8, 253–58; attitude toward Kalmykov, 166–67; attitude toward Derber group, 168–72; and Kolchak, 189–93, 204–7; economic planning and formation of a Siberian economic assistance committee, 217–18, 293–96; and Czechoslovaks, 243–47; 252; decision on Siberian expedition forced, 260–90; problem of priority, whether to relations with the West or to interests in Asia, 310–13; *see also under* specific names of persons, places, and subjects

——*Advisory Council on Foreign Relations (Rinji Gaikō Chōsa I'inkai*): organized, 23–27; rejects expedition to European Russia, 31; deliberates on Siberian expedition, 57–59, 122, 136–42, 224–25, 227–29, 269–90, 303–6; deliberates on reply to U.S. note of March 5, 136–42; informed about naval units to Vladivostok, 136; and Semenov, 183; accepts military agreements with China, 189; deliberates on reply to U.S. proposal for joint expedition, 274–85; deliberates on declaration to announce expedition, 286, 289–90; deliberates on reply to U.S. objections of July 25, 303–6; *see also* Gotō Shimpei; Hara Kei; Hirata Tōsuke; Inukai Tsuyoshi; Itō Miyoji; Katō Tomosaburo; Makino

Shinken, Motono Ichiro; Ōshima Ken'ichi; Terauchi Masatake
——*Army:* influence of, 11–15, 18–19; representatives on Advisory Council on Foreign Relations, 26; views regarding expedition to European Russia, 30–31, 227–28; plans for sending expeditions to north Manchuria and Siberia, 50–53, 101–6, 162–87, 267, 309, 329–58; negotiations with China and Joint Defensive Military Agreement, 52–53, 113–21, 161–65, 188–89, 292–93, 363–65; Japanese intelligence officers to China, 69; mobilization plan, 103, 104, 337, 341; plans for cooperation with navy, 104–5, 338–39, 342; problems of, preparatory to expedition, 161–87; and Semenov, 180–87, 199–203, 207–12; and Horvat, 201–3; proposal to secure control of Chinese Eastern Railway, 201–3; and Czechoslovaks, 254–59; and Terauchi, 291–93; *see also* Japan: Siberia Planning Committee; Kuroki Shinkei; Mutō Nobuyoshi; Nakajima Masatake; Ōshima Ken'ichi; Sakabe Tosuho; Tanaka Gi'ichi; Uehara Yūsaku
——*Cabinet,* 7; Terauchi's, 15–18; "transcendent" and "party," 19, approves army's rejection of European Russia expedition, 30–31; approves army's proposal to seek control of Chinese Eastern Railway, 203; decision on Siberian expedition, 266–67; refusal to revise declaration, 302–3; approval of revised declaration, 306
——*Diet,* 7; political parties in thirty-eighth, 20; in thirty-ninth, 23; representatives on Advisory Council on Foreign Relations, 26; Motono's speech to, 141
——*Foreign Ministry,* 10, 18, 26, 53–56, 217; *see also* Gotō Shimpei, Motono Ichiro
——*foreign relations, see under* Allied Supreme War Council; Allies; China; France; Gotō Shimpei; Great Britain; Motono Ichiro; Russia; United States
——*Navy:* ships at Vladivostok, 3–4, 39–40, 48, 60–65, 104–5, 143–46; representatives on Advisory Council on Foreign Relations, 26; marine landings at Vladivostok, 62, 66, 104, 105, 146–51; attitude toward Bolsheviks, 64; plans for cooperation with army, 104–5, 338–39, 342; negotiations with China and Joint Defensive Naval Agreement, 189, 366–67; support from, in Czechoslovak seizure of Vladivostok, 250–53
——*Privy Council,* 7; representatives on Advisory Council on Foreign Relations, 26; approves joint defensive agreements with China, 189
——*Siberia Planning Committee (gunji kyōdō i'in-kai):* organization of, 101–2; and prerequisites for Siberian expedition, 102–6; and Sino-Japanese military alliance, 116; and Sakabe's organization in Vladivostok, 166; and American proposal, 265, 287–90; agenda preparatory to Siberian expedition, 336–37; plan for sending an emergency detachment to Vladivostok, 338–39
——*Temporary Siberian Economic Assistance Committee,* 293–96
Japan Young Men's Association, 102
Jezierski, Count, 191
Joint Siberia Planning Committee, *see* Japan, Siberia Planning Committee
Jordan, Sir John, 168, 186
Jusserand, Jean Jules, 89–90, 133, 239*n*

Kadet party, 71, 76
Kaledin, A. M., 34
Kalmykov, Ivan, 80; flight of, 95–97; and Ussuri Cossacks, 109; failure of, 166–67, 206, 255, 256; ordnance supplied to, by Japan, 355
Kamchatka Bay, 123, 124
Kamigawa Maru (ship), 62
Kanai Kiyoshi, 177
Kantō (ship), 105, 153, 338
Karachens, 44
Karakhan, Lev, 159
Karymskaia, 76, 194
Katō Kanji (Hiroharu): commands squadron at Vladivostok, 62–65; "silent pressure" at Vladivostok, 65–67, 142–46; lands troops at Vladi-

Katō Kanji (*Continued*)
vostok, 146–51, 153; attitude toward
Derber, 171; quoted, 216; and Czechoslovaks, 245–46, 250–53
Katō Kōmei: as foreign minister, 11–
12, 13; rejected for premiership, 15–
16, 17; heads Kenseikai party, 20;
and the three-party declaration on
foreign policy (*1916*), 24; refuses to
join Advisory Council on Foreign
Relations, 25; and opposition to
Terauchi government, 298
Katori (ship), 105, 151
Katō Sadakichi, 62
Katō Tomosaburo, 18; member of Advisory Council on Foreign Relations,
26; agress to sending ship to Vladivostok, 62; attitude toward Motono's
negotiations, 138–39; restrains landing forces, 152–54
Kawakami Toshihiko, 106
Kenseikai (political party), 20–23, 25,
273
Kerensky, A. F., 44, 86, 240n
Khabarovsk, 35; Japanese forces to be
sent to, 51–52, 103, 331, 332, 340,
342, 343; taken over by soviet au-
thority, 74; Far Eastern Regional
Council of People's Commissars at,
74; Third Far Eastern Regional
Congress of Soviets at, 74; Far East-
ern Executive Committee at, 148
Khalka, 43
Khobdo, 110
Kiakhta, 110
Kiev, Czechoslovaks in, 234
Kikuchi Giro, 65–66, 95–96, 146, 147,
246
Kimura Ei'ichi, 217, 294–96
Kirgizov, Bolshevik leader in Chita, 81
Kirin, 110
Kirin-Changchun railway-loan agree-
ment, 115
Knight, A. M., to Vladivostok, 65;
urges Japanese reinforcements, 143;
supports Japanese landing, 146–47;
confers on Czechoslovak seizure of
Vladivostok, 247–48; supports Czech-
oslovak advance, 250, 252–53, 261,
263
Kodama Hideo, 298
Koike Chōzō, 13, 99

Kokuminto (political party), 20–23, 26,
273, 280
Kolchak, Alexander, 86–87; and Japan,
109, 189–93; and Semenov, 198–99;
fiasco of, 204–7
Konovalov, member of board of di-
rectors of Russo-Asiatic Bank, 191
Konshin, Captain, 240
Korea, Germany and, 32
Korean People, Central Headquarters
of the, 151n
Kornilov, General L. G., 44
Krasnoiarsk, 35
Krasnoshchekov, A. M., 160
Krupenskii, B. H.: and Kolchak, 191;
and appeal to Horvat, 268
Kudashev, Prince: and the Far East-
ern Committee, 84, 100–101; and
the British, 87–88; and Semenov,
87–88, 100–101; and the Japanese,
88; and Derber, 168; and Horvat,
168, 190; and the Chinese, 190; and
Kolchak, 191
Kuenga, 125
Kuhara *zaibatsu*, 13, 98–99
Kulikov, V. V., 240n
Kulusutai, 185
Kuo Tsung-hsi, 100, 189–90, 191
Kurihara Ken, 54n
Kuroki Shinkei, 92, 174, 197n, 211
Kurozawa Jun, 83, 92–93, 106, 180,
211
Kurskii, M., 256–57
Kurtovskii, V. M., 237
Kwantung Government General (of
Kwantung Leased Territory), 51,
267, 329–31, 334–35, 340–41, 346–
50
Kyūshū, 10

Lansing, Robert, 216, 219–21, 260–61
Lansing-Ishii agreement (Nov., *1917*),
15, 27
Lavergne, General, and the Czechoslovaks, 240, 243
Lazo, Sergei, 81; in charge of front
against Semenov, 85, 184, 195–97;
and Lin Fu-man, 111–12; agreement
between command of Chinese troops
and, 361–62; *see also* Soviet military
forces in Amur basin
Lebedev, V. I., 240

Lenin, V. I., telegram to Vladivostok Soviet, 149–50
Liang, Chinese minister of finance, 120
Lin Fu-man, 111
Lloyd-George, David, 34
Lockhart, R. H. B., 157, 221, 240
London, Declaration of: Japan's adherence to, 12; Russia's responsibilities under, 28, 34
Lu Cheng-hsiang, 115, 120, 164, 188
Lu Tsung-yü, 14, 115

Machida Kei'u, 13*n*
Maimaichen, 110
Makino Shinken, 10; member of Advisory Council on Foreign Relations, 26; noninterventionist views, 58–59, 137, 228, 272, 279–80, 286, 305–6, 307
Manchouli, 41; Semenov at, 46; Japanese matériel to be sent to, 99, 342, 344; Chinese troops to, 110
Manchuria, 5 (*map*); Prince Su's rebellion in, 14
Manchuria, northern: international agreements concerning, 40–41; Japan's plans to send troops into, 51–52, 101–6, 297, 329–31, 340–45; Japanese intelligence officers in, 69; Chinese in, 110–13; in Sino-Japanese defense agreement, 162, 164, 292
Maritime Territory, 5 (*map*), 43; Japan's plans to send troops into, 51–52, 101 6, 267, 329–33, 336, 340–52; efforts to drive Bolsheviks out of, 95–97, 257–58; *see also* Blagoveshchensk; Vladivostok; *and under entries beginning* Soviet
Markov, Social Revolutionary party leader, 240
Masaryk, Thomas G., 233–34, 239, 244
Matsievskaia Station, 111, 183
Matsui Keishiro: at Inter-Allied Conference at Paris, 33; and Pichon, 127–28, 296
Matsukata Masayoshi, 9–10, 155, 272
Matsumoto Osamu, 294
Matsuoka Yōsuke, 53, 217, 295
Matsushima Hajime, 53
Matveev, N. M., 185, 197*n*
Megata Tanetaro, 294

Meiji constitution, 309–10
Mensheviks, 41, 46, 78
Mikhailov, I. A., 237
Military, influence of the, in Japan, 11–15, 18–19; *see also* Japan: Army, Navy
Miliukov, Paul, 239
Minobe Shunkichi, 294
Mitsubishi *zaibatsu*, 20
Mitsui *zaibatsu*, 20
Miura Goro, 10, 24, 137, 154, 273
Mongolia, 5 (*map*), 14; Japanese intelligence officers in, 69; Japanese plans to send troops into central, 103, 336, 341; Chinese troops to Outer, 110; eastern, in Sino-Japanese military agreement, 162, 164
Moravskii, leader in Derber movement, 167
Mori Mikage, 106
Morris, Roland, 125–26, 297
Moscow, Czechoslovaks in, 234
Moser, Charles, 42, 107, 194*n*
Motono Ichiro: named foreign minister, 18; member of Advisory Council on Foreign Relations, 26; attitude toward expedition to European Russia, 31; his cliques plans for Siberian expedition, 53–56; and British naval vessel at Vladivostok, 61; attitude toward support of Semenov, 98–99; attitude toward Sino-Japanese coalition, 116, 117–21; negotiations with Allies, 122–35; Advisory Council on Foreign Relations and, 136–42; and landing of marines at Vladivostok, 145–46; replaced, 155–56
Muling, 206
Muramatsu Sen'ichiro, 48*n*
Murav'ev, Colonel, 44
Mushakoji Kimitomo, 54*n*
Mu-tan-kiang Station, 329, 341
Mutō Nobuyoshi, 174, 176–80, 197*n*, 208–9, 336

Nabokov, K. D., 29
Nagai, Colonel, 127
Nakajima Masatake: mission to Siberia, 67–69, 336; arrival in Vladivostok, 74; and Cossacks, 77–82; and Semenov, 94–95; in Harbin, 106; and Horvat, 106–8, 173; and Kol-

Nakajima Masatake (*Continued*) chak, 204–5; negotiations with railways, 293
Nakakoji Ren, 16–18
Nakamura Takashi, 295
Nakano Jiro, 48–49, 98
Natsvalov, Colonel, 194
Navy, Japanese, *see under* Japan
Nikiforov, leader of the Vladivostok soviet, 160
Nikitin, Colonel, 84, 94, 109
Nikolaevich, Russian businessman in Vladivostok, 176
Nikol'sk-Ussuriisk, 51; Japan's plans for sending troops to, 103, 332, 340; importance of, to anti-Bolsheviks, 250; falls to Czechoslovaks, 252; Horvat at, 255–56; Japanese supply system and, 333
Nishihara Kamezō: negotiations with China, 14, 18, 27, 115–16, 119–21; and proposal of a Siberian expedition, 48–50; and Semenov, 91–92, 98–99
Noda Utarō, 21
Noriyoshi, Yokoo, 80
North Manchuria, *see* Manchuria, northern
Noninterventionists: versus interventionists, 56–59, 269–74; capitulation of, 310; attitude toward the West, 311–12; *see also* Hara Kei; Makino Shinken
Noulens, Joseph, 240
Novo-Nikolaevsk, 73, 167

Obata Yukichi, 14, 294
Oishi Masashi, 49*n*
Oka Ichinosuke, 13*n*
Okorokov, A., 257
Ōkuma Shigenobu: resignation from premiership (*1916*), 11, 15; proposes Katō-Terauchi cabinet, 17; business and clan allies of, 20; inactive as genro, 156*n*
Okumura Naonari, 209
Okura *zaibatsu*, 13
Oloviannaia, 76–77, 85, 193, 197
O.M.O. (Osoboi Man'chzhurskii Otriad —Special Manchurian Detachment, 181; *see also* Semenov

Omsk, 35, 237–38
Onon river, Semenov's offensive to, 193–201
Oparin, Staff Captain, 45
Orlov, Captain, 174, 198
Ōshima Ken'ichi: war minister, 18; member of Advisory Council on Foreign Relations, 26; and Motono's plan, 59; on reconnaissance in Siberia, 68–69; on Japanese support of Horvat and Semenov, 203; and American proposal, 265, 269, 277–78, 291–92
Osoboi Man'chzhurskii Otriad, *see* O.M.O.
Otani Masao, 48
Outer Mongolia, *see under* Mongolia

Pao, military governor of Heilungkiang Province, 208, 209
Paris, Inter-Allied Conference at, 31–35
Patushinskii, G. B., 237
Peking: Russian diplomatic authorities at, 106, 109; Japan's military representatives in, 113–14; Japanese delegations to, 161; Horvat conference in, 189–91; Allied ministers in, 268
Pelliot, Captain, 91
Penza, 235
People's Commissars, Council of, *see* Council of People's Commissars
Pflug, V., 257, 268
Pichon, Stephen, 127–28, 130, 296
P'ing Kuo-chang, 53
Pleshkov, General, 174, 178, 198, 205, 206
Pogranichnaia, 41, 96, 97 166
Political parties: in Japan, 8–27, 310; *see also* Dōshikai; Ishinkai; Kenseikai; Kokumintō; Seiyūkai; Shinseikai
——in Russia, *see* Bolsheviks; Kadet party; Mensheviks; Social Democratic party; Social Revolutionary party
Polk, Frank L., 298
Popov, K. A., 83, 84
Prisoners of war in Siberia, 3; German and Austrian, 37, 45, 55,

114, 261, 263, 276, 277, 307, 308; Turkish, 45; Chinese protest against arming of, 112; in Lazo's forces, 196; Japan's plans to destroy, 334, 342–43, 344
Putilov, A., 87, 100–101, 191, 257

Rabulov, member of the Far Eastern Committee, 84
Railroad Siding 86, 111
Railways: American activities and Japanese fears thereof, 125–26, 214–16; Japanese army's plans to protect, 203, 332–33, 334–35, 340–45; Japanese army's draft agreement for use of, 356–58; see also American Advisory Commission of Railway Experts; Amur Railway; Chinese Eastern Railway; Russian Railway Service Corps; South Manchurian Railway Company; Trans-Baikal Railway; Trans-Siberian Railroad; Ussuri Railway
Rashin Ura, 151
Reading, Lord (Rufus Daniel Isaacs), 33
Red Army in Siberia, 109, 184; see also Soviet military forces in Amur basin
Red Cross, 253, 294
Red Guards, 73, 85, 109; in Vladivostok, 38; in Khabarovsk, 74; in Irkutsk, 75; in Chita, 76–77; in Blagoveshchensk, 108; in Tomsk, 108; ordered organized by All-Siberian Congress of Soviets, 184; in Lazo's forces, 196; see also Soviet military forces in Amur basin
Reinsch, Paul S., 210
Repington, Charles à Court, 29
Rinji Gaikō Chōsa I'in-kai: see Japan: Advisory Council on Foreign Relations
Riutin, Ensign, 46
Robins, Raymond, 157
Root, Elihu, 123
Rumania, 28, 32, 129
Rusanov, N. A., 170
Russia: secret treaty of 1916 with Japan, 12, 36; obligations under London Declaration, 28, 134; role in First World War, 28; Japan's inter-

ests in, 36–37, 214–15; see also Soviet authorities in Moscow
Russian Railway Service Corps, 124
Russian Revolution: Siberia's role in, in Soviet historiography, 6; initial reaction of Allies to, 27–35; problems created for Japan by, 36–38; attitude of people in Amur basin toward, 71–82 (see also under specific names of provinces, territories, and cities); as threat to Japan's China policy, 311–12
Russo-Asiatic Bank, 41, 100, 106, 122, 189–91

Saionji Kimmochi, 9, 19, 58; attitude toward Motono's plan, 155, 156; and Siberian expedition, 270–74, 307
Saitō Kijiro, 53, 88, 293; and Semenov, 89, 209–10; and Czechoslovaks, 254
Sakabe Tosuho: sent to Vladivostok for reconnaissance, 68–69; confers on Vladivostok landings, 146; intelligence organization reinforced, 166; recommends support for Derber, 171; reports on prisoners of war, 288
Sakanishi Rihachiro, 14, 53
Sakhalin: Japanese in, 4, 55, 309; U.S. interest in, 123
Samara, 237–38
Samura Masao, 166
Satō Naotake, 54n, 68n; attitude toward Domanevsku, 83; attitude toward Semenov, 92, 93–94, 200; Nakajima's conference with, 106; and Kolchak, 205
Satsuma clan clique, 8–10, 20, 26, 155
Savel'ev, Lieutenant, 77, 85
Sawano Hideo, 49, 91
Sazonov, A. V., 240n
Seiyūkai (political party), 9, 19, 20–23; representatives on Advisory Council on Foreign Relations, 26; noninterventionists, 58, 270–74
Semenov, Gregorii, 42–45, 46–48; activity among Cossacks, 76–77; quest for support, 85–87; Allies and, 88, 91, 169, 221–23, 231; and Nishihara, 91–92; in Harbin, 92–95, 105–6; and Nakajima, 94–95; Japan's support of, 97–100, 201–3, 231–32,

Semenov, Gregorii (*Continued*)
337, 351–55; cooperation with Horvat, 100–101; China's attitude toward, 110–12, 180, 183–84, 199, 207–12; bid for leadership, 180–87; Onon river offensive, 193–201; rescue of, 207–12
Seo Eitaro, 209
Shanghai, uprising at, 13
Shantung question, 117, 119
Sharasun, 180
Sharp, William G., 130
Shatilov, M. B., 237
Shidehara clique (diplomatic), 58
Shidehara Kijuro, 10, 175–76
Shigeno Shujo, 48*n*
Shil'nikov, Cossack General, 194
Shilov, Dmitrii, 81, 184
Shinseikai (political party), 23
Shōda Kazu'e, 14, 18
Siberia: political conditions in, 69–77; increasing power of Bolsheviks in, 108–9; and Czechoslovaks, 233–59; *see also* specific countries involved in intervention *and* names of territories, cities, and provinces
Siberian expedition, proposals for, *see* Allied Supreme War Council; Expeditions; foreign relations *under* France; *under* Great Britain; *under* Japan; *under* United States; Inter-Allied expedition
Siberian Foreign Trade Conference, 215
Siberian regionalists' conference at Tomsk, 72–73
Siberia Planning Committee, *see under* Japan
Sinkiang area, 110, 162
Slavin, Bolshevik leader of the Harbin soviet, 46
Social Democratic party, 71, 74, 75, 150; *see also* Bolsheviks; Mensheviks
Socialists, moderate, 71–73, 76
Social Revolutionary party: in Harbin, 41, 46; strength in Constituent Assembly election returns, 71–72; cooperation of left wing with Bolsheviks in Amur basin, 73–75; split in party ignored by Japanese, 78; protests Japanese landing at Vladivostok, 150–51; and Provisional Government

of Autonomous Siberia, 167; represented in Horvat government, 256
Sokolov, Boris, 81, 82
Sonnino, Sidney, 34, 296
South Manchurian Railway Company, 92, 97, 106, 165*n*, 178–79
Soviet authorities in Moscow: protest against Vladivostok landings, 4, 149–50, 159; withdrawal from war against Germany, 28, 34, 157; Allied assurances to, concerning Vladivostok landings, 157–59; Allied hopes for invitation to intervene, 157–59, 221–22, 226; negotiations for Allied military help, 157; appeal to China concerning Semenov, 207; and Czechoslovaks, 233–36, 241; Itō's evaluation of U.S. attitude toward, 281; for attitude of allied countries toward, *see under* France, Great Britain, Japan, United States
Soviet governments in Amur basin: seizure of power, 41, 45–6, 74–82, 108–9, 156–60, 184 (*see also* Central Executive Committee; Congress of Soviets; Council of People's Commissars; and under specific place names); driven from Harbin by Chinese, 46–48; protests against Vladivostok landings, 148–49
Soviet military forces in Amur basin: campaign against Semenov, 85, 111, 180–86, 193–97, 207–12; campaign against Kalmykov, 95–97, 258; negotiations with Chinese, 111–13, 180, 183–84, 207–8, 361–62; organization of, 184; campaigns against Czechoslovaks, 234–38, 247–49, 252, 255, 258; establishment of defensive fronts, 237, 258
Soviets, Congress of, *see* Congress of Soviets
Sovnarkom, *see* Council of People's Commissars
Special Manchurian Detachment, *see* O.M.O.
Ssu-Cheng railway-loan agreement, 115
Staal, leader in the Derber movement, 167
Stevens, John F., 123–24, 177
Su, Prince (Shan-chi), leader of a monarchist movement, 14

Suffolk (ship), 3, 61, 63, 158, 250
Sumitomo *zaibatsu*, 19
Syromiatnikov, Colonel, 240
Syrovy, Jan, 237
Sze Sheo-chang, 45

Tai-Ro Dōshikai, 48
Tai-Shi Rengōkai (China League), 13
Taishō Tennō, 8–10
Takeda Kakuzo, 255, 268
Takehazama Osamu, 178*n*
Tanaka Gi'ichi, 11, 49, 63; attitude toward military coalition with China, 15*n*, 52–53, 114, 116–17; Siberia Planning Committee, 101–6; attitude toward support of Horvat, 173, 175–76; and Chang, 188; and Semenov, 200–201; and American proposal, 265; and Siberian expedition, 288, 292
Tanaka Kunishige, 88
Tanigawa, Japanese military attaché in Washington, 264
Taskin, S., 194, 256
Tateba Tongo, 49*n*
Taube, Lieutenant General, 195
"Teidai" (Tokyo Imperial University) faction, 10
Telegraph system in northern Manchuria, Japanese interest in, 201–3
Temporary Siberian Economic Assistance Committee, 293–96
Terauchi Masatake: leader in Chōshū clique, 10; biographical sketch of, 16–17; appointed premier, 17; selects cabinet, 17–18; party allies of, 18–23; and Advisory Council on Foreign Relations, 23–27; reaction to British move on Vladivostok, 61–62; approves arms to Semenov, 98–99; encourages Sino-Japanese negotiations, 114; assurances concerning Motono's negotiations, 137; receives Yamagata's letter of March 15, 140–41; resignation discussed, 152, 154; restrains navy at Vladivostok, 152–54; calls for clarification of Allied policy, 224; agrees with army to use U.S. invitation, 264–65; wins cabinet approval, 266–67; discusses reply to U.S. proposal in Advisory Council, 269, 272–73, 274, 278, 283, 285; assures Hara

on government's intentions, 285; tries to bring army in line, 291–93; bitter about U.S. objections, 300; faces cabinet revolt, 302–3; accepts Itō's solution, 302–7
Tochinai Sojiro, 143–44
Tokonami Takejiro, 21
Tokugawa Iemasa, 13*n*
Tokyo Imperial University ("Teidai") faction, 10
Tomizu Kannin, 49*n*
Tomsk, 72, 77, 108, 237–38
Tosa clan clique, 8–10
Trans-Baikal Cossacks, 76–77; *see also* Semenov
Trans-Baikal Railway, 125, 176–80, 211
Trans-Baikal Territory, 5 (*map*); Semenov in, 42–45, 85, 194–95, 207–12, 359–60; Japanese army plans for expedition to, 101–6, 126, 267, 292, 334–37, 340–50; agreement between Lazo and command of Chinese troops in, 361–62
Trans-Siberian Railroad: importance of, 32–33, 38, 52, 129; Motono's plan for seizure of, 56; Czechoslovak seizure of, 236
Treaty of Brest-Litovsk, 157, 191
Trotsky, Leon, 236, 241
Ts'ai Ao, 13
Ts'ao Ju-lin, 14, 115, 120
Tsentrosibir', *see under* Central Executive Committee
Tsitsihar, 51–52, 331
Tuan Chih-kuei, 114, 188
Tuan Ch'i-jui, 14; loss of office, 27; Japan's effort to bring back into power, 113, 115, 120; return to Chinese premiership, 161; objection to proposals in draft defense agreement, 164; and Semenov, 210, 212
"Twenty-one demands," 12, 13, 114–15, 164

Uchida Kōsai, 213
Ueda Sentaro, 159
Uehara Yūsaku, 11; attitude toward military coalition with China, 15*n*, 52–53, 114; on reconnaissance in Siberia, 68–69; on Japanese support of Horvat and Semenov, 203; and

Uehara Yūsaku (*Continued*)
  American proposal, 265–66; and Siberian expedition, 291–92
Uejima Nagahisa, 48*n*
Uliassutai, 110
Ungern-Sternberg, Fedor: joins Semenov, 43, 45; leads Oloviannaia offensive, 76, 85
Union for the Regeneration of Russia, 239–40
United States: ship to Vladivostok, 3–4, 65; effect of Bolshevik Revolution on, 28–35; and Soviet authorities in Moscow, 33–35, 157, 221; in British proposal for action at Vladivostok, 40, 60–61; supports Horvat at Harbin, 42; refuses to support Semenov, 89–90; railway activities, 123–25, 177; rumors of concession-hunting in Amur basin, 123–25, 215–16, 293–94; pressed by Allied Supreme War Council to support Japanese expedition, 134–35, 262; protests Japanese landing at Vladivostok, 157–58; refuses to recognize Derber, 171, 249–50; Ustrugov charged with being pro-American, 172; Horvat-Stevens railroad agreement, 177; and Czechoslovaks, 244, 260–64; participates in protectorate over Vladivostok, 251; plans for economic assistance to Siberia, 294; *see also* Knight
——*relations with France*: Foch plan and U.S. rejection, 28–35; French urge Irkutsk expedition, 89–91; French urge support of Japanese expedition, 129–31, 133–35; *see also* Allied Supreme War Council; Allies
——*relations with Great Britain*—British urge: U.S. or Japanese expedition, 33; support of Semenov, 88, 189; support of Japanese expedition, 89, 129–30; common policy toward Soviet authorities, 157; that United States deplore Japanese landing, 158; *see also* Allied Supreme War Council; Allies
——*relations with Japan*: Lansing-Ishii agreement, 27; both oppose Foch plan of intervention, 28–35; Japanese fear of U.S. aims, 122–25, 177–78, 215–16, 293–94; Japan informed of

aims of Stevens mission, 124; Motono's proposal of expedition, 125–26; U.S. reply of March 5 to Motono proposal, 129–31; Japanese note of March 19, 140–42; United States protests Japanese landing, 158; rivalry for influence on Chinese Eastern Railway, 176–80; United States in Gotō's policy, 213–21; Japan's reaffirmation of March 19 note, 229–30; U.S. proposal of July 8 and subsequent negotiations, 260–64, 296–307
Urga, 110
Ussuri Cossacks: Nakajima and, 79; British and, 87, 95; Kalmykov and, 95–97, 109, 166–67; aid given by Japan to, 353
Ussuri Railway, 176, 356
Ussuri valley, 51
Ustrugov, L. A., 167, 168, 191, 257

Vanderlip, Frank A., 294
Verkhneudinsk, 44, 80, 344
Versailles Hotel (Vladivostok) incident, 66, 104
Vladivostok: Allied ships in, 3–4; threat of soviet take-over, 38–39; British proposal for joint intervention at, 39–40, 60–61; Japanese navy's plan of action, 39–40; Japanese army's plans for expedition to, 51–52, 103, 104–5, 331, 332, 336, 337, 338–39, 340, 342; British, Japanese, and U.S. naval units to, 60–65; Japanese navy's activities in, 60–67, 142–54, 159–60; Nakajima sent to, 67–69, 74; political situation in, 74; on Siberia Planning Committee's agenda, 102-3; Japanese navy's joint plans with army for preliminary operations in, 104–5; rumors of Japanese concessions sought at, 107; arrival of Russian Railway Service Corps at, 124; soviet authority established in, 142, 156–60; Japanese naval landing at, 146-54; Derber in, 167–72; Czechoslovaks in, 245, 247–50; Allied protectorate over, 251
Voitsekhovskii, Colonel, 236, 237
Vologodskii, P., 237
Vostrotin, S., 176, 256

Voznesensky, section chief in Soviet Foreign Commissariat, 159

Wang Shih-ch'ang, 53
Ward, John, 251
Willard, Daniel, 294
Wilson, Woodrow, attitude toward Siberian expedition, 133–35, 216, 219–20, 262, 298
Wireless-station loan to China, 116
Wonsan (Genzan), 151
World War, First, see First World War

Yada Chōnosuke, 293
Yamada Shunzo, 14
Yamagata Aritomo: influence of, 9, 10, 12; and Terauchi, 15–18, 21, 152–53; attitude toward Japanese expedition to Siberia, 139–40, 288, 301; and crisis at Vladivostok, 155–56; attitude toward support of Horvat, 173; and Gotō, 213; and American proposal, 266; and Hara, 270–74

Yamagawa Hashio, 154, 159
Yamamoto Gombei, 63
Yashiro Rokuro, 104
Yeo Shih-ching, 191
Yokota Sennosuke, 274, 298
Yonai Mitsumasa, 63
Yoshimi Enzō, 49, 91
Yoshizawa Kenkichi, 88
Young Men's Christian Association, 294
Yuan Shih-k'ai, 12–13, 14
Yunnan, rebellion in, 13

Zaibatsu, 8, 19, 20; Kuhara, 13, 98–99; Mitsubishi, 20; Mitsui, 20; Okura, 13; Sumitomo, 19
Zhevchenko, Lieutenant, 45; and Kudashev, 86; and Kolchak, 87; and the Japanese War Ministry, 91, 97–98; and Nishihara's representatives, 91
Zhigalin, Bolshevik leader in Chita, 81